1964

The Life of
ROBERT
SOUTHWELL
Poet and Martyr

The Life of
ROBERT
SOUTHWELL
Poet and Martyr

CHRISTOPHER DEVLIN

FARRAR, STRAUS AND CUDAHY
NEW YORK

First Published in America 1956

PRINTED IN GREAT BRITAIN
BY WESTERN PRINTING SERVICES LTD. BRISTOL

FOR

PATRICK AND MADELEINE

AUTHOR'S NOTE

WHEN modern historians of the Elizabethan religious struggle pay their just tribute to the losing side, two names are nearly always linked together in praise: Edmund Campion and Robert Southwell. Campion has already been the subject of a full-dress biography by Richard Simpson as well as of a conclusively brilliant study by Evelyn Waugh. But there have been only summaries so far of the life of Southwell. At the same time a great deal of work has been done to clarify and increase what is known about him. For both these reasons a full-length biography seems a timely venture.

The recent work done on Southwell has mostly had his writings as the end in view. Dr. Pierre Janelle's *Robert Southwell the Writer* and Fr. James Macdonald's *Bibliography of Robert Southwell* have proved invaluable for the winnowing of evidence and the establishment of sources; and behind these lie the research of several scholars of the Society of Jesus, notably Fr. Herbert Thurston and Fr. Hungerford Pollen. A very recent book from Yale University, *The Poetry of Meditation* by Professor Louis L. Martz, is an indication of the increased importance being ascribed to Southwell's verse.

My own predominant interest, however, in this biography is not Southwell as a writer but Southwell as a person. My intention has been to tell his story in chronological order as fully and as accurately as possible.

The settlement of some disputed points in Southwell's early life abroad I owe to Fr. Leo Hicks who most generously put all his *Southwelliana*, as well as several transcripts, at my disposal. A chapter hitherto unattempted in Southwell's life has been his stay at the English College, Rome; for inspiration and guidance on this subject I am indebted to Fr. Basil FitzGibbon. But I must make it clear that my use of the help given me on these points is my own responsibility.

A large number of letters from Southwell and Garnet, covering the period in England, were found in Rome very recently and are here used for the first time. I am most grateful to Fr. Philip Caraman for my knowledge of these important letters as well as for help in other ways.

To Mr. Francis Edwards I am indebted for the loan of transcripts, and to Miss Daisy Moseley for help with genealogies. I would also like to thank Fr. Lewis Watt, Mr. John Harriot, and Fr. William Lawson, Principal of Manresa College where this book was written.

CONTENTS

PART I

CONTENTS

APPENDIXES

PART ONE

CHAPTER ONE

England : the Fading Portrait

THE Southwells were a fairly old East Anglian family, originally from Barham in Suffolk, then branching to Woodrising in Norfolk, and in 1537 to Horsham St. Faith near Norwich. It was here that Robert was born towards the end of 1561, when Queen Elizabeth had been on the throne for just three years.

From the windows of his stately home he could see the bare ruined priory of Saint Faith which the last Benedictine monks, only seven in number, had left for ever twenty-five years before his birth. His grandfather, Sir Richard Southwell, commissioner for the suppression, had watched them go without rancour but with satisfaction. Of the four monastic properties which he and his brother had netted this was the site that pleased him best. While his new mansion rose near by, the stripped priory became a home for birds and cattle or a leaking shelter for husbandmen against the weather. From its walls there vanished under coats of dirt a great thirteenth-century painting of the Crucifixion, life-size; it was uncovered by modern research only a few years ago, startling in its ruined beauty. (1)

Indifferent to fading relics of the past, Sir Richard had pressed on to new conquests. Still living at St. Faith, a vigorous man of fifty-seven when Robert was born, he could look back upon a varied career whose watchword had been to serve the king and to save his own skin at whatever moral hazard. As a young man, it is true, he had faltered when called on for false witness against Sir Thomas More; but later on he came forward without a tremor as chief accuser of Henry Howard, the poet, Earl of Surrey, at

3

the trial which led to his death. This was a particularly shameful thing because the Southwells were hereditarily attached to the Howards and the two had been brought up as boys together.

In all the lethal changes of politics and religion that followed, Sir Richard slipped adroitly from one party to the other like a cormorant riding the waves. He even survived the transition from Mary to Elizabeth, for he had been a courteous escort to the captive princess who was now unchallenged queen. He kept his office of Master of the Ordnance for three years before he ceded it to the Earl of Leicester's brother. When he came to die in 1564, fortified no doubt by the rites of the Church, he could reflect—as a distraction from less promising thoughts—that he had left his family among the richest in the land.

He had seen his eldest son, also a Richard, well married: to Bridget, sister of Thomas Copley of Roughway, or Roffey, in Sussex. Thomas was a man of vast possessions including much property in Southwark and the valuable manor of Gatton in Surrey which could return two 'burgesses' (himself and friend) to Parliament; but what was more important, he and Bridget had been faithful companions of the Princess Elizabeth in the days of her sorrow. Thomas indeed had made a quixotic gesture of his devotion by boldly becoming a Protestant in Mary's reign. It was well known that Elizabeth never forgot her old friends, and this was soon proved in Thomas's case; for being affianced in youth to a sister of the elderly Lord Chamberlain, Howard of Effingham, he met a girl more of his own age, Catherine Luttrell, who 'liked him better for her beauty', and he jilted the Chamberlain's sister. The enmity of so powerful a person might well have proved fatal (and later did); but the Queen smiled on his new marriage, and stood godmother to the eldest son, Henry, who was born in 1560. His family and the younger children of Bridget Southwell grew up together on intimate terms. (2)

Through the Copleys, the Southwells were cousins of the Cecils and the Bacons, a relationship carefully noted by William Cecil, which acquired an unforeseen value for the other partners in it when it became clear who was to be the power behind the throne.

To Copley when he had fallen on evil days much later, William Cecil (then Lord Burghley) wrote: 'I was also the more inclined to conceive well of you because I knew you were of blood and kindred to my wife, so as your children and mine were to be knit in love and acquaintance by blood.'★

Old Sir Richard Southwell had the further satisfaction of seeing his brother's family, who had inherited the ancestral home of Woodrising, also growing up in firm friendship with the Cecils. Sir Robert Cecil afterwards wrote about Sir Robert Southwell—not the subject of this biography, but a cousin— 'He is a gentleman with whom in my youngest years I was bred in such love and friendship as I know none in Norfolk or Suffolk.' (3) The Southwells, thus, were well entrenched in that most privileged of all classes, not the precarious *haute noblesse* of Plantagenet creation, but the Tudor-made oligarchy founded on Church spoils. They kept a Marian priest in the house, at least in Robert's earliest years, as a sign of their attachment to the old ways; but it is unlikely that he ever preached on such texts as, 'If a man leave not father and mother . . .' or 'I come to bring not peace but a sword . . .' 'Religion', as Sir John Harington wrote of those years, 'brake not friendship, brake no allegiance, barred no good opinion.'

It is difficult at first to see why Robert at the age of fourteen should have chosen, as he did, a way of life quite out of keeping

★ The connection came through the family of Belknap, thus:

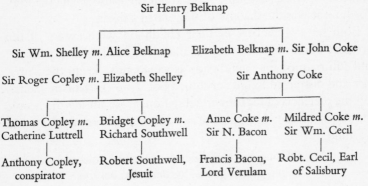

with his environment. The scraps of personal reminiscence that have survived belong all to his early infancy, not to the years of combative boyhood. The sensational event of his infancy was being kidnapped by a gypsy woman who had been captivated herself, so she said, by the beauty of his countenance as he lay in his cradle. In the panic that followed he was recovered by the devotion of a maidservant, whom he sought out long afterwards and cared for. (4) As a prophetic symbol of his future outlawry (Jesuits and gypsies were to be fellow victims of Topcliffe's rack) the incident has its significance, but not otherwise—unless one were to infer, which would hardly be just, that Robert was a neglected child. He was, however, perhaps a little lonely and unusually solemn. 'Even from my earliest infancy', he wrote to his father after he was a priest, 'you were wont in merriment to call me *Father Robert . . .*' (5) He was the youngest son of a family of eight, three boys and five girls. His brothers, Richard and Thomas, seem to have been a good deal older; the nearest to him in age and affection was probably his sister Mary, born about 1563 or 1564. (6)

In the background to his boyhood, perhaps, it will be possible to discover what influenced his choice of career. A misfortune which dogged the family in later years may have begun to cast its shadow as early as 1570, after the Bull of Excommunication. The authority on the misfortune is Sir Henry Spelman, the antiquary, who was born in Norfolk about the same time as Robert. Spelman had no doubts about the cause of the shadow. For him, it was the shadow of the ruined Priory.

Both he and Robert in their childhood were aware of the presence of one-time monks, old men who had lost their pensions and still roamed the countryside as vagabonds. From the scored face and distracted tongue of some poor Tom-o'-Bedlam, haunting the precincts of his former habitation, arose among the people the terror of the 'Monks' Curse', a new application of the old warning:

> Of long ago hath been the common voice:
> In evil-gotten goods, *the third shall not rejoice.*

The Southwell family tree, condensed from *Visitation of Norfolk* 1563 (Vol. I, ed. George H. Dashwood, Norwich, 1878, p. 127).

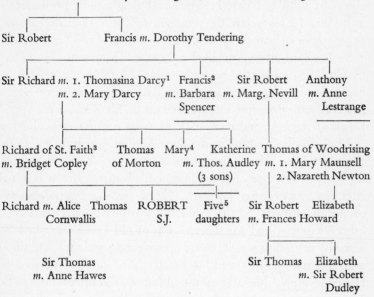

Richard Southwell *m.* Amy Winchingham, heiress of Woodrising

Sir Robert   Francis *m.* Dorothy Tendering

Sir Richard *m.* 1. Thomasina Darcy[1]   Francis[2]   Sir Robert   Anthony
     m. 2. Mary Darcy   *m.* Barbara   *m.* Marg. Nevill   *m.* Anne
                  Spencer   Lestrange

Richard of St. Faith[3]   Thomas   Mary[4]   Katherine   Thomas of Woodrising
m. Bridget Copley   of Morton   *m.* Thos. Audley   *m.* 1. Mary Maunsell
                      (3 sons)   2. Nazareth Newton

Richard *m.* Alice   Thomas   ROBERT   Five[5]   Sir Robert   Elizabeth
     Cornwallis   S.J.   daughters   *m.* Frances Howard

Sir Thomas   Sir Thomas   Elizabeth
m. Anne Hawes   *m.* Sir Robert
                                         Dudley

Notes

1. By Thomasina, Sir Richard had a daughter Elizabeth who married Sir George Heneage.

2. Francis's children are omitted for lack of space.

3. Richard's second wife was Margaret Styles by whom he had two sons: Henry (knighted by James I) and Denzany, who inherited Morton. Denzany's son Thomas, who died a Catholic at Louvain, is styled on his tombstone: *Pronepos R. P. Roberti Southwell Martyris.* Morton was the subject of dispute between Sir Richard's great-grandchildren.

4. Mary married William Drury, Judge of the Common Pleas; their son, Robert Drury, became a Jesuit.

5. ROBERT'S sisters: 1. Elizabeth *m.* 1. —Lister, 2. Giles Nanfan.
       2. Anne *m.* —Baskerville of Erdsley, Hereford.
       3. Frances *m.* William Lenthall: their son was the Speaker of the House of Commons.
       4. Katherine *m.* Leonard Mapes of Ipswich.
       5. Mary *m.* Edward Bannister of Iddsworth, Hants.

In his old age, after long research, Spelman wrote his macabre *History of Fate and Sacrilege* in which he traced disasters to the third and fourth generation of families that had robbed abbeys, especially those of Norfolk. The Southwells figured prominently in his list. Nevertheless, the mundane origin of their misfortune, as he relates it, was the peculiar married life of old Sir Richard.

Sir Richard, having married an heiress, Thomasine Darcy, had had his children by the heiress's cousin, Mary Darcy, relegating her in between times to be the wife of one of his serving-men called Leech. But after Thomasine's death, Sir Richard convicted Leech of bigamy, and took back Mary as his own wife; his last child, a daughter who became Kate Audley, was born in lawful wedlock. The slur on his sons seems to have been hushed up, for there is no sign of it in their coat-of-arms. But it resulted later in a bitter crop of lawsuits. The children and grandchildren of the illegitimate brothers and the legitimate sister sued each other viciously; and Mr. Leech—son of old Leech—justified his name by clinging fast to both sides, instigating and mulcting them with alternate perjury and blackmail. 'And this', concludes Sir Henry severely, 'brought all the filthiness afore-mentioned to be raked over again. And when they were all notoriously defamed by it, they all did sit down again without any recompense.' (7)

The crop of lawsuits did not mature till after Robert's death. But the seeds of blackmail had evidently been sown long before. Large drains of money had begun much earlier, and they were not due to recusancy fines. Robert's father was a competent man-of-affairs,* and by 1581 he was a conforming Protestant; yet in that year he had to grant an annuity of £40 for life on his lands to a rising young lawyer called Edward Coke—in return for legal advice. (8) After that his losses grew worse and worse. But they belong to a later chapter. An earlier mishap is more relevant as falling within the period of Robert's boyhood.

In May 1576, Richard and Thomas Southwell, who were staying with their cousins the Audleys in Essex, were summoned

* He helped to draw up a remarkably water-tight settlement for his brother-in-law, Thomas Copley.

before the Star Chamber. They had got into trouble with the bailiffs of Colchester on the information of one of Walsingham's eavesdroppers, for 'certain lewd and inconvenient speeches used of the Queen's Majesty, concerning the tilting at Killingworth'. (9)

The case was dismissed by the Star Chamber, but on payment of £200 security. It was an illustration of the way in which the Government was handling the rich families of their own class who were slightly suspect: benignly and carefully, as though waiting for a ripe pear to drop, and using informers to bestow a gentle prod every now and again. 'The widow Audley,' reported Walsingham's spy, 'the bastard daughter of Sir Richard Southwell, a very wealthy and dangerous woman.' The spy was inaccurate; for the widow Audley, Kate Southwell, was in fact Sir Richard's only legitimate child. She was also a more vigorous Catholic than her brother, Richard. She and her sister, Mary Drury,* lived near Wivenhoe on the Essex coast, and the spy's report of 1577 speaks of 'riotous assemblies of Papists there and nearabout' to hear Mass, 'twenty or thirty at a time'; and also of a certain shipmaster who 'carried Mrs. Audley's son and a Mass-priest from her house over the sea to Douay'. (10)

This brings us up against the crucial event in Robert's life. In May of the previous year, 1576, just when the Star Chamber case was on, he himself was making his way overseas to a life of exile, from which he was not to return for a full ten years—and then only 'like a foreigner', as he wrote later, 'finding among strangers that which in my nearest blood I presumed not to seek'.

From the time-serving comfort of his father's house to this state of harried outlawry was such a stiff and formidable step that one feels obliged to ask by whose decision it was made. One might imagine Richard Southwell sacrificing his youngest and most gifted son as a hostage to conscience, a sort of peace-offering to the shades of the monks. But as far as young Robert himself is concerned it is quite certain that he would never have gone for

* Mary Southwell, Robert's other aunt, married William Drury, Judge of the Common Pleas. They conformed after this to the State Church, but the Judge died a Catholic in 1588.

that reason. There is a paper in Latin among his private meditations, dated about 1580, which reflects a view of the Suppression
more in keeping with Sir Thomas More than with Sir Henry
Spelman:

> Consider frequently what harm has been done to the Christian
> Commonwealth by wicked, quarrelsome, and corrupt Religious.
> See what has happened in England, in Germany, or anywhere else,
> where nowadays for most people the names of 'monk' and 'scoun-
> drel' have the same meaning. And it is true that even daily we see
> numbers of them roaming from place to place, to the grave discredit
> of Religion. . . . It is our duty therefore—we who last of all have
> enrolled ourselves as Religious under the most Holy Name of Jesus
> —by the gentleness of our manners, the fire of our charity, by
> innocence of life and an example of all virtues, so to shine upon
> the world as to lift up the Res Christiana that now droops so sadly,
> and to build up again from the ruins what others by their vices have
> brought low.

Too much importance should not be attached to the youthful
rhetoric of this fragment in praise of the Society of Jesus; but it
does illustrate how his vocation was to him a glorious sunrise in
the future, rather than a muffled invitation from the past. Before
he left England, he had begun to be attracted towards this
nascent religious order, which mingled the new learning and a
new spirit of adventure with the old chivalric devotion to God
and His Blessed Mother; and it is known that he had also conceived a longing to be an apostle and martyr in 'The Indies'.
To look for this attraction in the environment of Horsham St.
Faith would be as strange as to expect a wild harebell to grow
from clayey loam.

If it is human causes that are in question they must be looked for
elsewhere. The Audley home in Essex is an obvious possibility.
But in fact such evidence as there is points in a different direction. (11) It seems that it was from a creek on the South coast
that he took ship in 1576; and there is evidence that in 1571-2
his mother was living at the Copley house of Gatton; (12) so it
may be presumed that Robert, aged ten, and his sister Mary

were there with her. At this stage, two events must be considered which separated Robert's childhood from his boyhood, a public event and a private. There was the Bull of Excommunication of 1570, and, following on that, there was an upheaval in the Copley household.

The cause of this went back to 1562 when Thomas Copley, staying at his town property of Rochester House, had a dispute with Bishop Jewell which set him reading books about the Council of Trent, then drawing to its close. As a result, having become a Protestant under Queen Mary, he became a Catholic again under Queen Elizabeth. It was a startling change from the usual order, and it sorely puzzled his friend William Cecil who had done just the opposite. But for the present the Queen's favour was not withdrawn.

Later on, when Catherine Copley had to go into exile she gave her youngest son to Bridget Southwell to bring up. It is a reasonable conjecture that earlier on Bridget had asked the same favour for *her* youngest son, to have him educated in the faith. There is certainly evidence of warm and early friendship between Robert and this attractive family whose charm reaches one easily over the centuries: Uncle Thomas, Lord Copley as he was called from an extinct barony, whose slightly Micawberish *panache* never wilted in adversity; Aunt Catherine whose sweet old letter is the only private one among Robert's Roman papers; and their colourful children: Henry, knighted by the King of France at the age of nineteen; Margaret, beautiful and heroic, twice sentenced to the scaffold; Anthony, the wayward poet and conspirator, whom Robert called 'my Anthony'.

From the Copley home at Roughway in West Sussex, he would have been introduced to a wide semi-circle of his mother's kinsfolk that stretched along the South Downs to the fringes of the New Forest: Shelley of Michelgrove and Shelley of Petersfield, Gage of West Firle and Gage of Bentley, Cotton of Warblington and many other allied families, who were soon to prove a most formidable rampart of recusant Catholicism. They were all Tudor-made families like the Southwells, and had risen to knightly rank through the Law; but in their case wealth had not extinguished the old traditions of medieval piety. It was of people like these that Robert wrote in later life:

> Let all history witness their sincere dealing, plain words, simple attire, frugal tables, unfeigned promises, assured love and amity, and most entire and friendly conversation one with another. Let us consider their large hospitality in housekeeping, their liberality towards the poor, their readiness to all merciful and charitable acts. Let us remember their assiduity and continual exercise of prayer, their straight observation of long fasts, their austerity and rigour in other chastisements of the body, and we shall find what different manners and fruits proceed from our belief, and from the doctrines of our new doctors. (13)

To such kinsfolk Robert's mother would naturally turn to safeguard the faith of her chosen one when disaster fell on her brother's family.

Copley was not implicated in any of the political disturbances that accompanied and followed the Bull of 1570. But it became clear to him that he was at the mercy of his ancient foe, Howard of Effingham, and that he could no longer live as a Catholic in England. He decided to go into exile to preserve his soul for himself and his estates for his family. His brothers-in-law, Richard Southwell and John Gage, were called in and they drew up a legal instrument which bequeathed his lands to his two sisters, to be held in trust by them for his wife and family. Then he fled. A later letter from Lord Burghley is a tribute both to the writer's amiability and to Thomas's motives:

> I always before your departure hence had a good opinion of you for your wisdom, virtue, and other good qualities, having never heard you touched with any spot of dishonesty or disworship. . . . And though I now perceive that your continuance away is grounded upon scruple of conscience for religion, yet I still think your first departure was occasioned by the extreme furious usage of the said Lord Howard of Effingham whom I found many times sore bent against you.

Parliament having passed a retroactive law against 'fugitives', Effingham made violent assaults upon Gatton while Southwell's mother was living there. The Queen however intervened with genuine clemency and allowed Thomas's wife and family to join him overseas without incurring his crime of 'fugacy'. Catherine thus retained her rights to the property, and it was handed over to Lord Burghley as President of the Court of Wards.

Meanwhile, if Robert had been staying with the Copleys till they left in 1572, where did he go next?

One place certainly suggests itself. When he left England in 1576, it was probably from one of the creeks between Hayling Island and Warblington, the house of his mother's cousin George Cotton; for he left in company with John Cotton, second son of the house, on the way to a Jesuit school in Belgium where Richard Cotton, the elder son, was already a student. This was the sort of transaction that required a good long spell of arrangement on the spot; and there would be long delays before the bribing of a ship-master could coincide with the wind and weather necessary for a secret crossing. Altogether, it is reasonable to suppose that Robert spent a good deal of the time between 1573 and 1576 with his second cousins at Warblington.

Two or three circumstances lend confirmation. His sister Mary, who is likely to have accompanied him to his mother's kinsfolk, afterwards married Edward Bannister of Iddsworth which is four miles from Warblington. And Robert, when he returned to England as a missionary priest, took the *alias* of Cotton. But the most persuasive circumstance is that this was the most likely place in England where he could have acquired his romantic enthusiasm for the Society of Jesus, and his early ambition to be a missioner to the Indies. It is worth while dwelling for a little on this circumstantial background.

In 1573, a year after Edmund Campion had made his reverberating decision, a Portuguese Jesuit, Father Alvarez, was carried ashore at Southampton Water on his way from Rome to 'India' —the West Indies, in fact, but to the average man of that time 'India' was an all-embracing term. He had with him some of those famous 'Relations' which described the adventures of missionaries in the marvellous new continent. In the enclave between the New Forest and the Sussex Downs, he found a knot of families who were organizing secret Mass-centres under the protection of Henry Wriothesley, second Earl of Southampton— 'the most illustrious and leading Catholic in England, and a great supporter of the faithful'. (14)

Prominent in this association was Mr. George Cotton of Warblington. There was also Swithin Wells, 'tutor' in Southampton's household, a genial and accomplished scholar who ran a private school for the sons of neighbours and tenants. But the outstanding member of the group was Thomas Pounde of Belmont, a cousin of Southampton. Reading Fr. Alvarez's letters from India, and conferring with him, Pounde conceived a lasting passion for the Society of Jesus; and he began to organize a number of young men whom he would lead into Flanders and thence to Rome, to join the new Order. Crossing by way of France was fairly easy from this part of England, because of the many little creeks hidden along the coast-line. But the only one who actually got across in 1574 was Pounde's page-boy, Thomas Stephens—from whose letters these facts are taken; he afterwards became a famous missionary in India, whose adventures are related in Hakluyt's *Voyages*.

Childhood history-books have accustomed us to Millais' picture of two boys, Walter Raleigh being one of them, listening spell-bound to a seaman's tales of wonders to be seen and done beyond the Spanish Main. It is not so well known that Catholic boys listened with no less rapt attention to equally wonderful, and perhaps more accurate, accounts of perilous journeys to heaven through the fabled other hemisphere. If Pounde's exploit had succeeded, India might have been converted by Englishmen, instead of being merely conquered by them.

Pounde however was caught in 1575. Released by the influence of Southampton, he was arrested again sixteen months later along with George Cotton. (15) This was just the period within which Robert Southwell and John Cotton made their successful em-

barkation. It is scarcely possible that they were not eager participants, at least in sympathy, in the adventures that preceded it.

The Catholics in this district were protected by the two most
powerful local families: the Earl of Southampton at Titchfield,
and his father-in-law, Lord Montague, at Cowdray near Mid-
hurst. Robert's connection with the Wriothesleys is worth
noting; his eldest sister and his eldest brother had married,
respectively, a nephew and a niece of the second Earl; he was
thus, loosely speaking, twice a cousin by marriage of the future
third Earl, Shakespeare's patron. The second Earl had been in
prison while his wife was with child; but, through the instances
of Lord Montague, he had been released in time for the birth and
for the Christmas of 1573.*

Since Robert's presence in this region is only known by
inference, not by any direct evidence, it would be foolish to try
and build up a factual narrative. But it is important that he should
have spent the years of awakening adolescence in a place like
Warblington; important for his poetry as well as for his religion.
It is described as:

> 200 feet square with a fair green court within, and buildings round
> the said court; with a fair gallery and diverse chambers, and two towers

---

*Marriage connection between Robert Southwell and the Wriothesley
family.

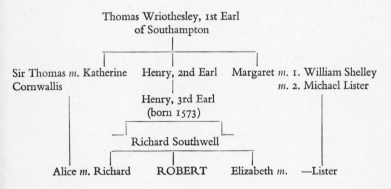

Thomas Wriothesley, 1st Earl
of Southampton

Sir Thomas *m.* Katherine   Henry, 2nd Earl   Margaret *m.* 1. William Shelley
Cornwallis   *m.* 2. Michael Lister

Henry, 3rd Earl
(born 1573)

Richard Southwell

Alice *m.* Richard   ROBERT   Elizabeth *m.* —Lister covered with lead; a very great and spacious hall, parlour and great chamber with a chapel and all other offices; a fair green court of two acres before the gate, and a spacious garden with pleasant walks adjoining, containing two orchards and two little meadows; and near the said place a fair fish-pond; with a gate for wood, two barns, stables and other outhouses. (16)

This was a place perhaps more favourable to his special kind of poetic imagery than was his father's house in Norfolk. In spite of his later study of didactic models he always kept a fresh and natural good taste such as can only have been nurtured in some remembered garden of his own, whose seeds were the sense-impressions of early boyhood or awakening adolescence. Here is an unpublished poem of his which can be dated most probably between 1581 and 1585:

> Behold how first the modest Rose doth pry
> Out of her summer coat in virgin's hew,
> One half in sight, half hidden from the eye;
> The lesser seen, the fairer to the view.
>
> But in her pride her leaves she doth display,
> And fades in fine, and seemeth not the same;
> It seems not she that was a dainty praye
> For every amorous youth and galant Dame.
>
> So with the passing of a sliding day
> Of mortal life the flower and leaf doth pass;
> Nor with the new return of flowering May
> Doth it renew the bounteous wonted glasse.
>
> Then crop the morning Rose while it is fair;
> Our day is short, the evening makes it die.
> Yield God the prime of youth 'ere it impair,
> Lest he the dregs of crooked age deny. (17)

The first fourteen lines are a translation of the song in Armida's pleasure-garden from Tasso's *Gerusalemme Liberata* (1581), which Southwell evidently read at Rome. Another version of it is

Edmund Spenser's 'lovely lay' which was sung as a lascivious invitation to the Bower of Bliss. Robert's youthful effort is 'drab' no doubt (to use Professor C. S. Lewis's term) by comparison with Spenser's.* But what is interesting is the tranquil ease with which the younger writer turns a temptation to vice into an incitement to virtue. He must surely have been someone whose boyhood memories were held in such gentle subjection that they could move freely in and out in the service of his theme. Memories of a casement window opening in the early morning on tree-tops and meadows and a walled garden; of brocaded dresses in the afternoon like moving rose-bushes; of a golden sunset fading over mellow walls and feathery orchards.

Along with a flowering in the imagination went a quickening of the intellect. Hitherto he had accepted his religion as (in his own words): 'the belief which to all my friends by descent and pedigree is, in a manner, hereditary'. The raw material of Grace and the nourishment of conscience had been the ingrained conservatism of boyhood. But now came the exciting realization that the Old Religion had renewed its youth like the eagle and was no longer on the defensive. The name most associated with the Catholic revival was 'the Society of Jesus'; but coupled with the word 'Jesuit', in mouths both friendly and hostile, was another of still greater significance for Englishmen: 'Seminaries.'

The English scholars from both Universities, but especially from Oxford, who had fled overseas constituted a band of writers whose talent and learning were as great as, if not greater than, those of any Protestant divines: Thomas Stapleton, William Allen, Richard Harding, Gregory Martin—and now Edmund Campion. Their apostolate had been confined to the pen until, between 1569 and 1572, William Allen founded a 'Seminary' or training-college attached to the University of Douai in the Spanish Netherlands. His object at first was the same as that of

---

* But its graceful economy compares favourably with Edward Fairfax's translation in *Godfrey of Bulloigne* (1600). It should be added that Robert's version is quite clearly taken direct from Tasso (editions in 1581 and 1584), not from *The Faerie Queene* (1590).

C

the Marian exiles had been—to have a trained clergy ready for the next swing of the pendulum in England.

The Jesuits also had a college attached to the same University; and Allen modelled his training upon their system. There was no intrinsic connection between the two colleges, and no question of any Jesuits being spared for England; but the two names, 'Jesuit' and 'Seminary', were coupled together from the outset—a whisper of hope to the recusants in England, and a shadowy menace to the newly-established State Church.

The English Government had been hoping that, as the old generation of priests ordained under Queen Mary gradually died off, the Catholic religion also would die of inanition without the need of persecution. This was actually happening until 1570; but after that date came a stiffening and an increase of 'recusancy' —that is, of refusal to attend Protestant worship. It is not sufficiently realized that this stiffening came from *within* the Catholic body in England. Allen had no idea of sending his priests back as missionaries, until, from England itself, came the demand for them: from pockets of resistance such as the one just described, in the region of West Sussex and East Hampshire.

The pattern there was the same as in many other places: a noble house, such as Titchfield or Cowdray, which provided a sort of bulwark; an adventurous layman, like Thomas Pounde, who collected Catholics for worship; and a schoolmaster, like Swithin Wells, who trained the young in the arguments for their religion. This is the pattern which Robert Southwell experienced; and, by a curious coincidence, he has left a description of it—by hearsay—as happening in quite a different part of England, in the Forest of Arden in Warwickshire. This is contained in a short biography in Latin of a friend and contemporary at Rome, Edward Throckmorton, who died there in 1582, aged twenty, with a reputation for great holiness. (18) The early part deals with his Catholic boyhood in the district between Coughton, the Throckmorton home, and Parkhall, where he stayed with his uncle, Edward Arden, who was High Sheriff of the county in 1575 and who later died—in Southwell's view—a martyr.

In the narrative Robert picks on just those qualities and experiences of his friend which he himself had shared and understood. He describes in detail Edward's affection for his old nurse, and his care for her when she was past work—which is one of the few things he related about his own childhood. He speaks with understanding of Throckmorton's father who, like his own, was Catholic at heart, yet attended Protestant services because such was more or less the accepted procedure; and he stresses the change that came over the boy's life when he was sent to live with an uncle and aunt who were recusants; how he came under the influence of a tutor who combined learning with ardent Catholicism; how other boys also flocked to him, and a school was started.

He gives a vivid picture, obviously drawn from similar experience, of the counter-reformation in miniature. A number of the boys formed a society, and pledged themselves to suffer all sorts of imaginable tortures rather than take part in any Protestant service. They canvassed the neighbours and tenants, and discovered other boys who attended the Protestant church only for fear of being flogged at home if they refused. The society would then invoke the secular arm in the person of Throckmorton's uncle; and if that worthy gentleman proved ineffective, the society would arrange for the boys to escape from their homes and live in hiding elsewhere. This was the sort of behaviour which won high commendation from our Victorian forebears, when it was practised by Puritans. But it was the recusants who first set the example of this *furor juvenilis*—just as it was the recusants also at this time who first got the idea of emigrating to America for conscience sake.

The narrative stresses the intense love of the poor which he shared with young Throckmorton.

When he caught sight of poor people, he used to run to the pantry, storeroom, or kitchen, to get something for them; and if he was refused or kept waiting, he pressed his demand earnestly and urged it with warmth. If the servants gave indeed but selected the worst, he cajoled them to throw in something better, repeating that what was given to the poor was given to God, and therefore ought to be of the best. Often too in winter time he led the children of the poor suffering from cold and hunger, with his own hands to the fire, and prayed the servants to make ready something to eat while the children were warming themselves.

This traditional charity—so superbly arrogant in modern eyes —is made more naïve and natural by a few deft touches:

Whenever in company with other gentlemen he was bidden to put down money for play, he always gave his winnings away to beggars. And when he had his choice of recreation, he was very fond of fishing in a pond close by the house, so that he might bestow on the children of the poor whatever fish he caught. Even when wearing silk and fine linen according to his rank, he avoided higher company when circumstances permitted it, and did not blush to consort with beggar boys.

A slight ruefulness is apparent in a reference to the *mauvaise honte* that was already beginning to be characteristic of English male youth:

This behaviour was all the more worthy of admiration in him, since the sons of persons of rank when young shrink exceedingly from this kind of virtue, especially in this poor England of ours where even a boy of thirteen finds it hard to save his soul.

A description of a priest arriving at a crowded house-party seems to recapture the young Southwell's own compassionate distress:

At once he hastened to meet him, and if the servants were not on the spot, he himself led his horse to the stable and pulled off the rider's boots—nay, even, sometimes he was not ashamed to clean them. And if on any occasion the crowd of gentry and visitors prevented the priest from sitting at table with the rest, he would at once run to his aunt and conjure her with many entreaties to give him leave to wait on him. If that were denied him, he implored at least to be allowed to dine in the room with him.

Finally, there is an unintentionally comic description of the solemn pomp with which the English Catholics set about committing the wholly illegal and felonious act of sending a boy abroad without permission:

> It is wonderful how many of his old school-fellows and of the common people and gentry assembled both to bid farewell to the object of their singular esteem, and congratulate him on his departure to a Catholic country. What tears started to the eyes of relations! What lamentations there were of servants, male and female! What weeping and grief of all! Each one bewailed the great loss which he foresaw he would suffer by the departure of Edward; and as though about to be deprived forever of one whom they held so dear, they accompanied him upon his way as if in a funeral procession, with many sad tokens of their deep affection.

In sober fact, however, there was nothing comic or sentimental about escaping to school overseas. There were sickening delays and dangers. Boys who were caught were liable to be whipped and starved, and even sent to Bridewell. The prospect of never seeing home or parents again was likely enough. In the case of Robert and his mother it was almost certainly so.

She was still alive in 1583, but after that nothing is known. His father married again—a parson's daughter, one of the maids of the house—to his children's great displeasure. (19) Perhaps that is why Robert does not mention his mother in the long letter to his father of 1589—except to say that it was from his mother's breast he drew his love for his father and his home. There is no certainty even that he saw her to say goodbye. In an unpublished poem, Mary's lament for the loss of her Child in the Temple, the last two stanzas run:

> And art thou slain, sweet Lord, with cruel death
> Through wretched spite and bloody tyrant's hand?
> Or dost thou live, dear child, and draw thy breath
> Yet haply hid in unacquainted land?
> If thou be dead, then farewell life for me,
> And if thou live, why live I not with thee?
>
> And if thou live, how couldst thou leave in woe
> Thy mother dear that brought thee first to light?

> How couldst thou leave thy mournful parent so,
> That for thy weale takes care both day and night?
> How couldst thou go some other where to dwell,
> And make no stay to bid her once farewell?

The last couplet may be more than just an embroidery on the Gospel story, and if so, then the lines become transformed with genuine pathos:

> How couldst thou go some other where to dwell,
> And make no stay to bid her once farewell?

CHAPTER TWO

'The Beautiful English Youth', 1576–8

IN the summer of 1576 the Netherlands were undergoing an uneasy interregnum between the death of Requesens and the dilatory approach of Don John, the new governor. But the two English boys, coming from Paris under the guidance of Mr. Covert, Dr. Allen's agent in France, were able to cross the frontier safely and reach Douai unimpeded. The Diary of the English College for 10th June records: 'Mr. Cotton and Mr. Southwell, noblemen's sons both, were brought to us by the same messenger from England.' (1)

The arrangement for Robert was that he should have board and lodging at the English College, and attend classes at the neighbouring Jesuit school. As Pierre Janelle has emphasized in his *Robert Southwell the Writer*, it was of the greatest importance that he experienced these two influences simultaneously, the English and the Continental. (2)

At the English College he was one of some hundred and twenty young men between the ages of fifteen and twenty-five. They were from all parts of England, and of varying social rank, but precedence was strictly by academic standards. The college was in fact an enclave, or a slip of Catholic Oxford grafted on to a foreign university. The tutors were all Oxford graduates, distinguished scholars many of them, such as Thomas Stapleton, translator of Bede, and Gregory Martin who was engaged on his English version of the New Testament. All, whether schoolboys or students, lay or clerical, were bound together by a sense of vocation and the prospect of danger; for Allen had recently

23

decided that the purpose of the College was to send back priests to revive the faith in England. Of the eighteen newly-ordained who had just left, six were to be martyred, beginning with Cuthbert Mayne in 1577, and others were to suffer imprisonment of the very worst kind.

The life was hard and the diet poor; but the response from England to Allen's decision had been amazing. Numbers were increasing so fast that he had gone to Rome to arrange for the foundation of a new College there.

On Allen's return, Robert, like everyone else, came under the spell of this genial patriarch, whom he himself styled later: 'He whom I venerate among the first, the father of his country, to whom is due all the good that is done here.' (3) For this gift of being a 'Father in Christ', if it were for nothing else, Allen ranks among the greatest of English Churchmen. A keen humanist, the trappings of scholarship—doctorates and degrees and so forth —had only real value in his eyes as a means to the conversion of England. In his training system, the stress was on practical or pastoral theology, and on the explication of Scripture in terse vernacular, so as to compete with the Protestant divines. Every night there were litanies in common for the conversion of England. Breathing in this spirit, Robert was prevented from ever forgetting his native land, in spite of his dreams of India. (4)

On the other hand, for the formation of his style, it was important that he should be studying rhetoric under foreign Jesuits. For, by a paradox, while the Catholic exiles were keeping up the tradition of plain, homely English, the influences actually at work in Protestant England were those of neo-classical rhetoric as practised on the Continent. The first voices, apart from the exiles, to break the long silence of English prose, were to do so in the honeyed accents of *Euphues* and the *Arcadia*; and these were to be the dominant influences until almost the end of Southwell's apostolate in England. (5)

The Jesuit school at Douai was the foremost of its kind in Belgium, numbering nearly a thousand pupils. In spite of presumable difficulties of language, Southwell was promoted rapidly from 'Humanities' (or 'Poetry') to 'Rhetoric'—the name of the top class in Jesuit schools. To be in 'Rhetoric' presupposed not only a thorough grasp of 'Syntax' and 'Grammar' (the names of the lower classes) but also a close acquaintance with the epistles and easier speeches of Cicero, with the easier books of Virgil, and with suitable extracts from Horace, Ovid, and Catullus. As the names of the classes imply, the principal subject was Latin—Ciceronian Latin. Greek seems only to have been studied as a means to Religious Doctrine, in which the books used were the New Testament and Chrysostom's homilies in the original. Otherwise, Latin held supreme sway; and other subjects—history, geography, modern languages, etc.—were dovetailed into it as 'accessories' or fields of illustration.

In a typical Latin class, the professor would first *declaim* a passage, say, of Cicero; then he would analyse its artistic structure with the stress on style rather than on erudition, descending from the ethical power of the piece as a whole down to the rhythm and *nuances* of particular words and phrases. Then, after a repetition, the pupil, in his own time, would produce a written exercise on the same lines—for example, turning Cicero's argument that a seditious mob is not the Roman People into a discussion of the attributes of a Christian gentleman.

A surfeit of Cicero was relieved by excursions into the 'accessories'. In Geography, in particular, the Jesuits had the advantage of first-hand missionary reports from mysterious continents, which nourished for a time Robert's early dreams of India. But monotony was chiefly broken by 'academies' and 'disputations', and also by an occasional dramatic performance before the notables and townsfolk.

The Jesuit 'theatre' was the product of a running contest between enthusiastic producers and cautious superiors. In Robert's time, dramatic dialogues were held in the Church of St. James, the subject being always some youthful Early Christian Martyr. Scenery was forbidden, but women's costumes were allowed, provided there was 'no frivolity in dress or action'. There is a programme extant for 7th October 1570, 'St. Catherine, Virgin-

Martyr' (the subject of one of Robert's early Latin poems). Later plays presented St. Laurence, St. Sebastian, St. Cecilia, St. Maurice and the Theban Legion. It is not certain whether there was a performance in October 1576; but an interesting fragment of reminiscence suggests that, if there was, Robert may have taken part in it: '. . . the people of Douai, when Robert Southwell was studying humanities there, used to call him "the beautiful English youth".' (6)

The people of Douai, though increasingly anti-Spanish, were still friendly to the exiled youths, so that the first few months at school cannot have been other than pleasant. (7) The hours were not excessively onerous. Day-boys began to arrive at a quarter to eight, the 'nobles' among them stacking their weapons in an armoury before entering. Schools were from eight till ten-thirty followed by High Mass, Dinner and Recreation; and again from one-thirty till four, with an hour and a half of study in the evening. Apart from the numerous feast-days to look forward to, every Thursday as well as Sunday was a whole holiday 'lest the pupils should have to go to school four days in succession'.

An occasional and honoured visitor at the English College was Robert's Uncle Copley who was living with his family at Louvain. Among Robert's English companions were several with whom he remained in friendship afterwards: Brooksby, Vavasour, Throckmorton, and two others with whom reunion at Rome was not to be so pleasant: Gilbert Gifford, an extremely clever boy with a corrupt mind and a deceptively innocent appearance, and a certain Hugh Griffin, 'who', noted Allen with unusual severity, 'for choler and other singularities was insupportable among his fellows here'. Among other companions, an unexpected name is that of Christopher Blount, who was later the Earl of Essex's adventurous and tragic lieutenant; his sister, it seems, married Richard Cotton, Robert's second cousin.

The schooling of the English boys at Douai was interrupted after the first six months by a political storm. A band of Spanish mercenaries, unpaid since the death of Requesens, broke loose in

November and stormed Antwerp with fantastic valour and appalling ferocity. 'The Spanish Fury' threw the Catholic population of Belgium into alliance with the Calvinists under William of Orange. The English exiles in the Netherlands, pensioners of the King of Spain and maintained by his bounty, were on the wrong side. The Calvinists had long since mastered, if they did not actually originate, the technique of mob-instiga-tion. Though the citizens of Douai were friendly to the exiles, the magistrates refused to be responsible for their safety. Thomas Copley arrived at the College with a story that the English Ambassador had determined to take advantage of the situation to get the exiles cleared bag and baggage out of Belgium. Allen decided to get rid of as many students as he could, especially of the younger boys who were not studying for the priesthood.

At the end of November a large party left for Paris. And there John Cotton and Robert Southwell began their schooling over again at the famous Jesuit college of Clermont—this time with no English cultural breakwater. They were fortunate, however, in coming under the care of one of the earliest English Jesuits, Father Thomas Darbishire, who was attached to the college; it was he who had just converted George Gilbert, soon to be the leader of Catholic youth in England.

The only authority for Robert's stay in Paris is the Jesuit historian Henry More, who, indeed, was under the impression that 'he spent *two years* there, sharing chambers with John Cotton'. More had letters of his—which are now lost—covering the period: hence his natural but erroneous inference. In fact, apart from a short stay at the beginning and end of the two years, his Parisian period is covered by the six months from November 1576 to June 1577.

Nevertheless, it was at Paris that two important things hap-pened to Robert Southwell. He began to form a literary style, and, much more important, he underwent a spiritual crisis.

Evidence of both is contained in his first known piece of writing, a prose-poem usually referred to as the *Querimonia*. Regrettably the English in which he wrote it has perished and there survives only a Latin translation made by More. The extract that covers the interior struggle at Paris is as follows:

> Thou with thy loving gentleness didst pull my heart to thee, and I must needs acknowledge me thy slave. For thou didst conquer me, Lord Jesus, yea, in double battle didst thou conquer me.
>
> For at thy first approach I fought thy holy inspirations, thinking it was for thy sake, not my own, that thou wouldst have me part of thy Society.
>
> Then didst thou spy my weakness, Lord, and with new engines rock the ramparts of my heart, until despoiled of every refuge, and beaten by necessity, after long struggle I surrendered, and humbled me beneath thy powerful hand.

Even from the retranslation the lyric ardour is obvious; but it throws only a little light on the conflict that was taking place. The whole piece was written at the end of the year, when his petition to enter the Society had been rejected; but the extract quoted looks back on the irony of his state of mind in Paris, when he was wondering, not whether the Society would have him, but whether he would have the Society. In retrospect it seemed a foolish question, but at the time and in fact it was the turning-point of his life.

Paris was evidently for him the city of decision, where he overcame the vague, nameless repugnance to a life of poverty, chastity, and obedience, and all that it implied. There was no question of his simply drifting into the Society as the obvious course. Over the crowded roof-tops of Paris he had to look up at the stars alone, and wrestle with eternal issues. There was no one among his friends who could help or advise. John Cotton was going back to a different sort of heroic life: that of a country squire keeping his ruined estate together so as to shelter priests whenever required.* William Brooksby, indeed, had felt the same call as Southwell, but he had evaded the issue temporarily, and returned to England where a fortune and a fiancée were awaiting him. For others, like Hugh Griffin, to enter the Church

---

* His father, George Cotton, remained in prison from 1577 to 1585.

still meant simply to secure a canonry, and live in as great comfort as possible out of England.

In Father Darbishire, it is true, Robert had a confessor well versed in spiritual things; in fact, before becoming a Jesuit, he had been deeply drawn to the Carthusian order. 'From Father Darbishire', writes More of Southwell, 'he learned to trust in God's kindness, and to believe that, whatever he honestly decided to do, he would be helped.' Father Darbishire does not seem to have tried to influence his vocation, but only to smooth away the element of fear in his perplexity. He encouraged him to a greater familiarity with God in prayer, so that he was able to overcome that awful apprehension of nothingness which sometimes accompanies a religious vocation—'lest having Thee, I might have nought beside'. Thus, he was more calm of soul, but still undecided in mind, when the next move in his outward life took place.

Don John, victor of Lepanto, new Governor of the Spanish Netherlands, had succeeded in restoring harmony, at least in the Catholic regions; and in the spring of 1577, the scattered English students began to return. The *Douai Diary* for 15th June records: 'Fr. Thomas Smyth came from Paris with his distinguished pupils, Southwell and the two Audleys.'

Just before leaving Paris, Southwell wrote some letters—perhaps to his parents, or to the Copleys, More does not tell us—hinting that his return to Belgium would help him to decide his future career. But he had not long been back at Douai before he found himself in a worse tangle than before. He was certain that he must dedicate himself entirely to God; but, now, like his late director Father Darbishire, he felt an overwhelming attraction to a life of complete solitude and contemplation in the Carthusian order. He speaks of it later as a temptation of the Devil, so that it may have been an unconscious subterfuge to escape his real vocation: on the principle of 'All or nothing: not all: therefore nothing.' On the other hand, no doubt as a boy in England he had had the experience of rapt adoration of invisible beauty; and this experience, informing the exercises of prayer and spiritual reading, seemed now a genuine attraction to the contemplative life. In fact, the two are not the same—may even be mutually exclusive—but the borderland is hard to find and involves humiliation. Southwell had certainly no Lutheran bent for posing as a lonely rebel tossed by incomprehensible desires; his clear-headedness made him docile so long as his reason was not violated. But in his present involved adolescent state he shrank from unburdening himself to a new director; and when he did eventually approach the Douai Confessor—a certain Father Columb, a Devonshire man—he received straight-from-the-shoulder advice which did not seem at all to reach the roots of his trouble.

Hitherto in this narrative he has been a more or less silent passenger. But now he begins to speak with a vengeance. In this first revelation of himself, he appears as a high-spirited boy, flourishing his intellectual ardour with an almost girlish elegance in a manner characteristic of Elizabethan youth.

He burst in on Father Columb one day, and told him that his methods were all wrong. Fr. Columb, restraining perhaps some justifiable indignation, turned away to the window, and then said suddenly: 'Look!' Robert looked, and saw, at first, his esteemed professor Master Leonard Lessius, and then, walking up and down with him, a Flemish youth to whom he felt an instant attraction. What the youth was like—whether he was pale and ethereal, or florid and overwhelming, or dark and intense—it is idle to speculate. His name was John Deckers, and he was to be an inseparable friend in the critical months that lay ahead.

The best thing now will be to let Southwell recall the scene himself as he recalled it in a letter written to Deckers in 1580, the draft of which is decorated with two very villainous men's heads. It is a long letter but the bulk of it must be quoted; it is young Southwell at his most characteristic:

I want you to know what first made me confide in you. I was in two minds about my vocation—tossed on a tide of suggestions, now making for the good ship 'Bruno', now for the ship 'Ignatius', and reaching neither; in fact I was drowning in a torrent of temptations, until at last I steered a sensible course and went to my Confessor.

But he would say nothing except the same thing over and over again in different words: 'Stick to the Society, stick to your first vocation.' This stilled my storm for the moment but did not over-master it; as soon as I left him it broke out again with new ferocity. Beaten thus with daily buffets and bewildered where to turn, I began to get quite ill with the unending struggle. I chose the Society, and at once the Devil with a new stratagem changed my mind. I turned to the ranks of the Carthusians, and immediately the pangs of conscience gripped me. For three whole months I had no peace of soul, strung up in this perpetual suspense and miserably swaying to and fro. But our dear Lord and Father Jesus Christ, who lets no man be tempted past endurance, at length incited me to one last assault upon my Confessor. 'Only one thing can do me any good', I told him, 'and that is to find someone with desires like mine, someone whom I can talk to naturally and freely, and settle the questions that every day keep cropping up.' Now, at the very moment that I spoke,—so the Divine Goodness had arranged—who should be walking up and down with Master Leonard but yourself, yourself whom our most loving Jesus from all eternity had destined to lend his shoulder to this weak and trembling athlete. 'Look,' said the Father, pointing me to you, 'there is a man who for a year or more has been as keen on serving God as you, but so far he has shown no sign of *your* weak-mindedness.' No sooner had he spoken than I felt a leap of joy, and every shadow of doubt left me, (I promise you) so that hardly ever, in fact never since, have I wavered about my vocation to the Society. I pressed my petition there and then scorning delay, and begged him to ask you if you would be my spiritual friend. . . . For a whole day I waited, between fear and hope: fear of the difference in our language and conventions, fear of the monstrous absurdity of my own behaviour: but hope, that once our wills were tuned to the same purpose, this would prove stronger than those obstacles, in bringing us together. . . . But I am going on too long. All that, and much more like it, I leave out. Just one thing more I *will* recall, for the glory of God: how the whole world clothed itself anew that day; so strange a splendour bathed my soul as she emerged from gloom, that I minded no longer the wounding battles of the past; the solace that I felt in the sole hope and expectation of your coming had wiped all scars away . . .

We met—at last; we opened to each other the deep desires and secrets of the heart. With what sweet talk of God and of his Company we set each other's souls on fire! Ah, what was dearer then to John than Robert, than John what dearer in the world to Robert, save this to both, that they should enter the Society? No day would pass, no time for meeting was let slip; yet every moment we could steal to talk together seemed all too short. Fervour in prayer began to grow, and private penances became attractive; the roughness of the hair-shirt, yes and of the scourge, became delightful. Let us remember these things, my dearest John, remember them and strive, that what we did in exile sighing for the City, we may do with still more fervour now that we are citizens enrolled. (8)

The events described in the letter belonged to the autumn and winter of 1577. Following on them, early in 1578, the two young men applied for admission to the noviceship at Tournai.

But just as Southwell was congratulating himself on having wrestled till daybreak and prevailed, the sword of the guardian of Paradise flashed out with unexpected cruelty. Its purpose may be guessed: to cut the bindweed of sentimentality. Deckers was accepted and his entry was fixed for 25th May. Southwell, however, was rebuffed, not once but repeatedly; and thereafter their paths diverged for two and a half years. Caught in a worse dilemma than before, he wrote the *Querimonia*: of which an extract has been quoted already. He wrote it in English, a sign perhaps that already he felt the rift—it was never a quarrel— between himself and his friend. He could not understand why God, having thrown a rope to him and pulled him from the depths, should now cut the rope just as he was reaching the surface.

The Jesuits indeed had not absolutely rejected him, but they had deferred him without any definite hope. He was a year younger than Deckers and he was an Englishman. There may have been difficulty about his parents' consent, but a greater difficulty was the political situation. In January, Don John, supported by Alexander Farnese, had defeated the Netherlands army at Gembloux. But this, by weakening William of Orange, had forced the extreme Calvinists into allegiance with Casimir of the Palatinate and his German mercenaries, who were now ravaging the country, allegedly on behalf of Queen Elizabeth. Burning and massacre began to spread through all the towns which could not defend themselves. The English students, of course, were marked down for destruction; but so also were those Religious Orders who had not renounced their allegiance to Don John.

Dr. Allen, narrowly escaping with his life, led a party of his men across the border into France, where the Duke of Guise gave them a shelter at Rheims in a building which was destined to become even better known in England than the College at Douai had been.

> Did he not draw a sorte of English priests
> From Doway to the Seminary at Remes
> To hatch forth treason gainst their natural Queen?

—wrote Marlowe in his pot-boiler *The Massacre at Paris*.

But it was some time before the College settled down at Rheims. At first all was confusion, with students dispersed in all directions. Southwell stayed behind with the Jesuits at Douai, hoping still to be admitted. He made a grave decision when he cut himself off from Rheims and his English friends who were going there. It meant that if the Jesuits would not receive him, he would have no alternative but to go home.

But the Jesuits themselves were in none too safe a position. Already in February they had been driven with violence and destruction from Maestricht. At St. Omer in April the citizens resisted and refused to expel them; and at Douai also they were to be brought back almost immediately. But the pattern of organized hooliganism seemed due to repeat itself in every town. Under these circumstances they would not admit an English boy of sixteen whose duty, clearly, was to go home to his parents.

On 25th May Deckers was duly admitted to the noviceship. But a week later the violence reached Tournai. On 3rd June the novitiate was closed, and the novices were sent back to their families.

D

At this juncture there is another clear glimpse of Southwell's character. The first touch of persecution came like a gust of native air from England. He abandoned his *Querimonia* and sprang into vigorous action. Perhaps he remembered the young Jesuit hero, Stanislaus Kostka, who ten years earlier, defying parents and pursuers, had walked to Rome from Poland. At any rate, afire with enthusiasm he confronted Deckers: 'Rome! Rome is where our vocation urges us.' But poor Deckers had been quite dazed and jolted by the turn of events. He seems to have been appalled by Southwell's vehemence and shocked by his contempt for *bourgeois* values. At least that is what one gathers from the rueful letter that he wrote to Southwell two and a half years later —the letter that drew the warm-hearted answer already quoted.

I beseech you, how came it about that we so like in age were so unlike in generosity. . . . I cannot conceal my insane error. Truly I wonder at it. Why were you so impatient of delay, why did you trample underfoot all those values which cause worldly men to hesitate, oblivious of your homeland, your parents, your colleagues, not to mention your costly property (*preciosae suppellectilis?*)? You answered: I am hastening without delay whither my vocation urges me. . . . Useless were the objections of those who sought to move you from your purpose. Vain was their energy, they beat the air with words, advising you to postpone your entry, or deprecating your setting-out for Rome. (9)

Even from this condensed excerpt it may be seen that Deckers did not favour an incisive style. He was a good friend to Southwell in later years, an invaluable if florid eulogist of him after his death, and a very worthy man in his own line—he became a professor of theology and a correspondent of the astronomer Kepler—but, at this crisis Robert turned to his fellow-countrymen.

There was an English student—hitherto unnoticed—named Matthew Marshall who was of like mind with himself, and ready for the hazard. Their enterprise once fixed became unexpectedly easy. While the Belgian Jesuits prophesied woe, the Englishmen who still remained at Douai gave enthusiastic support. In those early days it was considered an honour for an English College man to enter the Society. Perhaps good Fr. Columb, the Devonshire man, came into his own on this occasion: 'Go ahead, my boy; stick to your vocation, stick to the Society.' There was talk of two other young men, Harwood and Nicholas Smith, who were planning the same expedition from Paris. So Paris once more was the first step where they joined up with the other pair. Nicholas Smith was found to be a connection of Robert's, being a first cousin of the Copleys on the Luttrell side.

Mention of the Copleys recalls that they had moved from Louvain to Paris about this time, and were on the crest of a short wave of prosperity. The King of France had ennobled Uncle Thomas—in compensation for that extinct English peerage he had always claimed—and was about to knight his eldest son, Henry. It is a harmless conjecture that he gave his two nephews, Robert and Nicholas Smith, and their two companions a handsome send-off.

There was a fifth Roman pilgrim who seems to have travelled independently, Edmund Holt, already a priest and a distinguished man. For him, admission into the Society might be considered a certainty. But for the four boys, their journey to Rome was a courageous gamble. For Robert in particular, it was the last and decisive throw in a series of risks that had begun when he became a recusant at the age of fourteen, or probably earlier.

Since that time he had moved through a very strange countryside, fit to turn the head of a clever imaginative boy. On the one hand, looming always and sometimes actually leaping across his path, had been the dangers of arrest with torture to follow or of death by mob-violence; and on the other, the glittering and accessible rewards of a career in eloquence and letters. The effect of this life on his fellow-student, Gilbert Gifford, had been an intoxicating attraction to fantastic intrigue and corrupt pleasure. Robert had been preserved from this only because his primary motive had been not self-expression but the love of God.

The spirit of adventure and desire for the New Learning had played their part, but they had been canalized by the training he had accepted. From the sons of Saint Ignatius he had learned that prayer and solid virtue are the only ways to keep natural gifts from being wasted, and at Allen's English College he had become imbued with the spirit of loyal co-operation for the common cause.

God, working through nature as well as grace, had invaded the senses of his soul with sweetness, awakening wholly new powers. But the advice given by Father Darbishire he had now worked out for himself: that this mysterious love was given to him to diffuse among his fellow-men, and that in the Society of Jesus he would find the means for doing so. It is not too early to attribute to him the thoughts, if not the words, of his poem: *From Fortune's Reach*:

> Let fickle Fortune run her blindest race,
> I settled have an unremoved mind;
> I scorn to be the game of Fancy's chase
> Or vane to show the change of every wind . . .
>
> My choice was guided by foresightful heed,
> It was averred with approving will;
> It shall be followed with performing deed
> And seal'd with vow till death the chooser kill.
> Yet death, though final date of vain desires,
> Ends not my choice which with no time expires.

CHAPTER THREE

Rome : the Portrait Revived, 1578–81

THERE was no Dome upon Saint Peter's to catch the eye of the English pilgrims in 1578. But neither were they troubled by the ghosts of a dead empire whether crowned or otherwise. 'Do you wonder', Edmund Campion had written in the previous year to his friend Gregory Martin, 'whether life holds anything if all this wealth and beauty have come to nothing? Then think of the men who stood firm when these dissolved, and of the things that do remain. The relics of the Saints and the Chair of the Fisherman!'

On the Chair of the Fisherman sat the aged Gregory XIII, a Pope of great conceptions often marred by strange indiscretions or fits of apathy. He was a zealous patron of the new colleges for producing trained and cultured national clergies; and he had also a great vision of the Church being planted in far continents and growing up without European political interference. He was therefore a warm supporter of the new orders, particularly of the Society of Jesus. But he was surrounded by bureaucratic departments whose heads did not altogether share his enthusiasms. Hence great projects and heroic endeavours were often fouled by the cross-currents of palace intrigue.

Robert was made aware of dissension as soon as he arrived. His grand-uncle, Sir Richard Shelley, *doyen* of the English colony, had quarrelled violently with a certain Archdeacon Owen Lewis, a Welsh dignitary who stood high in favour with the Inquisition. The subject was the ill-advised expedition of Lewis's particular friend, the Marquis Stukeley, a picturesque ruffian who

37

had changed his profession from Protestant pirate to Papal bully. Sir Richard, having hotly denounced it, had been delated to the Inquisition and might have been seriously embarrassed if his friend Father Persons, confessor to the English in Rome, had not warned him in time. (1) The quarrel had then swollen into a general Welsh-English feud, which centred on the Pilgrims' Hospice where Southwell and his companions were staying; the Hospice had been founded in the eighth century—but by a king from Wessex or from Wales? It was a childish dispute. 'But who can stay young men, or old either,' wrote Persons to Doctor Allen, 'once incensed on both sides by national contentions? You know what passeth in Oxford on like occasions.' (2)

Robert Persons, late fellow of Balliol, was the unofficial leader of the rapidly growing number of English Jesuits. He was delighted with the four boys who had just arrived, and wrote to Edmund Campion:

> We are here at Rome now twenty-four Englishmen of the Society, whereof five have entered within this month: one named Mr. Holt which was once of Oriel College master of Arts; and the other four came hither from Paris, all excellent towardly youths, and all have ended the courses of philosophia. Two of them are your countrymen born in Pater Noster Row, one named Harwood, and the other Smith, little Doctor Smith the physician's nephew. One English of good learning is presently now herehence sent towards Japponia. I hope ere it be long we shall find a vent another way. . . . I pray you, Mr. Campion, pray for me, for I have great need of it. (3)

The Englishman 'sent towards Japponia' was Fr. Thomas Stephens, already mentioned. By 'a vent another way' Persons meant England. It seemed to him a tragic thing that some of Allen's best men should be leaving him to join the Society without the prospect of any return for his generosity. But the General of the Society, Everard Mercurian, was firmly opposed to Jesuits getting entangled with the English mission; there was so much to do elsewhere.

Another worry was this Pilgrims' Hospice which Allen had designed to convert into a new English College on the Douai-

Rheims model. Archdeacon Lewis had offered to use his talents and influence to further Allen's design. But between the intention and the action something had gone wrong.

The Hospice, situated in the Campo dei Fiori, was run by a number of venerable Chaplains, most of them church dignitaries of Queen Mary's day, who took it in turns each year to be Warden. Archdeacon Lewis had persuaded the Cardinal Protector of England to prolong the wardenship of another Welshman, Dr. Morice Clenock, a good but incompetent man. His plan was that, when the Hospice became a College, the existing Warden would become *ipso facto* Rector of it with the Archdeacon to guide his hand. A Welsh Barchester in renaissance Rome! (4)

The Chaplains did not object to sacrificing themselves for the good of their country; but both they and the new English students were complaining: that the place was becoming a club for retired Welshmen, and, more seriously, that they were not being trained for the English Mission. Some confirmation of these murmurs Southwell would have gained from the fact that his old schoolfellow, Hugh Griffin, who was the Archdeacon's nephew, was now in the College with no intention beyond that of securing a benefice and living comfortably abroad.

But neither Southwell nor his three companions were to be burdened with such worries yet awhile. Their minds turned longingly towards their goal on top of the Quirinal Hill overlooking the City. Here stood the house and garden which the Colonna family had given to St. Francis Borgia. It was called Sant' Andrea, after the little parish church which formed part of the property—Bernini's baroque masterpiece was yet to come— and it was the Roman Noviceship where St. Stanislaus had died ten years earlier. (5)

Robert and his friend Matthew Marshall entered Sant' Andrea together on 17th October. It was the vigil of St. Luke, afterwards invoked in his spiritual notes as 'St. Luke who didst write about the Mother of God and didst paint her portrait'. By a coincidence, it was also—according to English reckoning—the feast-day of St. Faith whose priory his grandfather had robbed. The inscription of his entry runs: *Robertus Southwell, circa* 17 *annorum, admissus Romae,* 170 *Oct.* 1578. More adds that he was not yet quite seventeen.

There were three other Englishmen already in the Italian novitiate to greet the four new arrivals. (6) The last to enter, on 25th April, had been Simon Hunt, the ex-schoolmaster of Stratford-on-Avon, who had come from Rheims. Six years later Persons was to petition for 'Robert' and 'Simon' to be sent together on the English mission. Robert was turned down because his intellect was too useful elsewhere, and poor Simon (who died the year after) was queried *'for lack of learning'.* Since he was probably one of Shakespeare's schoolmasters, he must clearly shoulder some blame for the alleged 'little Latin and less Greek'. All the same, the only schoolmaster Shakespeare showed any fondness for was the amateur one in disguise from Rheims: 'this young scholar that hath long been studying at Rheims, so cunning in Greek, Latin and other languages . . .'

England, however, was firmly banished from Robert's mind as he stood on the threshold of Sant' Andrea. The news broken to him by Persons had certainly come as a blow. This seems clear from a passage in his spiritual notes which evidently dates from the first days of noviceship, and which also shows that his deciding motive in joining the Jesuits and not the Carthusians had been the resolution to return and work for his kinsfolk in England. (7)

'*Why,*' he asks himself in some perplexity, 'why, then, should God have drawn me to the Society—and not to the Carthusians or some other solitary order—and drawn me with this one and only argument, namely that only in the Society and not in these other orders, could I be of any use to my country, to my kinsfolk, to my friends, etc., who do so seem to need my help?' He answers himself in the words of Christ: 'Thou knowest not now, but thou shalt know hereafter.' But some earlier lines in the same passage show that it was not without interior flinching that he braced himself to meet this new, strange, buried life: 'Do not be sad or angry whatever they tell you to do, even though they want you to spend your whole life in the kitchen or in the pantry or in abject drudgery. They would never tell you to do it unless it were God's Will.'

In the peace and interior stillness of Sant' Andrea he listened for the voice of the Holy Spirit. The stillness, however, was not the perfect and gracious silence of a Carthusian monastery. 'Stillness', indeed, is not the dominant impression a visitor would get from a Jesuit noviceship. It consists largely, as far as mere time is concerned, in a relentless rush from one duty to another, during which vocal silence is counterbalanced by a good deal of noise from other instruments—knives, plates, broomsticks, buckets, not to mention heavier objects. And silence-time itself, at Sant' Andrea, would be amply compensated by the pious but piercing din of an Italian recreation. It was the human, not the super-human or inhuman, element in the noviceship that provided its severest tests.

The shock that awaited sixteenth-century neophytes, most of whom were of high breeding, was the very absence of those noble weapons by which they had hoped to achieve heroic sanctity in a short time—enormous flagellations, nocturnal vigils, protracted fasts. Instead they had to settle down to a humdrum, rhythmic life: eating plenty, sleeping soundly, and achieving a smiling and modest efficiency at half-a-dozen tasks, among which those of scullion and pantry-boy loomed large. The kitchen was generally recognized as the battle-ground on which most sixteenth-century novices won their spurs. The kitchen comes up again a little further on in the same passage of Southwell's notes, with a hint of panic behind it: is he to be there all his life? But he settles the matter with a smile at his own vanity:

> God knows that your talents are made for mighty deeds, he knows your gifts of nature and of grace. He has examined them thoroughly and considered them from every angle. And he has come to the conclusion that the kitchen is the place that suits you best—at least, for the moment, though of course there may be needs in the future for which he will provide a different set of circumstances.

Later on, he still feels the need to rally himself against obstacles, and he does so in a discussion which is an interesting link between the sorrow at the beginning of the *Querimonia* and the joy at the end of the letter to Deckers. It also shows how potent a cause of vocations in a college is example. *Memento, nunc, Roberte*, is the keynote:

Keep continually in your heart that longing that made you so often beg admittance. Remember all the times, when you were repulsed, how you burst into tears, and had to sit in your bed-room alone, unable to keep down your sobs and sighs. How blissful, you thought, were those who had actually made their vows in the Society. How strict and sweet and gentle seemed to you the union between God and a son of the Society. How you admired them when you watched them praying. It never occurred to you but that they were rapt in the highest contemplation. And though you were like an exile and outlaw who could not be among them, how pleasant it was even just to try and imitate their prayer. Well, then, remember, Robert, the case is altered with you now. You *are* a son of Jesus Christ, a member of his company, and you who used to wonder at their virtues, must now be an example of the same to others.

Another note of a later date recalls those early resolutions on the threshold of religious life:

From today you are beginning. So you must think what you put to yourself on that first day when you did begin, how you did everything you were told by anybody, and bore yourself like a pilgrim and a stranger. When people blamed you, you said nothing, except to admit openly that it was your fault.

You have come like an outlaw from the world, all torn and filthy with sin, you have come into religion like a beggar, having no other place to fly to and take refuge from your enemies. . . . And God in calling you thus from the world has made this clear to you: that while before you were his servant, he now is asking more of you: henceforward, you are the servant of his servants. He made this very clear to you when on the threshold of religious life he gave you this keen desire: to be forgotten and ignored by all and put to work at all the meanest tasks.

In a community where everyone is liable to insist on being everyone else's servant, external humility can become the grotesque disguise of vanity and envy; the passage ends with a note which is evidently the fruit of experience: 'All the same, you should be guided by custom in this sort of thing, and avoid eccentricity. Always avoid eccentricity, for it is the ruin of any kind of social life.'

With this attitude of loving service, he soon discovered that the driving force of his vocation was not primarily a wish to build his character or shape his career; it was a longing, as the hind desireth the water-brooks, for union with God in prayer. He could now enter as of right into the Jesuit method of prayer. Not that there is, or was then, a special Jesuit method; Gagliardi, the chief Jesuit authority of those days, wrote: 'Every man has his own way of meditating.' But there is a general method commonly used in the Exercises, called active contemplation. It is roughly this: to soak the memory and the senses of the soul in the physical reality of Christ's words and actions, and then to let there be distilled, as it were, in the intellect a word of God, a confused apprehension of his divinity, to which the will 'with a blind and naked stirring' can adhere. Examples of this kind of prayer occur in several pieces of what seem to be his early noviceship writings. Here is one on the text: 'Wearied with his journey' (John 4: 6):

[Imagine that] Christ is following after me, crying 'Wait for me till I come and cure thee,' and coaxing now with sweetness, now with reproaches, now with inspirations. But all the while we run from him, and still we block our ears, so that he is forced to give up, *weary with journeying*. He has called and no one has answered, he has run and caught nothing, he has searched and has not found; and for that reason it is that *weary from the journey, he is sitting* there. . . . He is sitting, as one waiting, without hope. Follow me still, O Lord, follow me. Or rather, if thou wilt, let me come and sit also at thy feet. And give me the waters of life which quench the fires of lust. And wash me, Lord, wash me. Behold, I come. My God, receive me.

St. Ignatius, however, sets a double object before his disciple: 'the love *and* the service of God'; and though objectively these two are inseparable, yet it is not long before his disciple is aware that in particular subjects they seem to part company. The soul would have him sit absorbed in the mirror of God, forgetting and forgotten by all else. But the mind urges him to be up and doing and to exploit his talents to their best advantage. He must learn to keep trying to do both. His task is to keep his effective love of God at high pressure and at the same time to transfer all that latent energy into the daily activities of brain and volition.

Southwell's pursuance of this lifelong task began in earnest when, in his second year's noviceship, he was transferred from the seclusion of Sant' Andrea into the bustling life of the Roman College. Here he had to complete his noviceship under the direction of Fr. Persons, and also to make up his course of philosophy which had been somewhat scrambled between Douai and Paris. The difficulty of wrenching his mind from contemplation to the by-play of dialectics can be inferred from a note like this: 'O blush and be confounded, that while God is pouring life into you every moment, you should be offending his eternal majesty with that very gift you are receiving from him.'

At first he tried to regulate his thoughts by a meticulous spiritual time-table. But a more radical and Ignatian approach to the problem is indicated in the following note:

The reason why you relapse so easily seems to be this: that you think you can afford to do and say what you see other people doing as a matter of course, or what you hear them saying. But that is most untrue. For you know by this time that you are very easy-going by nature and prone to the line of least resistance; and you begin to get slack as soon as you omit the least bit of what your confessor and your superior have agreed to your doing. Your fickleness is a great drawback, too; you decide to do a thing and then not to do it, and do not stick to the resolution that you made with God's inspiration and your superior's consent. What does you much harm, also, is your own mental confusion. The only remedy for this is to persevere with one virtue, and to follow a method, especially in prayer, at Mass, and in your studies. For the present you must keep working at the first degree of humility, which consists in external composure and religious good-manners; and you may very well be encouraged in this by remembering how the good manners of Ours have caused or confirmed nearly all the vocations to the Society, and on the other hand, how some have been almost turned from their vocations altogether by the ill-regulated words and gestures of Ours.

The only difference between this and the ordinary type of noviceship resolution is that Southwell kept his. To the end of his life he was remarkable for gentle courtesy and composure even under the strangest circumstances. But the movements of the heart were, at first, not so easy to regulate, and use as means to an end. One note runs:

If you could love a friend so much, if *he* or *he* is so attractive that everything he asked of you, you would agree to; and if it is so sweet to sit and talk with him, describe your mishaps to him,—then with how much more trust should you betake yourself to God the God of goodness, converse with *him*, show *him* your weakness and distress, for he has greater care of you than you have of yourself, indeed he *is* more intimately *you* than you are!

And another recalls a moment at evening recreation indoors, when those who have been serving in the refectory come in from 'second table' and there is a reshuffling of places to make room for them.

So, when you are talking with someone, and you become aware that you would rather be talking with someone else, you must be very careful not to move your eyes towards that other person, and not to turn the conversation round to him; and if it is a question of making room for him, you need not be the first to do so; but you should go on talking to the person you are with, as if he were Christ—and do violence to your will.

These minor acts of abnegation were part of a very positive pattern, a glimpse of which is provided on the day that he came to take his vows, 18th October 1580: in Latin that could almost slip accidentally into English verse, he writes: 'Thoughts on

St. Luke's Day, after my vows: Unto the Crucified my soul is spouse, and she must likewise be, even with his body, crucified. For likeness is the cause of love, unlikeness of disunity.'*

The Roman College, where Robert completed his noviceship and continued his studies, was still on the site chosen for it by St. Ignatius at the foot of the Capitoline Hill. It had been originally intended simply for young Jesuits studying to be priests; but the quality of its teaching had caused it to outgrow its modest beginnings. Students were flocking to it from all over the known world, attracted by the fame of such professors as Bellarmine, Suarez and Clavius. New and more spacious quarters financed by Pope Gregory were already in process of construction, and it was about to assume its new title of the Pontifical Gregorian University. (8)

Among those who attended its course of studies were the young men from the German College and from the recently founded English College. Both these national colleges had Jesuit professors, and the German was from the beginning under Jesuit supervision; but it must be emphasized that their purpose was not to train more Jesuits, but to produce a cultured and disciplined national clergy. During the next two years that Southwell spent at the Roman College he had nothing to do with the English College.

In 1581 he crowned his course of philosophy with the ceremony known as a 'Public Defence', about which we have the enthusiastic evidence of his friend John Deckers: 'His excellent talents and abundance of divine light enabled him to make such quick progress that—I say so in all moderation—he was without a rival in philosophy among his fellow-students of the Roman College, which is the most celebrated in the world. And all can testify to that who witnessed his disputation in the whole of philosophy.'

But in spite of this scholastic triumph it is likely that his heart was elsewhere. In the spring of 1580 Edmund Campion had

* *Crucifixo desponsata est anima tua, unde et eam cum corpore crucifixam esse oportet. Sicut enim similitudo amicitiae, ita et dissimilitudo disunionis causa esse solet.*

come from Prague; and he and Robert Persons and the flower of
the English College had ridden out of Rome on the Flaminian
Way towards England. Campion, with whose talent and temperament Southwell had so much in common, he hardly knew
except to gaze with reverence during his short stay in the City.
But Robert Persons was an important element in his life. He had
been Southwell's spiritual director until he left with Campion
in the spring; and after that there seems to have been an understanding that Persons would try and get him on the English Mission
as soon as he was ordained. For the next few years no letter from
Persons came to Rome without a message for 'my dearest Robert'.

The first step towards England was that in 1581 he was transferred from the Roman College to the English College. He
carried on with his theology (the four-year course that follows
philosophy) at the Gregorian University, but he had to live at
the English College in the Campo dei Fiori, and to act as tutor
in philosophy to his fellow-countrymen, who were often as old
as he was and sometimes older. What had looked like a stepping-
stone became a fixed assignment. He spent the next five years
there, first as tutor and then as Prefect of Studies.

During those years he was raised to great heights of enthusiasm,
and he was also plunged into alarming depths of melancholy.
The whole experience did much to shape his character. It was an
experience closely bound up with events in the College; and
therefore those events will have to be treated at a length that
would otherwise be disproportionate. During Robert's year of
seclusion at Sant' Andrea, the College had passed through a
crisis; its government had been altogether changed, and changed
for the better, but a spectre of dissension remained which was to
haunt it intermittently during the next two decades.

The dissension between the 'English' and the 'Welsh' had
come to a head in March 1579 when the thirty-three English
students broke into open revolt. They were lifted above the level
of ordinary malcontents by the personality of their leader, Ralph
Sherwin—a typical Englishman of the best sort, good-humoured,
rugged, gentle, brave as a lion, and unashamedly pious—and by

the nature of their demand: '*We do not ask for freedom, but for discipline.*' They asked to be put, as the German College was, under the fathers of the Society, and to be trained as the Germans were, for the dangers and difficulties of their native land. But revolt against ecclesiastical authority is always a scandalous thing. From the General of the Jesuits the rebels received the very reverse of encouragement; and the Cardinal Protector and the Cardinal Secretary of State came down with all their weight on the side of Dr. Clenock and Archdeacon Lewis. Behind them was the shadow of the Inquisition and the Papal prisons. But the Englishmen did not flinch. Persons, an agonizedly neutral spectator, could not restrain his admiration:

> This act of theirs before the Cardinal was straightway known and talked of all over Rome, for there were at it all the family of the Cardinal and did wonder to see such liberty of speech before so great a personage. And albeit I think there must needs pass many excesses amongst so much as was spoken in that place, of so many youths; yet many men did imagine to see a certain company of *Lawrences*, *Sebastians*, and the like intractable fellows, who brought Emperors and Princes to desperation to deal with them, for that they could neither with giving nor taking away, neither with fair words nor with foul, bring them to condescend to any one little point that they misliked. Many also strangers made this consequent: if these fellows stand thus immovable before such Princes in Rome, what will they do in England before the Heretics? And many said that they doubted before of things reported of English Priests in England, and of their bold answers reported by letters, but now they could believe anything of them. (9)

At the crucial moment when all seemed lost the Pope himself —'this good old Gregory' as Persons called him—intervened dramatically on their behalf with large, decisive gestures. Archdeacon Lewis was promoted to be administrator to Cardinal Borromeo (St. Charles) in Milan. Dr. Clenock vanished peacefully. The General of the Society was commanded, against his will, to take over the College. In the space of a week the situation was completely reversed, while the Cardinal Protector and the

Cardinal Secretary of State shrugged their shoulders and adjusted their points of view. The new Rector was a Jesuit from Siena, Alphonsus Agazzari, who had been very well liked as a lecturer; during the troubles he had worked himself to the bone raising alms for the students after they had been put out onto the street. The governing rule of the new order, which destroyed the dreams of Dr. Lewis, was that every student had to take an oath to return as a priest, if sent, to his native land whether England or Wales. The scholastic year 1579-80 opened with fifty students.

To Dr. Allen, who had hurried to Rome, the solution seemed a particularly happy one, since he had always hoped that the Society by taking over the College would bind itself irrevocably to England, thus fulfilling the pledge which St. Ignatius a year before his death had given to Cardinal Pole. But under the circumstances happy forecasts were premature. Owen Lewis still enjoyed considerable prestige in influential circles, particularly with the Inquisition. Outwardly he accepted the situation with suavity and grace, but under the surface he had received an incurable and festering wound.

In the final report on the English College written by the Papal Visitor, Cardinal Sega, after eleven years' observation, the whole source of its recurring trouble was traced to the 'machinations' of Owen Lewis. Even if this judgement is deemed too harsh, there is no doubt that Lewis became the rallying-point for a number of men of tarnished character who put themselves at the disposal of Walsingham's spy-system in order to wreck the English Colleges both of Rome and Rheims. (10) Among those whose names will recur at a later point in this narrative were: Solomon Aldred, Thomas Morgan, Gilbert Gifford, William Gifford, and Edward Grately.

These 'Seminary Stirs' have become something of a *cause célèbre* in English Catholic history because they flowered monstrously into the discord that poisoned the recusant body in the seventeenth century. According to one view the troubles were the instinctive revolt of the English character against the alien policy of the Jesuits. According to the other they were the work

E

of a hired minority that in no way represented the English Catholic clergy and layfolk.

Southwell was involved in the troubles of 1584–5 only, and not with their more serious aftermath; but his evidence, so far as it goes, is strongly in favour of the second point of view, and therefore it is only fair that it should be given in its right context. Its main interest, however, as has been said, is in its delineation of his character. Roughly speaking, it may be said that his first two years were a transforming inspiration, and his next two were a confirming test: consolation and desolation.

By 1581 the corrupting influence of Aldred and Gilbert Gifford had been removed. Dr. Allen had arrived and had persuaded the General of the Jesuits to let Persons and Campion head the first mission to England. The astonishing results of this enterprise swept all discord clean out of the College; and the years 1581 to 1583 were the most glorious in its Annals. Then trouble followed. It began with the return of Solomon Aldred early in 1584 as a secret agent of Walsingham, and it came to a head with the return of Owen Lewis at the end of the same year.

CHAPTER FOUR

The English College, 1581–3

I N 1581 a stream of young Englishmen came over the Channel
to Rheims. (1) Twenty-two of them passed on to Rome, bringing with them the death-story of Ralph Sherwin who had
ridden out the year before. All the twenty-two had been directly
inspired by Campion and his companions; many had seen
and spoken with them; and some had been their hosts and
guides.

Henceforth the life of the College, now overflowing with
seventy students, was geared to a heroic pitch. From being the
subject of raised eyebrows among the Romans, it became a
sanctified spot where Sebastians and Laurences were to be seen,
not painted on church walls, but walking about in the live colours
of flesh and blood. They were for the most part youths of high
talent and gentle birth who had dared death already in their
escapes. Ten of the seventy were to be martyrs; twenty more
broken by imprisonment; and ten—a tragic proportion—were to
die of consumption before they had finished their studies. Over
their delicate features shone something which might be described
as 'fey' or '*exalté*', or simply as the aureole of heroic sanctity.

The sanctity was heroic enough in most cases; but the aureole
was partly a matter of due publicity: that is, of fitting the youths
into the tradition of Early Christian Martyrs, as Christian Art had
pictured them through the centuries. A good deal of this publicity was the work of Robert Southwell.

He was captured heart and soul by the spirit of the College.
But he also added something to it by being able to express it.

All the time he could spare from his tutoring and private studies was devoted to the work—indeed, more time than he should have spared; for, eventually, there came an admonition from Father Persons: 'Tell Robert not to spend so much time in writing news-letters, but to get on with his studies.' (2)

Catholic propaganda played an important part in the religious struggle which was now reaching its height. Its purpose was not only to raise recusant spirits in England, but to win sympathy— and alms—from Europe. The Jesuits through their colleges had means of reaching France, Flanders, Portugal, and those states in Italy, the Empire and Eastern Europe where the preservation of the Faith depended largely on popular feeling and freedom of speech, and whose friendship the English Government was anxious not to alienate. Southwell's news-sheets were among those of which Lord Burghley complained bitterly that they were making the name of England detested over the Continent. The Catholic practice, however—and Southwell was an example of it even at this early stage—was always to distinguish between the English people and the government.

Not many of these early writings of his have survived as separate entities. His *Life of Edward Throckmorton* has already been mentioned; there is extant a lively news-letter sent to Naples, and there is mention of other such sent to France and Flanders. But probably a good deal of what he wrote was in collaboration and is contained in the *Annual Letters* of the English College 1581–4. These *brochures* are concerned mainly with the adventures and hardships of the incoming students who had escaped from England, and with the work and suffering of those old *alumni* who had returned there as missionary priests.

The author uses bold colours to tell the adventure stories of the incoming students of 1581 and 1582. Some had journeyed in rags through the forests, like Edgar in *King Lear*, living on roots and berries until they reached the coast. Others had been sent to the frightful house of correction at Bridewell, or imprisoned twice or even three times, before they got clear. A number of them— one is edified to note—were middle-class boys ('but gentlemen', the writer adds staidly) who defied their parents at the cost of much indignity both physical and mental. One, after many floggings, had been driven by his father with a stick towards the Protestant church; but he ran past the church, and kept on running, till his home was far away.

For Robert's private rejoicing, there were reunions with several old friends from Douai days. Chief among these was William Brooksby who, with his brother Edward, had acted as guide to Campion; he had joyfully left a large inheritance behind, but had experienced considerable distress at having actually to run round the girl he was engaged to, who had been posted by her parents, not of her own volition, to stop him getting out of the house.

By far the most famous of the young men who acted as guides and hosts to the missionaries was George Gilbert. He was broken in health when he arrived, and had not long to live, but he seems to have irradiated the place with spiritual energy. He had the pictures of former English martyrs painted in the chapel; and he left behind him a most remarkable memorandum on ways and means of carrying out priestly duties in England. But what was most impressive was to hear him, in his slightly stammering but momentous voice, insist on the only possible mood and temper that would do for a priest in England: 'Let them say of you as they said of the Apostles: "These men are full of new wine." Depend upon it, my brothers, this strong inebriating wine of perfect love is there for you to draw, from the side of Christ Crucified which was opened and pierced for all.' Almost his last words as he lay dying were: 'Why are you weeping? You, who have the chance of martyrdom—while I am lying on a soft bed.'

A host of small details reinforced this attitude. Mr. Stephen Brinkley, Campion's printer, arrived in Rome, bringing with him the ropes with which Campion was racked. Someone else had a passing reminiscence which Southwell noted down—foreshadowing his own arrival in England—'Many Catholics make a habit of going to the City Gates or to London Bridge where the heads and quarters of the martyrs are exposed; to avoid suspicion they ask the bystanders who these traitors were, and then venerate them in secret and put up a silent prayer.'

In the news-letter to Naples, Southwell—quoting, perhaps, information from his cousins, the Cottons or the Shelleys—dwells at length on the courage and suffering of the common people in Hampshire; and in accounts of the executions of the *alumni* of the College, he stresses the rough sympathy of the crowd: 'His neck being in the noose, he continued till his last breath to exclaim with indescribable joy, and with a smile on his countenance: "Jesu, Jesu, be to me Jesus!" while the crowd cried out: "May the Lord receive thy blessed soul, good Sherwin."' (3)

Another indication of Robert's position as the College scribe is a 'relation sent to Fr. Southwell in the English College at Rome by a friend who was present . . . but is not named'. Intended doubtless to be translated and publicized, though its rugged English would have been sadly spoiled by the effervescent Latin of the time, it is a stark narrative of the martyrdom of George Haydock and a companion, lately students at Rome. Although too long to be quoted here, there are two points about it which have a bearing on a question that must now be glanced at: the interior discipline of the College.

The first is that George Haydock, and indeed all those whose heroism has been mentioned in this chapter, were devotedly attached to their Jesuit preceptors, and in particular to the Rector Agazzari. The second is a special feature of these executions: the dramatic last-minute appearance of a spy from the English College with evidence of conspiracy not presented at the trial. Under the gibbet, in order to counteract the people's sympathy, the Sheriff said to Haydock: 'There is worse matter found against thee since thy arraignment.' Haydock, a shrewd and stalwart Lancashireman, replied: 'So belike I was wrongfully arraigned!' Then, as on previous occasions, a way was made, and the actor and hack-dramatist Anthony Munday flounced up to the cart and accused Haydock of saying to him at Rome that he would like to kill the Queen. 'But Mr. Haydock, moved with these foresaid talk and speeches said as followeth: "I am presently to give an account before God, and as before God I shall answer, I never spake nor intended any such thing. And, Munday, if thou didst hear me speak any such thing, how chanced it thou camest not to the bar to give this in against me on thy oath?" "Why," said Munday, "I never heard of your arraignment." ' (4)

Anthony Munday had been a confederate of Aldred and the others in the early attempts to corrupt the English students just after the Jesuits took over the College; his pamphlet *The English Romayne Life* has been quoted as an authoritative source by those who take the view that the Jesuit regime was alien to the English character.

The presence of hostile agents must always be borne in mind when considering the Seminary regime. The College was bound by the medieval traditions of the Hospice to give hospitality to any English visitor who asked for it. The only protection from corruption both within and without was a strict interior discipline *voluntarily* undertaken. The rules were such as could only be maintained by the free co-operation of those who accepted them.

The candidate had ten days' residence as a guest to see what was in store for him; and the College reserved its judgement on his fitness during four months of probation. Companions for walks were allotted. Visitings and visitors could be checked at the Superior's discretion. The prefect system was employed; an older student, already in orders, was in charge of each of the seven or eight dormitories. Silence was to be absolute between night-prayers and Morning Mass; and there were other fixed times of prayer amounting to an hour a day.

Those who have experienced modern seminary training at Rome, or elsewhere, may feel a familiar shiver at some of these items. But in Southwell's day such restrictions, though more explicable in view of Walsingham's activities against the Colleges, were much more startling in their novelty, at least in comparison with the free-and-easy life of English Universities. Southwell himself was under no illusion on that score. Ten years later, replying to an accusation of Lord Burghley's that the Seminaries produced 'a multitude of *dissolute* young men', he wrote:

> We must limit our minds to the restrained and severe course of the Society of Jesus or the Seminaries, where the place is in exile, the rules strict, the government austere, our wills broken, the least fault chastised, and most absolute virtue exacted. And who can imagine those to be of so *dissolute* humours who thus determine to abridge themselves of all causes of dissoluteness, and to imprison their affections within the precinct of a regular and straight order? And lest haply it may be imagined that we say more than in proof we find, it is known to thousands and daily witnessed by travellers that we are there tied to so precise terms in diet, apparel, exercise, and all other things, that we are much more shortened of our scope than in any College of our English Universities.

He then goes on to point out that the regime would have been pointless if it had not been part of a voluntary process of self-conquest, undertaken by resolute men who had their eyes on the labours and temptations and tortures that awaited them. The rule of life, apart from being a security measure against spies, had a mystical purpose, expressed in the words of St. Paul: 'to be hidden with Christ in God'. Small penances and privations were a means of union with Christ in the humiliations of his Infancy, the subjection of his Hidden Life, and the temptations of the wilderness: thus pointing forward by an access of supernatural strength to the heroic zeal of his Public Life, and finally to the Passion and Death and Resurrection.

The English Government helped greatly towards delineating the final pattern; for the weapons they employed—false witnesses, bullying judges, strippings, scourgings, and suspension by the wrists with the murderous constriction of breath and blood and muscle—were very easy to assimilate to the Passion by which was wrought our Redemption.

It was a mystical purpose which by no means excluded the humanist ideal of self-conquest as a means to self-fulfilment. Two final quotations from the *Annual Letters*, possibly written

by Robert himself, bring out how potent was the desire to be
clean and whole and strong:

> Twenty of them have this year made the Spiritual Exercises, with-
> drawing from all company for a few days to take account of their
> past lives, and to contemplate the life and example of Christ as the
> model they are to copy in their future conduct. They also think out
> different ways of progressing in virtue: for example, how to over-
> come the desire for esteem and to advance in humility. Like prudent
> wrestlers, they use the practice of secret self-conquest to fit them for
> encountering one day the implacable hatred of the heretics and with-
> stand their cruel assaults . . .

—and how the near presence of the enemy within the gates was
a motive for steady discipline and *esprit de corps*:

> This College can count as a high honour the cunning arts by which
> the English Government tries to overthrow it, as well as the failure
> of these wicked plans. For it is thereby clear that the Queen of
> England stands in greater dread of the *spiritual* war waged by these
> two Colleges (of Rome and Rheims) than of the hostilities of the
> most mighty Princes. And not without good cause: since those
> trained in them are so high-hearted, so on fire with zeal, as not to be
> deterred by threats of racking, or by the still more grim and shameful
> tortures that may lie ahead.

The only private letter of Robert's that has survived from these
two years echoes the sentiment in the extract just quoted: that
only by *spiritual* means was England to be converted. Writing
to Fr. Persons early in 1582 he says that all at the College have
studied Campion's answers at his trial on the subject of loyalty
to the Queen in temporal matters, and are enthusiastically
agreed that this is the precedent to be faithfully followed. It
was, indeed, in order to establish this precedent that Allen had
obtained from Pope Gregory the suspension of Pius V's decree
against Elizabeth; complete abstention from political activity was
thereafter explicitly imposed on all Jesuits and missionary priests
going to England. Allen and Persons—whatever political negotiations they were engaged in—never allowed them to interfere

with the purely spiritual impulse of the Seminaries, difficult though the dilemma later became. Without the integrity of this impulse—as Southwell pointed out at length in his *Humble Supplication* of 1591—the Seminary training would have been psychologically impossible. This letter of 1582 is evidence that his views did not change in the ten years that intervened; they were the views of all the genuine missionary priests and were in complete accordance with the wishes and commands of their superiors.

The rest of the letter is concerned with his father and brother who, he fears, have lapsed from the Church, and with his own desire to return to England as a missionary. 'Some future day, if health and means permit, and Signior Claudio will give leave, I should like to join you and have a share in your toils and profits.' (5) (*Signior Claudio* was the new General of the Society Claudius Aquaviva who, unlike his predecessor, was in favour of supporting Allen with all the means he could.)

Two other fragments about Southwell at this time have a certain interest. Robert Middlemore, a Roman student, to his cousin Robert Throckmorton of Coughton, in an intercepted letter of April 1582 wrote: 'Mr Southwell, otherwise known as Father Robert, and others desire their commendations.' (6)

'Father Robert' was what his father had laughingly called him in early childhood; and the nickname—which had no reference to the priesthood—was evidently carried over to Douai and thence to Rome.

The other fragment is an elegant reference by John Pitts in his Latin book *On the Famous Writers of England*, much quoted in Fuller's *Worthies*. 'He was a familiar friend of mine at Rome', wrote Mr Pitts kindly of his ex-tutor, 'and there he made praiseworthy strides both in philosophy and theology. He also wooed with considerable eagerness the graces of the mother tongue both in prose and verse.' (7)

Apart from their intrinsic interest, these fragments indicate the friendly quality of Southwell's relations with the students; and it is worth noting that the writers were both young men who did not at all share the prevalent desire for martyrdom. Middle-more paid his own fees rather than take the oath, while Pitts, though a Pope's pensioner, slipped away to a lucrative job on the Continent. 'He left for England', is the comment in the College Diary, 'but he has not yet arrived.'

It goes without saying that there was a lighter side to the English College than that which has hitherto been stressed. Apart from the stream of pilgrims passing through the hospice, there were many celebrations when the house was crowded with visitors and rules went by the board; and the College's polyphonic choir was a centre of attraction which filled the little church to overflowing on Sundays and feast-days.* For holidays they had a former hunting-lodge of Pope Julius, given them by Gregory, with an estate and vineyard attached, though many of the students pre-ferred to spend their summer in walking tours over Italy, to raise alms.

The Rector was a warm-hearted Umbrian of commanding personality and great integrity who, nevertheless, took a naïve delight in providing small and unexpected treats. He evidently put personal relations before literal observance, and it is possible that he had favourites. There are letters from two very heroic Englishmen, George Haydock and Christopher Bailey, written to him in terms extraordinarily childlike and touching which suggest that he was able to help and sympathize in ways that might have been impossible for a more taciturn Englishman. Allen held him in very high esteem.

Robert's attitude, apart from implicit obedience, was one of mingled affection and amusement; and Agazzari, for his part, reposed in him an absolute trust. It is not certain at what date he took on the office of Prefect of Studies; (8) but it is certain that in 1584 he was acting as Agazzari's right-hand man with the students under conditions that put an excessive strain on the College.

* A later complaint on this score alleged 'that when the young students sit as they do every feast-day in the Canons' stalls in the church, which is a small one, a number of ladies come and sit quite near, almost facing them, and other young men and gentlemen from outside come and look at them very immodestly, before the eyes of the students . . .'

The stream of young men to the colleges overseas was still very large in 1583. In the month of August, Dr. Allen had more than fifty applications. Many of them were scholars and graduates of the two Universities. He could not bear to turn them away, especially as they represented the continuity of English Catholic culture which he had so much at heart; but some of them caused grave misgivings to himself and his Prefect of Studies, Dr. Barrett. There was a small but deadly faction at Rheims that kept in touch with Gilbert Gifford and Thomas Morgan, and looked to Gilbert's cousin, William Gifford, as their leader within the College. Allen was afraid that the newcomers would be tainted by the faction before they could get the true spirit of the College. He appealed to his good friend Agazzari to take some of the more difficult ones, especially those who were over the age-limit (eighteen to twenty-five); and Agazzari, confident of his success with English youth, replied with an expansive gesture of welcome.

So it came about that a distinguished but formidable company of twenty-five assembled at Rome during the scholastic year 1583-4. The fact that they were mostly University men made them cling together. It was touch and go whether they would recoil in unison at the shocking difference between the Roman seminary and an Oxford College, or whether each on his own would:

> At downright 'No or yes?'
> Doff all, drive full for righteousness.

A glance at the future of fifteen of the twenty-five who came that year provides a clue to the stresses that prevailed during it. Seven of them afterwards joined the Society, while three were intimately attached to it. But five were so permanently estranged that they were afterwards prepared to help the English Government against it; and there are indications that three or four of the remainder veered in the same direction. Between two such opposite poles there was bound to be tension.

Three especially, who were over the age-limit, call for a short note, because it is possible that one or two or all of them were *saboteurs* from the start: Christopher Bagshaw, John Cecil and Stephen Gosson.*

Bagshaw had been a fellow of Balliol along with Robert Persons, and had lent himself—unhappy omen—to manœuvres against him. Since that time he had become a prebendary of Lincoln, and Principal of Gloucester Hall—as Worcester was then called. Although a busy reformer—or perhaps because of that— he had not been popular with his fellow *domini*: 'A zealous Protestant', was the verdict,'but troublesome in his public disputes, and in his behaviour towards persons.' (9) This rasping attitude in personal relations was to prove Bagshaw's lifelong disqualification, except for work demanding indefatigable rancour. The verdict of the heretics was very soon confirmed by the papists at Rheims. Barrett wrote to Agazzari in August 1583: 'Your prudence will be needed to deal with him dexterously, for with us he could not bear the least word that had any note of reprehension or admonition.' (10)

Agazzari had thus an admirable opportunity for bringing out the best in an involved but able character. But Agazzari, unfortunately, was otherwise engaged. As Superior of the Hospice as well as of the College, he felt a responsibility to try and secure pensions from the Pope for deserving exiles. Of late there had been a storm of these demands, and he was kept running from the apartments of one Cardinal to another, and the pensions that he did secure for some only increased the complaints of favouritism from others. He was losing his health, and neglecting the College. By the time he realized this, the troubles inside the College had got well under way. (11)

It seems that Robert Southwell had to bear the brunt of them during the first six months; for early in 1584 he felt obliged to write to Father Persons—about Bagshaw in particular. Persons was in the Netherlands with the Prince of Parma. He was suffering sorely himself from the Morgan faction, which had now been joined by Charles Paget, and at first he did not take the Roman

* They are all noticed in the *Dictionary of National Biography*.

troubles so seriously as he later did. In a letter to Agazzari of 24th March 1584, he wrote: 'All the things that my dear brother Robert has written to me about the College *and about Father Bagshaw* are not strange to me or unexpected; because God Our Lord has given me some experience of what the devil can do to strew thorns and obstacles in the way of good.' (12)

After Easter things became more difficult for Robert. Several of those who were most congenial to him, like Henry Walpole and William Brooksby, left to join the Jesuit noviceship in Naples or in peaceful Sant' Andrea. These departures to the Society produced distinct sparks of resentment; and in the Easter intake of newcomers there was more matter for combustion. Among those who arrived in April were Gosson and Cecil.

Stephen Gosson was a reformed playwright. Turning from the stage in disgust he had written *The School of Abuse* and *Plays Confuted* (dedicated to Sir Francis Walsingham in 1582). *The School of Abuse* provoked the immortal *Apologie for Poetrie* from Sir Philip Sidney, and this has tended to eclipse Gosson's literary merits in the eyes of posterity. The example of other London men-of-letters who had dealings with the Seminaries (Anthony Munday, Thomas Watson, and Christopher Marlowe) would suggest that Gosson was a hired trouble-maker sent by Walsingham—especially as on his return he became lector in the Parish Church at Stepney without incurring any penalties for his flight overseas. Moreover this was a period of great spy-activity in Rome; the English Government was using Solomon Aldred in a complicated intrigue—to be noticed later—which deeply threatened the Seminaries. In any case, judging by Gosson's age (he was almost thirty) and by the acrimonious tone of his pamphlets, he must have been a difficult subject. (13)

John Cecil was of a different calibre from either Bagshaw or Gosson: far quieter and more able. He was a man of very pleasant manners, keen intellect, and considerable self-control. Being a graduate of Trinity, Oxford, he was held in special admiration by two young companions from that college, John Fixer and William Warford. It is not certain exactly when he first offered his services to Walsingham as an agent, though 1588 is the first known date. (14) A later account credited him with being a main source of the trouble at Rome, but at the time he escaped overt criticism;* the chief complaints of the Rector were against his two admirers, Fixer and Warford. Both these young men came from Rheims with high characters. Warford afterwards justified his, breaking with John Cecil. But Fixer, who remained Cecil's constant companion, acquired a very scabrous reputation among the English Catholics, not only for treachery, but for seduction and blackmail, and became in Persons's words: one of those 'lost and wandering lads, that otherwise might have been good and learned men if this faction had not been'.

Without antedating future scandals, it may be gathered that the delicate machinery of the Seminary, described earlier in this chapter, was in danger of being tampered with from the inside.

* For an interesting light on Cecil's part in the troubles, see his letter to Lord Burghley, quoted in Appendix 'A'.

CHAPTER FIVE

The 'Stirs' of 1584–5

THE former Principal of Gloucester Hall was naturally looked up to by his fellow Oxonians. His first grievance, which was taken up by several, was that the Roman regime was fit for children and not for mature University men. For some this was the honest grumble of men anxious to be in the mission field: that Allen's rule at Rheims was more liberal yet Rheims sent more than Rome to England. But for others, including Bagshaw himself, it was just the opposite. The complaint at being debarred from higher degrees and doctorates, with their prospect of livelihood abroad, was in reality an obscure move *against the oath to go to England*, that is, against the whole *raison d'être* of the College. It was the perception of this that caused Southwell to write in alarm to Persons for advice.

Hitherto the 'short' course (three years of moral and controversial questions) had been far more popular with the students than the full course of seven years, because it brought them nearer to England. Now the opposite view was asserting itself, laudably and yet insidiously. Southwell's view, tinged by memories of his martyred companions, was ruthlessly pragmatic: Catholic England was the end and studies, higher or lower, means to the end. With the notion of study as a career he had no sympathy. In a later letter from England to Agazzari, recalling the bitter days of internal strife that were now happily over, he added: 'It is true that all priests are useful here, but especially those who are well skilled in moral and controversial questions. As for other branches of sacred learning, they may gratify fastidious ears, but they are rarely of any use to us here.' (1)

There is evidence that it was his stand in this matter that first brought him up against the trouble. Three students of high intellectual ability, Pormort, Woodward and Thornhill, though they had come to Rome in the famous year of '81, were prominent in supporting Bagshaw's complaint. The variation in their subsequent careers is instructive. It discloses in miniature the unconscious motives behind the discontent and, in one case at least, Southwell's accurate and sympathetic diagnosis of the discontent.

All three did in fact go on to higher studies. Woodward's animosity then vanished; he volunteered for England and became a close friend of John Gerard.

Thornhill, on the other hand, became a querulous Canon at Vicenza. He, too, pined for England, but in a different manner. In 1604 Dr. William Gifford offered him to Cecil (Lord Salisbury) as an 'intelligencer' against the Jesuits.*

Pormort's story, which throws a backward light on Southwell and the opposition he encountered, belongs mostly to a later chapter. Here it is enough to say that a warm friendship had existed between the two in the years 1582-3. But in 1584 when Robert suggested that the other's true vocation lay in England, the result was a serious estrangement. Afterwards a calumny was spread about in the College that Pormort had been driven to his death, not only by persecution in Rome, but by Southwell in England also. How loathsomely false this was Pormort clearly proved in England both by word and deed. But at the time the rift seemed permanent. Pormort left the College in 1586 and took refuge with Monsignor Owen Lewis. (2)

The name of Owen Lewis was already being conjured up by the discontented party. Forgotten was all the 'Welsh' dispute. It was only recalled that Lewis had wished to run the College on lines suitable for mature University men.

As the bitterness of Bagshaw's faction increased during the year, it found issue in a more savage accusation. (3) The Jesuits

* On being discarded by Salisbury, he returned, complaining that the Jesuits had thwarted his zeal for souls. See *Letters of Thomas Fitz-Herbert*, ed. Leo Hicks, p. 72, n. 4 (*CRS*, XLI).

F

it was said, only promoted the studies of those whom they hoped to capture for their own Order; others, for whom they had no use, they were content to send as gallows-fodder to the mission-field. In particular, it was alleged, they concentrated their favourites in the Sodality of the Blessed Virgin, and used them to spy and report on the others. This accusation touched Southwell very nearly, for—at least in 1585—he was Prefect of the Sodality. There is a letter of his to the General—to be quoted later—in which he complains with some bitterness that students are being *prevented*, and injuriously prevented, from joining the Society. Once again, his standpoint is diametrically opposed to that of the complainants. This important fact has never been pointed out before: that Southwell, personally, was a main target of attack by the disturbers; and the Pormort calumny suggests that it was an attack of a poisonous and vicious kind. (4) Another letter from Persons, in July, reveals that Southwell had aided the Rector in some strong action which had temporarily silenced the malcon-tents: 'God bless the zeal of your Reverence and of Father Southwell. It is very welcome news . . . I am very glad that you have scotched Father Bagshaw and his companions, but I am inclined to think that more drastic measures will be necessary.' (5)

Persons's reference to 'Father Southwell' shows that, in the midst of these troubles, Robert had passed through the great moment of his ordination to the priesthood. There is no mention of it in his scattered spiritual notes. But the last batch of them undoubtedly belong to a time when he was wielding authority in the College, and they throw much light on the strain he was under during that year. (6) There is one passage in particular which shows how difficult it was for him to break his relations of easy equality with the students, to report one and admonish another, to abstain from familiarity with those he loved because of accusations of favouritism; and on what a razor-edge of recti-tude he had to live. He speaks to himself, as he so often does:

By the bowels of Jesus Christ and that most sacred blood which flowed from his wounds, I beseech you to take yourself in hand; insist on the most thorough examination of yourself; and be what you must seem to be, the light of the world and the salt of the earth. You know too well how free from stain and blemish those must be whose duty it is to mark the faults of others, to rebuke them, and to punish them in deed as well as words. . . . For the man who professes to bring not only himself but others to the height of perfection, to observe the faults of others, and either to correct them himself with the proper remedies or make report of them to those that will—for such a man, I say, what might not be a fault in others is a fault and worse in him. A wandering eye, an empty laugh, an unregulated act or gesture, in him is tantamount to mortal sin, so much is his behaviour spread out for all to scrutinize and judge.

The accusation that the Jesuits had no conception of the horrors to which they were cheerfully sending the students—'All very well for this boy with a soft career in the Society in store for him!'—must have come with all the keener irony, since to him England and all its dangers seemed a paradise compared with this Roman Inferno.

The Long Vacation did not bring its expected relief. Fever raged. Everyone in Rome, we learn, was sick or weak that summer. Perhaps it was now that a new complaint was added to the list: that the Jesuits neglected the health of the students; indeed, that some were left to die in their beds during the holidays, when the College moved to its Villa. The death-roll had certainly been tragically high both at the English College and among the young English Jesuits. Scarcely a year had passed since 1581 without Robert seeing some friend or dear companion carried off by consumption: Matthew Marshall, Edward Throckmorton, George Gilbert—to be followed by William Brooksby in 1585 and Simon Hunt in 1586; while others, like Nicholas Smith, had had to leave with only an uncertain prospect of being readmitted later.

One or two of his later notes are about pain and illness:

Fear grips you sometimes when sickness hovers near. Sick men, you argue, are useless to the Society, a burden to others, good for nothing. And—and this is the rub—if you fall sick of that particular disease which parches the chest and lungs, farewell to all your hopes of England, and all your hopes of doing great deeds for Christ.

Physical death had no terrors for him. He faced it on this occasion with the same text that he used again at a moment of the greatest danger in England, and once again in his speech from the scaffold: 'Whether we live or whether we die, we belong to the Lord.' What tormented him was the thought of his own sinfulness, and the fear of not being able to wipe it out by the supreme act of love in martyrdom. Desperately he tried to forestall disappointment by long and subtle arguments on the theme:

Inspirations are sent by Almighty God for various purposes, and not always that they may issue in act. . . .

For example, though the desire for martyrdom may be constant, fervent, humble, and devout, yet I should not take for granted that this inspiration is a guarantee that I am to die in defence of the faith. . . .

And pathetically he wrestled with himself on the question: 'Is it better to offer myself or to remain silent?'

I have been wondering which would be better, to manifest my desire, after prayer, to my superior, so that he may decide whether it be from God or not, or to leave the whole matter absolutely to the disposition of God.

The question whether he should be sent straight to England, now that he was a priest, formed a small part of the much larger pattern that came under the survey of the General of the Society, Claudius Aquaviva, that autumn. In spite of world-wide cares —India, Japan, Brazil, Ethiopia—and of even sharper problems pressing on the heart of things at Rome, Aquaviva kept in his mind a clear and privileged place for England.

The Jesuit mission there had almost ceased to exist. Everyone had agreed that with a few more missionaries like Campion there would be a landslide back to the old religion. But the striking successes of Campion and Persons had not been followed up. Jaspar Heywood who succeeded them was a brilliant— though somewhat eccentric—man;* but the English Government, declining to make a martyr of him, had shipped him overseas, after torture, in 1583. William Weston, who had moved

* Known to posterity as a translator of Seneca, and uncle to John Donne.

unnoticed into his place, was to show himself one out of a hundred in worth. But the fact remained that he *was* only one during the years 1584 and 1585, when more than a hundred priests were sent from the Colleges.

Persons, who felt this situation acutely and had himself been refused leave to return, wrote urgently in September 1584, asking that Henry Garnet might be appointed to lead an expedition, and adding: 'I should be glad of Father Simon Hunt also, *and of Father Southwell*, if Father General would agree.' There was thus a definite chance of Robert escaping to his heart's desire before the new scholastic year. But Aquaviva hesitated. His hesitation was partly due to a lack of men for other posts. But in the case of Southwell he had a more telling reason. The *morale* of the College was being so seriously threatened that if he were withdrawn it might collapse; and, on the other hand, if he were sent to England, he would be helpless in the web of intrigue and treachery that was now disfiguring the English Mission.

The Government was making a great effort to subvert and discredit the colleges overseas; the method used was to involve disaffected students in regicide plots which could then be exploded in England with the maximum anti-Catholic propaganda value, the eventual object being the execution of Mary Queen of Scots. The pattern of this sort of intrigue became very clear at Rheims during the following year. How it led up to the 'Babington Plot' is a matter of history, recorded by Dr. Conyers Reade in his life of Walsingham:

> In the year 1585, Walsingham was trying his best to widen the breach between the factions which divided the English Catholics in France, the Jesuits and the Seculars. To that end he was negotiating secretly with Dr. William Gifford, one of the leaders of the Secular Party.* It was in connexion with these negotiations that Gilbert Gifford, the *agent provocateur* in the events which followed, appeared on the scene. . . .

* Dr. Reade is a victim of the misinterpretation of the term 'Secular' as equivalent to 'anti-Jesuit'. The leader of the Secular Clergy was, of course, Dr. Allen. Gifford was his secretly-disaffected subject.

Walsingham's intrigues with the English Catholics in France were not directly designed to entangle Mary Stuart, although he probably hoped that damaging evidence might be secured against her by that channel. At any rate, it was through these English Catholics, or rather through one renegade among them, that he was finally enabled after some eighteen years of ceaseless effort, to bring her to her reckoning. (7)

Walsingham's agent with the disaffected Rheims men was Solomon Aldred, who had retired from playing the same part in Rome the year before. Barrett indicated in a letter to Agazzari how Morgan and Aldred went about this work of corrupting the colleges:

> They keep an extraordinary watch on anyone who has a complaint or difference with superiors. . . . They approach him with the utmost urbanity and tact; give him money if he needs it; invite him to meals, and never let him go. Fr Gifford they count as wholly theirs, and I think he is. (8)

But Aldred's work at Rheims in 1585 was not so noxious as it had been at Rome in 1584, because at Rome it reached right into high places. Aquaviva and Allen had to look on aghast while Aldred conducted negotiations with the Cardinal Secretary himself (whose mentality, it must be confessed, was unworthy of his high office) and with officials of the Inquisition. The terms appear to have been a measure of toleration for English Catholics *in return for* the complete withdrawal of the Jesuits from England and English affairs. But neither side can have taken the terms very seriously, because, at just the same time, the Parry Plot was in progress. Parry belonged to the same firm as Aldred, but he peddled a different line of goods. (9) While Aldred offered terms for a compromise between Rome and London, Parry offered, in terms of pious vagueness, to murder Queen Elizabeth. Allen and Persons both denounced him, but, supported by the faction, he obtained a Plenary Indulgence through the Cardinal, and hastened back with it to the English Government which employed him.

It looks as if both sides, Rome and London, had been attempting to deal each other a mortal blow under cover of a flag of truce. But London at least knew what it was doing. It waited till the plot—and Parry, too, because he was getting dangerous—could be exploded at just the right moment. In the event, the explosion caused a wave of Protestant and patriotic feeling that quite upset the Catholics; the *Bond of Association* against Mary Stuart was made legal; and the terrible Statute was passed decreeing death for any who sheltered a seminary priest.

Parry himself had not dared to come to Rome, where the English Jesuits would have openly denounced him. But two others of the same faction had been there in September, 'consorting principally with Chr. Bagshaw', just when Aquaviva was making up his mind about Southwell and Garnet. These two were John Ballard and Anthony Tyrrell. Ballard was to be the chief agent of the Babington Plot; and Tyrrell afterwards concocted a story that during this month at the English College he had been instructed (by Agazzari!) to murder Queen Elizabeth. (10) It is not suggested that Aquaviva foresaw all this. But he certainly saw two things: that England was no place at the moment for unskilled innocents like Garnet and Southwell, and that the troubles in the College were going to go on and get worse, as long as the sources of them had protection in high places.

In October he replied to Persons that it was out of the question to release Garnet: he was destined to succeed Clavius in the Chair of Mathematics. Having turned down another candidate, Aquaviva added: 'I am very uncertain who should go in his place. Father Simon seems to lack sufficient learning; and *as for Robert*, he is still in the midst of his studies which I do not wish to interrupt, especially as he is destined *for a much more suitable post.*' (11)

As the new scholastic year came nearer it became evident that Robert was to continue as Prefect of Studies; and it is even likely that the General gave him a hint that his future life-work was to be with the English College in Rome. It may have been the prospect of another year more strewn with thorns and pitfalls and potential sins than before, that wrung from him a long and strange threnody entitled, 'To die quickly is a safe thing; to live long in pain for Christ is a holy thing.' It is prefaced by the cry of the Psalmist: 'Woe is me that my sojourning is prolonged! I have dwelt with the inhabitants of Cedar: my soul hath been long a sojourner'—of which the succeeding verse is 'With them that hated peace I was peaceable: when I spoke to them, they fought against me without cause.' In spite of its lyric ardour, it is the nearest that he ever came to cold despair:

> It is a noble thing beyond all doubt to suffer toil and torment for the love of God. It is a noble thing to work for souls and live religiously in a daily round of penance and self-conquest. But if I cannot do these things without offending God, then I would leave them all and quickly die, rather than go on slighting God with daily faults however small. I am not afraid of work; I do not shrink from pain and torture; I would not seek to escape this cramped, confined and dreary life—except that true love cannot bear the loved one to be hurt, either in great things or in small. . . .
>
> I am straightened between two ways, desiring to be dissolved and to be with Christ, for that is better far. Yet if I must remain in the flesh for the sake of others, let thy will be done, for I am thy servant and the son of thy handmaid. . . .
>
> I do not know whether I deserve to be loved or hated. One thing only I know, that other men have fallen, and I am worse than they; and whether I will fall as they have fallen, I do not know. But I am afraid. For thou O God, seeing their ingratitude, hast let them fall from sin to sin. On this I ponder, and I see no way of hope. Ah, dearest Jesus, help and rescue me. I ask for no relief except a good and timely death. Canst thou not kill for pity one who longs to die? Life and death are in thy hand, and giving either is no loss to thee; but death is gain for me. Then quickly let me die and come to thee, dear Jesus, and, free from sin and danger, cry in Heaven: *Gloria in excelsis Deo*.
>
> Yet not as I will, but as thou. Thy will be done. (12)

How seriously should this threnody be taken? Pretty seriously. It was the death of youth. He attained his twenty-third year by climbing into the maturity of middle-age.

In the troubles at the College he had encountered, for the first time, the terror and anguish of raw human nature when it felt the pull of sanctity, not as a sweet attraction, but as a throttling rope; when it plunged wildly in all directions except the one intended. He felt the conflict both within and without. This was his baptism of fire. He emerged from it a ruler of men. But for a moment the sudden and unexpected contrast between the song of the Angels and the howl of the Beast was unnerving. All the joys of religious life, the innocent familiarities of companion-ship, and even the delight of solitary prayer became smeared with the all-pervading taint. And hence it was that Hamlet-like—though wearing his rue with a difference—he could see no way out of the pestilent congregation of vapours except a speedy death.

But no hint of this conflict appeared on the surface. His two offices of Prefect of Studies and Prefect of the Sodality brought him right up against the two main accusations: of favouritism in promotion to scholastic honours, and of spying on those who would not submit to Jesuit spirituality. But between the lines of More's account there is a glimpse of how he carried out these two offices, his care in coaching being all the more attractive because of the glittering sharpness of his mind, and his gentle appeal to virtue being backed by a compelling personal example:

> The English College at that time was crowded with young men most distinguished by the variety and brilliance of their minds; they could not be easily led except by one who gained support from all the ornaments of learning. Now this Southwell lacked neither sharpness in the quick conception of things, nor soundness in judging them, nor ease of expression in explaining them clearly; and besides there was in him an innate suavity and modesty joined with gravity, and a ceaseless striving after virtue amidst the heat of studies; and thus both in ruling the studies with authority, and in inciting souls to virtue, he bound to himself the will of everyone. (13)

'The will of everyone' is a pious exaggeration on the part of More who studiously avoids all mention of the troubles. But where Southwell's influence was probably decisive was upon the nineteen new arrivals of 1584–5. Had these continued the pattern of Bagshaw's year, the College would have been disrupted. But in fact, out of nineteen, only two adhered to the faction. One of these was Anthony Major who soon afterwards became a spy for the Earl of Huntingdon in the North. (14) The other was George Foster who, according to a later entry in the Rheims Diary, was suspected of having been a Government agent while still a student. (15) All the rest took a firm stand for righteousness. Among them were four of Southwell's future fellow-martyrs: Christopher Buxton, Edmund Duke, John Ingram, and Polydore Plasden.

Thus in the attitude of the new men to the authorities there was a remarkable cleavage between light and darkness, spies on one side, martyrs on the other. In the case of one new arrival, Southwell's influence must be reckoned more than an inference; that was Anthony Copley, who came in September 1584. Anthony was by nature a rebel; but as long as his cousin was in Rome, his rebellious instincts were enlisted firmly on the side of the Angels.

In this way, the challenge when it finally came proved not so formidable as might have been expected. In December 1584 Archdeacon Owen Lewis arrived with his servants to stay at the College he had helped to found. (16) As he gazed round the refectory he saw no one who had first-hand knowledge of 1579 —except Agazzari. Their positions seemed now, with a fine artistry, reversed. The old complaint against Lewis, that he was turning the College into a quiet academic centre, was now the burden of a growing chorus in his praise. The grievances were culminating in a demand that the College be removed altogether from Jesuit control and entrusted to a distinguished churchman of the English (or British) nation.

In the same December or the following January, 'after Dr Bagshaw had been in the College about fifteen months', as Persons wrote in his memoirs, 'there ensued such tumults there as had never been known before'. (17) What form they took is not known. But they were such as to rouse the normally easy-going Protector, Cardinal Buoncompagni. Early in January he descended like a bolt from the blue and commanded *viva voce* that Christopher Bagshaw and a youth named George Potter should depart from Rome within three days, the reason for Bagshaw's expulsion being 'that he would not take the oath and would not behave himself'. (18) In 1579 in support of Ralph Sherwin the entire body had walked out of the house. But no one accompanied Bagshaw on his melancholy journey.*

The dissidents were relying mainly on influential help from outside. Gregory XIII was nearing his end, and it was confidently expected that his successor would reverse his policy towards the Society. Only such an expectation could explain the recklessness of the charges that began to circulate in Rome: that three times as many students were decoyed into the Society as were sent to England, that a third of the students were coughing blood as a result of Jesuit persecution, and finally that the Jesuits were embezzling the funds.

Aquaviva at this juncture seems to have asked Southwell for his views. Southwell's reply, dated 23rd January, is extant. Pointedly ignoring the recent disturbance, he praised unreservedly the fine spirit of the student body and their confidence in the skill and understanding of their Rector. He added however a sharp complaint: that the best spirits among the students were longing to join the Society, but were being deliberately thwarted. This was a striking reversal of the charge that they were being *victimized* to join the Society and were (literally) spitting blood as a result. Southwell asserted exactly the opposite, and he attributed the illness of one in particular (who actually had been coughing blood according to a later medical report) to his being *refused* any hope of admission to the Society. 'I am aware,' he added, 'and bitterly aware, that things have come to such a point that students cannot be publicly admitted to the Society without danger of scandal; but all I ask is that some way be found of

---

* Bagshaw did proceed to England, but in the service of Morgan and Paget. Reports from Aldred, William Gifford and Grately advised Walsingham to make use of his services, 'for he has an excellent wit and knows the proceedings of the Jesuits'. (*CSPD*, 1580–1625, pp. 175, 179.)

affording them relief; for if we do nothing to assuage their mental anguish, we shall be responsible for their breakdown in health.' (19) It is worth remarking that the Society by turning away many promising candidates, so as to avoid the charge of proselytism only incurred (and still incurs) the opposite reproach: that the number of Jesuits in England was contemptible as compared with the number of Seculars. The main interest, however, in his letter is its implicit assertion that the real troubles were manufactured from outside the College. This was soon to be borne out by the sequence of events.

In April, Gregory XIII, beloved of the English Catholics, died, and after a very short conclave, the Franciscan, Cardinal Montalto, was elected as Sixtus V. When it became known that a complaint against the Jesuits was to be addressed to the new Pope on behalf of the English College, there was a counter-stir of great indignation among the main body of students. Hitherto they had kept silent, bearing patiently the provocations of the minority. But now the senior among them drew up a remonstrance which was afterwards signed by forty-nine out of the total of sixty-seven students:

> Whereas a report is abroad that the scholars of our English College, with a degree of inconsistency, desire that the Fathers of the Society, whom they before so earnestly demanded, should now be removed from the direction of this College: it is deemed good by the consent of all whose names are here-to subscribed, to declare to your Eminence that the report is wholly groundless. We consider it unjust, as in other communities, so in this our College, that the imprudence of a few should be allowed to prejudice the solemn judgement of the many. We were the sons of the Society for the full term of seven years, nor, by the help of God, will we ever withdraw from the duty of upright children towards their loving parents. (20)

A nearly three-quarters majority was enough to nullify the substance of most of the mutineers' complaints. But their petition had already got beyond their control, and was part of a larger weapon in the hands of those who hoped to profit by the new

Pope's supposed dislike of the Society. Sixtus V, however, though an autocrat, was an impartial one. He was suspicious of the Jesuits, but his suspicions took the form of a fact-finding commission headed by Monsignor Sega. Sega's first report was a dry and factual affair compared with his later denunciation of Lewis. But it was conclusive. And here too the episode may be concluded, with the brief notice of it by Pastor in his *History of the Popes*:

> The common view in Rome, and even more abroad, was that Sixtus V was not well disposed towards the Jesuits, and that he would change their constitutions. Above all, those who were either the declared opponents of the seminaries, or were unwilling that they should be in the hands of the Jesuits, saw in him one who shared their views. A visitation of the Roman seminaries directed by the Jesuits, the German and English Colleges, the Roman College, and the College of the Maronites was actually ordered in 1585. The careful investigation however turned out in favour of the Jesuits. (21)

Since the main object of this chapter was to outline the context of Southwell's spiritual development, it may well end with the last of his spiritual notes. These close abruptly with resolutions on obedience, and they reflect some great decision made in the light of prayer.

> In case it should ever happen, which God forbid, that I am shaken in my resolution, I now, in full tranquillity and serenity of mind, lay down for myself the following clear rule in all matters; especially those referring to my vocation and my duty of obedience. I am to turn my eyes back to my present determination, I am to regard seriously and without thought of self the will of God as declared to me at all times and in every circumstance by my superiors. I have had regard to my soul's health and I have understood the necessity for me of the religious life and the obvious dangers that are in the world. In the light of these considerations, true, good, reasonable and pleasing to God, I have made the firm and inviolable resolution, in the sight of God and of all creatures, that it is absolutely the best, the most necessary, the most suitable thing for me, to live and die, for the praise and glory of God, in no other state that exists or might exist, but only in the Society of Jesus. All this and everything else I understand in accordance with the Constitutions of the Society.

Southwell's obedience had behind it the full power of his critical intelligence and his autonomous free will. Compared with unthinking obedience, or with petulant rebelliousness, it was like dynamite to butter.

Yet the very last entry of all, the one that concludes his notes, though it is on a softer key, is no less revealing. It shows him descending from the harsh heights of eternal issues into the flat plain of daily life. It is a short comparison of the life of the Fathers of the Desert with his own immediate vocation:

When the fathers in olden times had fallen into any fault or error, they used to remove the occasion of it. So, for example, if one had erred in his speech, he would stay within the walls of his house and no longer mix with men. This was certainly a mark of great virtue. But a still higher level is placed before *us*. They, when they saw the enemy, saved themselves by flight, and taking refuge in their strongholds, removed themselves from his power.

But *we* must ever keep our enemy before our eyes, always be in touch with him, always be fighting with him, and yet never be beaten or conquered by him. The faults we commit in speech we must correct, not by keeping silence altogether, but by speaking with greater caution; and motions of impatience, not by fleeing from occasions, but by stout resistance to them, and so on—

FOR THE GREATER GLORY OF GOD (22)

CHAPTER SIX

Life in Rome, 1585-6

THE experience just described might have proved fatal for Southwell's poetry. The struggle with unruly passion might have tempted him to suppress all poetic inspiration as erotic in origin; or alternatively his success in subduing passion to reason might have engendered a wholly utilitarian view of verse. But it did not. His simple view of inspiration, the same as Sidney's 'Look in thy heart and write!', is revealed in one sentence: 'I know that no man can express a passion that he feeleth not, nor doth the pen deliver but what it copieth out of the mind.'

The sentence is from the dedication to his *Mary Magdalen's Funeral Tears*, begun in Rome and later published in England. The choice of this theme, made in Rome, is significant. (1) Mary Magdalen was the type of the indestructible Eros, purified by contrition and thereafter made capable, through affective union with Christ's human nature, of the divine love of the Creator. The note that Southwell strikes all through is the divine acceptance of genuine human love however misguided.

But alas why do I urge her with reason, whose reason is altered into love, and that judgeth it folly to follow such reason as should any way impair her love? Her thoughts were arrested by every thread of Christ's sindon, and she was captive in so many prisons as the Tomb had memories of her lost master: Love being her Jailor in them all, and nothing able to ransom her but the recovery of her Lord.

Phrases like 'her thoughts were arrested by every thread of Christ's sindon' show that while Southwell's judgement had matured, his poetic 'sensibility' had not been blunted.

79

It is true that the qualities he strove for above all in his verse, as in his conduct, were clarity and control. But he always made allowance for the spontaneous leap of nature to its origin and end; and that is what diffuses a lovely, lilting quality through much of his otherwise pedestrian verse; it is a lilt impossible to locate particularly in rhythm, imagery or diction; it pervades the whole because it is the effect of his personality. His personality, on the highest level, was spontaneous as personality must be and independent of all except its lode-star, God.

Thus, in the struggle for self-conquest, the figure of Robert Southwell emerged from the dust of battle with the plume of beauty nodding proudly and gaily above the helmet of righteousness. It was a victory won, of course, at the price of unceasing vigilance and tension. But this was just what would put him in tune with the best spirits of his age, both Catholic and Protestant. It was the age between the High Renaissance and the Baroque, when Vignola built a masterpiece that might equally be a monastery, a fortress, or a pleasure-resort, and Sir Philip Sidney sought to combine the careers of hermit, courtier, and man-at-arms. Integrity, after the bewildering expansion of the half-century, was what they felt the need of, and integrity was what Robert Southwell had achieved.

Another passage in the same dedication brings out, like an early renaissance sculpture, the lithe and muscular knotting-together of all the passions to a single purpose. It is very long, but an extract must be quoted because it is a sort of engraving of himself:

Love is but the infancy of true charity, yet sucking nature's teat and swathed in her bands, which then groweth to perfection when faith besides natural motives proposeth higher and nobler grounds of amity.

Hatred and anger are the necessary officers of prowess and justice, courage being cold and dull, and justice in due revenge slack and careless, where hate of the fault doth not make it odious, and anger setteth not an edge on the sword that punisheth or preventeth wrongs.

Desire and hope are the parents of diligence and industry, the nurses of perseverance and constancy, the seeds of valour and magnanimity, the death of sloth, and the breath of all virtue.

Fear and dislike are the scouts of discretion, the harbingers of wisdom and policy, killing idle repentance in the cradle, and curbing rashness with deliberation. Audacity is the armour of strength, and the guide to glory, breaking the ice to the hardest exploits, and crowning valour with honourable victory.

This remarkable balance of cold intelligence with fearless ardour was what the English Government particularly dreaded in the incoming Seminary priests; it was the reply to the alliance between the reformed religion and the renaissance. But there was more to it than that. The personality of Robert Southwell as a poet was an even greater menace to the Government than his virtue or his learning. For the strength of the new establishment did not any longer consist in its learning and virtue, in truth and goodness. It consisted in a force completely non-clerical, and even anti-clerical, which for want of a better word may be called 'beauty'. The old tradition of Courtly Love, with all its Arthurian trappings, had been revived and centred on the Virgin Queen. To the older generation of Catholic exiles, Elizabeth was the equivalent of a gangster's moll, desecrating the throne of Saint Edward; but in the eyes of the rising generation she was being built up in the likeness of a beleaguered Princess in the white tower of England. If Spain could be prodded sufficiently into playing the part of the dragon, a scene would be set to which Catholics more than any others must instinctively respond. By tradition and temperament they could despise the new religion, but the appeal of chivalry was much harder to resist. It was precisely the element of knight-errantry in Edmund Campion, honouring the Queen and turning the heretic Government into the dragon, that had swung the sympathies of young Catholics back to the Old Faith. 'The greatest number of papists is of very young men', wrote Lord Burghley in chagrin to Elizabeth in 1584. He noted also an extraordinary thing: their *personal* devotion to the reigning Pope, Gregory. (2)

G

Robert Southwell had seen this at once. 'This is the line we must all follow', he had written, about Campion, in 1582. He was deliberately training himself to be a courtly poet: to circumvent the luxuriant return of chivalry and bring it back to its Catholic setting. He had all the encouragement he needed for this, both in the Ignatian letter ('to go in at another's door and come out at your own'), and in the peculiar spirit of the sublime vagabond of Montserrat who remained a knight-errant at heart to the end, seeing the Church as the Bride of Christ chained to a Rock, the Rock of Peter.

This is the place to reflect how Southwell's eight years at Rome enabled him to translate both the grandeur and the weakness of the Church into terms of his own poetic experience: heavenly glory striving to win free from mortal decay. The Protestant caricature of Archimago was eclipsed in the mirror of his soul by the truer and more compelling symbol of the wounded Fisher King, the world's hope in abeyance.

The Pontificate of Gregory XIII, in spite of many blemishes, did really mirror the New Jerusalem in a way unequalled for a long time before or since. The impeccable Montaigne, who visited Rome in 1580 and found the cookery distressing, was moved in his own way by its grand universality:

> The sovereign of Rome embraces all Christendom and makes laws for all. At his court it matters nothing whence men come. At Venice the independence of the government and commercial interests attract many foreigners; but they are there in the house of a stranger. Here, everyone is at home. (3)

Gregory himself, in his long views, was well fitted for his office of godfather to the whole human race. The Gregorian Calendar, one of his special concerns, was a gift to the entire world; it enabled scientists on both sides, Danti and Clavius in Rome, Kepler and Tycho Brahe in the north, to wave understandingly to each other above the clamour of sectarian invective. The other achievement which bears his name, the Gregorian

University, has already been mentioned; the new building was solemnly opened in 1584 with speeches in twenty-five languages. Less spectacular, but more significant of a long and world-wide view, were its supporting national colleges. The men of the English College could feel that, hard pressed as they might be, they were part of a great victorious advancing army. Close beside them was the German College which was already being carried on the tide of Catholic revival. Farther off, the Greek College, the Maronite College, and a college, even, for converts from Jewry and Islam, were reminders that the return of the whole Monophysite and Nestorian Middle East seemed a reasonable probability in Gregory's reign. From farther off still, from America, from India, from Africa, came prospects of world-conversion that seem fantastic nowadays; and yet they were solidly based at the time and even on the way to accomplishment.

A fitting climax to his reign came in March 1585, a month before his death, with the arrival of the native Christians from Japan under the care of their Jesuit tutors. Three princes and a band of young nobles, they were fêted through Italy and had a tumultuous reception in Rome: slim and modest in their white silk coats embroidered with birds and flowers in different colours, wide-sleeved and open at the front, with rich scarves crossed over the breast and round the waist again as girdles. Gregory wept as they knelt to kiss his feet, and said, 'Now thou dost dismiss thy servant in peace . . . because my eyes have seen . . .'

Another great occasion for Jesuits in Rome was the completion, after a forty-year delay, of the church known as the *Gesù*. It was not what Michel Angelo had promised Saint Ignatius to build as a labour of love; it was not even quite what Vignola, his successor, had planned; but it was a great gesture by its donor, Cardinal Farnese, the grand old man of Rome, who had turned from renaissance luxury to piety and good works. Eight hundred pupils of the Jesuits took part in the ceremonies of consecration.

How fresh and powerful still was the spiritual appeal of the Society of Jesus was shown in November 1585 when the young prince Luigi Gonzaga, having overcome all opposition, entered the Novitiate of Sant' Andrea as the best way of renouncing the world and following Christ.

But, in many quarters, this strange power of attracting power by the very act of renouncing power seemed alarming and subversive. Already, after only fifty years of life, the new Order was being compared to the Knights Templar; hostile elements of the most diverse sort were coalescing, and the theme of 'Suppression' was in the air.

Yet it was the new Order that was mainly responsible for the success of the Counter-Reformation.

The trouble was that the Counter-Reformation was like a splendid sword-blade in a cracked hilt; the blade was spiritual heroism, the hilt was temporal power.

Thus Rome generated in Robert Southwell a sense of wonderful expectation, but also of agonized frustration. Momentous issues of world-conversion might hang in the balance of some palace intrigue, like the rocks in his poem *A Vale of Tears*: 'Huge massy stones that hang by tickle stays.' The atmosphere of precarious strain was emphasized by the actual insecurity of Roman life. Brigandage was rife right up to the walls of the city, and within it there was the perennial problem of the Teverine mob. Montaigne, who noted with surprise the piety of the Roman upper classes, found the populace more frightening than that of Paris. Bound up with this insecurity was the severity of the penal code. Gregory, though disliking it, did little in mitigation, and under Sixtus it was considerably intensified.

Southwell witnessed at least one public execution: the great *auto-da-fé* of February 1583. Sixteen men were sentenced at the Church of the Minerva on varying charges of judaizing, black magic and heresy—the same Arian heresy, apparently, for which Kett and another were burnt alive at Norwich a few years later. In this case, some were sent to the galleys, some whipped, some banished; but the three judaizers were burnt, two alive and one dead, in the *Campo dei Fiori* just behind the English College. Southwell recalled the scene, non-committally, four years later. (4)

The Jesuit formula of self-conquest is accused of tending to spiritual complacency and callousness. No doubt it may do so, and has done so—especially in prosperity. But it did not often do so in the Jesuits of Southwell's generation, who courted death for themselves, not for others ('being too well acquainted with the smart of our own punishments', as Southwell wrote later, 'to wish any Christian to be partaker of our pains'), and were more often the accused than the accusers in tribunals, including the Inquisition. It is obvious that the burning of heretics, and the Papacy's temporal power in general, aroused in him no conscious disagreement—'justice in due revenge being slack and careless, where hate of the fault doth not make it odious, and anger setteth not an edge on the sword that punisheth or preventeth wrong'; but, unconsciously, the discord in the New Jerusalem, between the ideal and the actual, formed part of that profound sadness and self-disgust which breaks out again and again in his poetry.

> By force I live, in will I wish to die;
> In plaints I pass the length of lingering days;
> Free would my soul from mortal body fly
> And tread the track of death's desiréd ways:
> Life is but loss where death is deemed gain
> And loathed pleasures breed displeasing pain.

The truth is that the Jesuit discipline, in the design of St. Ignatius, sets up an interior tension which can only be resolved by crucifixion. At the heart of it there is an element of supernatural wildness expressed in his famous rule,

> . . . to recoil from everything that the world loves and embraces: to allow and long for, with the whole heart, whatever Christ Our Lord loved and embraced. . . .
> . . . So much so, that if it could be without any offence to the Divine Majesty and without any sin on the part of another, we should desire to suffer insults and calumnies and violence, to be held for fools and posted as such (but without ourselves giving any occasion for it), because of this great longing we have to be in some sort of way conformed and assimilated to Jesus Christ Our Lord and Creator, and to put on his garments and livery.

What Rome did principally for Robert Southwell was to bind him inseparably to the Society of Jesus and to settle him in a fixed desire for martyrdom. But it also clothed his shy impulsive boyhood with a new urbanity and *savoir-faire*. This is illustrated by a suit which he successfully urged in favour of his uncle, the Baron Copley. (5)

Uncle Thomas had enlisted his aid in a somewhat delicate transaction. He had left Flanders for France in 1577 after some disagreement with the Spanish authorities; but he now found it necessary to leave France and return to Flanders. Would the Spanish King renew his pension which had been broken off? And would he recognize the barony conferred on him by the French King? For Thomas Copley, it may be imagined, the second consideration was just as important as the first. Now, the Governor of the Spanish Netherlands was the great Prince of Parma. And the uncle of Parma, and head of the family, was Cardinal Farnese at Rome. So off went Southwell, at a most difficult time, when the ante-chambers were thronged with petitioners and accusations of 'favouritism' were thick in the air, to play the part of suitor and diplomat.

The Cardinal was graciousness itself; and Thomas Copley's last year of exile was softened by an honourable reception from the Prince of Parma who bestowed on him the empty titles of Baron of Gatton and Grand Master of the Maze. (The Maze was Copley property in Southwark, just east of London Bridge.) His son Anthony was offered a post as page in Parma's court, but he hankered after Rome where his cousin Robert lived. So off went Southwell again, to procure a pension from the Pope—with assurances of repayment of course when the Baron's affairs were more settled—and Anthony duly arrived in September 1584.

Thomas Copley died in the same September, still wrestling with Lord Burghley—who did not now intend to honour the Queen's promise—about the manor of Gatton. His last letter to Burghley was an effort to repay his nephew's good offices: if his wife Katherine were not allowed to live at Gatton, let it go to his sister, Southwell's mother, 'Her Majesty's old servant of near forty years continuance'.

His letter shows that Bridget Southwell was still alive in 1583, and it is a reminder that Robert was being drawn to England not only by supernatural desire for martyrdom but also by cords of native affection more attractive than the successful career at Rome that might have been his had he desired it. It is unlikely, however, that his mother lived to hear of his return. The only family correspondence that has survived is a letter of affectionate gratitude from his aunt Katherine Copley. 'To my very loving Nephew, Mr Robert Southwell, of the holly Societie of Jhesus, at the Inglish Colledge at Rome.' She wrote it in April 1585 on the eve of departure from Dunkirk to see if she would be allowed to live in peace with her family in England. Its simple piety and gentle courage were another reminder to Robert that his work lay at home.

There is a characteristic letter of his, about the same date, which shows how he coupled detachment from his own wants with loving courtesy towards others. In the grim month of January 1585, his old friend John Deckers passed through Rome on his way back from Naples to Flanders; and Robert seized the opportunity to write to the great theologian Leonard Lessius who had helped him so much at Douai, and at Rome also in the previous year. The letter, written amidst a buzz of conversation, is a pleasing picture of the Flemish time-table entangled in the Italian *dulce desipere*: Deckers impatiently waiting to be taken a walk through the sites of Rome, and Agazzari bustling in and out with fresh messages and 'small gifts':

Amantissime Pater—In the most desperate throes I am scratching off this letter to you, much too short, but it comes with all my love. I am so glad you had a happy homecoming, and may you live long there in strength and prosperity. Everything here is going on all right. I am not in the very best of health, myself, but fairly well, thank God. Father John Deckers is at my side, urging, insisting, *ingeminating*, that I should finish. Love is a little word, but too big to be expressed in letters. Still, for the lover, as for the wise man, one word is enough. Father Rector salutes you—over and over again—and is sending you some small gifts—as a token of his good will—along with many thanks for your letter. Goodbye, my Father! And be mindful of me, for I am never unmindful of you. 8th January, 1585,

Your brother and servant in Christ,

Robert Southwell. (6)

A fortnight later he was writing in bold and solemn terms to his General, Claudius Aquaviva. This was the letter (already quoted) about affairs in the English College. But in the concluding paragraph, Southwell made the formal petition that he had so long and anxiously debated within himself:

About myself I will add only one thing: nothing is more in my prayers, and nothing more welcome could ever happen to me, than this. It is Your Paternity's decision that I devote myself to the English here in Rome. May it also be your decision, by God's inspiration, that I do the same for England herself, with the supreme goal of martyrdom in view. I will not cease to strive with God in prayer that he may grant me this in his mercy, and that he may keep Your Paternity long years to rule over us. X Cal. Feb. 1585.

Such was his irrevocable request. In the autumn of that year it took a sudden leap towards fulfilment. Dr. Allen and Fr. Persons, the two men whom after Aquaviva Southwell most reverenced, arrived in Rome for a stay of several years. It was now no longer possible to withstand the desperate appeals of the English Catholics for more Jesuit Fathers to assist Weston. (7)

Weston had held the fort during this difficult period, 1584-6; and in the swirling and deceitful currents of intrigue, he was looked on by all the Catholic body, and by many Protestants also, as a rock of fidelity and a beacon of discretion. But already he was feeling the strain of physical exhaustion, loneliness and crushing responsibility. The 'exorcisms' in which he was then engaged were a disquieting symptom. Some of the Seminary priests from Rheims who were most attached to him had brought over a gruesome ritual of doubtful orthodoxy for curing victims of hysteria; and Weston had seen it as the beginning of a genuine spiritual revival. Historically, it was a less noxious form of the contemporary craze for witch-hunting; and psychologically it expressed the longing for supernatural direction that is felt by an oppressed minority. But the great temporary emotional success that it was having was likely to provoke bitter reactions.

What was needed was something more liberal and expansive, a revival of 1581. There was need also for a brilliant organizer, a man of special intelligence and tact. The men that Allen chose and, through Persons, pressed for, were Henry Garnet, the mathematician, and Robert Southwell, the poet.

Aquaviva was very loath to let them go. The reasons which were given for his reluctance in 1584 were even more valid, as will be seen, in 1586. But he had already promised Allen that whenever the need was imperative he would comply. So he consented, though it grieved him severely. 'Lambs sent to the slaughter', he murmured when he thought of it.

On 2nd February 1586—so it would seem—is the last entry in Southwell's handwriting in the *Liber Ruber* of the English College. Before the next entry, 10th March, he had evidently been withdrawn from the College, and was being briefed for England.

CHAPTER SEVEN

The Road to England, 1586

IN the early morning of the 8th May (29th April by English Style), three horsemen faced each other by the Milvian Bridge, two miles north of Rome. It was a scene graven for ever afterwards on the memory of Robert Persons. It was by his efforts that his two companions were now on their way to England. His choice had weighed with Allen, and his persistence had persuaded Aquaviva. He had ridden out with them, thus far, to say goodbye.

'Two arrows shot at the same mark', said Southwell jauntily, as they talked together by the bridge, meaning that if one were arrested the other might still get through; but Persons remembered the words in a different sense, twenty years later, when Garnet had followed Southwell to the gallows. (1)

It was fortunate that the two companions had taken a strong liking to each other. Garnet, when called from his professorial studies to prepare for the mission, had come a little nervously, but as eagerly as other professors have done in recent years when told to parachute into some strange land and organize resistance. He was the youngest and perhaps the brightest of that brilliant constellation (including Sanders, Rastell, Harding, and Stapleton) with which Winchester and New College had adorned—unofficially—the recusant cause. His was one of those mathematical minds with a fondness for music, which combines a lucid judgement and an immensely patient grasp of detail with a preference for human contacts, and a tendency to base important decisions on feelings and intuitions rather than on logic. His mild tran-

quillity had caused him to be termed the 'Pecorella', or 'little
sheep', by the Professors at Rome. He enjoyed the nickname
and after he had eluded capture for several years, sent a message
to Bellarmine to tell him that 'the little sheep' was not doing so
badly. He had an unfailingly shrewd and chatty sense of humour
which was a useful foil to the Copley strain of quixotry in Robert
Southwell.

Garnet had been appointed 'superior' of the dual expedition
until such time as they could find Father Weston at liberty in
England. Weston's exact whereabouts were uncertain, but he
was known to be in close contact with several old friends of
Campion and Persons in London; and to these Persons now sent
his parting messages. There was the indomitable Thomas Pounde;
but he was not the best person to maintain security. There was
also Lord Vaux at Hackney, whose son Henry had taken George
Gilbert's place as leader of the recusant lay organization. And
there was Francis Browne, Lord Montague's brother, at whose
house the first secret printing-press had been set up; it was a
house easy of access, on the south side of London Bridge, beside
St. Mary Overies (now St. Saviour's).

Persons recalled his own arrival in London in 1580. Iron-
nerved as he was, he had quailed before the many-mouthed
City gaping to engulf him. Reaching Southwark at four o'clock
in the morning, he had wandered about the bankside, till at last
he stepped boldly into the Marshalsea Prison, and found the
ebullient Thomas Pounde, ready to give him the names and
whereabouts of staunch Catholics. (2) Prisons, Persons reminded
them, were excellent information-centres for Catholics: that is,
not the grim City gaols, but the easier establishments of Southwark, the Marshalsea and the Clink.

Finally, and somewhat hesitantly, he added a personal request.
His mother, who was very old, had now no one to look after her.
Would it be possible to find out where she was living, and to see
that she was cared for?

They promised faithfully, and knelt for his blessing. Then
they mounted again and, crossing the bridge, continued on the

Flaminian Way. Persons watched them go along the road where he had gone with Campion and Sherwin, in May six years before. Then he turned and went back to his desk in the City.

Allen and he were facing a manifold crisis on the English Mission. Up to 1583 their hopes had been of a quasi-constitutional move to establish Mary Stuart as the acknowledged heir—a sort of Catholic '1688', at least as Whig historians have glorified that episode. These hopes had been dashed, partly by King Philip's refusal to supply the necessary shipping, and by the subsequent change of regime in Scotland, but even more by the covert alliance between the Lewis-Morgan faction and the English Government.

Mary's captivity was now so arranged that, while Allen was cut off from all communication with her, Morgan, with his insidious plans, had free and encouraged access. Priests of the faction, Grately, Ballard, Tyrrell and others, were spreading scares and snares up and down the country so that the very name of 'seminary priest' was becoming an object of distrust to the English Catholics. In Rome itself the intrigues of Lewis and Aldred had had their effect. The new Pope was suspending judgement as to the value of the missionary movement; and Allen was kept waiting in vain for an audience.

The only remedy, as Persons saw it, was that Allen should have complete authority to silence opposition, that he should be made Cardinal of England. On 20th May, twelve days after he had said goodbye to Southwell and Garnet, he wrote to King Philip's Secretary of State. Lamenting the lost opportunity of 1582, he concluded:

> However that may be, there is one thing which I will tell your Excellency in all sincerity and in the sight of God our Lord; and I will tell it before it comes to pass, for afterwards there will be no remedy for it. It is this: unless 'the enterprise' is carried out forthwith, and unless Mr. Allen is raised to a certain dignity so that he can keep the nation united in the hope of a future good, it is a matter of absolute certainty that in a very short time all the friends who rely on His Majesty in those parts will be completely ruined, and there

will be such a change of outlook of people and affairs in that country, that there will be no longer any hope of proceeding by the means that up to now have been used. (3)

The 'change of outlook' which Persons accurately foresaw was that the English Catholics, alienated by the regicide plots of the faction, and weakened by new Government pressure, would soon be both unable and unwilling to help themselves. Any new political move on their behalf would have to rule them out as participants. But 'the enterprise' to which he was alluding was still the old one just described; it was not the 'Spanish Armada' as it afterwards materialized. As far as can be gathered from Persons's writings, he did not sympathize with the foreign invasion of 1588. Persons indeed took a far smaller part in political dealings than has customarily been assigned to him; his main interest was always the maintenance and increase of Allen's colleges. (4)

All that this question involves is too complex to be discussed here; and it is clogged with four centuries of harsh feeling and distorted views. Nevertheless it should be possible for modern readers to reach a common ground: the ground at least that was common to Lord Burghley and to Robert Southwell.

The Elizabethan government was not the equivalent of the Nazi or 'Iron Curtain' regimes of this century. Elizabeth's statecraft may have been non-Christian, but it was not anti-Christian; it was classical and machiavellian,* and to that extent it was shared by most European states, Catholic or Protestant. At the same time it is clear from the controversy between Allen and Burghley in 1583 that Burghley was not sincere in his protestation that Catholics had only to abstain from politics in order to enjoy freedom of worship. The truth which is apparent from his far-seeing, but strictly private, memorandum of 1584 was that if the old religion were allowed to survive, it would also revive; it would revive and spread till a Protestant government would be unable to go on governing. (5) Burghley was much more

* See Burghley's memorandum of 1584, discussed in Appendix 'B'.

afraid of Catholic piety than of Catholic plots. His aim was to abolish the Mass, but by guile and attrition if possible, not by violent persecution. To make martyrs, as the memorandum insisted, was to admit defeat. Priests should be laughed out of court, not raised to the altars. In effect Burghley had issued a challenge to the Church: 'The English people do not want you. If you don't believe it, come and see!' And the Church had *de facto*, though not *de jure*, accepted the challenge on those terms.

The common ground of the unequal struggle was, thus, the moral sense—broadly understood—of the English people. The propaganda that the priests were foreign spies* did not represent a genuine issue but just a move in the struggle to gain the support of right-thinking Englishmen. That, at any rate, is the only interpretation that makes sense of the life-work of Robert Southwell.

The Catholics who did interfere in politics, up to their necks, were those of the faction who devised the so-called Babington Plot. Something must be said about this, both because Southwell was walking right into it unawares, and because he afterwards made it the subject of a detailed study.

There had already been several contrivances to get the Jesuits to burn their fingers in attempted regicide. There had been the attempt of George Gifford in 1583, (7) and the affair of Aldred and Parry, alluded to in the last chapter. But this one of 1586 was the plot to end all plots, to incriminate the Jesuits and Seminaries up to the hilt, and to finish off the Scottish Queen once and for all. It was marked by the same sinister and apparently contradictory conjunction as the others: between an intrigue to disrupt the Seminaries and an attempt to murder Elizabeth.

Its chief agent, Gilbert Gifford, was certainly working hand-in-glove with Walsingham. But it is hard to believe that Thomas Morgan was not aware what his henchman, Gifford, was about.

* Aquaviva's instructions to English Jesuits after 1581 were explicit and unqualified: 'They are not to mix themselves in affairs of States, nor should they recount news about political matters in their letters to Rome or to England; and in England they are to refrain from talk against the Queen, and not to allow it in others.' (6)

There is a good deal of evidence still not evaluated in this business. On the whole it is highly probable that Thomas Morgan, the *originator* of the Babington Plot, was Walsingham's ally from the beginning. Morgan's end and object was to ruin the Jesuits, and as a means to this end he was prepared to aid Walsingham in entangling Mary Stuart—especially when it became clear that she would not lend herself to the faction. For Walsingham, however, the end was always the killing of Mary, and the means was any bait that might entice the renegade Catholics necessary to his schemes. Morgan expected Walsingham to attribute the plot to the Jesuits, that was part of the bargain; but, in the event, Walsingham found it simpler and more straightforward to attribute it to Morgan. (8)

It is not, however, necessary to accept this radical solution in order to appreciate the peril in which the Jesuit missionaries were to be placed. It is enough to consider the intrigues that were actually taking place in the month of April 1586 when Garnet and Southwell were preparing to go to England.

(A) Morgan and Gilbert Gifford were at that moment briefing Ballard and Savage for the final stages of what came to be known as the 'Babington Plot'. Ballard, who, though one of the faction, was probably a genuine hot-head, was to tour England, involving as many leading Catholics as possible; another priest, Grately, was being employed in an especial manner to incriminate the Earl and Countess of Arundel; other renegade Catholics such as Poley and Berden had similar tasks.

(B) At exactly the same time, Morgan, by means of Solomon Aldred, was arranging for Dr. W. Gifford to meet Stafford, the English Ambassador who was representing Walsingham. The plan was that Dr. Gifford should lead a schism in the Seminary at Rheims, and come over to England under Government protection, presumably to start a rival branch of the Catholic Church there. Aldred's despatch included the following promise by Dr. Gifford: 'that he has five or six scholars of the best that will surely follow him and that he does not doubt to bring Dr. Allen himself into this action, after he has set Persons and him at variance'. (9)

Gifford's boast about Allen was, of course, completely baseless and in the event he shrank from coming to England. Walsingham was annoyed. He had him condemned to death as a prime instigator of the Babington Plot, and *at the same time* (August 1586) he informed his cousin Gilbert that Dr. Gifford had 'deserved' that 'we both write and speak bitterly against him'. There is a contrast here of public and private utterance which stinks to high heaven. Walsingham has the man with whom he has just been negotiating branded as a regicide, and at the same time he sends him a half-apologetic message saying in effect: 'Well, it was your own fault for not playing fair!' Conyers Reade was right when he wrote of this affair: 'Dr. Gifford's reputation has received a dark stain from the part he played in it.' (10)

(C) The essential link, from Morgan and Gifford's point of view, between the proposed disruption of the Seminaries and the regicide plot was the book of anti-Jesuit slanders which was then being drawn up by Grately and Gilbert Gifford for Walsingham. (11) It included the assertion that an assassin had been commissioned *by Father Persons* to do the murder. (It may be recalled also that Tyrrell, another of the faction, had a story in readiness about the plot having been hatched at the English College, Rome.)

As things turned out, the Jesuits had reason to be grateful to Mr. Secretary Walsingham that, through all his tortuous schemes, he preserved a certain flint-like integrity and economy of purpose. He demurred from inventing crimes against innocent persons when he had so many genuinely wicked dupes to hand. But that eventuality did not diminish the dire peril which attended the coming of two Jesuit emissaries from Rome, both of whom were young and utterly unused to intrigue.

Even before they had got clear of Italy, the news of their coming was being carried to Thomas Morgan. Nothing could have suited his plans better. He sent the news across to Gilbert Gifford, as will be seen, and Gifford communicated it to Walsingham.

Garnet and Southwell, after a detour to pay their devotion to Our Lady at Loretto, had made for the Alps, stopping on the way at the Jesuit houses of Modena, Parma, Piacenza, and Milan. At Modena they met a priest, Jonas Meredith, of somewhat dubious associations. A partisan of Owen Lewis and Morgan, he had come over from England on the ship on which the Earl of Arundel was captured—apparently by the treachery of Grately. He had been sent to Rome by Morgan and Paget to answer charges brought against them by a Catholic layman in Paris. Supplied with alms by the English College, he had left Rome on 9th April, a month before Garnet and Southwell. He was to arrive in England two weeks ahead of them, supplied by Morgan with the Government safe-conduct which Walsingham had intended for William Gifford. It seems likely that he was the channel by which Morgan heard of the mission which the two Jesuits were most anxious to conceal.

From Milan Southwell wrote to Agazzari:

Collegio di Brera, 26th May. . . .* At Modena we ran into two priests, Father Shaw and Father Meredith, who lodged at the college and remained there one night. They encountered us again at Parma and at Piacenza, and were made welcome along with us. . . .

He concluded with a careful thought for the horses:

Tomorrow morning, Whit Tuesday, we intend leaving for Como. . . . The horses are doing us good service, but the sore on William's† mount is not yet healed; and I am afraid for the chestnut too, which has been galled by the baggage since we left Loretto. . . .

Your dear son and servant in Christ,

Robert Southwell. (12)

By June they were in the Low Countries. Douai, Allen's first foundation, was a spiritual home to Southwell for many reasons, not least among them that his friend Deckers was there, at the College where they had first met. Once again their time together

---

* Southwell's dating follows the Gregorian Calendar till his arrival in England, when it changes to the Old Style as used there.

† 'William' was a Flemish lay-brother who accompanied them right up to the English shore.

H

was hurried and all too short. By the end of June the two missionaries had left Douai, and were at St. Omer; the Jesuit Fathers there were to arrange for the ship that was to take them across. Southwell wrote from there to Deckers, a severely practical letter which betrays signs of nervousness.

From St. Omer, 2 July, 1586. I promised, five days ago I think, to write to you; and I am doing so now in case there is delay in the post. We have heard nothing of the letters we expected from Rome, and this is most inconvenient, for we may have to stay here longer than we can safely lie hid. If they do not come soon, we shall be off on our journey. Meanwhile, I beg of you, do not let any English people know where we are or that we have been there, until I write to you from the Port, or let you know in some other way what is happening to us. . . . In case any English people should hear of our coming to you, keep secret at least where we are now; and if they already know that, conceal the reason for it, until I write to you again under my own hand. Meanwhile, my most beloved Father, farewell, and pray for me. Father Henry sends his greetings. (13)

Their security precautions may have been satisfactory as regards the Low Countries. But Morgan in Paris was already well informed. On the day following, 3rd July, he sent a message—probably by Meredith—to Gilbert Gifford who, he very well knew, was in consultation with Walsingham about the proposed book of anti-Jesuit slanders: 'There are two Jesuits sent into England. Both very young men. Father Southwell and Father Garnet.'

And he added hypocritically: 'May God prosper them!' (14)

The letters from Rome arrived shortly afterwards; and they were directed, perhaps unexpectedly, not to a Flanders port of embarkation, but to Boulogne. Their attack was to be a frontal one, although, in the past year, twelve priests had been taken on the coasts of Kent and Sussex. But this apparent rashness may have proved a blessing in disguise. For Walsingham, by some other source, had received information that one Southwell (mentioned by name), with an unknown companion, was due to land somewhere on the coast of Norfolk, his home county.

There followed ten days of waiting: days of nervous fretting for Robert; but Garnet perhaps, more philosophically, used them to tick off the units that separated the Gregorian Calendar from the Old Style. At last on 15th July (the 5th by English reckoning) came the orders to sail next day. Robert wrote his last Continental letter, the one he had promised to John Deckers. It is a remarkable letter. There is a tone about it which might be called ecstatic or merely hysterical, according to one's sympathies. But one thing is clear from it, in either case. He was going through the experience common to brave men on the eve of a great enterprise they have long planned and dreamed of. He was terrified.

Faced with the last encounter, from death's ante-room I write to you, my father, for the help of those same prayers of yours that once awakened life in me when I was dead in spirit: pray now about my body's death, that either I may usefully escape it, or manfully endure. It is true I am being sent 'amongst wolves', and likely enough 'to be led to the slaughter',—I only wish it were 'as a lamb'—for His Name's sake who sends me. I know very well that sea and land are gaping wide for me; and lions, as well as wolves, go prowling in search of whom they may devour. But I welcome, more than fear, their fangs. Rather than shrink from them as torturers, I call to them to bring my crown. It is true that the flesh is weak and can do nothing, and even now revolts from that which is proposed. Yet God who is mighty in battle will be at my right hand lest I be shaken. He who holds up the model, will not hold back the means. He will not fail the challenger, who himself has framed the challenge. But do you, my father, compass me with flowers (the prayers that ascend in the odour of sweetness); prop me up with the apples of your good deeds, so that if I languish, then with love I languish, not with fear. Indeed, indeed, I do not dare to hope what I so violently desire; but if I reach, God willing, the lowest rank of happy martyrs, I will not be unmindful of those who have remembered me. My helpers will not find I am less pleasing in heaven, I, who on earth would do anything to please them. Plead, then, for me, my father, (perhaps it is the last time I shall address you), plead my cause to our common father, the Lord JESUS, for it is your cause too, the cause of all the church, that I who play His part may so sustain it; as God Himself, as the Angels, as the Society expects of me; and throw away my life-blood, if I must, with fortitude and faith.

This I commend to God, along with myself and all of you. Greet Father Rector from me, please, and the other fathers and my brothers. Goodbye, as we leave the port, 15th July, 1586. (15)

In the decade when Southwell wrote, the art of pathetic understatement was not yet in use. Even if it had been, it would not, in him, have been a sign of sincerity. Pathetic understatement has to do with feelings that cannot be trusted. But Southwell's feelings ran in and out, like children in an Italian church; and were accustomed, when they wanted words, to find them. But if there was no understatement in the letter, there was no overstatement either.

A list of the twenty-five priests from Rome who were in the London district in July shows that his chance of survival was one in three. The numbers from Rheims were double those of Rome, but the proportion in prison (about thirty in July) was much the same. (16)

But the chief threat that he had to fear was that of walking straight into the fine-drawn net of the Babington Plot, before he had had time to spread his wings: of being strung up, not as a martyr, but as a twisted little conspirator, the 'second murderer' from Rome, amid howls of execration, a disgrace to religion and a source of scandal and despair to English Catholics. The very day that his ship was preparing to set sail from France, Wednesday, 6th July,* marked the opening of the decisive stage of Walsingham's long preparations.

On this day Ballard returned to London from his tour of the counties, a broken man. Not one of the substantial Catholic squires had yielded to his blandishments. Sir Thomas Tresham had threatened to denounce him. Morgan, his employer, had disowned him. To the English Government which had long been observing him with interest, his usefulness, apart from his arrest and torture, was now over. The role of chief cat's-paw in

* From now on the Julian Calendar, or Old Style, is followed.

the plot passed to the self-dramatizing young aristocrat, Anthony Babington, who, distracted and half-hypnotized, had just had his second interview with Walsingham.

On the same Wednesday, Walsingham released a letter from Queen Mary which Phelippes, his handwriting expert, had intercepted some days previously; it was her reply to Babington's earlier offer of his services, and it gave away nothing. It was brought to Babington by the Government spy, George Gifford, who insisted on taking back an answer that evening. Robert Southwell, in his *Humble Supplication* written later, averred that the bearer brought the answer 'ready penned' for Babington to endorse. Much depended on the answer, and Walsingham was not disappointed. Out of context, and quite falsely, Babington wrote that he had six gentlemen ready 'to despatch the usurper'.

On this same Wednesday, Anthony Tyrrell, who had been arrested two days earlier, wrote a letter to Lord Burghley promising 'to certify your Honour of that of the which you shall be full fain'. (17) The subsequent *questionnaire* of Lord Burghley elicited, among other things, the fiction of a Jesuit plot to murder Elizabeth, hatched in the English College at Rome.

Finally, on this same Wednesday, the Council ordered a general search of the houses of Catholic recusants, and a special watch on the ports. Instructions were also given to clear the London and Southwark gaols of small fry, in preparation for a larger haul.

On the whole, if Garnet and Southwell had sat down and planned it out, they could hardly have chosen a less propitious moment to sail. They weighed anchor at two next morning, and all night the wind was hard against them, as if in warning of what was in store.

But with sunrise, as Garnet's first letter from England reported, the wind changed and dropped. The sailors looked kindly on them as luck-bringers. They sailed towards the distant shore as it were upon a broad river. The lilt of the sparkling waves lifted their spirits as the Foreland came in sight. Off a lonely stretch of the Downs, between Dover and Folkestone, the ship's boat was lowered. (18)

PART TWO

PART TWO

CHAPTER EIGHT

'The Birds of the Air have their Nests—'

IN the same hour before sunrise, two days later, Robert stood at the Southwark entrance to London. Somewhere to the left was Rochester House that had once been his uncle's, and on the right the Manor of the Maze. But all seemed strange and disembodied at this hour. Tall houses on either side of him, wan and shuttered, blinked in the half-light like candles at a Requiem. And in front of him, blocking his path, stood something like a giant altar-piece, or a blurred figure of the Redeemer with a crown of thorns.

But just then the morning wind twitched the last overlap of mist and darkness, parting them like the curtains before a puppet-show. He saw what he had seen so often in his dreams. It was the towering Gatehouse of London Bridge, with its spiky coronet of human heads.

'To win you to heaven or to die upon your pikes'—had been Campion's splendid phrase. Here were the pikes, and here, when the play was played, his head would rest at last.

But a broadening band of sunlight travelled across the river and touched the tips of a larger coronet: the spires of many churches that seemed cushioned against the green heights beyond. The great bridge stretched out in all its splendour, the river took on colour, and the gardens awoke. All at once it was possible to exclaim: 'London, thou art the floure of Cities all.'

The Flower of Cities stirred, wearily at first with a few street-cries, and then abruptly and energetically with a great banging of shutters and sloshing of water. From one of the many handsome inns that flanked the street, a stable-boy, whistling sleepily, came forward to take his horse. But the ordered sequence of early-morning sounds was broken by a more insistent clamour: shouts of command and trampling feet. It was the search of recusant houses ordered by the Council and carried out by the myrmidons of William Gardiner, the usurer, magistrate of Southwark.

'On reaching London', wrote Southwell, in his earliest letter to Aquaviva, 'I had my first meeting with Catholics—between drawn swords; and then afterwards in a certain prison: portents to me, if it is lawful to take portents, of a fate most welcome.' (1)

The file of armed men, with captives between them, crossed the street on their way to the prisons of the South Bank. With a sense of moving in a preordained pattern, Robert followed them down the alley-way in front of St. Mary Overies, and round the walled gardens of the palaces to the sprawling prisons. His purse was the magic key. Blank doors and gaolers' faces opened wide. Proudly, like stall-keepers, they displayed their costly wares.

In the large prisons on the South Bank a man had as much or as little hope as when Selden told his story:

> The Keeper of the Clink . . . had priests of several sorts sent unto him. As they came in, he asked them who they were. 'Who are you?' to the first. 'I am a priest of the Church of Rome.' 'You are welcome', quote the Keeper, 'there are those who will take care of you. And who are you?' 'A silenced minister.' 'You are welcome too, I shall fare the better for you. And who are you?' 'A minister of the Church of England.' 'O God,' quote the Keeper, 'I shall get nothing by you. I am sure you may lie and starve and rot before anyone will look after you.'

Gerard, later on, described his move from the Counter to the Clink as a translation from Purgatory to Paradise, where he was able to say Mass for a crowd of Catholics who 'all of them had the keys of their own doors'.

In the Clink, on this occasion, were two priests from Rome, Edward James and John Lowe, both soon to be martyrs. James had parted from Southwell not many months before; and Lowe

until recently had been Weston's intimate companion. The
whole problem that had weighed on the incoming Jesuits—how
to establish their credentials and get in touch with Father Weston
—vanished with the pleasant inconsequence of a dream.

A certain dream-like quality, like the opening of Dante's
Purgatorio, had enveloped all these first days in England. There
had been a sense of protection ever since they saw the white
Foreland through the mist, and stepped on to the forbidden coast.
Garnet's first letter records their first adventure:

> On a high bluff overlooking the beach, we caught sight of a man;
> he was scrutinizing us carefully and obviously asking himself who
> were these people who landed at this unusual place so far from the
> harbour. I must say we felt a thrill of fear. However, the die was
> cast, and we must try our luck—which we knew was not mere luck,
> but the watchful appointment of divine goodness. So we walked
> straight up to him and began to complain gravely about our boat-
> man who had put us down at the wrong place and left us here.
> The man, who was some sort of a shepherd and a very honest
> fellow, was most indignant at the wrong done to us—much more
> indignant than we were. He described to us at length the places
> round about, and the right way to get to them; and he assured
> us that he felt towards us as if we had been his own kith and kin,
> and this he confirmed with a very hearty oath. So our first adven-
> ture was a merry one.

Their next adventure had come as they drew near their first
town, expecting with trepidation that searchers would bar the
way. But before they reached it, they were caught up in a
friendly, jostling crowd that quite masked their entry and exit.
Snatches of conversation told them that this was the day when all
Kentish folk flocked to the traditional Fair; and then they understood. It was the feast of the translation of Saint Thomas of
Canterbury. The guardian of England, patron of martyrs, friend
of pilgrims, had taken them under his protection. Garnet wrote
in a reminiscent letter fifteen years later:

> I remember that we had said the first vespers of St. Alexis (17 July),
> but on the following morning as the sun was rising, we landed on

the feast-day of St. Thomas—ten days earlier! And in his diocese, too, between Dover and Folkestone, so as to have his holy protection, though at the moment we did not realise it. Yet this was the reason of our safe journey, the great crowds that flocked to and fro for the Fair.

So we made our confessions to each other as we walked along, and then we separated. Next morning, he, more fortunate than me, passed me on the high-road on horseback. Then the morning after, we met each other in London, at breakfast, in one of the prisons, where we were both safe from danger; and we obtained directions where to find our friends.

So it seems that Garnet, who had taken the tilt-boat from Gravesend, rejoined Southwell at the happy moment when he had discovered his Roman friends in prison. Southwell, after his harrowing forecasts of ravening lions and prowling wolves, was finding Elizabethan England a surprisingly kindly and easy-going place—so far.

By collating Government reports for this month one gets a picture of the Catholic families in London who came to welcome the missionaries during these first days when they were waiting for Weston. The spies only mention notable persons, so one has to remember that there were crowds of lesser folk sheltered by the houses of Lord Vaux at Hackney, the Brownes (Lord Montague) at St. Mary Overies, and the Wriothesleys at Southampton House. The Vaux family, according to Robert's early biographers, was the first to welcome him. Close friends were the Arundells at Clerkenwell whose chaplain, Father Cornelius, had known him well at Rome. Information for July 1586 runs: 'Francis Browne and his brother altogether governed by Edmonds (Weston's *alias*) and Cornelius.' The Close of St. Mary Overies which belonged to Francis Browne's brother, Lord Montague, is indeed likely to have been the scene of Garnet's and Southwell's first Mass on Sunday the 10th. It was a place of great resort for Catholics. Lady Vaux put up there when her husband was in prison near by; and it was frequented also by Robert's Hampshire cousins: 'The names of those that were present at this mass: Mr Browne (my lord's brother), Mr George Cotton, Mr Bannister and his wife . . .' This last report is of some years later; but a strictly contemporary one notes that among those frequenting Southampton House were 'a Mrs Gage and a Mrs Bannister'—probably his sister Mary. Swithin Wells, who lived very near, at St. Andrew's Holborn, was also under observation. (2)

Southwell was overwhelmed by his reception. The hunger and devotion of the recusants brought out the hitherto-unrealized splendours of his priesthood. He wrote in his first letter:

We have had the happiest possible arrival in England. . . . Our coming has marvellously cheered and inspirited the Catholics; for previously they had been complaining that they were practically abandoned by the Society; and they were full of misgivings that their shepherds, dismayed by difficulties, were abandoning the flock that never stood in greater need of their care.

Garnet had the same to say, but on a more apprehensive note:

Things would be terrible here if we had only our enemies to think of, and wonderful if there were only the Catholics and their fervour. They show no fear of sheltering us at any time; and so great is our friends' opinion of the Society that we are forced to conceal that we are of it, 'lest the whole of Jerusalem be disturbed'.

Garnet was right to be apprehensive. Allowing for the intricacies of the secret post, it was just about 8th July that Morgan's message, passed from Gifford to Phelippes, was handed to Sir Francis Walsingham. (3)

The danger they were in is shown by another sentence from Southwell's letter, in which he was plainly unconscious of the full significance of what he was writing:

The news of our coming has already spread abroad; and, from the lips of the Queen's Council, *my name* has become known to certain persons. The report alarms our enemies, who fear heaven knows what at our hands, so nervous have they now become.

The 'lips of the Queen's Council' in this case were the lips of Sir Francis Walsingham. The persons to whom he had made known Southwell's name—though he was ignorant of his where-abouts—were Anthony Babington and his shadow Robert Poley.

Next Wednesday, 13th July, Walsingham was giving them orders to discover the whereabouts of the Jesuits whose entry had eluded him. For Babington this was not too difficult; he still moved on the fringe of recusant circles; and among those who had recently joined his set was Southwell's cousin, Robert Gage, lodging at Southampton house, whose brother John was engaged to Margaret Copley.

Southwell, who was less aware of danger than Garnet, con-tinued in his letter, with an *insouciance* that afterwards earned him a mild rebuke from Aquaviva:

> At the Queen's Court they say that there is a business in hand which, if it succeeds, will mean ruin for us; but, if it fails, all will be well. To the Catholics, however, these are but bugs to frighten children, for they are driven so far already that there is no room left for further cruelty.

The first sentence is an astonishingly apt description of the real nature of the Babington Plot. But the second sentence shows that he was simply repeating the gossip of Catholics with friends at Court.*

The Court, during this week-end, was moving upstream from Greenwich to Richmond. It was high time for the sober and resourceful Father Weston to make his appearance.

The date of his arrival can be reckoned between the 11th and the 14th, and was probably the 13th. (4) His extreme joy at seeing them was almost equalled by his alarm at the dangers to which they were exposed. He had no foreknowledge of the Babington Plot, but he had a highly-developed sense that there was danger in the air. He had, in fact, been carefully avoiding Babington, although he liked the young man, because of his association with Poley whom he distrusted profoundly. 'He was

---

* The artificial character of Walsingham's contrivance was an open secret; he himself complained of the Queen with respectful bitterness: 'I am sorry the event fawleth out so yll. I dowbt greatly her majestie hathe not used the matter with that seacracye that apperteynethe.'

so obsequious in his manner', he wrote of Poley, 'that he made me recoil as at an unpleasing smell.'

Weston removed his friends at once to his own lodging, which was probably a house lent him by Mrs. Francis Browne, in Hog Lane, Norton Folgate, where Bishopsgate runs into Shoreditch. (5) But hardly had he got them safely ensconced there than a visitor was announced. With a shock he saw that it was Anthony Babington.

Babington's subsequent report to Walsingham, which was a very accurate one, suggests that Southwell and Garnet were actually in a different room of the same house when he was talking to Weston. *'Myself might have seen them'*, he told Poley.

> Those shipped at Boulogne came from Rome. The captain of Boulogne had a commandment to embark them in secret, they should be landed on what coast of England they would require. They landed on the Downs. Two of them are Jesuits, and are in London, very close. I myself might have seen them; but in regard they are so suspected to be dangerous men, I durst not without knowledge of Mr. Secretary's faith and pleasure. (6)

Walsingham's first step had been to pick out one of his feigned Catholics, a spy called Berden, and put him on the track of the Jesuits. But a further idea had occurred to him which might kill two birds with one stone. He was anxious about Anthony Babington's fits and starts, and uncertain as to how far he was playing the part of a 'spy on both sides', and he was uneasy at having to rely so completely in this matter on the nefarious Poley. A meeting between Babington and the Jesuits might be a test and a trap for both parties. If Babington betrayed them, it would mean he had no further plot than that which Walsingham already knew. And if the Jesuits betrayed themselves to Babington, even if only by a rash gesture or foolish speech of sympathy, they would have only themselves to blame. It was no doubt Walsingham's intention that Berden should be near at hand during the meeting, to arrange for the arrest.

On that very forenoon, the 13th, he had summoned Poley and told him to fetch Babington to Barne Elms. It was their third interview. The Secretary was quite frank. If Babington played fair, he said, he need have nothing to fear; but he was not yet satisfied with his loyalty. To prove it, he asked for this small service against two enemies of the State recently landed. Babington returned by river from Barnes to London with Poley, in a state of great agitation. But Poley calmed him, saying that they still had the Secretary on a string; Babington must continue to do these small services; it was all part of the great game of politics.

Babington's mentality, before he called on Weston that evening, had been like that of a drug-addict. Sometimes he seemed to himself the arch-politician round whom the world revolved. At other times he knew that he was caught in a quagmire, sinking steadily. His moral sensibilities had become blunted. Yet he still had a finer Catholic strain in him than any of the Morgan-Paget crowd. To write, or sign, a letter in a sort of daze was easy; to betray a holy and defenceless priest was not easy.

In Weston's account, he appears as pitiable but not odious. He made no overt reference to the plot, but, in a state of great distress, presented a case of conscience. All he wanted, he said, was to go abroad and live in peace. Walsingham had promised him a travel-permit in return for certain services. How far could one lawfully go, he asked, in giving information about Catholics, provided one took care that the information would do them no harm?

Weston replied kindly but firmly that once he started that way, he would fall miserably between two stools as others had done before him. Babington continued to plead. Had Weston hesitated and asked for further details, had he interfered and tried to save some of Babington's young associates, he and his companions would have been ruined. Weston, however, was a man of rocklike principle and blessedly limited imagination. He was sorry for Babington, but not as sensitive to his distress as Garnet or Southwell might have been. He closed his eyes firmly, issued some sound spiritual advice on general lines, saw Babington to the door; and then, summoning his two companions, departed with speed and secrecy out of London. (7)

It was a bold move, and a lucky one. Berden, who was distrusted by Walsingham's regular team, was taken off his guard; and Babington, to his credit, delayed making his report. Indeed, he told Poley later on that he would go no further in this matter against priests. Poley took to his bed on the 14th and remained there for three days.

On the 18th, Walsingham had leisure to summon him and inquire what Babington was doing about the Jesuits. It was then that Babington sent his report that has been quoted, asking for further authority. Walsingham sent peremptory instructions for him to proceed, and ordered Berden to collaborate. But on the 21st a querulous report reached him, unsigned, possibly from Poley, more probably from Berden:

> I have many times given notice of the place where the Jesuit hath resorted at the time of his being there, but no great account hath been made thereof. . . . And when some priests have been by my directions apprehended, it hath been so handled contrary to my directions as I hardly escaped without being discovered to be the author thereof. *Henly Park* is never without three or four priests, and the Jesuit is there at this present, but never searched that I can hear of, though I have often required it when there have been a certain number there. (8)

Henly, or Henley, Park, in Surrey, Francis Browne's country house, was a shrewd guess on Berden's part. But it was not in fact correct. Thanks to Weston's vigilance, Garnet and Southwell, who were both so fond of an apt text to illustrate their progress, might have used those words of the Psalmist: 'Like a bird from the nets of the fowler our soul has been snatched; the snare was broken and we were set free.'

Early on the 14th they had taken horse at St. Giles-in-the-fields and were riding up the Oxford Road past Tyburn. At Brentford they took the left fork by Hounslow Heath, and then across the alluvial meadows of the Colne. With the towers of Windsor on their left, they carried on over the Thames by Maidenhead Bridge; and then by a narrow woody way through

I

the Great Frith, or *fruticea sylva*, studded already with early apples, till they saw the river again at a ford called Hurley.

They were entering an enclave of Buckinghamshire between the Thames and the Chiltern foothills where several of Weston's hosts had their houses: to the north, Lord Compton at Woburn and Lord Windsor at Braddenham; to the east, old Sir George Peckham of Denham, William Fitton and John Gardiner of Fulmer, 'obstinate receivers of priests'. The Babington Plot was to catch them all in its net. These rose-red, early Tudor houses were all too vulnerable behind the delicate wrought-iron tracery of their gates. City Puritans were to take them over and desecrate their treasured chapels. The presence of the three Jesuits in their neighbourhood on this occasion, though it was never proved, was a prelude to their ruin.

No sooner had the three crossed the river than their actual objective came in sight. It was Hurleyford, a lonely but spacious mansion set amidst great woods. Its owner, a recent convert of Weston's, had been a favourite of the Earl of Leicester, but had grown sick of the life. On returning from the wars in Flanders, he had retired to this solitary house where he and his wife could practise their religion in peace. Tyrrell's information to the Government supplies his name. It was Richard Bold, of a well-known Lancashire family that had owned this mansion in the south for generations. Tyrrell himself had been there a few weeks earlier, on an exorcising expedition with Weston, conducted by Edmund Peckham. (9)

But now the travellers were to enjoy an exorcism of a much better kind. Richard Bold was an ardent musician. He had in his house a chapel, a choir, and all sorts of instruments; and among his guests was none other than William Byrd, the Father of English music. Weston, in his enthusiastic description of their reception by Mr. Bold, has recorded casually this meeting with Byrd, which must have meant so much both to Garnet, the musician, and to Southwell, the poet:

We were very happy and our friends made it apparent how pleased they were to have us. . . . During those days it was just as if we were celebrating an uninterrupted octave of some great feast. Mr Byrd, the very famous English musician and organist was among the company. Earlier he had been attached to the Queen's Chapel, where he had gained a great reputation. But he had sacrificed everything for the faith.

Dr. Fellowes, the authority on Byrd, has remarked that his presence was quite natural on this occasion; for he was engaged on the collection of music known as *Lady Nevile's Book*, which kept him to and fro between Windsor and his house at Harlington on the Bath Road. Moreover the helping of his fellow-Catholics was always uppermost in his care and interest. His connection with the persecuted family of Tregian is well known; and it is possible that there was a little musical enclave also in this corner of the Thames Valley: an interesting passage in the State Papers for 1584 records the capture, in the Buckinghamshire parish of 'Stoke', of a 'popish song-book' which contained a letter from William Byrd of the Queen's Chapel to Mr. William Fitton, already mentioned. It is not correct that Byrd was struck off the roll of the Queen's Chapel; but Weston is right in saying that his career suffered through his religion. He was certainly subject to numerous vexations; his house was to be ransacked in August of this year, at the same time that Richard Bold was arrested— almost certainly in connection with the meeting here recorded.

The meeting began a lifelong friendship between Byrd and Garnet. The beauty of church music was one of the chief means by which the recusants kept up their spirits. Between Southwell and Byrd there is no record of any further meeting; but it is natural to suppose that there were many. Byrd was engaged at this time in setting to music the poems contained in his *Psalms, Sonets, and Songs of Sadness and Piety*, which did more than anything to preserve the medieval lyric in English poetry; and it was probably with his help that Southwell first became acquainted with contemporary English verse in its current manuscript form. One thinks particularly of Raleigh's 'Farewell, false love', and Dyer's 'My mind to me a kingdom is', which have obvious echoes in some of Southwell's poems.

But apart from music and poetry, and their priestly ministry, there was other serious work to occupy them during this unexpected and delightful holiday. Weston had a premonition that his days as an apostle in England were numbered; and he set before them a detailed plan of all the Catholic houses in England, as far as he had been able to get to know them in his wide and frequent travels. This was what Garnet had been waiting for. From this council may be dated the beginning of an amazing change in the English Catholic situation. It took years to accomplish, and only occasionally, as in the autobiography of John Gerard, do we catch glimpses of the transformation actually at work; but its magnitude may be judged by its terms. In the years between 1581 and 1586, of the 150 priests sent into England the majority had either tumbled into prison almost immediately, or were clustered uncertainly around London; whole shires in the interior were destitute of spiritual help; and, in addition, for many Catholic gentry with the best will in the world, the very name of 'seminary priest' had become an object of distrust. But ten years later, despite the intensest counter-measures by the Government, there was to be a network of country houses which provided accommodation and a radius of fruitful labour for 300 priests throughout the land; and when the organization was broken in places, as it was bound to be, not only Catholics but Schismatics (i.e. secret Catholics) and even Protestants, helped to restore it.

As a beginning, it was arranged that Garnet should go either to Lord Vaux's house in Northamptonshire, or to his daughter's in Leicestershire, from there to organize centres of worship in the neglected shires; Southwell was to stay near London, in Lord Vaux's town house at Hackney; part of his task there, when he had found his feet, would be to provide shelter for incoming priests, and to direct those who were willing to places in the interior which Garnet would have arranged; he probably also had under his own charge the county of Sussex, where he had so many friends and relatives. In all this there was no question of encroaching upon anybody's authority, for there was no authority to be encroached on; there was a chaotic situation urgently crying to be set in order, and the Jesuits alone had the influence and ability to do so. What they did was done voluntarily, and they were the better able to do it, because at this time the only priests in England who were not friends, and indeed admirers, of the Society were men like Grately, Bagshaw, and John Cecil, who from a Catholic point of view were thoroughly unreliable.

The climax of their eight days' holiday was to be a *Missa Solemnis* (one of Byrd's perhaps) sung on 22nd July—'on the very feast of St. Mary Magdalen', wrote Southwell in his letter, 'with a wonderful accompanying harmony of different instruments and voices. But', he continued, 'it was postponed to the following day, and I could not attend, as I was invited to another place.'

The 'other place' was London again, where his activities at the time of writing (25th July) are thus described: 'I am devoting myself to sermons, hearing confessions, and other priestly duties: hemmed in by daily perils, never safe for even a brief moment.'

It was probably fortunate for him that Walsingham's team was fully occupied during these days with the final arrangements for arresting Ballard and for keeping track of all Babington's young associates. Even so, Robert's guardian angel must have been kept hard at work. On the 21st the spies had reported his escape from London, and on the 22nd he rode back into London and went about *preaching sermons*.

There is a suggestion, too obvious to be rejected, that the sermon from which sprang his *Mary Magdalen's Funeral Tears* was the engagement that called him from Hurleyford on the 22nd. On that evening there was a 'banquet' in the Marshalsea Prison at which one or two priests and several ladies and gentlemen were present, and at which the *pièce de resistance* was a sermon on St. Mary Magdalen. Walsingham's secretary passed on a spy's report of it in shocked tones to his master:

Among other guests were three gentlewomen very brave in their attire, *two of them daughters to Sir John Arundell.* . . . It was Magdalen's day, and the priest catechized the company with the doctrine of popish repentance, taking for his theme the story of Magdalen, absurdly applying the same to his purpose. Yr Honour sees how well these kind of prisoners are looked to by their keepers. (10)

Now, it was to Dorothy Arundell that Robert dedicated his book. Only a very special occasion could have brought the two sisters into the sordid precincts of the Marshalsea 'very brave in their attire'. The suggestion is that at Dorothy's persuasion, Robert had returned to preach the sermon which she afterwards entreated him to make a book of: 'To the worshipful and vertuous Gentlewoman, Mistress D.A. Your vertuous request, to which your deserts gave the force of a commandment won me to satisfy your devotion in penning some little discourse of the Blessed Mary Magdalen . . .'

The English Catholics, starved of culture and piety, were ready to dare all hazards to hear the sort of sermon that Campion could preach. Campion had been unique. But now this young man had arrived, noble of birth, beautiful to look upon, but of an evident simplicity and holiness that transcended and transformed his earthly advantages, and gifted with an eloquence, not so lithe and pointed as Campion's, but perhaps more appealing to hearers of that day. The last pages of his book sound exactly like the peroration of a sermon. They are too long to quote. It must be enough to say that when one has become attuned to their melodious accents, they have a grave and haunting loveliness that vividly recalls their author (11).

To encourage him in his literary apostolate he could not have found better company than the Vaux family who were now his hosts. Lord Vaux, son of the poet of that name, was calmly facing material ruin, but in happier times he would have been a great patron of the arts. Edmund Campion who at the height of his Oxford fame had been tutor to the elder children, Henry and Eleanor—'a matchless pair', he called them—has left a beautiful portrait of this gentle and cultured household.

Henry Vaux's poems have survived, perhaps significantly, in the same manuscript volume as the completest edition of Southwell's. He was one of that shining band of young recusants who might have seemed altogether fitted to embody the Spenserian dream of chivalry. But across his retired, Platonic world had sounded the appeal that Ignatius of Loyola caught and transmitted in his *Contemplation of Christ the King*: the call of the Wounded Lord of Earth and Heaven, 'A Moi!': the return of chivalry transformed. He had relinquished his birthright so as to be free to join the Society of Jesus as soon as he could be spared from England. It may have been a secret grievance of Elizabethan statesmen against St. Ignatius, that he had stolen so much of the fire that might have kindled a national religion of myth and monarch-worship.

Eleanor, who rivalled Henry in the graces of scholarship, was the young widow of Edward Brooksby, Campion's chief shelterer and brother of Southwell's overseas friend. She, unlike her sister Anne, was very timorous by nature, and this throws into all the brighter relief her persistent loyalty as a priest-shelterer. With her was a little cousin, Frances Burrows, whom she had adopted after her husband's death. Frances, though aged only eleven, was to prove an important member of the household, for it seems likely that on one occasion she saved Robert Southwell's life. Eleanor was to be Garnet's hostess in the country in the following year, but there is evidence (the chronicle of the convent where Frances became a nun) that she was in London this winter with her father and brother.

Hackney in those days was not much more than a line of houses on either side of the old Knights-Hospitaller church that is now St. John's. Borough history has failed to trace the mansion once so well known to pursuivants as 'Lord Vaux's house in Hackney'. At a guess, it was on the site of an eighteenth-century 'Hackney House'—which has now also vanished—just east of the church, between Tresham Avenue and Brooksby's Walk.

From the Vaux's house Robert went out daily to work in London. One of his first tasks was to find Persons' aged mother and provide for her. An intercepted message to Persons, surviving as a garbled abstract in the State Papers, conveys his news of the indomitable old lady: 'Desires to be commended to one

Roberts, a Londoner, and speaks much in praise of that Roberts' mother, and that she looks for her son's coming and desires it.'

In his other letter Southwell had spoken of being 'hemmed in by daily perils, never safe for even the briefest moment'. But that had been written on 25th July. In ten days time the situation was to be incomparably worse.

CHAPTER NINE

'And the Foxes have their Lairs . . .'

IN the early days of August, the Babington Plot burst wide open. Up to this time Southwell had had one or two narrow escapes; but the weeks that now followed were his real baptism of fire. On every side of him people he knew and loved were being seized and hurried off to the rapidly-filling prisons. The first casualty had been Father Weston, on 3rd August. Then came another event that touched him closely: the fate of Robert Gage, whose brother John was engaged to Margaret Copley. Robert Gage seems to have been a young man mentally distraught and tired of life; he had joined Babington's friends only a day or two before Ballard's arrest. When asked at his trial why he had taken to the woods with Tichbourn and the others, he answered fiercely, 'For company!' and would say no more. His inclusion in the plot threw a shadow of suspicion on all his relatives who had frequented Southampton House with him. His brother John was arrested. So was Swithin Wells. And there was a raid upon the Copleys' house at Gatton. A priest, Nicholas Smith, Southwell's old companion of noviceship days, was found there; and the whole family was sent to prison.

The next to go were Southwell's late hosts in the country. Richard Bold was taken to prison, at the instance of the Earl of Leicester. William Byrd, the musician, and Francis Browne had their houses searched, but escaped arrest. Meanwhile, with ominous accuracy, the Government picked up the two seminary priests who had been most closely connected with Father Weston. All these names, and many more, were included in a long and rambling statement by the wretched Anthony Tyrrell who had broken down completely on seeing the crippled form of Ballard being carried in a chair for fresh examination. (1)

Southwell was expecting arrest at any moment. But a story of Garnet's suggests that it was perhaps his very indifference to danger that gave him a charmed life.

> A traitor once caught sight of our Robert and, instead of pouncing at once, followed him for a long time, so as to track him to the house where he was going and make a larger haul. But Robert, who liked to walk at a good pace, though he was quite unaware of the spy's presence, suddenly increased his stride and disappeared from view altogether. So there was no flattering reward for the traitor when he got back to Walsingham but hard words instead. (2)

This picture of Robert changing speed to match his thoughts and escaping absent-mindedly round a corner seems to belong to his earlier and more care-free days in London.

He seems to have moved quite fearlessly from prison to prison. His letter to Agazzari sent news of many former students he had visited. There were special messages for Anthony Copley who was becoming restive at Rome: 'His mother begged me earnestly to write to him that he must on no account leave the college, for she added solemnly that she did not know what would become of him if he were here. Poor dear lady, she has so much to bear and was reduced to such straits that I had to lend her ten pounds ...'(3)

Soon there were the executions: first the protracted butchering of the Babington 'conspirators', Robert Gage among them, and later the martyrdom of three seminary priests, including Father John Lowe. Southwell had to work his way through the crowd as near the scaffold as possible so as to give the last absolution which the victims would be counting on. Then there were the many houses of Catholics in or around London who were demanding his presence now more than ever. He wrote to the General:

> More than ever, the Catholics have a holy hunger for the Sacraments, and count themselves most hardly used if they have to abstain

even for a short time. . . . It is their only solace amid all these
turmoils and dangers, to refresh themselves with the Bread of
Heaven; and if that were taken away, many would grow weak and
torpid whose courage and holiness is so great when nourished
by it. (4)

At night he would slip back through the streets he was beginning to know by heart. At some appointed place he would meet
Henry Vaux, his 'angel guardian', and they would ride up the
ribbon-built road of Shoreditch, past the old Priory of Holywell
and the new Theatre, then, turning right, across open country to
the house in Hackney where the door was opened by friends
whose love grew the stronger the worse things became. No
wonder he could write in his letter: 'In the midst of perils it is
marvellous how good God is and how bountiful of his comforts,
insomuch that danger itself groweth sweet.'

The final test could not be long deferred. The London Magistrate, Young, was pressing Tyrrell hard to discover the whereabouts of this new Jesuit who had so strangely evaded him, who
was heard of in so many places in London, but never seen.
Tyrrell, not yet definitely suspected by Catholics, had the freedom
of the Clink to wander round and pick up information. But he
had been in prison since early July and could not connect the
name of Southwell with any priest he knew. From his episodic
confessions it appears that his captors suggested the name to him
without further specification, and that the suggestion originated
with the Queen herself.

His first essay was a bad blunder. He brought information
against Sir Robert Southwell, recently knighted, who had married the Lord Admiral's daughter. When Young told him that
the Queen was surprised at his story, he amended it and said he
meant 'Young Mr. Southwell who married Mrs. Southcote.'
But that did not hit the mark either. His final venture was more
by luck than knowledge. On Friday, 4th November, he 'gave
information of one Mr S——, (5) a priest that for certain did lie
at the Lord Vaux his house, by which means Justice Young went
himself thither in the morning and made a search.'

The raid was timed for an early hour in the morning when it was known that Mass would be in progress. (6) It was carefully planned and carried out in force. Before the usual warning could be given, the doorkeeper was overpowered, and men with drawn swords rushed into the hall, led by the chief pursuivant Newall. Justice Young himself seems to have kept in the background. The chapel—where Mass was indeed being said—was just above the portico through which the searchers had entered; but it could only be reached by a narrow staircase at the far end of the hall. The family and the priests (there appears to have been one other besides Southwell) heard the noise of feet scuffling in the hall below. Frances Burrows rose swiftly and left the chapel. As the searchers beat against the priest's chamber on the ground floor and blundered towards the stairs in the half-light, they too heard the sound of feet, running lightly down towards them from the gallery above. They shouted and held their swords ready. Framed in the flare of their torches stood a little girl who seemed to be the least perturbed person present. 'Put up your swords', she said in shocked and authoritative tones, 'or else my mother will die, for she cannot abide to see a naked sword.' As if in confirmation of this warning Eleanor, who had followed Frances, stood swaying, deathly pale, on the stairway, and seeming about to swoon at any moment.

The constables hesitated, and even began sheepishly to hide their swords. Newall, exasperated, pressed on; he had hoped to storm the Mass-chamber and catch the priest and family *in flagrante delicto*; but it was difficult for a crowd to pass in a hurry without doing positive harm to the swooning lady on the stairs and her indignant daughter. At the head of the stairs Lord Vaux appeared, and held up Newall with a wrath and dignity that overbore the pursuivant's: if there was to be a search, let the warrant be first produced and the thing conducted in decent order, not in the manner of felons breaking in under cover of darkness. Meanwhile, with speed born of practice, the Mass-things were being cleared away, and Lady Vaux was hiding the sacred vessels in her little casket whose resting-place was known only to the most trusted servants. By the time the *posse* arrived in force at the chapel, Henry Vaux had seen the priests into their hiding-holes. But in the priest's chamber there were two letters of Southwell's for Rome which Henry had been hoping to get rid of that day, and he was caught with them on him.

Meanwhile Newall, having failed to make a clean catch, had no recourse but to send his men round the house, knocking over the furniture, banging on the walls and ripping the panels where they sounded hollow. This went on for hour after hour. Only the power of prayer—or rather, the fact that his hour had not yet come—can have saved Southwell on this occasion. In a later letter he writes:

> Twice I was in extreme danger. The pursuivants were raging all around. . . . I heard them threatening and breaking woodwork and sounding the walls to find hiding-places; yet by God's goodness after four hours' search they found me not, though separated from them only by a thin partition, rather than a wall.

Late in the day Newall was forced to retire baffled. But he sent Henry Vaux away under guard to answer before the Council; and he left a ring of men round the house to examine all who came or went. Inside the house a hurried consultation was held. Southwell, presumably, would have insisted on giving himself up to liberate Henry. But that was clean against the Vaux code. Finally, Sir Thomas Tresham and his lawyer from nearby Hoxton were allowed to enter the house. They seem to have decided that Henry knew how to look after himself, and would soon be released. In fact, he was not released till May of the next year, and then only to die in the following November. The letters, which were in Latin and signed *Robertus*, were at once handed over to Tyrrell for translation and comments. It was feared that the dreaded Robert Persons had returned to organize resistance. Tyrrell gave it as his opinion that Robert Persons was indeed the writer. Afterwards he realized that it was Southwell, and said so. But the belief persisted for some time in Government circles that the elusive *Robertus* was Persons once more at large in England. (7)

Pressure was kept up for a week or more against the house at Hackney. Southwell, practically confined to his hiding-hole, anticipated some of the hardships of imprisonment, as he wrote, continuing the same letter:

> The house was in such sort watched for many nights together that I perforce slept in my clothes in a very strait and uncomfortable place. In this wise while we are yet free, we are trained to bear confinement.

The pursuivants swooped again in the hope of effecting a surprise, and again little Frances figured prominently: this time in an incident which is best related in the words of the Chronicler of her convent:

> A pursuivant thinking with terror to make her disclose the secret places of the house, caught her by the arm, and holding his naked dagger at her breast, threatened that if she would not tell him where the priests were, he would stab her in the heart. She, undaunted, as not apprehending anything of death, bade him if he durst, and with courage said, '*If you do, it shall be the hottest blood that ever thou sheddest in thy life.*'

It was an answer that might have come straight off the Elizabethan stage. Without detracting from Frances's heroism, one is reminded that Lord Vaux still kept a private company of players. A sentence from Robert Southwell's writings of this date suggests that there had been a performance at the house while he was there; he is referring to the borrowed finery that was a noted peculiarity of English actors:

> . . . Children seeing the stage-players in costly attire think them happier than the rich gentleman that goeth plain, because neither consider they the players base condition, otherwise, nor their shameful profession, but only their fayned glory. (8)

But if Frances was the stage-struck child in question, she knew, like the youthful St. Teresa, how to translate her day-dreams into action; and the catch-poll, to his credit, recognized the authentic note. The chronicler concludes:

> The pursuivant, perceiving that death could not fright her, offered a hundred pounds to have her, for to make a present to the Lord Bishop of London, saying it was a pity a maid of her courage should be spoiled with papistry.

The pursuivant's geniality was perhaps a sign that the searches were being finally abandoned. But once again Southwell had the bitterness of knowing that another man was led into captivity to pay for the freedom which it was his duty, not his inclination, to preserve. He wrote on 21st December:

> The time that I was sought for they led off two of the household; one of whom, because he would not attend the conventicles of the heretics, they cruelly beat and forced him by day with great toil to turn the treadmill along with vagabonds and the like, and to lie at night on the ground, without bed, mattress or coverlet; neither could he obtain that food or bed or clothes should be supplied him by his friends. After this sort he is afflicted even to this day, by whose means I have escaped.

This is clearly a description of the dreaded prison, Bridewell, instituted under Edward VI for the correction of vagabonds and harlots. It seems likely that the brave man who faced it was Mr. Harris, Henry Vaux's confidential clerk. The only commitment to Bridewell for refusing to 'attend the conventicles of the heretics' runs as follows in the prison lists of 30th November: 'To be committed to Bridewell: *William Harris* an obstinate recusant that will not receive conference.' (9)

Earlier in the month, however, Southwell had slipped away from the besieged Vaux household, and had gone down into the country—probably to his relatives in Sussex or Hampshire. His aunt still languished in prison. But his cousin Margaret had been set free, together with John Gage, and the young couple were married about this time. They were cousins within the forbidden limits by the pre-tridentine code. Later on, Southwell wrote to Rome in perplexity to know whether power to dispense from these impediments was included in the faculties given him.

While he was in the country he arranged for a secure way of sending and receiving letters across the Channel. His next letter to Aquaviva, of 7th January, shows that he could rely on messengers between France and England: 'Would you please send some small gifts for our hosts. I know that, coming from us, they will be a source of much pleasure to them. If they can be sent to our procurator in Paris, I have reliable friends who can get them over to us.'

Aquaviva, in the next few months, seems to have arranged for a friend in the French Embassy to transmit the letters. But at this stage Southwell was probably relying on his relatives in Sussex and Hampshire. A certain Mr. Robert Barnes who acted as steward to Southwell's cousin Shelley of Petersfield and later to Lord Montague at Cowdray, was afterwards accused by Topcliffe of slipping to and fro across the Channel. He recurs once or twice in connection with Southwell's movements, and was evidently a key-figure in the lay underground movement for helping priests and organizing Mass-centres. He and Swithin Wells and John Shelley were later accused of 'carrying a priest up and down the country' disguised as a servant in Lord Montague's livery. 'They shift such persons between them.'

Swithin Wells, an elderly man now but still young in spirit, was another of the underground messengers. In March 1587 he was arrested for colporting devotional books from overseas. As the consignment included presentation copies for Lady Vaux, Lady Tresham and others, these were probably the 'small gifts' asked for by Southwell. (10)

The inquisition into Swithin's movements revealed the names of several of Southwell's Sussex-Hampshire cousins:

I came on Shrift Monday last to Mr Paulet of Heriot where I lay the night. From thence the next morning I came to Mr Coles's house in the parish of Berington where I lay that night. The next day I came to my cousin's George Cotton's of Warblington, there I lay that night. From thence to Mr Kemp's of Slindon, there I lay that night. The next day to Michelgrove [the Shelleys] where I have remained till this day. (11)

Robert Southwell's maternal cousins, and his connections with West Sussex and East Hampshire.

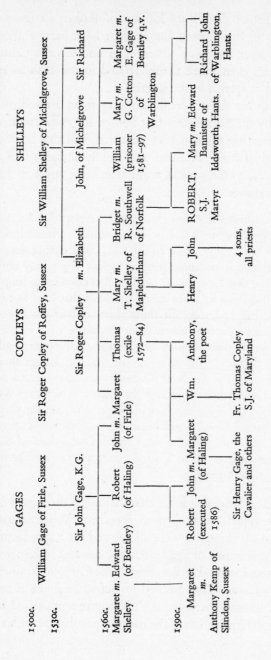

No further details are known of Robert's contacts with his relatives in this region; but it must have been a great comfort to him, after ten years' absence, to find George Cotton and all the others even more firmly rooted in the faith in spite of all that had happened in the interim.

During his absence in the country news arrived of a rumour spread by the pursuivants that he—or someone credited with his London activities—had been captured, and that no more would be heard of him. Amused and mildly indignant, Robert hastened back to the capital, from which he wrote in his letter of 21st December.

> I am informed that there is a general report that I am taken, and, hearing this while I was yet free, I smiled to think how gratifying that would be for a time to my foes, until 'having slept their sleep, they should find naught in their hands'. They may say as often as they like that I am taken; but I shall endeavour, as long as I escape their hands, to let them know by deeds that I am not taken. Not that I shall undertake anything that can hurt the State; but I am determined never to desist from the works of my calling, though these when done cannot long escape their notice; and they will know that there still lives one of this sort whom they have not taken. . . . The souls of Catholics are more precious than our bodies; and when we reckon the price at which they were bought, it should not seem much to endanger our lives for their salvation. That Sacred Blood is still warm, those wounds still open, and those bruises may still be seen, with which God redeemed the souls that we are tending. At such a sight dangers may well be scorned, lest such precious pearls be lost.

It is clear from this letter that the ordeal through which he had passed had had a marked effect upon him. When he first set out for England his thoughts were all centred on a speedy martyrdom; but now the taste of aggression had aroused in him a vigorously combative strain. The devotion of the Catholic families had come as a revelation. They needed his active help just as passionately and for the same reasons, as the Government desired his capture. He was determined to make the best possible use of his native wit and courage to avoid capture, to build up a tough and flexible organization in and around London, and only to sell his freedom at the longest price obtainable. Already there are observable the lineaments of a figure somewhat different from the passive victim he is generally supposed to be. Along with his gentle exterior and intense holiness there were signs of an ice-clear brain and nerves of steel that were to achieve for him a feat unrivalled by any other missionary. In the heart of London, where no one else could long survive, he got through six years of active work and outwitted a six-year intensive search.

It is worth stressing here, incidentally, that his remark about keeping clear of politics was amplified in a covering letter to Persons: 'About Parliament I say nothing, as I desire my letters, like my soul, to have absolutely nothing to do with matters of State.'

Another result of the ordeal was a determination on his part never again to imperil his generous friends and patrons. On his return to London—probably early in December—there were many Catholic families most anxious to receive him. But he had decided on his plan of life for the next year or two. He must find a place of refuge where he would be virtually unknown and undisturbed; from there he would issue only at night to 'perform the works of his calling', and by day he would devote himself to prayer and to the writing of books which—he now felt—was in an especial way his apostolate. While he was hesitating and hoping for a sign from God, a gentlewoman touched him on the sleeve and delivered a message which was the answer to his prayer. It was a request to visit the house of the Countess of Arundel and Surrey in the Strand.

Arundel and Surrey—proudest titles in the peerage—were carried by a lady who might have been a wraith, so little was she known to the multitude or heeded by the great. She was Anne Dacres, daughter of a great northern family. Her husband, Philip Howard, having got back his earldoms after the attainder of the Duke of Norfolk, his father, had plunged into a life of gaiety at

Court from which she was completely banished. While *she* remained in obscurity, longing for the old-fashioned ways of the north, *he* became one of Queen Elizabeth's chief favourites at the time of the proposed French marriage. His abominable uncle, Henry Howard, schemed to make him the figurehead of a conservative movement against the hardly less abominable Earl of Leicester; but when the French marriage failed, Arundel's favour declined. He himself cared very little for politics, but, by a coincidence, he began to be attracted to the purely spiritual aspect of the Old Religion. It was almost a case of telepathy, for Anne a little earlier had secretly returned to the faith she had never willingly abandoned. She was dreading her husband's displeasure when he should hear the news; but instead, for the first time in their married life, she found him gentle and even penitent. To complete his downfall in the eyes of Elizabeth's court, he began to live with his wife; and she bore him a child, a daughter, in 1583. They were both, at that time, aged twenty-six. They had a brief eighteen months of bitter happiness together, during which they were both at different times under house arrest. Then, in April 1585, Philip, trying to cross the Channel to confer with Dr. Allen, was seized and taken to the Tower*—which he was not to leave till his death ten years later. He never saw his wife again, nor did he ever see his little son who was born just after his apprehension.

Deprived of Howard House and of most of her income, but still hoping to get access to her husband, Anne was living in Arundel House, which was her jointure. It was a pleasant place with a garden reaching down to the river and private landing-stairs. But it was hemmed in and overawed by the mansions of great Protestant potentates: the house of Leicester, her husband's arch-enemy, on one side, and Somerset House, the Queen's resort, on the other, and Cecil House a little farther up-stream. It was hardly a suitable environment for a Catholic chaplain, let alone for a Jesuit who had been violently hunted since the

* The Catholics believed that he had been decoyed by a false message, concocted by Grately for the Government.

Babington Plot. But in fact the Countess had no intention of acquiring another resident chaplain. Her only previous experience in that regard had not been a happy one, for in 1585 the spy Edward Grately had lived with them. When Grately disappeared a very good secular priest, Martin Array, a friend of Ralph Sherwin, used to visit her when she asked for him. But he had been captured in June, and since that time no request for a priest had come from the silent house in the Strand.

Then in November or December, when the storm of the Babington Plot was subsiding, she sent her gentlewoman to inquire of her Catholic relatives, the Vauxes and the Arundells, what priest there was in London who could bring her the Sacraments. They had no hesitation about whom to recommend.

For Southwell the invitation was a momentous one. The Earl's conversion had made him the obvious leader of all Catholic England. There was no capital charge against him, he might be released at any moment; on the other hand he might waver and compromise; he knew very little about the religion he had so recently embraced; there was an imperative need to comfort and sustain him both for his own sake and for all the English Catholics. It was a task to which Southwell felt peculiarly drawn. Although his grandfather had betrayed Philip's grandfather,★ the Southwells were hereditarily attached to the Howards. And Philip was a poet too: not in the same class as his grandfather, it is true, but lively and sensitive and a great patron of letters. Here was a heaven-sent chance of approaching him through the written word. But the chance depended wholly on his bereaved lady who was an unknown quantity to the English Catholics; a mysterious figure, wrapped in grief, and obviously difficult to approach.

It was probably with some trepidation, not caused altogether by the bustling lictors at Leicester House, that Southwell followed his guide through the courtyard next door, and was ushered into the presence. He saw a tall, graceful, fair-haired woman with a fresh complexion like a girl's, but otherwise rather faded in appear-

★ See Chapter One, opening.

ance, without any jewels or ornaments except a little gold cross. Her manner was at once ceremonious and shy, deferent and remote. It was by no means a chilly welcome, but there was none of the alert friendliness of the Vaux household. There was perfect willingness to meet his demands, but there was no anxiety to forestall them. After a day or two he was still in the position of a week-end guest whose imminent departure is regretted but taken for granted.

The origin and solution of this mild initial *contretemps* is best told in the stately words of the Countess's biographer:

She caused one of her servants better acquainted amongst Catholics in London than herself, to make enquiry for some Priest by whom she might sometimes receive the Holy Sacraments; but neither intending that he should make his abode with her, nor thinking it possible, by reason of the inconveniency of her house, and the small number of Catholics about her; though she did not manifest so much to the servant employed therein. Who, understanding upon enquiry that Father Southwell in the company of Father Henry Garnet was not long before come into the Kingdom from Rome, found means to speak with him, and to declare her Lady's desire of having him to come to her; and he in discourse demanding if her Lady's meaning were, whether he should reside with her or no, she answering affirmatively, he remained with that persuasion; and thereupon after a few days, being with the Countess, he began upon occasion to speak of procuring some secret convenience to be made in some part of the house, wherein himself and his few books together with the Church Stuff might be hidden in case any sudden search should happen to be made, as it was usual in most Catholic houses where any Priest had residence. She wondered to hear him speak in that manner, not knowing what her servant had said unto him; but out of Respect made no reply, not doubting that himself within a little time would find by experience how unfit and inconvenient her house was for him or any other Priest to make their residence. And well it was she did not then declare her thoughts; for had she but made the least insinuation that her meaning was not to have him live with her, he never would have offered it, but settled himself somewhere else, as he told her when after some years she discovered to him in pleasant discourse, how the matter passed; he no less wondering than she rejoicing at it, as reason good she had: for had he not remained with her, both she and her Lord and many of their friends had wanted that great help and Comfort which they found in him in all occasions. (12)

So began for Southwell a ghostly twilight life, but one for which both his temperament and his training in sanctity and scholarship uniquely fitted him. He was given a little room in an unvisited part of the house, which, at the same time, allowed him safe access to the Countess's private apartments when Mass and confession were required, and also enabled him to slip out on to the street, or to the river, under cover of darkness when his services were needed by other Catholics in London. In this room he stored his books and papers: the Bible and Saint Bernard and many long written extracts from the Greek and Latin Fathers; and from this room he never stirred a foot during the daytime. He lived so quietly, never showing himself at the window and never moving about except soft-footed, that for nearly two years no one knew he was in the house, except the Countess and one or two trusted servants who provided him with the necessities of life.

The one who mostly looked after him, and who might be called his landlady, was, surprisingly, not a Catholic—though 'otherwise', comments the Countess's biographer wonderingly, 'of moral life and not addicted unto heresie'. She was an old retainer, a northern woman possibly, and wholly devoted to the Countess; and she soon became attached to her mysterious lodger. They used to argue amicably about religion, but she would not budge an inch. It was not till many years later, when she lay on her death-bed, staring into the unknown, that she suddenly said, 'Oh, Blessed Father Southwell', and asked for a priest.

One cannot suppress a sneaking hope that this admirable woman—whose name one would give a lot to know—compensated for her religious indifference by an extra attention to hygiene, and that she kept the room reasonably aired in summer and warm in winter. Not that her lodger would have caused her much trouble; though he was living like a mouse, he had a cat-like cleanliness and self-sufficiency. 'My mind to me an *empire* is',

he sang softly to himself, remembering perhaps a manuscript
poem that William Byrd had shown him.

> I feel no care of coin,
> Well-doing is my wealth;
> My mind to me an empire is
> While grace affordeth health.

If his landlady ever tried, with feminine malice, gently to
exploit his captivity as a help to her argument, and to provoke
those nervous explosions of anger, greed and so on, which sometimes make a man's religious profession look rather ridiculous,
she would have been disappointed.

> I wrestle not with rage
> While fury's flame doth burn;
> It is in vain to stop the streams
> Until the tide doth turn. . . .

> Spare diet is my fare,
> My clothes more fit than fine;
> I know I feed and clothe a foe
> That pamper'd would repine.

Southwell had a smooth philosophic armour, made up of
apophthegms and proverbs, for dealing with the minor difficulties of life; it was only in major issues that he uncovered the deep
fire of his religious love. There is sometimes an apparent discord
between his cold common-sense in the ordinary problems of life
and his glowing ardour in the face of death and wounds; but in
practice he kept these two tempers running easily together on a
loose rein of philosophy that might be summed up in St. Augustine's line: 'Lord Jesus, let me know myself, in order to know
Thee', the knowledge of self and of human weakness, and the
knowledge of God and of Divine Charity. In Southwell, as in
the saints, the two had become inseparably correlated.

With his mental operations finely ground between these bare
essentials, with his retentive memory richly stored with Scripture
and the Fathers, and with few—as yet—of the many worries

that were later to come on him, his pen simply flew over the paper when he sat down to write his letters to Earl Philip.

But as these letters increased and began to take the form of a treatise and were passed round to other readers, a bold idea took shape in the minds of his friends, the small band that still survived in London. There had been no native Catholic literature since the printing presses of Campion and Persons had been hunted down; but the stir they had caused throughout England was still vividly remembered. Was not this the time, now when all seemed lost, for a similar gesture?

CHAPTER TEN

The Secret Printing Press, 1587

As Southwell made his way secretly about London by night, at the beginning of the new year, he realized the full extent of the ruin that had come on the recusant cause through the Babington Plot—'that wicked and ill-fated conspiracy', he cried, 'which has struck such a blow at the Catholic cause that even our enemies, had they had their choice, could never have devised anything more ruinous to us or agreeable to themselves.' (1) Very soon he was to modify his verdict when he realized how far the enemy had indeed devised it, and used it to destroy Catholic strong-points, and, even more effectively, to attach a moral stigma to the Catholic name.

Materially, the damage was considerable. There were great gaps in the list of houses that Weston had given him; places he could no longer in conscience approach, where the owners had been imprisoned, or lay crushed by fines at the mercy of blackmailing informers. A particularly heartrending example was the Bellamy household of Uxendon Manor, near Wembley, which, out of compassion, had given food and clothing to Babington's young men when they were on the run. Two sons of the house, though they had no knowledge of the plot, were done to death, a third suffered torture and exile, and the aged mother died in prison. (2)

'There is weeping almost unto death', wrote Southwell on 12th January, 'among wives who have no husbands, and families with no support, where religion has no champions, and chapels no loving hands to tend them.' (3)

Yet it was the moral desolation which was worse. The actual death-roll from these months of persecution was not large. The Government had stopped short, on purpose, of this last extremity.

There is an interesting note among Walsingham's papers, dated December 1586:

> The execution of them, as experience showeth, in respect of their constancy, or rather obstinacy, moveth men to compassion and draweth some to affect their religion, upon conceit that such an extraordinary contempt of death cannot but proceed from above, whereby many have fallen away. (4)

Burghley had admitted the same in his memorandum of 1584. It was an admission that the attempt to disguise the old religion as treason was still failing to deceive many.

But now they hoped that with the death of the Scottish Queen the scandal of more martyrdoms would not be necessary. The passive Catholic body could be crushed silently by fines and humiliations and by all those methods which Burghley had outlined in his memorandum, such as separating children from their parents—'as hostages, under colour of education' he had written cynically. The main thing always, however, was to cut them off from spiritual succour by their priests. For the first time since 1580, this aim looked likely to be achieved. So many priests had vanished into prison or banishment that London was to all appearances quite free from Mass and the Sacraments. As to the laity, they had had the full degradation of their liability for High Treason brought home to them. Hitherto it had been possible to feel the tide of public opinion secretly in their favour; but now it seemed set strongly and rancorously against them. In pursuance of a further part of Burghley's programme, the apocalyptic anti-Roman fervour of the Puritan preachers was being turned on at full blast. Southwell noted a great spate of licensed propaganda of the most diverse sectarian nature.

> But all agree in one cry: that traitors and assassins such as we should not be tolerated in the State, that we are plotting the ruin of the gospel and of all sacred things. And we are to conclude that our own ruin has come upon us because we are hateful both to heaven and earth.

He noted also the public and shameless falsehoods by which the Government immobilized the French Embassy in January so as to seal the fate of Mary Stuart. (5) 'It is an axiom for liars', he commented grimly, 'that what is won by lies must be kept and confirmed by lies.' His eyes were now opened to the real nature of these regicide plots, he saw *which* Queen was their intended victim. Behind everything now loomed the coming tragedy of Fotheringhay. With Mary's neck would be severed the last temporal hope on which, inevitably, even the most spiritual Catholics had depended.

It was the very darkest hour, fitly symbolized by the thick January nights in which he crept from house to house, trying to gather up the fragments. But a revelation awaited him. He was greeted at first with amazement as one risen from the dead, for the report of his capture had been widespread—and then with exultation. The Mass had returned! As he wrote in the same January letter,

> *And yet* the faith is still alive! The Church exults! The families are *not* falling away.* The work of God is being pressed forward— often enough by delicate women who have taken on the courage of men. For as the sufferings of Christ abound in us, so also through Christ abounds our consolation. Only priests are lacking. It is clear and certain that, whatever storms are raging, the Bark of Peter is moving forward, and moving steadily, *and very many are seeking access to her.* Let them come, then, those who are to come, so that the fruits of our toil may be greater.

He saw with certitude that the mystical Passion of Christ and His Resurrection, perpetuated in the Mass, were at work around him—and through him. It was the old lesson once more. The real contest was not over, it was only just beginning.

To share the understanding of this, as far as in him lay, with those suffering in prison, he arranged his writings into twelve chapters, each one being a reason for comfort in tribulation,

* An extraordinary example of this was Richard Bellamy, the sole surviving son, who set up house again with his wife and family at Uxendon, and began to rebuild his shattered fortunes, and to receive priests cautiously.

reasons drawn from philosophy and history and contemporary events, as well as from prayer, from dogma, and from mystical theology; and to the whole he gave the title: AN EPISTLE OF COMFORT *to the Reverend Priests, and to the Honorable, Worshipful, and other of the Lay sort, restrained in durance for the Catholic Faith.*

But it was his friends who first suggested the daring and seemingly impossible notion that it should be printed and published in book form so as to make the vitality of their resistance even more strikingly apparent. He had evidently a rush to get it finished in time: 'Having written this Epistle of Comfort to an especial friend of mine, and not thinking at the first to let it pass any further, not only the time to which it principally serveth, but the entreaty of diverse, enforced me so far that I could not but condescend to the publishing of the same, though it cost me no small labour in altering the style.'

But this calm reference to 'the publishing of the same' covers a baffling question. *How* was it published? And when? And where?

Before any attempted answer, an important sentence in his letter of January deserves attention: 'The work of God is being pressed forward—sometimes by delicate women who have taken on the courage of men.' The emergence of women was beginning to be a marked feature of recusant resistance. With Henry Vaux's capture, his sisters Eleanor and Anne stepped forward to take his place. With the Earl of Arundel shut up in the Tower, the Countess began, softly and hesitantly at first, to use her means and influence in his stead. She was supplying Southwell with money and other helps for destitute families. She lent him a little house, probably at Acton, Middlesex, where he could offer shelter to incoming priests. And it seems that it was by her influence that his book was published.

The evidence about it comes from three very different sources: first, a pamphlet by 'Martin Mar-prelate', published early in 1589, referring to events two years before; secondly a spy's report, catalogued under 1588–9 but also referring to the early part of 1587; and finally a reminiscence by John Gerard of his first meeting with Robert Southwell.

'Martin Mar-prelate' was the pen-name of a group of Puritan pamphleteers who, with the support of powerful courtiers like Sir Francis Knollys, ran an illicit press up and down the country in the years 1588 and 1589, issuing violently abusive attacks on the Anglican bishops. It might be thought that the Puritans and Catholics would have struck up a pragmatic sympathy against a common enemy. But there never seems to have been the least likelihood of this; the chief plank in the Puritan platform was a barbaric and almost delirious hatred of Rome. The complaint in the Mar-prelate pamphlet was that Archbishop Whitgift, while enforcing the Star Chamber decree of 1586 against the brave Puritan printer Robert Waldegrave, had *on two occasions* in 1587 allowed 'popish' printers to escape unscathed. The printers named were 'Popish Thackwell' and 'J.C., the Earl of Arundel's man'.

The occasion of the first accusation—it is now known—was a genuine and very gallant little Welsh Catholic press which carried on in a cave in the mountains; its apparatus was thought to have been supplied by a printer in London called Thackwell; the cave was tracked down and captured in April 1587; but Thackwell, though questioned, seems to have been released for lack of evidence. The mar-prelates, therefore, though their facts were distorted, knew what they were talking about. (6)

Their second accusation was against another printer for supplying the Earl (or rather, the Countess) of Arundel with an illicit press in February of the same year:

And, good your grace, I do now remember myself of another printer that had press and letter in a place called the Charter-house in London in *anno* 1587, near about the time of the Scottish Queen's death.* Intelligence was given unto your good grace of the same by some of the Stationers in London. It was made known unto you what work was in hand, what letter the book was on, what volume (viz: octavo, in half-sheets), what workmen wrought on the same: namely, *J.C.* the Earl of Arundel's man and three of his servants with their several names, what liberality was bestowed on those workmen and by whom . . . but to this day the parties were never called *in Coram* for it. (7)

* 8th February.

It is pretty certain that this book was Southwell's *Epistle of Comfort*, for three reasons. Internal evidence limits its composition, certainly to 1587, and probably within the first three months of that year. (8) It was the only book with which the Earl or Countess of Arundel was connected in that period. The earliest known edition of it is an octavo volume evidently printed surreptitiously and in haste. It is marked IMPRINTED AT PARIS, but this is an obvious blind.* Where, then, *was* it printed?

J.C. was John Charlewood, a well-known publisher enjoying the monopoly of printing play-bills, who styled himself, at least until 1585: *Printer to the Rt. Hon. the Earl of Arundel*. His shop was 'in Barbican, at the sign of the Half Eagle and Key'. But Martin did not accuse him of printing the book in his shop, but of supplying the machinery and labour for printing it in 'a place called the Charterhouse', that is, Howard House. This seems incredible, because Howard House had been mostly taken over by the Government after Philip's arrest; and, although his brothers the Lords William and Thomas still had lodgings within its large enclosure, the Countess had lost all her rights there. Nevertheless, once again it may be supposed that Martin knew what he was talking about, up to a point. He knew, that is, that Charlewood used to print privately for the family in the days before the stringent Star Chamber decree against unlicensed books—the evidence for this is an early book by Lord Henry Howard, printed by Charlewood, and marked *From Howard House* on the title page (9)—and he inferred that there would still be an old disused press in the Howard brothers' lodgings at the Charterhouse. Though Martin could know nothing—obviously—about where the press was taken to and worked, he was probably right in his guess where it came from.

The spy's report is some confirmation. (10) Like most spies' reports it is a sprawling and ambiguous document. Its subject is illicit Catholic books and the occasion of it seems to have been the large consignment of devotional works, referred to in the

* According to Fr. Pollen the 'pot' or chalice in the watermark is of a type that denotes English paper.

previous chapter, which were smuggled in from France in March 1587; they included sumptuous presentation copies for Lady Vaux, Lady Tresham and others. But the spy also refers to *the late impression* of such books, and to a priest whom he thinks to be 'acquainted with the impression'. Of this priest he says: 'He useth much to Doctor Atslow and to the Charter-house, but to which of the brethren I am not certain.' Dr. Atslow was a famous physician, devoted to the Earl and Countess of Arundel. The 'brethren' were the Lords William and Thomas. The priest, or another one, was suspected of visiting Lord William on the pretext of teaching him French. The report is vague, but for what it is worth, it is independent evidence that the Charterhouse was suspected in connection with the printing of Catholic books.

John Gerard's evidence is very brief, but quite clear. He is describing his arrival in London in the winter of 1588:

> We then had few friends in a position to help us. Father Southwell alone had a great benefactress, and . . . he was able with her help to maintain himself and some other priests, as well as keep a private house where he usually received the Superior on his visits to London. It was there that I first met them both; *there too that Father Southwell had his printing press, where his own admirable books were produced.**

The term 'private house' (*domus privata*) rules out the Charterhouse as the final home of the press—though not as its place of origin. The Countess at different times had two small houses where she retired, perforce—according to her biographer—when the Queen came to stay at Somerset House. One of these was near the Hospital outside Bishopsgate; the other was at Acton, Middlesex. It was probably at one of these—and more probably at Acton—that Gerard saw the illicit press.

So what seems to have happened is this, though it can only be a conjecture: the Countess persuaded her brothers-in-law, who in turn persuaded and bribed Charlewood, to allow the old Howard press and letter to be transferred from the Charterhouse to the house at Acton. It was dismantled and carried piece by

---

* The italics are not in the original.

piece, no doubt; and Charlewood and his assistants helped to set it up, and instructed the amateur Catholics how to use it. Charlewood's chief assistant was probably John Roberts who succeeded to his copyrights and his monopoly of printing play-bills; that perhaps is why Roberts afterwards printed the first copyright editions of Southwell's verse.

John Roberts's connection with playwrights is interesting, because the only traceable *official* reference to the *Epistle* occurs in a 'Remembrance' that was used against Christopher Marlowe in 1593. The statement runs: 'This book is in custody and is called AN EPISTLE OF COMFORT and is printed at Paris.' (11) But the context implies that the book was in secret circulation before its capture. There are nine or ten copies of this secret edition (marked IMPRINTED AT PARIS) now known to exist. Mar-prelate's pamphlet had accused Whitgift's searchers of being duped or bribed by the printers; so it seems likely that the edition was successful in getting abroad.

It is a pity that not more is known about this exciting episode. But it seems tenable, on the evidence, that just when the Catholics appeared doomed, after Mary's execution, this book came out to reaffirm the purely spiritual and indestructible nature of their resistance. Southwell's literary apostolate was launched.

Although his book had the aspect of defiance stamped on it by circumstance, intrinsically it is a work of rare value and scholarship. It revived in the language of his own day the grand tradition of English medieval devotion, like the restoring of a great Cathedral window before the art of those glowing colours had been forgotten.

It is not possible here to confirm this judgement by illustration, because the periods are too sustained to permit short quotation. But an idea of the clarity and rhythm of the style may be gathered from a passage that begins like this:

> One that understandeth the course of Christian behoof cannot but think it a most comfortable thing to suffer adversity for a good cause, seeing it is not only the livery and cognizance of Christ but the very principal royal garment which he chose to wear in this

L

life. And therefore can it not be taken of a soldier but well to be clad with his captain's harness, or of a disciple to be like his master.

And a sentence like the following shows a strained simile transfused by personal devotion, in this case by the sense of God's fatherhood:

Yet the clean and chaste dove, abhorring such a loathsome abode, without this ark cannot find any rest: but with the wings of penitent heart and longing desire flickereth still at the window, until it please our *Noe* to put out his merciful hand, and receive it into the Ark of his heavenly felicity.

There are also abundant signs of strength, as when he indulges the range of Elizabethan melancholy in a manner reminiscent of Webster:

Our infancy is but a dream, our youth but a madness, our manhood a combat, our age a sickness, our life misery, our death horror.

Or when he touches the same vein of tragic pathos as Shakespeare:

Where the Prince (sayeth Cassiodorus) in so great agony mourneth, who would not weep when he weepeth, and sigh when he lamenteth: when instead of his royal crown, he is covered with dust, and his head is hoary with ashes, not with age.

There is indeed one chapter of controversy full of clean and vigorous hitting; and there is a lively address to the persecutors which has this sentence:

When England was Catholic it had many glorious confessors. It is now for the honour and benefit of our country that it be also well stored with the number of Martyrs. And we have, God be thanked, such martyr-quellers now in authority as mean, if they have their will, to make Saints enough to furnish all our Churches with treasure when it shall please God to restore them to their true honours.

But for the rest, one must refer the reader to Janelle's appreciation of the work in his *Robert Southwell the Writer*—adding only this bit from the introduction, where Southwell as a novice apologizes for addressing an exhortation to veterans:

For as to the wayfaring pilgrim wandering in the dark and misty night, every light though never so little is comfortable: and to the stranger that traveleth in a land of divers language, any that can (though it be but brokenly) speak his country tongue, doth not a little rejoice him: So peradventure in this foggy night of heresie, and the confusion of tongues which it hath here in our Island procured, this dim light which I shall set forth before you, and these my Catholic, though broken speeches, which I shall use unto you, will not be altogether unpleasant.

Arising out of the *Epistle of Comfort*, there are a number of phrases and turns of speech which suggest that a fair amount of Southwell's verse may have been written during this year. There is indeed one poem—almost the only one that can be definitely dated—which belongs exactly to this period. It is his ode *Decease, Release*, on the martyrdom of Mary Queen of Scots, which expresses what he and the English Catholics in general felt about the cause for which she suffered. A manuscript copy of it among Anthony Bacon's papers at Lambeth (12) is endorsed in French in a contemporary hand: *Some verses by Mr. Southwell on the Scottish Queen, received in the month of February*, 1586—that is, 1587.*

Two of the stanzas will be enough to show that Robert was already an accomplished versifier during his first year in England. The last lines are felicitous enough for any contemporary sonneteer to have envied:

> Alive a Queen, now dead I am a Saint;
> Once Mary called, my name now Martyr is;
> From earthly reign debarred by restraint,
> In lieu whereof I reign in heavenly bliss . . .
>
> Rue not my death, rejoice at my repose;
> It was no death to me but to my woe;
> The bud was opened to let out the rose,
> The chain was loosed to let the captive go.

Although Southwell ranged and experimented more widely in his verse than is often realized, a large number of his poems do consist of variations on the 'Decease-Release' theme, written

---

* Bacon, who was a cousin of the Southwells, seems to have been at Bordeaux about this time, but he kept the English custom of dating the new year from March 25th.

either in the old-fashioned ballad style or in conventional penta-
meter sestets (the stanza of *Venus and Adonis*).

They vary in mood according to his state of consolation or
desolation: consolation, as understood by St. Ignatius, being the
soul's awareness of its native beauty restored by grace:

> Retired thoughts enjoy their own delights
> As beauty doth in self-beholding eye;
> Man's mind a mirror is of heavenly sights,
> A brief wherein all marvels summed lie:
> Of fairest forms and sweetest shapes the store,
> Most graceful all, yet thought may grace them more . . .

while desolation is the groan of nature in bondage to original sin:

> Who would not die to kill all-murdring grieves?
> Or who would live in never-dying fears?
> Who would not wish his treasure safe from thieves,
> And quit his heart from pangs, his eyes from tears?
> Death parteth but two ever-fighting foes
> Whose civil strife doth work our endless woes . . .

The central theme is the same as that expressed by Sidney in
the words 'erected wit' and 'infected will'. Southwell would
have much appreciated—had a manuscript copy ever reached his
hands—that famous passage in the *Apologie for Poetrie* on the
image of the Creator and original sin. And on Sidney's side it
would have been interesting to see how he, who had been so
deeply drawn to Edmund Campion, would have felt towards
Robert Southwell. But Sidney was dead. On 16th February his
magnificent funeral cortège had passed through London, leaving
behind a large debt which neither the Queen nor Leicester was
disposed to pay.

'He was my godson', wrote King Philip in his painful hand;
and with the words a line was scored, as it were, through his
unavailing efforts, often against his conscience, to maintain friendship with England. Now that Mary Stuart, the rightful heir to
the throne, was dead, both conscience and commodity dictated
a different line of attack.

CHAPTER ELEVEN

Rumours of War, 1587–8

AFTER the daring publication of the *Epistle* it was all the more necessary for Southwell to lie as quiet as a mouse in his tiny room between the great mansions of the Queen, of Leicester, and of Burghley. The year of close confinement that followed proved less easy to endure than the first adventurous six months. He was, after all, only twenty-five, and brimful of energy. It was harder than he had expected to remain physically inactive when there was so much work to be done, such increasing opportunities of conversion.

Four of his letters to Aquaviva during this year are extant: two written in August, and two in the following January. (1) The August couple show him still keeping melancholy fairly well at bay; they reflect the uneasy lull that followed the execution of Queen Mary, with the Government hesitant to strike decisively as long as war with Spain was uncertain, and yet unwilling to spare:

> We hang in the balance, not yet safe, but not unduly nervous. . . .
> I do not know how it will all end. The distress of our people is very great, but their resistance remains constant and ready for the worst. This last tempest of persecution has added several persons of note to our ranks; it has also blown away some chaff, but the good solid grain stays firm in the barn.

His confidence in the revival of the old religion was reiterated frequently in both letters; but at the same time his attention was compelled by the strength of 'Puritanism' in London. The term

149

'Puritanism' at that time comprised three quite different elements. There was the presbyterian movement within the Establishment; there was the separatist movement which aimed at disestablishment; and there were the extreme sectaries who carried private inspiration to the pitch of anarchy. The stories he has to tell relate to the second and third of these groups.

A Puritan named Wigginson* was preaching a sermon in one of the churches against episcopal dignity, when he was reported to the bishop of London. Catchpolls burst into the church while he was actually preaching, pulled him out of the pulpit and began dragging him to the bishop. At once up rose the apprentices, seized their preacher from the catchpolls' hands, and administered to the catchpolls themselves a most handsome beating. Then, that same day, they took their man off to another church and listened to him preaching there, and still he has not been arrested. The minister in whose church he preached was thrown into prison, but behaved with great courage, affirming that there were twenty thousand men in London who were ready to risk their lives in the same cause. Thus far has Puritanism made progress.

His second incident came to him by hearsay from his native town of Norwich, where burnings seem to have been not uncommon. Besides this case mentioned by Southwell, there was Matthew Hammond in 1578, John Lewis in 1583, and Robert Kett in 1589. (3)

He denied the divinity of Christ and the Holy Spirit, and the Motherhood of the Blessed Virgin; and he prohibited the taking of oaths, the existence of magistrates, and the baptism of children—after the manner of anabaptists. Condemned to death by those who were very little different from himself, he was burnt at the stake—with a great show, I am told, of stubborn and misguided zeal. Yet a little while after, of his bones and even of his ashes there was nothing to be seen; these foes of holy relics were so eager to get possession of his remains.

* This would be Giles Wigginton who, along with Udall and Penry, was reckoned among the most fiery of the extremist preachers and tract-writers. (2)

Southwell was not unduly alarmed either by the growth of the Puritans, or by the counter-claims of the anabaptists to martyrdom. He believed that what really threatened the mass of the people was a drift from all standards of religion and morality, and that when the better elements came to themselves, it would be to the Catholic religion that they would turn—provided there were priests at hand to teach and to encourage. Commenting on the Norwich burning, he wrote:

> Although they chastised this poor little man under colour of zeal, yet it is certain that the great majority—indeed, the mass of the people—is ready to deny not only that the Son and the Holy Spirit, but also that the Father is God: in other words, they are atheists who worship pleasure. The neglect of all religion and the turpitude of their lives is my evidence for this. And the awareness of this is of the greatest advantage to the Catholics, who are all the more confirmed in their faith by seeing that those who reject it plunge headlong into sin.

He had already boldly affirmed this point of view in the *Epistle*:

> But we need not range far for examples of good life. For, God be thanked, even our adversaries themselves are so fully persuaded of our good behaviour, that if a man in company be modest and grave in countenance, words or demeanour, if he use no swearing, foul or unseemly speech, if he refuse to join in lewd company and dishonest actions, he is straight suspected for a Papist. And, on the other side, if there be anyone ruffianly, quarellous, foul-spoken and lewdly-conditioned, he is never mistrusted for a Papist, but taken for a very sound and undoubted Protestant.

On the day after he finished his first letter, his obscure life was radiated by a double joy. Henry Garnet came up to London, and at the same time there arrived the long-delayed and expected letters from Aquaviva containing full confirmation of all their faculties. Both Southwell and Garnet sat down at once to reply. Their letters are a spontaneous proof of the filial love they had for their great General. Robert's began:

> I cannot tell you in words what a joy it was to receive your letter of February 20th, with the list of our privileged faculties. It was

like the long-looked-for star to storm-tossed mariners, like the messenger in the nick of time to souls hanging on the brink, it was like what it was—a pleasant story of home to distant exiles. We felt at once what it is to have a loving father, a skilled and wary captain, and the spirit of the Society which is what we need to keep us going . . .

and so on for several lines more; but he meant every word that he said.

Garnet's last visit had apparently been in February. Already they had agreed on what afterwards became a vital feature of their missionary life: a meeting at least every six months for a renovation of spirit and discussion of plans. February and August were later changed to Easter and October. The meetings for the first few years were in London, presumably at the house in Acton which Southwell kept open for incoming priests. About the printing press there, however, there is no mention in any extant letter, and its further activity remains a mystery.

Southwell now had many priests working with him in London. From Rome there were his former pupils, Richard Leigh, Christopher Buxton, Robert Moreton, Robert Charnock, and Robert Gray; and from Rheims, two magnificent missionaries, Anthony Middleton and William Gunter, the one posted at Clerkenwell, the other in Fleet Street, where Southwell had many friends. Robert Charnock, one of the factious students at Rome, was to cause him grave embarrassment later; but the others were all men after his own heart, and five of them outran him on the road to Tyburn. He ended his letter on a note of lyric confidence: 'In spite of all, faith grows stronger under the strain, and our Ark rides the waves, exulting.'

By the time that he was writing his next letter, however, there were signs that something else besides the Government cat-and-mouse policy was having a wearing effect on his nerves. 'We seem to have fallen upon times', he wrote, during the winter of '87-8 (the letter is undated), 'full of grandeur in their promise, and very mean in their performance.' He was thinking not only of the uneasy calm in religious affairs, but of the loudly-publicized and hitherto abortive preparations of Spain. The two, in fact, were connected. Though the English sailors might be relying on another devastating swoop like Drake's of the previous spring, the Queen and Lord Burghley were hoping for negotiation with the Prince of Parma; and for that reason the extremes of persecution were being most carefully avoided. Southwell saw the situation with gloomy but startling clarity. His own cousin, Sir Robert, who had married the Admiral's daughter, and Arundel's brother, Lord Thomas Howard, were both ardent sailors, and semi-Catholics; so it was probably from them that he derived his well-founded conviction of the English superiority at sea. (4)

He writes:

> The Tower of Babylon stands sure of itself and contemptuous of shadowy and spectral rumours. . . . There has been a mighty preparation for war here, and they are still maintaining it with the utmost diligence; but now they blame their former fears, and boast themselves secure and unafraid. The threat from Spain, which once was formidable, they now reckon they can either break up or turn aside. And as for France, the present tumult there means undoubted peace for them. But let us leave these things for them to discuss,

he concludes abruptly with an evident taste of sourness.

His state of mind was one that is easy to guess intuitively, but difficult to analyse objectively. The prospect of invasion touched him at the one point where the English Catholics were uniquely vulnerable—the point of honour. In St. Ignatius' parable of the earthly king's appeal applied to the heavenly king's, come the words: 'And anyone who would reject the appeal of such a prince so generous and so comradely, how deservedly he would be contemned by all for a recreant and a coward.'

The emotional trappings of this appeal were to be displayed to full advantage by the English Government—but on the wrong horse: the white horse that the Queen would ride to Tilbury. It was not possible, of course, to be deceived; but it was possible to feel a sense of sick frustration, not for himself but for his gallant friends among the laity. The English Catholics were in for a period of humiliation worse than death.

Continuing his letter, he had not the heart to speak as formerly of heroism and exultation, but resumed briefly: 'In the meantime, we are hardly dealt with, as usual, vexed by fines and threats, and, as usual, we bear them constantly trusting in divine aid.' He then turned to chronicle such books of interest as had recently appeared. But even from these the shadow of war could not be banished. 'Several books have appeared, not printed but written. One of them argued at length the problem whether war or peace was more to the advantage of the kingdom, and came down on the side of war as plainly necessary to stabilize the commonwealth.' This sounds like Sir Walter Raleigh's *Discourse of War*, drawn from Machiavelli: 'When wars are ended abroad, seditions begin at home, and when men are freed from fighting from necessity, they quarrel through ambition.' (5)

The second book recalled an incident that had caused much heart-burning in England: the surrender of Deventer by Sir William Stanley, one of Elizabeth's best generals, which Cardinal Allen had publicly praised as faithful to the traditions of Christendom and the Law of Nations:

> The second book is a reply to His Eminence's defence of the action of Sir William Stanley; and it has met with much applause. To me I must confess, it seems a vapid production, quite alien to a Christian sense of justice: the work of some atheist or agnostic courtier who is playing at theology and mistaking military precedents for moral principles.

But the controversy had a tail to it which touched Southwell more intimately than he was aware. The tract seems to be the same as that which was exported abroad under the mendacious title, *The Answer of diverse Catholick English Gentlemen to a certain seditious book veiled with the name of D. Allen*—with the object of persuading the Continent that the English Catholics were not only loyal but contented. The author of it was none other than the apostate Gilbert Gifford who was possibly still in the pay of the English Government. Unknown to Southwell, Gifford introduced his tract with a letter purporting to come 'From a Jesuit in London' to his superior, Father Persons. Writing with con-

siderable irony, Gifford's pseudo-Jesuit refused to believe that
Allen could have written a defence of Stanley, and requests
Persons to have it exposed as an impudent forgery. His letter
began circumstantially:

> Reverend Father ... The matter is, that of late being at M.O.
> house, there came to see me diverse gentlemen who, incontinent,
> after dinner, fell into disputation whether a catholic man might
> lawfully serve against the Spaniards in the present wars of
> Flanders. ...

And having pronounced the sense of the meeting to be violently
against the defence of Stanley, it ends with a suitable flourish:

> In the mean time the chiefest of our Catholics have by common
> consent set forth an answer to the pretended letter of Dr. Allen,
> declaring to the whole world they utterly defy the seditious doctrine
> of his resolution. Which book of the Catholics herewithal I send
> you, beseeching Almighty God to bless you with desired felicity.
> London, 23 Oct. 1587. (6)

Gifford then signed the letter, with typical spy-ambiguity,
'S.T.' But the only Jesuit at that time in London was Southwell.

Gifford's fraud was exposed almost immediately by Allen and
Persons. But a certain interest attaches to the verisimilitude at
which Gifford's forgery was obviously aiming; it may be a
falsified or imaginary version of a discussion which actually took
place, and at which Southwell was really present and was called
on for his decision.

The locality named by Gifford, 'M.O. House' (that is, presumably, Montague House or Mary Overies), was a likely one
for such a discussion. Old Lord Montague was still, in a sense,
the spokesman of the English Catholics at Court, since he was
the only recusant Peer to whom Elizabeth showed favour. It
was always his earnest endeavour to combine his religious fidelity
with a display of most meticulous loyalty; and there can be little
doubt that he *was* distressed by Allen's book.

There is, of course, not a scrap of real evidence of any such
discussion or any such question put to Southwell. But if there

were, it would only have been the foreshadowing of a much more urgent question that he would very soon have to answer. Was it lawful for English Catholics to take up arms against the Spaniards, not to attack Flanders, but to defend their own homeland?

To escape, perhaps, a premonitory shiver, Southwell turned for some light relief to the third and last book on his list. This was the massive and long-matured reply of Dr. Whittaker, Regius Professor of Divinity at Cambridge, to the *Quaestiones* of Robert Bellarmine, surreptitious copies of which had been working havoc among the undergraduates. It was the beginning of a long sequence of sledge-hammer blows with which the Doctor pursued his good-humoured adversary, so that it was said of him, since he was also very much a married clergyman, *quod mundo quotannis librum et liberum dedit*. A book and a baby every year! 'The Pit of Rome', wrote Dr. Whittaker—in an extract from his introduction which is here drastically curtailed—

> ... from the time it was first opened hath not ceased to exhale perpetual smoke to blind the eyes of men, and hath sent forth innumerable locusts upon the earth, like scorpions, who have wounded with their deadly stings all men upon whose foreheads the Seal of God was not impressed. ... Among these locusts—that is, amongst the innumerable troops of monks—none, as we have before said, have appeared more keen or better prepared and equipped for doing mischief than are the Jesuits at this present day. ... (7)

There followed a long and unwittingly complimentary passage on Bellarmine as the arch-locust-scorpion. Southwell at Rome had been an enthusiastic admirer of Bellarmine, and he was delighted now to send him messages through Aquaviva, with the familiarity of an old pupil, to tell him what a terrible figure he had become over here in England, how

> ... not only Reynolds at Oxford, but Whittaker at Cambridge, have abandoned their former ritual of teaching, and are panting in the wake of Bellarmine, following faithfully the order laid down by him. He would laugh to hear how they vie with each other in

extolling him to the skies so that their own erudition may bask in his reflected glory. Much of the worthy Whittaker's book consists in large passages of Bellarmine appropriated without acknowledgment, and the rest is a denunciation of Bellarmine in terms which are a description of himself—a liar and a sophist. As for Reynolds, he has managed after many months of labour to discover three falsehoods in the Book of Tobias, but has fallen into three hundred himself in the process, so that even his most faithful disciples are beginning to look the other way.

Southwell, an ex-professor himself, had evidently been violating the trade-union rules of that fraternity by listening to stories from undergraduates. Some confirmation of his gibes comes from the deposition by an unnamed but patriotic Cambridge man at the process for Bellarmine's beatification. This witness deposed unhesitatingly:

> During my student days at Cambridge, England's foremost University . . . I remember well the fame which Bellarmine enjoyed amongst the undergraduates. When we wanted to know how any don had succeeded with his sermon, we used to ask whether he had launched forth against Bellarmine. If told that he had, we knew without further inquiry that the sermon must have been a fiasco.

The accession to Southwell's side of brilliant young men from the Universities and Inns of Court was a factor which changed his missionary outlook. It may have begun as early as this. Something, at any rate, was enabling him to laugh where before, in spite of his resolutions of gentleness, he could not help raging. Himself the most accomplished disputant of his year in the Gregorian University, the thought of an Anglican divine triumphing by default over the Catholic cause had been supremely irritating. In the previous winter, crouched in his dark little room, a silent fugitive, while the waves of anti-Catholic propaganda carried the day by mere brute force, he had written with indignation in his *Epistle*:

> This is not the way in christian charity. . . . The way of God's church hath always in such cases been: to give free liberty to the very hereticks to have publick disputation before sufficient Judges, and

if they were there convicted, or refused to come, they have been subject, and that worthily, to temporal punishment. But hitherto could we never have any equal conditions of disputation granted Unless it be equal for a man to be brought from the rack to dispute!

But another year of English experience enabled him to end his letter impishly:

What is very comic in Whittaker's book . . . is the bravery with which this *miles gloriosus* demands that the Chancellor (the Lord Treasurer!) should allow a proper disputation between his party and ours, as if a proper disputation—which his party so far has studiously avoided—would prove them the stronger. As if *we* were the ones buttressed with every material help, and *they* were the poor victims caught unarmed in a merciless ambush.*

His aspersions on Whittaker's learning and courage were unjust, but this vein of mocking irony was more salutary for his peace of mind than frustrated emulation.

Although public disputations were not allowed, the Catholics and Protestants carried on an unofficial contest which might be described as exchanging salvoes in the form of Acts of God. If a notable persecutor fell down in a fit and died foaming at the mouth, a whisper of delighted awe ran through the Catholic body. On the other hand if a seminary priest could be brought to apostatize publicly, the affair was celebrated in a spate of Protestant sermons and pamphlets. Southwell played this propaganda-game with gusto, and a surprising turn in it caused him to write a fresh letter to Aquaviva, very different in tone from his previous mood of depression.

An *auto-da-fé* had been arranged for the unfortunate Anthony Tyrrell on 21st January at Paul's Cross, where he was to read his recantation preceded by a sermon from Dr. John Reynolds, the Oxford puritan divine. But the Catholics had been secretly at work on Tyrrell and repentance had won the day in his tormented bosom. A scheme had been devised for turning the tables, a

* Italics and exclamation-marks added.

cheme in which evidently Southwell was a participant, for his
etter was written on the day immediately following the incident:

His plan succeeded to perfection. They brought him to the Cross of
St. Paul's, where there is always a most crowded concourse, of
magnates as well as of the multitude, to attend the sermons. The
minister climbed into the pulpit; he intoned Psalm 6. Tyrrell . . .
was lifted above the crowd to a place just under the pulpit. He rose
to his feet and began to speak:

'I have come before this assembly, dearly-beloved,' he said, 'in
order that I may abjure that ancient faith which I sucked in with my
mother's milk and which I have reverenced since my tenderest
years. But what I do now vehemently bewail is that other faith
which so long and so wickedly I made pretence of, knowing that
it was false; and what I now proclaim and embrace with all my heart
is the religion of the Roman and Catholic Church, from which by
the instigation of the devil I fell away. To her I now return, and in
her defence I am ready by God's help to die, counting myself happy
if by this pain I might cancel the heavy burden of my sins.'

But as he was speaking, the Lord Mayor rose to his feet, the
aldermen all cried out together, and Young—that noted persecutor
—came rushing up. They clutched up at the man, and tore him
down, and tumbled him about and then carried him off through the
air in the midst of a great thunder-cloud of thronging and excited
people. But in the meantime he had torn his false profession into
tiny pieces, and he scattered among the crowd certain other writings
which he had kept hidden in his doublet.

Persons, who received another account from an eye-witness,
has described it in his own racy English prose:

But in the main space all was in marvellous hurly and burly at
Paul's Cross, where the people had heard three sermons in one hour,
all contrary the one to the other; the first of the preacher in praise
and credit of Tyrrell; the second of Tyrrell himself in derogation of
the preacher; the third of Justice Young threatening death to those
that should believe Tyrrell. But the concourse of people was so
unruly as Tyrrell was carried away on men's shoulders to the gaol
of Newgate, by St. Nicholas' shambles in Newgate market, the
Protestants crying out vengeance upon him, and he weeping bitterly

and knocking his breast and affirming that he had done nothing that day but upon mere force and compulsion of his conscience. And the concourse was so great about the prison as they were forced to change him within two hours after to the Counter, where none came to him but Topcliffe and Young. (8)

The dramatic success of the incident had been completed by Father Richard Leigh and a Catholic lawyer who had been waiting in the crowd. In the confusion they had hastened off with Tyrrell's flung papers to the Middle Temple, where a scrivener made copies for secret distribution. But the mention of Topcliffe in Persons' account was an ominous note. Southwell had reason to conclude his description with the words: 'I beg you to pray that he may persevere.'

Before he posted his letter he was able to record a fresh demonstration of Catholic solidarity. The occasion was the passage through London of the priests on their way to Wisbech. Among them was Father Weston who, having refused the Countess of Arundel's earnest offers of a ransom, was setting out for another fifteen years of crippling imprisonment. Southwell described the scene:

> Before the departure, leave had been given to the priests to visit and receive visitors; and there was such a throng to see him, with so many invitations, that I would scarcely have believed it if I had not seen it with my own eyes. . . . May God grant that we follow in his footsteps. I will write again when there is more to tell. Farewell, on this feast of Saints Vincent and Anastatius, 22nd January, 1588.

The Government policy of consigning the priests to contemptuous oblivion was not succeeding so easily as had been hoped.

In the spring of 1588 Garnet relieved Southwell in London and stayed there till the middle of July. He had a large and cheerful view of Catholic prospects and did not share Robert's keen premonition of a coming crisis. So unaware was he of what was happening that he looked forward to a *gradual* relaxation of the persecution. 'We are hoping', he wrote to Aquaviva on 9th June, 'that soon the moment will come which with sorely-tried patience we have long awaited: when the persecution will be relaxed just sufficiently to allow a wider field for our excursions.'*

His travels had convinced him that if the present lull continued, then, with better organization and more priests, 'an infinite number' would return to the Church. He was anxiously awaiting the reinforcements promised by Aquaviva: namely, Fathers John Gerard and Edward Oldcorne, whom he could use for opening up new regions.

> This is the plan we have agreed on for the glory of God, when there shall be a greater number of ours here. Two should be stationed at London—or one in London and one in the environment. The others should have assigned to each one a province or county in which each can work for all he is worth to promote religion. There will not be lacking other priests, men of outstanding holiness and learning, who will come to their assistance—and to this we most of all can testify by experience. The field will be theirs to take over from our labours, and the harvest from it will be beyond measure, owing to Him who guides the work of our hands unceasingly.

He ended with an earnest request that the prayers and merits of the Society might be extended to include formally

> all those whose energy and devotion make our life here possible: I mean, our hosts, or rather I should say our protectors and defenders; and also those priests, whose number is large, who wish to be members of our Society.

This division of England and Wales into provinces might seem to foreshadow the grievances of certain secular priests (fomented by our old friends Bagshaw and John Cecil) at the end of the century. But the shadow was non-existent at that time either in the mind of Garnet, or of the devoted priests who co-operated with him, or of Cardinal Allen who had chosen the Jesuits precisely for that work they were best qualified to do: the opening up of regions that had hitherto been closed to priests. Garnet's plans were certainly to produce a wonderful harvest in the succeeding decade. But in the immediate future there was a valley of death to be traversed, which he did not seem to suspect.

* *Paulatim* is the word he uses, showing his complete unawareness of the coming Armada.

M

CHAPTER TWELVE

The Spanish Armada

IN the backwaters of 1587, Robert Southwell, though faithful and industrious as ever, had been uneasy and depressed. But as soon as he felt the tug of the millrace in 1588, his spirits rose and his nerves tingled at the approaching conflict. Early and clearly he saw that the supreme trial for the Catholics would be the imputation that they were siding with a foreign invader. This was the gaping hole in their frail craft which would make it hopeless to ride the flood, however expert the steersmanship. His quick sense of dramatic values made him resolute, first, to plug the hole, and then to dare the flood. This at least is the clear impression that is flashed off phrases in his letters and his book *An Humble Supplication*.

The flood of patriotic fervour let loose by the Armada's defeat was the ambient of a three-cornered religious struggle which, in a way, was just as fateful as the naval battle. The Established Church was naturally best fitted to navigate the flood, because a nationalist *mystique* was precisely what it needed to give it life. But actually it was the Puritans, the least in numbers but most powerful in the Council and in Parliament, who bade fair to capture popular favour, because of the sanguinary Old Testament turn that was given to it. The Catholics alone seemed predestined to ruin. The story of how they weathered the storm, and emerged at the end of it—incredibly—in better shape than the Puritans, is revealed, if only partially, in Southwell's next batch of letters.

The first event he described was the internment of the leading Catholic knights and squires, first at Ely and later in some dozen 'concentration camps' throughout the country. This began with the beginning of the year, when rumours of invasion were in the air. From a modern standpoint it might seem a reasonable pre-caution. But Southwell referred to it as something far worse than ordinary imprisonment. One can see why. Compared with the Puritans who were about to launch their campaign against the Queen's church, these Catholics were the pillars of traditional loyalty in their parishes or counties; they were now publicly branded as traitors and their lives forfeit as hostages, 'so that at one stroke may be accomplished what otherwise could not have been brought about without the support and consent of many'. (1)

But for the next six months an uneasy lull prevailed. The Armada, after two false starts, put back to port in May. There were rumours that the death of Santa Cruz had taken the heart out of the expedition. Elizabeth opened negotiations with the Prince of Parma who was reported to have the gravest doubts of success. The English admiral, Lord Howard, who was chafing to repeat Drake's exploit at Cadiz, was ordered not to stir beyond the Channel. The cloudy peace, or 'cold war' as it would now be called, seemed likely to continue indefinitely, when, about Mid-summer, suddenly and dramatically, things began to happen. (2)

In June, the English spy-service in the Netherlands, by a smart piece of work, secured a copy of a broadside *Declaration* being printed in English at Antwerp for distribution if the Spanish army were to land. It was by Cardinal Allen: a summary of his short book, the *Admonition*, which he had written the previous April at the instance of Philip of Spain. Denouncing Elizabeth in harsh terms as a female tyrant unguided by moral principles, it proclaimed that King Philip was to give effect to the decree of excommunication which previous Pontiffs had been unable to execute; that England was not to be subjugated, but set free; and that all should rally to the Prince of Parma on his landing. (3)

Obviously it was only intended for publication in the event of Parma's landing in force, and in that event as a safeguard for

Catholics against the 'Spanish Fury'; but by 12th June a copy of Allen's book was in Burghley's hands, and a copy also of the broadside *Declaration* reached him before the 24th.

On the 22nd the die was cast. Howard got the orders he was longing for; he set sail and, with a little more luck, would have crippled the Armada as it lay along the coast of Biscay. As it was, he had to return and await its slow arrival in the Channel. In the meantime, while most of the other Councillors were engaged in fervent preparations by land, Lord Burghley had been meditating how to make the best use of the *Declaration* that had come into his hands.

Five years before he had urged the Queen to frame an oath of allegiance that would split the Catholics on the hypothetical issue: what they would do if a Papal army were to land in England.

> Hereof this Commodity would ensue. That those papists (as I think most papists would) that should take this oath, would be divided from the great mutual confidence which now is betwixt the Pope and them by reason of their afflictions for him. And such priests as would refuse that oath no tongue could say for shame that they suffered for religion if they did suffer. (4)

The majority (as he hoped), having lost the link with Rome which was the channel of its spiritual strength, could be dealt with at leisure; while the obstinate minority could be quickly exterminated with popular acclaim and no undue scandal. The moment for putting this policy into effect seemed now at hand.

His first thought, however, was a counter-stroke on the same lines as Gifford's counterfeit answer to Allen in the matter of Deventer. He wrote to Walsingham on 12th June,

> I could wish some expert learned man would feign an answer as from a number of Catholics that notwithstanding their evil content-ment for Religion should profess their obedience and promise with their lives and power against all strange forces offering to land in this realm. And to advertise the Cardinal that he is deceived in his opinion to think that any noble man in this land, or any Gentleman

of possession will favour the invasion of the realm. And that such a rash writing may give cause of danger of life to all that are reputed Catholics, specially to all recusants. (5)

A strange contradiction is apparent in his words. He is confident of the loyalty of all the influential Catholics and their followers. Yet at the same time he envisages the possibility of having them all massacred. It might be unfair to press his words —which were written understandably, as he said, 'in choler'— if it were not that they correspond with the policy which he had outlined five years before, and which he afterwards followed in cold blood.

The first part of his proposal, the counterfeit answer from the leading Catholics, was embarked on forthwith. It took shape as the famous *Letter . . . to . . . Mendoza* which has deceived historians down to the present day, though there are drafts of it in Burghley's hand among the Lansdowne manuscripts. (6) As Pollen notes:

> Amongst infinite other errors the writer states that many copies of 'The Bull' (i.e. the *Declaration*) had been introduced into England. It was probably through this widely-spread letter (which was translated into foreign languages and circulated on the Continent) that the false idea of the Pope having again excommunicated Elizabeth was popularized among non-Catholics and anti-papalists.

The second part of his proposal, the preparation for a massacre, was launched with the *Proclamation* of 1st July, 'against bringing in Bulls from the See of Rome', which was particularly designed to rouse mob-fury. (7) The stress was on Rome, not on Spain. The Cardinal's *Declaration*, though it was kept secret, was described as a Bull issued with the Pope's spiritual authority.

It was not a Bull, as anyone could see who had a copy in his hands; and even as a Cardinal's pronouncement it lacked all binding force, since it was never promulgated. Burghley, however, could argue with reason that if it had been promulgated the Pope would have backed it up. This was sufficient; for it was his intention to catch the Catholics in a *hypothetical* dilemma, to make their guilt hang on their answer what they *would* have done *if* . . . the Pope with the plenitude of his spiritual power gave them orders to side with the invasion.

The question was an old one; it had been in use since 1577. But this was the first attempt to bring it into judicature, to make a man *legally* guilty if he could not answer it. For the Catholics it now became the notorious 'Bloody Question' in the form that Gerard remembered as put to him:

> If the Pope were to send over an army and declare that his only object was to bring back the kingdom to its Catholic allegiance— what would you do? And if he stated at the same time that there was no other way of re-establishing the Catholic faith, and commanded everyone by his apostolic authority to support him? Whose side would you be on—the Pope's or the Queen's? (8)

It was a well-set trap, biting very deep, and at the same time largely and liberally framed. If the victim said 'The Pope's', he was making an answer that no Catholic Prince of that day would have countenanced if turned against himself; and he was giving the Government *carte blanche* to sentence him as a traitor. If he said 'The Queen's', he was denying inclusively the whole principle for which up to now he had suffered: the principle that the Pope was the supra-national guardian of the Christian conscience. But by far the most insidious feature of the trap was the poison of doubt that it distilled. The extent of the Pope's power was still a disputed matter among theologians. It was not conducive to martyrdom to know that one might be dying horribly for the wrong side in a scholastic debate.

It is not known at what date Burghley consulted the Crown lawyers about the legal framing of the question. But it was 20th July, the very day the Armada was sighted off the Lizard, that they sent their reply.

Before considering that, however, one must ask how little or how much the Catholics were prepared to stand the test.

Their cruel dilemma has, of course, been blamed directly upon Allen's *Declaration*. But that is a superficial view, mistaking an undivulged occasion for a cause. Southwell had no knowledge at all of the *Declaration*, he did not even know that the Armada

was on the sea; but ten days after the *Proclamation* 'against
bringing in Bulls from the See of Rome', he knew that this was
the moment which the enemies of the Faith had long been waiting
for.

'Now at long last the Serpent's Eggs are hatched', he wrote on
11th July, 'and a poison is gushing out that looks likely to be the
ruin of many . . .'

There followed a harrowing description of the state of Martial
Law, or rather mob-law, that had been proclaimed: how the
vilest informer—and there was plenty of competition—had only
to plant a book in a gentleman's house in order to have him
condemned instantly and have half his goods as his own reward.
Yet it must be confessed that his letter ended on a note of anima-
tion rather than alarm: 'This looks like the last stage before the
expected end; and it puts us, as some fear and others hope, very
close to martyrdom.'

Garnet's letter of the same date was in curious contrast. It
contained no word of martyrdom and no note of indignation,
but only a sad regret for the ruin of his careful plans and a nostal-
gic gratitude for the good they had been able to do, against all
expectation, in the past two years. 'Robert is telling you the still
unfinished story of what wickedness is being planned against us.
So I will write of pleasant things instead.' (9)

But he was equally aware of what Southwell was so anxious to
convey: that the moral life of the country was being gravely
wounded. 'And captive good attending captain ill.' Writing of
these events a little later, and describing the ruin of the Fitzherbert
family by Topcliffe and how it coincided in time and place with
the pardoning of a batch of hardened criminals 'because in these
troubled times the Queen has need of such men', he commented
sadly: 'How happy she would be (and I would she were) if it
were the other sort of men that she had need of.' In this single
line he packed with rare simplicity the whole complex state of
mind of the English Catholics.

There was no doubt—he admitted—that as a result of the
Proclamation many secret Catholics were falling right away and

coming out savagely in public against those they had formerly
supported. A notable example was the Earl of Shrewsbury, whose
violent change of front sent a bitter wind through Derbyshire.
Another was probably Arundel's half-brother, bluff Lord Thomas
('fore God I am no coward') Howard, who cut a good figure as a
sailor, but a very poor one later as Earl of Suffolk. Clearly it was
the parting of the ways for the great mass who had hitherto been
secret sympathizers. The leaves were blowing fast in the hurricane, and the only question that remained was whether the naked
boughs could stand the shock and strain.

That they did so was the work of Divine grace, but aided by
human prudence. The inner ring of their resistance bears the
marks of Jesuit contrivance; it consisted of a prudent withdrawal
and evasive action on the issue of the Pope's power, coupled with
a clean and unshakeable defence of the Mass and the ultimate right
of conscience. But how it came to be effective, against all probability, is a story that can only be pieced together from such
evidence as remains.

Various phrases in the autumn letters of Garnet and of Southwell suggest strongly that a consultation was held whose results
were communicated to as many Catholics as possible, especially
to those in prison. '*Consultius iudicatum est*', wrote Southwell in
August to Aquaviva, praising the uniformity and moderation of
the Catholics' answers at their trials: 'It was judged most advan-
tageous, since no doctrine of the Faith was at stake, that the
answers should be such as were truthful yet not offensive to the
magistrates.' And Garnet, praising the integrity of the leading
Catholics who were not able to consult with priests beforehand,
wrote with apparent approval: 'They relied on the Papal concession which allows duty and reverence to be paid to the Queen
as Queen . . .' (10)

The consultation was held, presumably, during the months
that Garnet was in London, between Easter and July, at Southwell's private house, since that was the only safe meeting-place;
and it seems likely that it was attended not only by representative
priests but by Catholic lawyers as well.

As usual, the priests found that the laymen were ahead of them in their resolution to stand firm. 'The resolute patience of the Catholics', Garnet had written on 11th July, 'is a model to us; truly, they are like rich fields, we receive from them more than we give.'

What the priests were most concerned about was lest their answers might provoke the wholesale massacre that was generally rumoured to be imminent. What the laymen were most anxious for was to have the certainty for their own comfort, and for posterity if possible, that if they were to die, they would die for Christ and not for Spain.

The answers outlined by Southwell in his August letter may be taken as the gist of their resolutions. There was nothing original about them, but in the existing atmosphere of turbulence and panic, they were a surprisingly cool and accurate stroke in the only direction that offered any hope for the future.

Unknown to themselves, their hope was receiving encouragement from a strangely unexpected quarter. The lawyers consulted by the Privy Council were Fleetwood and Egerton, who signed the paper in that order: at first sight an unpromising choice for Catholics. William Fleetwood, Recorder of London, was well known for his scathing gibes at the trials of 'massing-priests'; and Thomas Egerton, the Solicitor-General, was an ex-recusant anxious to live down the fact. Their reply showed a great anxiety to oblige the Government. At the same time it took up a decided stand against the law being stretched to cover hypothetical future intentions; it may not be unfair to attribute this part of it to Fleetwood.

Fleetwood was a typical old English man-of-law—a phenomenon rarer in Elizabethan England than is perhaps commonly supposed. He could really have figured with equal ease in the tales of Chaucer and the plays of Shakespeare (though not as a lawyer in the latter), in Defoe and in Dickens; and there is even a slightly Shavian ring about his lecture to the martyr, Blessed Thomas Alfield, in 1585, on the impropriety of an Old Etonian being hanged and quartered.

And then did the Recorder call him forth, and . . . told him that he wondered that his father in King Henry's days being an usher of

Eton and of good Religion and had brought up many learned divines and other that served the Queen in temporal causes, whereof hundreds, the Recorder himself was one of the meanest. And that the same prisoner passed through the same College, and so to the King's College, being both of the Queen's high foundation; and now he had so unnaturally and beastly behaved himself that he was become the first that ever was arraigned of felony of any that ever passed those Colleges by the space of these fifty years and more. (11)

But the old chin-wagging bully, already many times disappointed in his career, stood firm when he came to his last chance of advancement. The central part of the reply to Burghley was unequivocal:

And albeit it cannot be otherwise presumed but that all such as will not dutifully clear themselves upon these questions, by professing their loyalty and obedience to her Majesty are (at this time specially) exceeding dangerous persons. *Yet* if they do either obstinately refuse to make any answer at all, or subtly (as many in like cases have heretofore done) excuse themselves that they are unlearned and ignorant and so not able to answer herein, or that they ought not to be examined of things future or to like effect: *Then* upon such manner of answer made by them, they are not comprehended directly within the compass of the law for any proceeding to be had against them in case of Treason or felony in respect of that their answer only, unless some other action drawing them in danger of the law may be proved against them. (12)

In other words, the Catholics, if they answered as directed—as Southwell avers they almost all did—could not be convicted for aiding a foreign enemy. The prosecution would have to fall back on the old Statutes, particularly that of 1585 which had decreed the penalty of High Treason against priests ordained abroad, and of felony against laymen who aided the priests. But this was precisely what Burghley had wanted to avoid. The Statute of 1585 was virtually (since Marian priests were now almost extinct) a decree of death against the saying and hearing of the Mass. With convinced Protestants it might be popular; but to the larger part of the nation it was still repugnant; it created the nightmare situation that what had been good and laudable in itself since the beginning of English history could become High Treason overnight by Act of Parliament.

A condemnation for aiding the enemy would have been quick and easy in the atmosphere that prevailed after the Armada. But to rake up evidence of the saying and hearing of the Mass was a difficult and dreary business. The Government had thus to face a private dilemma of its own: the legal verdict would be unpopular, but the popular verdict was illegal.

How the dilemma was solved may be gathered from the papers of the Crown advocate, Puckering, a political lawyer now well on the road to becoming Lord Keeper. In a list of forty-seven prisoners, questioned between 14th and 20th August, their sentences (generally, '*susp.*', i.e. let him be hanged) have been written against their names—before trial—in terms of the Bloody Question; guilty, that is, if they had not definitely said they would take the Queen's part against the Pope under any circumstances. But the verdict on the formal charge, that of being or of aiding priests, was added later, after the trial. (13)

As a short-term expedient this was successful. It preserved the Queen's command that the Papists were to be proceeded against only 'according to the law'. At the same time it enabled the prosecution to take all its colouring from the popular persuasion that the victims were Papal spies and Spanish agents: a persuasion fomented by the imaginary Bulls of Burghley's proclamation, and reflected in the refrain chanted by the London mob at the first batch of executions:

> This priest for the Pope
> Is hanged with a rope.*

* With which may be contrasted the popular ballad—one of the last of its kind—composed for the three Derbyshire martyrs of 24th July:

> When Garlick did the ladder kiss
> And Sympson after hie,
> Methought that there Saint Andrew was
> Desirous for to die.
> When Ludlam looked smilingly
> And joyful did remain,
> It seemed Saint Stephen standing by
> For to be stoned again.

The executions began on 28th August, thirty days after the decisive battle off Gravelines, and eight days after the great thanksgiving service at St. Paul's. The victims suffered singly, or in twos and threes, in the various parts of London where each had been most known. There were eight on the 28th, and six on the 30th. The rest were kept for later.

On the 31st, in a strangely mingled state of misery and exaltation, of lacerated nerves and emotional clarity, and with that visionary shrewdness which never deserted him in times of crisis, Southwell wrote to Aquaviva in Rome. The reek of the Cauldron was still in his nostrils, and the brutish howls of the mob deafening his ears; yet his letter is the clearest living picture of the situation that we possess; that must be the excuse for quoting it at such length:

> I could not make up my mind whether or not to write to you, my Father, about the slaughter which has just occurred. Would it not be better to weep alone for the woes of my motherland than to let the misery of one island spread abroad to other nations? I know that the story of our sorrows cannot fail to stir their pity; but I am very much afraid that the tyranny of our persecutors will excite more loathing for the name of England than the bravery of our martyrs will win for her honour.
>
> Yet in the things that have just happened I see a sign that the storm and trouble of our time will not be calmed by the uproar of battle, but by the prayers and tears of faithful souls; and I have less reluctance in exposing the savagery of the oppressors because of the light which it sheds on the condition of the oppressed.
>
> When the danger of the war at sea was over, and the army conscripted upon land dispersed, our rulers turned their weapons from the foe abroad and plunged them into the bowels of their own nation. The hatred stored up against the Spaniards they are wreaking with a sort of bestial fury upon their own fellow citizens and subjects.
>
> Those whom they hold in prison . . . are dragged in gangs to the court-house, and there examined, not simply about what they have done, but about *what they would be likely to do*—what intentions would they have if this or that were to occur? If they are reluctant to answer, it is counted against them as rebellion and high treason;

if they say they would never do anything against their just and bounden duty to Queen and country, they are reviled as hypocrites and liars. Whatever they say there is only one answer that will satisfy their judges, and that is the one that will serve for their condemnation. Nevertheless, they all made their answers to the court very gently and with every effort to avoid bitterness, affirming constantly their duty and loyalty to their Queen and country. Their object in thus avoiding arguments and ampler discussion of opinions was so as to give no impulse to our enemy's lust for blood, because he was clearly endeavouring to twist their answers into a verdict against all Catholics in this matter. Since, therefore, there was no question of the Faith at stake, and since the priests' answers might turn to the ruin of the whole body, it had been judged best to use expressions which were the exact truth and yet not offensive to the magistrates. So the priests replied that they were clerks in orders to whom warfare was forbidden, but that they would pray God to favour that side on which his justice stood. The laymen, for their part, pledged themselves to fight for Queen and country against all unjust aggressors whoever they might be. But these answers were of no avail; for the death penalty had already been decided on by the judges, on the charge that either they were priests, or had helped priests, or had been reconciled to the Church.

Describing the trial of the first batch of prisoners—six priests, seven laymen, and one woman—he added:

The charge against the laymen (that they had sheltered priests) was based on such slender evidence that the judges on the bench (after the sentence was passed) protested weightily to each other, and made open complaints about the shameful conduct of the case.

One of the judges who protested, as will be seen later, was William Fleetwood.

In describing the executions that followed, Southwell cited several instances of men and women who cried out in sympathy from the crowd, and were promptly arrested. He commented:

So this is what the majesty of the law has come to—and it is a thing to be wept for with tears of blood—that only at the peril of one's life can one pray for priests, or ask their prayers, or even show a sign of surprise at the cruelty of their persecutors.

Among those who suffered were his friends and fellow-workers, Father Gunter on the 28th, and Father Leigh on the 30th. Southwell was evidently present on both occasions. Of the first he wrote:

> There was an extraordinary concourse of citizens, crowds surging together from all sides. But what they were thinking, I do not know. The martyrs were hung in different groups here and there about the city, by twos and threes and even singly, on six specially erected gibbets, but on the same day.

Father Gunter was separated from the rest, and taken up the long road from Bishopsgate to Shoreditch, where the new Theatre stood in the former precincts of the Benedictine Nuns' Priory of Holywell. The gallows had been set up opposite the Theatre. 'On either side of the street', writes Father Pollen, 'was a wide extent of fields and gardens, and hence the spot was adapted in every way for the melancholy spectacle of an execution.'

The word 'melancholy' applied to the execution recalls the strangely serious scene in Shakespeare's *Comedy of Errors*—'A Street before a Priory' where an onlooker describes—

> the melancholy vale,
> The place of death and sorry execution,
> Behind the ditches of the abbey here.

An American Shakespearean scholar, Professor T. W. Baldwin, anxious to prove that the *Comedy* was written before 1589—for which indeed there is internal evidence—has evolved the theory that in the execution of Aegeus, happily averted by the Abbess, there is a flickering reflection of the scene that Shakespeare might well have witnessed from the Theatre. (14) It is one of those theories that can never be really proved, but, as stated by the Professor, it sounds plausible. If it were true it would shed an interesting light on the man who could interrupt his *Comedy*, as he does, with just and sober reflections on the clash between the Statute and natural law, at a time when—as Southwell testifies—it was practically death to show the slightest sign of sympathy with 'Papists'.

Southwell in his letter gives another instance of the prevailing terror:

A certain lady went to a man of importance asking him to use his influence that the death of one of the condemned might be delayed. The first question was whether the person whose cause she pleaded was guilty of murder. She replied that he had not been condemned for any such thing, but only for the Catholic religion. 'Oh dear,' said the gentleman, 'For his religion! If he had committed murder I should not have hesitated to comply with your request; but, as it is a question of religion, I dare not interfere.' So hateful has become the name of Catholic, or as they call it 'Papist', that murderers are more easily pardoned than Catholics.

Nevertheless Southwell was right in his guess that the Government had overrated the blood-lust of the Londoners. The executions ceased abruptly after 30th August; and, when they were resumed a month later, most of the condemned were taken from the city to places on the south coast where the spectacle might be more appreciated.

Certainly, the executions on the second day, the 30th, were such as might have moved the toughest sightseer. Richard Leigh, a very gallant young man, was taken with three men and a woman to Tyburn. Among the men was Edward Shelley, of the Sussex family related to Southwell. The woman was Margaret Ward, lady-in-waiting to a person of rank. Of her, Southwell wrote:

Among them was Margaret, a maiden among a thousand, in whose frail sex shone a courage hard to parallel. Together with her friend, an Irishman named Roche, she suffered death for supplying a priest in prison with the rope whereby he escaped. She had been flogged and hung up by the wrists, the tips of her toes only touching the ground, so that she was now crippled and half-paralysed; but the tortures had only served to strengthen this most shining martyr for her last struggle.

All five sang the *Te Deum* as they were drawn in the cart to Tyburn. There Father Leigh, who was the last to suffer, blessed each one in turn as they mounted the scaffold. It is no wonder that a certain exaltation crept into Southwell's otherwise sad letter; he had seen the glories of the Early Church restored in England as they had been in no other country in the world since the days of Diocletian.

The last paragraph of his letter is interesting and touching; clearly, he had not remained unmoved by the surge of patriotism when England braced itself to meet the Spaniard; but in it he had caught a vision of how beautiful the English character could be if its impulses were softened and ennobled, as they had been in the old days, by the influence of the true Faith. He begs the General —that great and holy statesman, Claudius Aquaviva—not to judge the English character by this latest display of corrupt barbarity:

> Meanwhile, I would like you, my Father, to think of the tenacity of our Catholics as of something close to the heart of this people which still hungers after goodness; and to judge the frenzied cruelty of the multitude, not as a stigma on the whole nation, but as an infection of this heresy which does violence not only to religion but to the very laws of nature. Thus you will see the good deeds of some Englishmen in so lovely a light that the ignorance of the others will deserve a deeper pity.

The thought is subtly woven, by allusion rather than by statement; but the emotional colour of it is evident. He was determined that, as far as he was concerned, not all the propaganda in the world would drive a wedge between the Faith and England.

He was still—as all the Catholics were—expecting the executions to be protracted to the extent of a general massacre:

> I will end my letter now, for I shall have more to write of very soon. Our enemies are determined to root out every Catholic if possible; and the Catholics are equally determined, when the moment comes, to suffer any extremity rather than deny the Faith. So their inflicting death and our welcoming of it will soon present a most remarkable spectacle to God, to angels and to men.

But writing a week later, he reported that the sudden and unexpected death of the Earl of Leicester was likely to change the situation:

> I think that now that the Queen is freed from her slavery to this man, she will adopt a milder policy towards us.

A more likely explanation of the lull, perhaps, is that Burghley saw that the executions were no longer serving his purpose. The answers of the martyrs at their trials, and their behaviour on the scaffolds, had united the Catholics and their priests instead of dividing them. Puckering's legal botchery had failed to hide the fact that these men and women were dying for the Mass, not for the Armada. As a result, many secret Catholics who had lapsed for 'patriotic' reasons were filled with remorse when they realized the truth. Moreover, the evidence on the formal charge was often so inadequate that the judges on the bench protested. Finally, the Queen, whose prestige was then at its height, seems to have registered disapproval after the second batch of executions. It is now for the first time in the missionaries' letters that the Queen begins to figure as a person distinct from the Government.

An interesting passage in Garnet's letter of October describes what was probably the turning-point in these trials, and throws a favourable light upon both the Queen and Fleetwood. Garnet's tone may—or it may not—be half-ironical, but his purport is obviously sincere:

> Among those martyred was a woman, for supplying a priest with the rope he escaped by. Her fate is said to have touched the Queen's womanly and tender heart. And it was for that reason that recently she pardoned two other women who had borne themselves before the tribunal with singular courage. But it was the intercession of Fleetwood, the Recorder of London, that chiefly compelled her. Fleetwood saw that Young, his rival in hunting down Catholics, had brought these women to judgement out of private malice. He could not of himself reverse the gruesome verdict of the jury, (against Catholics, as you know, the juries make up their minds beforehand); but he told Young openly that unless in future he brought better evidence against his victims, he must look for some

N

other magistrate to pronounce sentence. This god-fearing man then went straight to the Queen, and the result was that she reprieved out of her mercy those whom Young had impiously condemned.

The total number executed for religion, following the Armada, was thirty-three—much less than at first had seemed likely. But Burghley was at this time filling the Continent with his spurious *Letter to Mendoza* about how loyal the recusants were (which was true enough) and how no man suffered in England for religion merely. So as soon as the religious character of the executions became apparent, they had to be abated.

What he had succeeded in creating was the myth in which the old religion figured as foreign tyranny and the brand-new Genevan one as traditional patriotism. Yet the pragmatic effects of his policy were not successful. As the sense of national well-being decayed and turned sour during the last fifteen years of Elizabeth's reign, (15) the hacked root of Catholicism flowered—incredibly —and began to spread. Not that there was any connection between recusancy and sedition. The Catholics were frequently at pains to emphasize their remoteness and abhorrence from the swelling mob of needy desperadoes which was infecting the country. But, in the general disillusionment, while the worser spirits turned to disaffection and crime, the nobler turned to the only religion in England which bore any marked resemblance to that of the Crucified and Risen Christ.

The best account of this growing attraction of noble minds towards the Catholic Faith is given in the famous *Autobiography* of John Gerard. So it was symbolic of things to come that in the darkest hour before the dawn, in the dead winter of 1588, John Gerard and his companion Edward Oldcorne came ashore to a rain-soaked wood on the Norfolk coast.

'At the first watch of the night we were rowed ashore in the boat and dropped there. *The ship spread its canvas and sailed on.*'

CHAPTER THIRTEEN

A Wandering Minstrel

WITH the present-day experience before our eyes of priests in conquered countries, and with the different but perhaps no less harrowing ordeal of the French worker-priests in mind, it would be interesting to know something of the psychological strain which the two Jesuit missionaries underwent and the remedies that they adopted. Unfortunately their letters are so extrovert that only a fragmentary clue emerges here and there.

A good deal probably underlies a remark of Garnet's in his November letter: that he had come to stay in London for a while, and that Robert—'has gone journeying, to get a breath of some more healthful climate'. If only physical health had been in question, midwinter travel on the English roads would hardly have been the best remedy. 'I have been on horseback', wrote Robert on his return at the end of December, 'round a great part of England in the bitterest time of the year, choosing bad roads and a foul sky for my pilgrimage, rather than waiting for the fair weather when all the Queen's messengers are on the prowl, much worse than any rainstorm or hurricane.'

Whatever oppression may have gathered in his soul as the result of his year of close confinement and suspense, crowned by the nightmare of the Armada massacre, it was all washed away by this drastic remedy. The very act of riding out of London put him in touch again with happier things: memories of Italy, the sense of a world-wide Church, and the vivid hope of heaven. He had written in an earlier letter:

I am off on my journeying, caring nothing for foul weather; the storms which the heretics raise up every now and again are much

worse; *and worst of all is that winter in the soul*, which we must at all
costs avoid. By your prayers, my Father, we hope to easily drive
it off; and that spring-time will be always at hand, with the flower
appearing and our vineyards breathing forth their fragrance. We
aim at this as much as we can, in this stony and desert land, by hearing
each others' general confessions every six months and by renewing
our vows; and though we are too few to make much of it, yet we
have the greatest consolation of all, that our small efforts are forming
part of that mighty mountain which is being built up by the good
deeds of all just men throughout the universe. (1)

Another good effect in him was the moderating of his excessive
desire for martyrdom, which had been stoked into a terrible flame
by the butchery of his friends. But now it was tempered again
to the gentle rhythm of his day-by-day philosophy. The lines
of his poem, *Time goes by Turns*,

> Not always fall of leaf, nor ever spring:
> No endless night, yet not eternal day:
> The saddest birds a season find to sing,
> The roughest storm a calm may soon allay.
> Thus with suceeding turns God tempereth all
> That man may hope to rise yet fear to fall . . .

were echoed in the opening of his first letter from the country:

Such is God's loving care of us from day to day, so gently He
arranges all things, that our enemies now relax their efforts, and go
no further in their cruelty than He judges fit for His chosen ones.
So sometimes our little ship is tossed up and down on the most
terrible waves, and at other times, when the storm is over, she sits
smiling on a quiet sea, and is carried peacefully on her course. A
month or two ago, things were being done against the Catholics
which only the filth of heresy could have conceived. But now this
horrid cruelty has fallen back upon itself, and though it has not
ceased to be cruelty, yet there are degrees in cruelty which make it
able to blush at itself.

He then goes on to describe the slackening-off of the persecution after the last excutions in October—which incidentally
had carried off his very dear companions Edward James and

Christopher Buxton, both members in desire, though not in name, of the Society of Jesus.

It was early in November that Garnet sent him off on his tour of 'a great part of England', and he was away about seven weeks. He thus missed the actual and long-expected arrival in London of Fathers Gerard and Oldcorne, though he returned in time to see them before they left. He also missed the magnificent coronation-day Procession of the Queen from Somerset House to St. Paul's, of which Garnet, an equably-minded eye-witness, has left a most lively and valuable account. But in compensation he had rare experiences that opened up a new vista in his missionary career. He had the actual sensation of God's graces to men springing like flowers wherever his feet trod; he felt the pulse of the Old Religion trembling through the whole of 'the great part of England' that he traversed; and he found scores of friends and admirers—many of them young men and heirs of famous houses —who were to help on his work, both apostolic and literary, in London.

He was so deeply impressed that, for the only time since his first days in England, he wrote a letter describing his own success. Unfortunately it is couched in such prim and modest terms as to be more tantalizing than satisfying. But since it is the only known letter of his in which he gives more than the merest hint of his own exploits, it is worth quoting in full. It is dated 28th December 1588.

Now that I can rest a little after the daily toil of travelling, my first thought is to write and tell you of the progress we are making. I have been on horseback round a great part of England . . . and have visited a great number of Catholics, whom I found extremely eager for our services: they desire and expect so much of our Society. Everywhere, according to my small capacity, I preached sermons, and I refreshed very many with the bread of heaven. Now, truly, although I have often felt it before, I know with the certainty of proof the extraordinary estimation of the men of our Society which is planted deep in the minds of all. So much so, that people who up to now would not even speak to a priest, much less admit one to the house, do not only receive us but press us to come and stay with them. With people of this sort I have been able to do a truly useful work, because, although it was men of our Society whom they most of all demanded, yet, in the present scarcity of ours, I have brought them by the grace of God to receive others without annoyance. In the majority I have found a wonderful keenness and contempt of worldly values: men of noble family and great possessions, surrounded as they are by every advantage, are yet more and more ready to risk their lands and liberty, and make nothing of them.

This paragraph of his letter is a striking confirmation of the point already made by Garnet—and afterwards amplified by Gerard—that the opening up of new regions to the Seminary Priests was a work for which the Jesuits were peculiarly fitted.* All the same, reading between the lines of Southwell's next paragraph one can gather that his own personality had much to do with his success. The young and the ardent were attracted to him as to something which they longed for above all things in themselves:

In the arrangements for my tour and the risks it involved, there have been two young men, both burning with desire to join our Society, whose good breeding and intelligence and personal appearance have greatly helped me. And indeed there have been very many—the sons and heirs of great personages—who have continually been ready to give me not only their companionship but their personal service. I have sometimes been to call on the Protestant Sheriffs to look after secret Catholics in their households; and they, seeing my fine clothes and my bevy of aristocratic youths, and suspecting nothing so little as the reality, have received me with imposing ceremony and truly sumptuous banquets.

'In this way', he added primly, 'we sometimes trick the Wicked One with his own snares and enticements.'

How much one would desire to have more details about these escapades, which must have been more coolly audacious than

* The reference here is not to the Society as a whole or in modern times, but only to that small band of exceptional men who were Southwell's predecessors and contemporaries.

anything in Gerard's exciting narrative! The glimpse of Southwell, charming with his urbane conversation the Sheriffs whose
lurid proclamations against Jesuits were still posted everywhere, is
a truly tantalizing one. But to himself it was no more than an
amusing side-show, for he continues:

> I managed in the meantime to do a good deal of work for our
> prisoners, and was able to help and console those who were not in
> too strict confinement.

Prisons were always his first care; and there is little doubt that
he was happier in the slush of a cobbled gaol-yard than in the
heated splendour of a banqueting-hall. But the banqueting-halls
could not be neglected. From a Mass-centre in the Great House
religion could radiate out to the peasantry, yeomanry, and lesser
gentry, whom otherwise it would be impossible to reach. Even
if the owner of the Great House were not a fervent Catholic, if
he were only a Schismatic* or a lax Catholic with a hankering
for the old religion, he could still be of much use; there would be
times, if he were a magistrate, when he would persecute to prop
up his reputation; but there would be many other times when he
would turn a blind eye on the members of his family or household
who were active Catholics. Some of the best work of the Jesuits
and Seminary Priests was done under these conditions of mild or
intermittent persecution; and up to a point, a crypto-Catholic
was more of a menace to the Government than an avowed
recusant.

Part of Southwell's work on his tour was undoubtedly to
restore the equilibrium and awake the conscience of these people
after the scare of the Armada; it was a work requiring great
courage of heart and delicacy of touch. The variety of tasks he
had to accomplish is indicated in the succinct and abstract summary with which he closed his account of the tour:

> In short, throughout my journey, I have striven my utmost to
> strengthen the weak and wavering, and to spur on the fervent to

---

* A 'schismatic' was strictly speaking one who favoured the Henrician settlement; but in practice it meant one who conformed to the new religion but
preferred the old.

even greater heights; to rebuke those who were setting a bad example, and to raise up those who had fallen; to be to all what each one needed, either a father, or a shepherd, or a judge. And now let me turn to other matters . . .

and so he finished all he had to say of these eventful seven weeks.

This part of Southwell's biography is written almost wholly in the light of his letters; and since these, as has been said, are so predominantly extrovert, inevitably the light is upon what he *did*, not what he *was*. But after quoting this last letter, one has to pause and ask, with all reverence, the same question as the disciples of Our Lord: 'What manner of man is this?' What sort of a person was this Robert Southwell: who was feasted sumptuously (*incognito*) by the great ones of the land, and then crept out to visit the sick and imprisoned; who chose foul weather to travel in, yet brought sunshine with his presence; who was pressingly welcome in so many places, but never stopped long enough to rest; who desired above all things to die, and yet found life so interesting; who had the brain of an expert lawyer; the daring eye of a cavalry-commander; the humdrum regularity of a faithful drudge; the sensibility of a high-born lady; the dumb endurance of a hardened foot-soldier; the manners of an accomplished traveller; and the heart of a little child. Could anything be more eternally youthful than his little poem, *A Child my Choice*?

Let folly praise that fancy loves, I praise and love that Child
Whose heart no thought, whose tongue no word, whose hand no deed defiled.
I praise him most, I love him best, all praise and love is his,
While him I love, in him I live, and cannot live amiss.
Love's sweetest mark, laud's highest theme, man's most desiréd light,
To love him life, to leave him death, to live in him delight.
He mine by gift, I his by debt, thus each to other due,
First friend he was, best friend he is, all times will try him true . . .

Robert Southwell must be the despair of a modern hagiographer, because there is no outstanding quirk or eccentricity that one can catch hold of to pry in: no mark of 'nature's livery or

fortune's star'. Yet a glance at him shows that this lack was no
lack of humanity. Quirks make one *exclusively* human by contrast, say, with the angelic nature. Southwell was very *positively*
but not exclusively human. His humanity merges into godliness
so gently that all is suffused light and no shadow. Those who
would most like to sketch him arrestingly are deprived of the
power to discriminate; and those who most detest the views he
stands for are equally helpless to criticize, because his views were
so clearly framed in reason, and expressed with just the requisite
amount of passion that makes reason human. All one can do is
to mark, about this period of his life, a new interior stage of
rounded, or many-sided, detachment, of gem-like *tagliatura*.

Perhaps to this period belong those poems, about Christ's
Infancy and kindred subjects, which do betray an increased
detachment. Forsaken is the conventional sequence and forsaken
too the introspection and the melancholy. The poem or hymn
has become a thing on its own, easy and clear-cut, because it has
been written for others, to bring good news to simple people
long starved of food for their simple piety. About this time, one
may guess, his poetry became a more operative part of his
apostolate. From now on he is a wandering minstrel, peddling his
wares *gratis*.

The main outline of his winter tour is hidden; but there are
some wavering indications. The two young men he mentioned
in his letter were almost certainly the two Wiseman boys, Thomas
and John, whose home was Braddocks, near Saffron Walden, in
Essex. The family, though recusant, was influential in the county;
it enjoyed the friendship of Penelope Lady Rich, the Earl of
Essex's wayward but goodhearted sister. Lord Rich was perhaps
one of the great personages who feasted Robert *incognito*, 'suspecting nothing so little as the reality'. There is also in his letter a
description (omitted for economy's sake) of the Catholics in Ely
prison. Braddocks to Ely makes a line through the university
town of Cambridge: an obvious place for him to have met his
'bevy of aristocratic youths' with their irreverent stories about

Dr. Whittaker; among them no doubt was the young Earl of Southampton, a Catholic still in spite of his wardship, connected with Robert in several ways, and soon to be a distinguished literary patron.

But after Cambridgeshire Southwell's tracks vanish. He did not go into Norfolk—that much is known; so one can only conjecture him disappearing west into the Midlands. Here he would have found some regions, such as Rutland, quite bare of friends; others, like Leicestershire and south Oxfordshire, rich in ancient Catholic homes and in memories of Campion. But wherever he went he was never alone. When he left hurriedly after Mass while it was yet dark, he could feel in the frost-bound countryside the echoing of that Heart whose Blood was still hot on his mouth. And it was in the air all around him.

As the huddled rain-stacks of November gave way to the snow-bleached fields of December, and the end of his tour came closer with the end of the year, one can imagine a setting for his most famous little poem, *The Burning Babe*, the one that begins:

> As I in hoary winters night stood shivering in the snow,
> Surprised I was with sudden heat which made my heart to glow;
> And lifting up a fearful eye to view what fire was near,
> A pretty Babe all burning bright did in the air appear . . .

and that ends:

> . . . For which as now on fire I am to work them to their good,
> So will I melt into a bath to wash them in my blood.'
> With this he vanished out of sight, and swiftly shrunk away,
> And straight I called unto mind that it was Christmas day.

The roots of this poem are deep in medieval England. It is as detached as an Emblem; but unlike Emblem verses, it is not the working-out of the picture that matters so much as the visionary flash transfusing the whole; it recalls and perhaps suggested Shakespeare's 'And pity like a naked new-born babe, Striding the blast . . .' For Ben Jonson it was the poem he would have destroyed many of his own to have written. One can see why. The invention is so rare, yet there is so little sign of labour.

Here, at the cost of digression, a very little must be said about
Southwell's range of verse. Edmund Bolton, the Jacobean critic,
wrote of his 'never-to-be-forgotten' poems: 'the English whereof
as it is most proper, so the sharpness and Light of Wit is very rare
in them'. Another of his Christmas poems, *New Heaven, New
War*, has just that quality of 'wit' that was prized by the Tribe of
Ben and recalls Crashaw also and the earlier Marvell:

> . . . This little Babe so few days old
> Is come to ryfle Sathan's fold;
> And hell doth at his presence quake
> Though he himself for cold do shake:
> For in this weak unarméd wise
> The gates of hell he will suprise . . .
>
> His Camp is pitchéd in a stall,
> His bulwarke but a broken wall:
> The Crib his trench, hay-stalks his stakes,
> Of Shepherds he his muster makes;
> And thus as sure his foe to wound
> The Angel trumps alarum sound.
>
> My soul with Christ join thou in fight,
> Stick to the tents that he hath pight;
> Within his Crib is surest ward,
> This little Babe will be thy guard.
> If thou wilt foil thy foes with joy,
> Then flit not from this heavenly boy.

At the same time, in some of the last stanzas he wrote, *On
Prayer*, it may not be fanciful to catch an almost Miltonic reso-
nance. Certainly they show an increased flexibility in the use of
stress and caesura:

> Like Abraham
>   ascending up the hill
> To sacrifice,
>   his servants left below
> That he might act
>   the great commander's will

Without impeach
to his obedient blow:
Even so the soul
remote from earthly things
Should mount salvation's shelter,
mercy's wings . . .

Nothing more grateful
in the Highest eyes,
Nothing more firm
in danger to protect us,
Nothing more forcible
to pierce the skies,
And not depart
till mercy do respect us:
And as the soul
life to the body gives,
So prayer revives the soul,
by prayer it lives.

Finally, there is that mysterious poem, *A Vale of Tears*, which has a wilderness of echoes from *Gawain and the Green Knight* to G. M. Hopkins.

Janelle has written of it, perhaps a shade over-enthusiastically:

The *Vale of Tears*, which in a way sounds so incredibly modern, is not unlike some of Wordsworth's poems in its association of the high thoughts of a pure and loving soul with the aerial solitude of the high hills; it may compare for exactness and intensity of feeling with the finest descriptions in Shakespeare's plays; it may even be said to rise to a sense of the mysteriousness of nature, of the spiritual reality beyond material things, which Shakespeare never reached. Southwell was not thirty when he wrote this piece—undoubtedly his most valuable composition. His poetic personality, matured by the hardships of his jeopardous life, was beginning to assert its power. A rare combination of artistic beauty with moral greatness was in the making and would soon have been perfect.

Certainly it is a prophetic poem. With the cracking-up of the great medieval edifice of Ceremony and Philosophy, there was soon to be no half-way halt to check and soothe the wayward passions. In Southwell's vision, Nature, guided seemingly at random by God's creative hand, steps in and touches a deeper vein of soothing resignation. His valley was a real valley, described with quaint and sensuous accuracy; but it was also a balanced state of soul where his emotions could be at rest until such time as the Sun of God's supernatural consolation should break the clouds again.

He returned to London at the end of December in time to greet the two new arrivals, John Gerard and Edward Oldcorne. A passage in Gerard's *Autobiography* throws an interesting light on Southwell:

> I stayed with the Fathers some time and we had frequent discussions on the methods we should follow in our work. Splendid advice on ways of helping and saving souls was given us by Father Garnet, and also by Father Southwell who excelled at this work. He was so wise and good, gentle and loveable.

Most priests when they arrived in England were only too glad to apply immediately for aid to Garnet or Southwell. It was typical of Gerard, however, that he had already arranged for himself a fruitful mission-field in Norfolk, where he had been issuing spiritual direction and even dispensations in a manner that caused Garnet to raise his eyebrows somewhat; and there was evidently a mild rebuke not mentioned in Gerard's *Autobiography*. 'It is not a serious matter', Garnet wrote to Aquaviva, 'but it might have been. Those of ours who come in future should be told not to neglect opportunities of doing good on the way, but not to delay too long.'

But Garnet soon came to appreciate the sterling qualities that went with the large manner. There was some truth as well as much modesty in Gerard's insistence in his *Autobiography* that if other priests had written theirs they would have had far more remarkable stories to tell. Southwell's short letter of 28th December is a proof of this; and so is the little that is known of the spectacular work done in Yorkshire by the Rheims priest, Father John Bost, martyred in 1594.

Nevertheless there was something about Gerard that must have come to the hard-pressed missionaries in the south like a breath of reviving air. He was returning, after only two years' absence, to an underground campaign he was already well versed in. He had complete *savoir-faire* and an irrepressible confidence that the Old Religion was the native and proper faith for Englishmen. No time could have seemed more hostile to this belief than the aftermath of the Armada with its branding of priests as foreign agents. But the robust wind of Gerard's coming helped to blow away the hateful illusion like a miasma.

There was a buoyant quality in Southwell also that responded joyfully to Gerard's assurance; and it is clear that the two, as soon as they did meet, became fast friends. They made a number of journeys together, in which they shared several hair-breadth escapes as well as some private jokes. From this time on, Southwell was to lead an increasingly wandering life, owing to a sudden crisis in the affairs of his patroness.

It was the news of this crisis, actually, that had brought him back in a hurry. He had heard while on his tour that the Earl of Arundel, after three years' imprisonment, was to be brought to trial for High Treason. Both the Earl and the Countess were in urgent need of his help and advice.

CHAPTER FOURTEEN

Philip and Anne, 1589

THE arraignment of Philip Howard seems to have been a concession to the more radical elements in the Privy Council restive at the new measures against Puritanism. (1) It has all the appearance of a cynical act of appeasement: 'Give up the marprelates and you can have Arundel.'

Entrusted to a commission of his worst enemies, the case was carefully built up by Wade, clerk to the Council.

Earlier on, Philip had been moved from his evil-smelling prison in the Beauchamp Tower to more spacious quarters in the Lanthorn Tower where he could communicate with his fellow-prisoners—among whom was Sir Thomas Gerard—and arrange for Mass to be said. The celebrant was an old Marian priest named Bennet. Among the prisoners was one John Snowden, lately introduced.* He was a pseudo-Catholic informer. From then on, the familiar pattern of Elizabethan justice became all too evident.

In July Snowden made his report to Wade. In August Wade cornered Bennet and forced him to admit that he had been saying Mass. Bennet, an old man of weak fibre, collapsed. The statement that Wade finally made him sign was that the Earl had told him to 'say a Mass of the Holy Ghost for the success of the Spanish Fleet'. Wade then cast about for a second witness.

---

* In 1591 'John Snowden' was the *alias* of John Cecil who had offered his services to Walsingham in 1588. But it cannot be affirmed that he was the 'John Snowden' of this incident.

He concentrated his attention on Sir Thomas Gerard, who at first held out firmly. After three or four months of pressure he was brought to impute certain words to the Earl that might have a disloyal construction put on them; but he denied the story of the Mass of the Holy Ghost. In December (or thereabouts) the commissioners, trying shock tactics, cross-examined Philip with great violence and bitterness; but he maintained stoutly—'and disdainfullie' according to Wade—that he had done nothing disloyal to the Queen in act or intention. Meanwhile Bennet, under moral pressure from his fellow-prisoners, had recanted his first confession. The case hung fire and Philip was moved back to the Beauchamp Tower.

It was probably at this juncture that he managed to get letters out to his wife and to Southwell. He was troubled about how far he could truthfully say that he had not sided with the Spaniards. His letters, which are quoted in part by the author of the *Life*, are a tribute to his innocence and strict conscience. He admitted frankly to Southwell that he had 'wished well to the Spaniards', though he could not recollect in what form of words, if any, he had given expression to his thoughts. It is easy to understand his scruples. He was a godson of the Spanish King and held him in regard as a great monarch. Years before, as a Protestant, he had corrected Drake in public for speaking insultingly of King Philip. No doubt there were Catholic prisoners, like Sir Thomas Gerard, who were just as belligerently anti-Spanish, at least in words, as Drake had been; and Philip may well have used expressions in private which did not represent his settled convictions. But as to the main charge, on which the prosecution rested, the Mass of the Holy Ghost for the success of the Armada, he was quite positive that he had not ordered it; and he added in his letter to Southwell a circumstance that sounds very natural and convincing —'that he was so newly made a Catholic before his imprisonment, that he knew not there was any such Mass as of the Holy Ghost'. Southwell's reply is not extant, but its tenor was undoubtedly to confirm him in the rectitude of maintaining his loyalty; for, at his subsequent trial, in answer to the 'Bloody Question', he said constantly that he would take the Queen's part against any foreign invading army. There is no reason to believe that this did not represent the settled conviction of his duty; but his purpose in maintaining it was not to save his life—which was forfeit as soon as a trial was decided on—but to ensure that he should lose it for the Faith and not for political opinions.

At the beginning of 1589 preparations for the trial were begun again. Bennet, a demoralized creature, was soon brought to heel; but it was not until February that Sir Thomas Gerard broke down and put his hand in shame to a joint confession which included the principal charge. Other witnesses were raked up, from the depths of the spy-world, whose rambling innuendoes might receive a colour of treason once the main charge was accepted. They even brought up, to prove Philip's evil disposition, an incident of his youth, when for a bet he had dressed up as a minister and preached a sermon that quite took in the congregation.

During the collecting of evidence, Lord Burghley wrote a little note to Sir Francis Walsingham. Philip had been Burghley's ward; he looked on him always as a fatherly friend, and Burghley encouraged this ingenuous confidence. Yet in March, just before the trial, Burghley wrote this note to Walsingham. He had no material evidence to offer, but he suggested that if the reports of a certain spy in 1586 could be dug up, they would put Philip's attempt to go overseas in a more ugly light.

But not in so ugly a light as this note puts Lord Burghley. As in the case of other great politicians of the same *genre* as himself, the façade of the Elder Statesman was apt to crack sometimes, and to reveal the mentality of the blackmailing footman. While one side of his sepulchre should justly extol his civic achievements and domestic virtues, the other might well bear the words of Tacitus: '*Jus regium servili ingenio exercuit.*' 'He wielded the power of a despot with the mentality of a slave.'

At the trial, broken in health through his malodorous confinement, hounded by the four leading advocates of the bar, bewildered by a variety of accusations he had never heard before, Philip

o

could do little to defend himself except challenge the faith of the two chief witnesses against him. But he was not allowed to cross-examine them. They were brought in only to acknowledge their signatures. Gerard did this with averted face, never looking at the Earl, for it seems that up to the last he had promised not to appear against him. With the appearance of Bennet, however, there was a dramatic scene. Philip drew forth his one slender, amateur bit of evidence, which he had kept next his skin lest he should be searched and deprived of it (says the official record)—Bennet's letter of recantation—and threw it into the Court. But he was told that it was not for him 'to daunt the Crown witnesses'.

As to the trial in general, it is enough to quote Pollen on the Indictment:

> Apart from an historical clause here and there, as that such a law was passed or such a proclamation made, the whole is false everywhere both as to fact and as to intention . . . and the indictment manifests the truth of the Earl's declaration: 'The Catholic Faith . . . is the only cause . . . for which I am now . . . to be executed.'

After the peers had risen in turn to pronounce him *guilty*, the Earl made request 'to talk with his Wife, and to see his Infant, born after his Imprisonment, whom he had never seen'. But neither of these requests was ever granted. The official record continues:

> Then my Lord's Grace pronounced judgement, That he should be conveyed to the place from whence he came, and from thence to the place of execution, and there to be hanged until he were half dead, his members to be cut off, his bowels to be cast into the fire, his head to be cut off, his quarters to be divided into four several parts and to be bestowed in four several places: and so (said my Lord Steward) the Lord have mercy on thy soul.
>
> To this the Earl of Arundel said, as it were softly to himself, *Fiat Voluntas Dei*. And so having made a low obeysance to the State, the Lieutenant took him away; Mr. Shelton going before him with the edge of the Axe towards him.

Shortly after the trial, Garnet came again to London for the twice-yearly renovation of vows—presumably again in Southwell's

house at Acton. Gerard* and Oldcorne were there, and several
other priests not named. There is a letter from Garnet to Rome,
describing the popular anger at the Earl's condemnation, which is
interesting, as probably the facts were supplied by Southwell.

There was a crowd outside Westminster, waiting for the
verdict; among them the Earl's innocence and misfortune, his
nobility and gifts and manly bearing were widely commented on.
When the Earl came forth from the Hall with the axe-edge
turned towards him, there was a loud uproar of remonstrance,
and people said openly that, even if the charge were true, things
had come to a pretty pass when a man could be convicted of
High Treason for what he said in his prayers. This was precisely the point which had divided the jury of peers, and on which
they demanded from the judges some ruling. But the judges—
'that bench once so venerated, but now of all most infamous',
writes Garnet who had himself studied for the bar—threw the
responsibility back on the peers. The waverers were finally
brought round by private assurances from the Treasurer that the
Queen only wanted the sentence, not the execution of it. This
last piece of information, if it is correct, can only have come to
Southwell through some peer—or some peer's wife—bringing
sympathy to the Countess at Arundel House.

The Elizabethan Government was quick to see when it had
gone too far. Not only did the persecution greatly slacken during
the next year, but the Earl's sentence remained indefinitely in
suspense—owing, it is said, to the protests of his kinsman, the
Lord Admiral, who had not, of course, been on the jury.

For the next few weeks, however, every day was expected to
bring the summons to execution. This was the period of Southwell's greatest intimacy with the Arundels, and of his usefulness
to them. Philip sent him several letters. In one of them, signed
'Yours till the last moment', he wrote:

My Dear and Reverend Father, This being the last time that I think
I shall ever send unto you . . . I beseech you for the love of God,

* For Gerard the situation must have been a painful one; Sir Thomas, the
Earl's unwilling accuser, was his father.

procure me to be remember'd in the morning of my Execution in as many ways as you can by that meane which you know most effectual to do me good, and by one of them [that is, a Mass] at the hour of my last conflict as near as may be conjectured.

There is a strange, ghostly appeal in the friendship of these two men who, so far as is known, never saw each other in life, and whose grandfathers had spat hatred at each other in the crowded tribunal when death-sentence was passed on the great poet. Now the grandson of Surrey's accuser used all his heart and intelligence to try and make up to Philip for the loss of those comforts which as a human being in a Christian country he had every claim to expect—the sight of his wife and children before he died, and the presence of a priest to give him the Last Sacraments. Unfortunately, only one letter of Southwell's has survived, and that in a Latin version made by the historian More. As the tribute of a friend it may be biased, but it is a remarkable revelation of how the English priests taught themselves to face execution—not penitentially, but with joy and high spirits, once the torture and uncertainty were over:

Your cause—by whatever name it may be disfigured in the eyes of men, by whatever colour deformed—is religion. The form of the accusation itself speaks this; all men of peace and judgement think it so; the rest of the charges prove it. . . .

Let therefore neither fury nor fiction nor the sword, nor glory of splendid attire, nor bribes, nor entreaties, nor any other violence seduce thee from the charity of Christ. Thou wast born to be God's; by Him thou livest, and for Him thou art to die. It is a death that will confirm the wavering and make the strong yet stronger still. Friends applaud, strangers admire, enemies are confounded, whilst you beget for yourself in both worlds an eternal name. . . . The cause is God's, the conflict short, the reward eternal.

Lastly to treat of the affairs of your soul. I would not that you afflict yourself much by fasting, prayers, and penitential works, in order that you may be stronger for the last combat. Your desire for confession—the means of which are denied you—and the contrition of a humble heart, expressed by your bloodshed in this cause, will remit all sins and their punishment as fully as in baptism, so great is the prerogative of martyrdom. I desire you the happiest issue of the conflict begun. Let us hope by the help of God to see each other hereafter in glory. Farewell.

The Earl had not the same facility of self-expression as South-well. His deeply sincere and almost contemplative spirit could only find the stately formulas of custom in which to write what he felt. The refusal to let him see his wife was particularly painful because he had so much to say to her which he could not write. After years of neglect, he had just begun to know and love her in 1585, when the shadow of the Queen's Majesty fell between them; and now his intense desire to make up to her was matched by the pain of not being able to tell her so. He did write to her, as well as he could, but a fragment of a letter to Southwell shows how he felt the inadequacy of his words:

I call our *Lord* to witness that as no sin grieves me any thing so much as my offences to (her), so no worldly things makes me loather to depart hence than that I cannot live to make (her) satisfaction according to my most ardent and affectionate desire. Affliction gives understanding. *God* I hope of His infinite mercy who knows my heart and has seen my true sorrow in that behalf has remitted all, I doubt not, and so has (she) of her singular charity to my unspeakable comfort.

The indefinite postponement of the Earl's execution was part of a periodic reaction among the more conservative of the Queen's Councillors against the obvious dangers of extreme Puritanism. But it was a reaction which was liable to cease as soon as the Catholics showed any signs of recovery. In the meantime the more violently Protestant among the Councillors were allowed to compensate themselves for the relaxation of the public laws by acts of private ferocity; hence the rise to power at this time of the unofficial persecutor, Richard Topcliffe. In 1590 Lord Hunsdon, one of the Earl's bitterest enemies, moved into Arundel House. The Countess and her family were at first restrained to the use of a few rooms there, and then evicted altogether. She rented a house outside Bishopsgate, in order to be as near her husband as possible, and lived there on an allowance from the Queen which was sometimes paid and sometimes not.

Clearly this marked the end of Southwell's stay in Arundel House. It may also have marked the end of his period as the Countess's resident chaplain, for the rented house at Bishopsgate cannot have provided the same facilities for lying hid as the great mansion on the Strand. It is probable that for the last three years of his missionary life, he moved about finding a temporary resting-place in different houses. But it was by no means the end of his friendship with the Arundels. He continued to look on them, and to write for them, as his principal patrons to whom he was bound by duty and affection. In September 1591 there died Philip's favourite sister, the Lady Margaret, at the age of twenty-nine. She was married to Robert Sackville, afterwards Lord Buckhurst and Earl of Dorset, son and heir of the famous poet and politician. In spite of much pressure from her Erastian father-in-law, she had remained a devoted Catholic and friend of the Countess Anne. On her death, Southwell wrote an elegy in prose, for the comfort of Philip in prison; it was afterwards published, under Sackville patronage, as *Triumphs over Death*. Shortly after this he wrote the *Rule of Good Life*, for the Countess and her children, as a tribute of his lasting affection.

These works will be mentioned again in their own time. But since his work outside Arundel House was now moving into a wider sphere, and the figure of the Countess slips into the background, this will be a convenient place to say something of the deep and enduring effect of their friendship.

When he first met her, in the winter of 1586, she was somewhat in the position of Shakespeare's Olivia:

> The element itself till seven years heat
> Shall not behold her face at ample view;
> But like a cloistress she will veiled walk,
> And water once a day her chamber round
> With eye-offending brine.

But shortly after his arrival she began to show signs of the formidable personality that had been so long obscured by sadness

and hesitation. With surprising initiative and skill she established
ways of communicating with her husband in prison. Then she
began to throw herself into the dangerous work that Southwell
was doing; she made possible the first printing of his books; she
sent secret help to innumerable Catholics, going out herself on
foot sometimes to do so; she kept a place ready for hunted priests
to take refuge. Her graceful shrinking from life was replaced by
a calm and queenly presence of mind that astonished her enemies
as much as it baffled them. One glimpse of Southwell's part in
this transformation is afforded by her biographer:

> And I remember to have heard her often say when (as being by
> nature very apprehensive) she was afflicted with the apprehension
> of any future adversity, *Now I must betake myself to Blessed Father
> Southwell's remedy*, (for so she always called him after his death);
> which was to persuade herself that what she apprehended would
> really succeed, and resolve to be willing and content to endure it for
> the Love of God. This she ever did in all such occasions, finding
> therein much quiet, and indeed, she never could have quiet till she
> had resigned herself in that manner, which was an occasion unto her
> of great merit, and making many noble resolutions.

Another glimpse of how firm and delicate was their understanding of each other is provided by this: that he made her solemnly
promise that, if he was captured, whatever stories she might hear,
she would not attempt to ransom him or procure his liberty.
She promised; but when the stories did reach her, the promise
must have cost her even more than she expected.

With the help of devoted servants who refused to leave her,
she so managed her shattered estate that, when James succeeded
Elizabeth, and her son was restored to favour, he was able to take
the place that his rank required. With returning prosperity, her
benefactions to the schools and seminaries overseas became
enormous; and at the same time she kept up her innumerable acts
of personal charity which recall the saintly queens of an earlier
and simpler age—as when she walked three miles and back
(having no coach), from Acton to Hammersmith, to rescue a
poor woman who was in childbirth 'in the common open cage

of Hammersmith that then stood in the midst of the street which is the high road way to London'. Protestants and Catholics alike came to look on her as an angel of mercy, and even heretic ministers (says her biographer as a final proof of her charity) were saved from disgrace on more than one occasion by her kindly intervention.

The accession of James was the occasion of her first appearance at Court, and she caused something of a sensation as she passed before the painted ladies and padded lords like a resurrection of the old Northumbrian world of Bede and Caedmon and St. Hilda. A nobleman who was present on that occasion said:

> I do not know how to rank my Lady of Arundel, whether amongst the old Ladies or the young: because the beauty and freshness of her face makes her seem young [she being then betwixt forty and fifty years], but the gravity of her countenance, carriage and attire move me to think the contrary, and that she is the eldest in the company.

Although her manner of life was an offence to the standards of James's court, it won her the admiration of the younger members of the royal family. Princess Elizabeth, the 'Winter Queen', corresponded with her up to the time of her death in 1630; and the comparative peace which the Catholics enjoyed under King Charles was certainly in part the result and the reward of her long life of self-sacrifice.

'Some who knew her in her younger years have told me', her biographer wrote, 'she was then very fair and beautiful which may very easily be believed, because even to her last sickness her countenance was comely and her colour and complexion more fresh than many women's is at forty. She was taller of stature than the common sort . . . but without deformity, it rather adding a kind of graceful comeliness and majesty: the which had she endeavoured to improve and set forth with art and ornaments as too many do, doubtless it would have seemed and been esteemed extraordinary.'

Though in the building of her character she owed much to Southwell, his own debt to her was not only a material one. She

was a sort of exemplar of all that he was working for. The
memory of her may have been at the back of some lovely lines
that he wrote sighing for the day of Resurrection:

> Fair soul, how long shall veils thy graces shroud?
> How long shall this exile withold thy right?
> When will thy sun disperse his mortal cloud,
> And give thy glories scope to blaze their light?
> Oh that a star more fit for angels' eyes
> Should pine in earth, not rise above the skies!
>
> Thy ghostly beauty offered force to God;
> It chained him in the links of tender love;
> It won his will with man to make abode;
> It stayed his sword and did his wrath remove.
> It made the rigour of his justice yield
> And crownéd Mercy empress of the field.

In the autumn of 1589—to conclude the year with the chapter
—Robert got news of a crisis in the Southwell estate. He made
it the occasion of the solemn *Letter to his Father* which he completed on 22nd October. The longing to bring spiritual help to
his family had played a great part in his vocation to an active
order and his return to England; and he tried to explain to his
father that 'it is not the carelessness of a cold affection nor the
want of due and reverent respect that has made me such a stranger
to my native home and so backward in defraying the debt of a
thankful mind, but only the iniquity of these days that maketh
my presence perilous and the discharge of my duties an occasion
of danger. I was loth to inforce an unwilling courtesy upon any,
or, by seeming officious, to become offensive . . .'

But he did not hesitate now that they were in such material
distress. Horsham St. Faith had been sold in the previous year to
the lawyer Hobart, afterwards Lord Chief Justice. Money troubles
had begun as far back as 1581 when Edward Coke was granted
an annual payment of £40 in return for legal advice. But the
most recent calamity was the enormous debt of the second son

Thomas, to whom Robert addressed a shorter letter of apparently the same date. Thomas had borrowed vast sums from London merchants, which would be easily explicable if he were the same Thomas Southwell who, with Edward Dyer, had been backing the alchemical experiments of Dee and Kelley in Prague. Dee's quarrel with Kelley and return to England in the autumn of 1589 had ruined any hope of recovery from that quarter; and no doubt it is the same Thomas Southwell who is found despairingly offering his services to Sir Francis Walsingham on 3rd November of that year. He was sent to the Fleet Prison shortly after; and his father and elder brother were left groaning under his unpayable debts. Already they had mortgaged lands to the value of £9,000, but two years later the debts were still unpaid, and Thomas still in prison.

Robert had already seen too many rich and noble houses made desolate for the matter to be any longer one of surprise. But what irked him was to see his birthplace sold, not as a free and generous sacrifice for the Faith, but as a despairing effort to keep up appearances at Court and avert temporal disgrace. What a shocking bargain, he exclaims to his father, which endangers eternal salvation and secures financial ruin instead. 'You have long sowed in a field of flint which could bring you nothing forth but a crop of cares and afflictions of spirit, rewarding your labours with remorse, and for your pains repaying you with eternal damages.'

But there is no note of scolding in the letter; it is a masterly mingling of the stern warnings of a priest, 'God's vicegerent', with the loving loyalty of a younger son. When he hints at his father's past excesses and the shame of his o'er-hasty second marriage, it is only in order to point out a quick and bold path to final recovery—as in the beautiful last paragraph:

Howsoever, therefore, the soft gales of your morning pleasures lulled you in slumbers; howsoever the violent heat of noon might awake affections, yet now in the cool and shade of the evening retire to a Christian rest, and close up the day of your life with a clear sunset; that leaving all darkness behind you, and carrying in your conscience the light of grace, you may escape the horror of eternal night, and pass from the day of mortality to the Sabbath of everlasting rest: and humbly desiring that my sincere affection may find excuse for my boldness, I here conclude . . .

What the immediate effect of the letter was on Richard Southwell is not known. During Robert's imprisonment, he was apparently still keeping his place at Court. But towards the end of the century he was in the Fleet Prison; and in 1600, in a postscript to a letter of 1st July, Garnet wrote: 'Mr. Southwell Robert's Father, has just died a Catholic.'

PART THREE

CHAPTER FIFTEEN

The Rise of Topcliffe, 1590

THE comparative lull in sanguinary persecution came to an end while Robert was actually writing his new year letter to Aquaviva. (1) But it was still holding when he began; and at first he could find nothing to write about except the great storm on the Epiphany, and a couple of first-class portents—'though *what* they portend, I must leave to your judgement.' On the north coast five whales, varying from forty to sixty feet in length, had been washed up over a quarter-mile of the shore-front; while 'on the west coast, a woman formed like a fish from the waist downwards (or a fish like a woman from the waist up) rose from the sea, and, sitting on a rock, sang so sweetly as to ravish all the thousands who flocked to behold her. Eventually some of the spectators loosed off a shot which wounded the singer, and with a loud and very piteous wail she dived from the rock and was seen no more.' No doubt as he wrote, Robert could imagine with some nostalgia Father Claudius welcoming these tit-bits as topics for recreation, and giving them the requisite turn to make them, as a Jesuit writer recommended such topics should be, 'agreeably religious or religiously agreeable'.

His professional news was at first restricted to one short but interesting sentence. 'We are all looking after our different "provinces", and working hard for souls with great profit.' Garnet's plans were evidently taking shape. Forty priests (ten of them future martyrs) had found their way over since the Armada; but instead of being scattered haphazard as previously, most of them now were in residences where they could work with the maximum advantage. Such a situation was too good to last; and even in the first part of his letter Robert put his finger on the seed of future trouble: 'We are liable to fresh trials because our enemies are afraid that war is still threatening.' Before he concluded on 16th January, he had to report that Father Christopher Bailey, who had been working with him since December 1588, had been captured in circumstances of sudden ruthlessness that heralded the approaching storm.

But before it broke with full fury, he had one spring-time holiday to remember with gladness. Late in February, when the daffodils were budding, he set out with John Gerard on the hundred-mile cross-country ride into Warwickshire. Gerard could boast later on that from one end of England to the other there were so many friendly 'stations' that on his longest journeys he never needed to stay a night at any tavern. But in their earlier journeys together they seem to have had to mix with a good deal of bawdy and bucolic company. It was on these occasions that Gerard's youthful proficiency at sport came to the rescue. When they had to sit at table with 'Protestant gentlemen', says Gerard, 'who had practically no other conversation except obscene subjects or rant against the saints or the Catholic Faith . . . there is often the chance of bringing the talk round to some other topic simply by throwing out a remark about horses or hounds or the like.' (2)

Robert, who had been cooped up in Rome while Gerard rode free in the Lancashire dales, had not the same hearty technical assurance. 'It is an easy thing to trip up in one's terms, as Father Southwell used to complain', continued Gerard with a reminiscent grin; 'frequently, as we travelled about together, he would ask me to tell him the correct terms, and worried because he could not remember and use them when need arose.' Robert, slight and inconspicuous, trotting along beside his imposing companion, was at least an earnest pupil; in a preface he wrote in 1591 there are several elegantly-worded metaphors from falconry.

In the very Catholic district of Arden, the Vaux sisters had taken a lease of Baddesley Clinton, ancient home of the Ferrars family—where Adam Shakespeare, thought to be the poet's progenitor, had once been a tenant. The house, protected by a ring of friendly neighbours, had been rendered doubly secure by the genius of Garnet's little carpenter-servant, Nicholas Owen, who represented if anyone did 'the constant service of the antique world, when service sweat for duty, not for meed'; he was one of a number of remarkable men who were attaching themselves at this time to the Jesuits in the capacity of 'temporal coadjutors', or lay-brothers.

Reunion with secular priests from Roman days, with Eleanor and Anne, and with Frances Burrows, now a young lady of fifteen, was for Robert a wonderful experience. He wrote on his return on 3rd March:

> It was a delight to be all together again for a few days, keeping our ancient custom, helping each other, and exchanging views. We opened our mouths and drew in the spirit. It seemed to me that I was looking at the cradle of our Society new-born in England, and that we are sowing the seeds in tears whereof others coming after us will gather the sheaves. We have sung the songs of Our Lord in a strange land; in this desert we have sucked honey from the rock and oil from the hardest flint.

The security of Baddesley Clinton was of course only relative. His letter continues:

> Sorrow pounced on us at the height of our joy, we scattered in some alarm, but escaped fortunately with more danger than damage. My companion and I, having avoided Scylla, proceeded to steer into Charybdis; but by a special mercy of God we circumvented both, and are now riding safely at anchor.

There are no details of this particular escapade—it was eclipsed by a more dangerous one in the following year—but it seems to have proved more exhilarating than depressing. He certainly needed all the encouragement he could get. By the time he returned to London, the reign of terror had begun. It was to last,

P

with one or two intervals, for the next five years, and is closely associated with the name of Richard Topcliffe. (3)

Topcliffe has not been reckoned among the 'Great Eliza-bethans' by modern panegyrists of that age. Yet he had at least two assets that might have qualified him. He had the same sort of demoniac energy and courage as Sir Richard Grenville; and one can imagine him rivalling Grenville's exploits if his career had lain on the high seas instead of at court. But, unlike Grenville, Topcliffe—and this was his second asset—*was a favourite*. That is to say, he enjoyed the Queen's favour to an extent not warranted by either his talent or his character.

From 1590 onwards he is found exercising a bewildering variety of functions. He has a private army to whom he promises the spoils of his victims beforehand, and he is the chief pursuivant who leads his raids against them in person; he acts as the prison-governor who prepares them for trial, with all the horrors involved by that, and at the trial he takes the part of an assistant-prosecutor, deferred to by the judges; and finally he is at the scaffold to see that the disembowelling is performed when the victim is properly conscious. The only title he ever possessed for all these functions was that of the 'Queen's Servant', but it was sufficient to gain him access to her Privy Chamber, independently of Ministers or Council. Perhaps his raw-blooded, bristling man-hood, undaunted at fifty-eight, was a pleasing contrast in her eyes with the younger generation of courtiers, remote and subtle, who dropped a mask, as it were, over their countenances before they approached her. Certainly, Topcliffe's devotion to her, based as it was quite frankly upon servile fear, was something she could rely on absolutely.

'*Homo sordidissimus*', wrote Garnet, measuring his words: 'This most unclean of men has attained, now for some time, such favour with Her Highness that he always has easy access to her, and need not fear the power or influence of any Councillor or Minister.' (4) It was as if the stage of *Titus Andronicus* had been widened to include the whole of London, with Topcliffe as 'Aaron the Moor'.

It is outside the competence of this biography to account for his ascendancy. But the opinion may be hazarded that the Queen had need of such a person because of the lone hand she was playing in her religious policy. Alarmed by the secret growth of Presbyterianism, especially among the gentry, she had discarded Burghley's policy of favouring 'the preciser sort', and was putting all her weight behind the Established Church in order to stamp it with the seal of her own balanced agnosticism and popular appeal. At the same time, although she may have preferred the Catholics to the Puritans, she still cherished Burghley's maxim that the only people a Prince can never trust or favour are those whom he has irrevocably injured. This obsessing fear, sedulously agitated by the Cecils, was to prove the perennial death-knell of the Catholic recusants. In suppressing the Puritans she automatically needed a new counter-weight against the Catholics, because only the Puritan gentry had the requisite zeal and ferocity to enforce fully the savage penal laws. In Topcliffe, no Puritan but a born hunter, with more than the extra brutality which the average magistrate lacked, she found the necessary counter-weight. Moreover, if he used the Catholics so badly as to satisfy the blood-lust of even the most extreme Puritans, then the main grievance against the Established Church (of favouring Papists) would be cut away at the start.

This would seem to be the reason for the new choice of *Bridewell* as the special prison for recusants. Southwell, with his usual quickness, had seen this before he concluded his January letter:

Almost all who are taken now may expect to taste of Bridewell, that place of shame; it is a slaughter-house where the cruelties inflicted are scarcely credible. The tasks imposed are continuous and beyond ordinary strength, and even the sick are driven to them under the lash. Food is not only of the scantiest, but so disfigured that it cannot be swallowed without retching.... Bedding is straw matted with stinking ordure.... It is the one Purgatory that all we Catholics dread, where Topcliffe and Young, butchers, have complete licence to torture. Yet whatever happens to us, I know we shall be equal to it ... and our Lord will speak peace to His people that His glory may dwell in our land.

One can sense the shudder that ran through him as he adjusted his mind once more to the physical details he knew he would have to endure. Bodily agony becomes infinitely worse when its deliberate purpose is the corruption of manhood. 'The nature of our nation', Sir Thomas Smith had written, 'is free, stout, haughty and prodigal of life and blood; but contumely, beating, servitude, and servile torment and punishment it will not abide.' The excuse (not justification) for the hideous promiscuity of Bridewell had been the supposedly brutish insensitivity of its usual inmates. It was never intended as a torture-house for extracting secrets from intelligent men. Yet here was the general warrant issued to Topcliffe in January 1590, and endorsed for the Keeper of Bridewell:

> Another Warrant from their Lordships to Richard Topcliffe and Richard Young Esquires to examine the said person Christopher Bayles a Seminary priest, John Bayles tailor, Anthony Kaye and John Coxted from time to time and, if they see further occasion, to commit them or any of them to such torture upon the wall as is usual for the better understanding of the truth of matters against Her Majesty and the State . . . (5)

But *was it usual?* Only three years back, Harrison's *Description of England* had been re-issued, with the words: 'Our gaolers are guilty of felony by an old law of the land if they torment any prisoner committed to their custody, for the revealing of his complices.' Hitherto, an aura of dreadful respectability had surrounded the use of torture; its purpose was limited to the public safety of the realm; a warrant was required for each application; and it took place in the Tower of London. But what was being enacted here was the official wedding of the moral corruption of Bridewell to the grim secrets of the Tower.

'*From time to time . . . torture upon the wall . . . as is usual . . .*': each phrase would seem to mark a fresh degradation of Justice.

The 'Christopher Bayles' of the Warrant was the gentle little scholar Christopher Bailey, whose execution in Fleet Street

Robert had returned from Warwickshire in time to witness. In his March letter he wrote:

He had been hung by the hands for twenty-four entire hours with only the tips of his toes touching the ground. All the time they kept plying him with questions. . . . From Bridewell, once reserved for harlots and ruffians, but now the slaughter-house of Catholics, he was taken to another prison, and . . . condemned to death for being a priest sent to England by the Pope's authority. . . .

When he had mounted the scaffold he said, 'Far be it from me to glory except in the cross of Our Lord Jesus Christ.' Then lifting his eyes to heaven he made the sign of the cross as well as he could with his bound hands. 'You have come', he said, 'to see a man dying, a common spectacle; and that man a priest, a common spectacle too. But I wish that as you watch my body, you could see into the inmost feeling of my heart. I think that if you could see my soul taking its flight, instead of these curses you are now uttering, you would sigh and rejoice with me in sympathy. I ask pardon of you all, and I forgive you all.' Then he turned to his prayers, and, a little while after, with an untroubled air, he went strongly and steadily through his death. He suffered on Ash Wednesday in one of the most crowded streets of London. Very many people, heretics included, were in praise of his holiness and courage.

With him suffered two citizens, Nicholas Horner and Saunder Blake, accused of sheltering priests. Over their heads was put a placard: 'For Treason and aiding foreign enemies', though this lie had less appeal than it had in 1588. They were the first of twenty-six (nineteen priests and seven laymen) who suffered in this year and the next, the majority in London; but that does not count the many, like those mentioned in the warrant above, who disappeared into prison and are not heard of again.

Nevertheless, it says much for the London organization that during the rest of the year only two priests were taken there; and those two, Anthony Middleton and Edward Jones, repaid the generosity of their hosts by absolute silence under torture. On the scaffold in Fleet Street, Topcliffe solicited Middleton with the places he had been in—'Yonder' (pointing to a house by the Conduit) 'and in Gray's Inn Lane, Shoe Lane, and other places

—you know I know where.' But Middleton answered, 'You know, Mr. Topcliffe, I never approached any man nor confessed any place. Therefore you wrong me.' He had been working for four years in Clerkenwell where he was greatly beloved. He remained alive, praying, till his heart was pulled out to be thrown into the cauldron.

In contrast with Middleton's gentle patience, Jones was a man of fiery courage who, as a Protestant, had been arrested abroad by the Inquisition, and then converted by Fr. Simon Hunt. At his trial, over which Topcliffe practically presided, he quoted, despite a storm of interruptions, one of Burghley's pamphlets about no Englishmen suffering death for conscience sake, and said that things were being done in England which no other Christian country would countenance. He had reason for his words; for against his name in an old Martyrs' Catalogue are the words: 'tortured in Bridewell by the privie parts'. (6) There are other known instances of this practice, and it is listed by Southwell as a common occurrence in his *Humble Supplication* among those things which 'we presume that Your Majesty seldom or never heareth the truth of'.

It is mentioned here once and for all—and will not be alluded to again—because it helps one to commiserate more with those few who failed under torture. At the same time, it gives an idea of why the Topcliffian persecution itself was a signal failure. By trespassing so flagrantly against the laws of nature, it encountered a rugged and holy grandeur in the English character, nurtured by a thousand years of Christianity, which the last century of Tudor State-worship had somewhat obscured, but which now shone out like granite in a storm. This was the hour of battle and God gave to the London Catholics the ancient angelic strength of good against evil.

It was a broadly based resistance, chiefly in the thickly populated fringe of the City—Bishopsgate, Aldersgate, Newgate, Black-friars; and farther out where the rule of the City Fathers did not reach: Southwark, Shoreditch, Clerkenwell, Holborn. (7) The majority on one list of shelterers is composed of shopkeepers: the tally-house in the Strand, the barber over against St. Clement's, the shoemaker in Ivybridge, the carpenter in Aldersgate, the haberdasher opposite the Poultry, the grocer by the Conduit in Fleet Street; to whom might have been added several invaluable innkeepers. But there were also the town-lodgings of the fine-racked country squires and their younger brothers and sons, lawyers, physicians, schoolmasters, men of many wiles, inured to danger.

The centre of resistance was the Ward of Farringdon, which might be described as a square subtended from the old west wall of the City, with diagonals from Blackfriars to Holborn Bars, and from Temple Bar to Greyfriars, or Christ-Church Hospital. Within this square were captured eighteen priests and laymen in the next two years, and within this square they were executed, with the special object of striking terror into the surrounding inhabitants. It is in this square, also, that Robert is reported as actually walking, in the only direct and localized evidence about his movements that has survived: 'There is one Mr. Southwell a Jesuit that useth to Mr. Cotton's in Fleet Street, and sometimes to Dr. Smith's.'*

Mr. George Cotton of Farringdon (Robert's old friend, or a cousin of the same name) had his house close to St. Bride's Church; Dr. Smith was Nicholas Smith's uncle ('little Doctor Smith the physician of Paternoster Row') who lived between Paternoster Row and Christ's Hospital. By the old-fashioned method of accompanying Robert on this walk, and by continuing round the rest of the square, one can get a survey of the places in London with which he was most associated.

Stepping out of Mr. Cotton's house, he was standing by the Conduit in Fleet Street, at the bottom of Shoe Lane. Opposite him, by the sign of the Hanging Sword was the back entrance to Lord Buckhurst's handsome town-residence, Sackville House, once the Bishop of Salisbury's, whose gardens reached down to the River. To this house Robert was at least a secret visitor, for here

---

* This report was not handed in till January 1592. It was out of date by that time, but was probably true of an earlier period.

lived Lady Margaret Sackville when she was in London; and it was just about this time that he was translating for her Estella's *Hundred Meditations* on the love of God, of which it was recorded in a subsequent dedication to Margaret's daughter: 'Mr. Robert Southwell . . . wrote and meant to have printed them for your

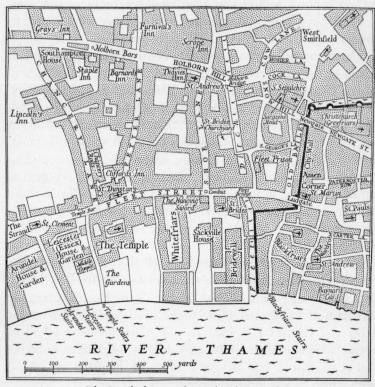

The Ward of Farringdon with Adjacent Liberties
(Drawn from Stow's *Survey of London* and Nordern's *Map of London* of 1593)

holy Mother's devotions, singularly by him honoured and affected.' (8)

Next to the walled garden of Sackville House, along the River Bank, was the precinct of Bridewell with its horrible prison. And next to that, joined by a 'bridge of sighs' across the sewage-stream of the Fleet, was the precinct of Blackfriars, the old Dominican Priory. In the Gatehouse, whose wings merged indefinitely into the Priory, was the lodging of his sister Mary and her husband, Edward Bannister of Iddsworth. The Gatehouse under its tenant at that time, young Mr. Fortescue of Racton, one of the Sussex-Hampshire ring of interrelated families, was a most famous centre of recusancy. Behind it was the Priory Mansion itself, owned by the Earl of Northumberland whose country seat was at Petworth, Sussex; and right in front of it lived Fortescue's uncle, Sir John Fortescue, Master of the Wardrobe. Both these personages turned a blind eye to what was going on in their households, especially after Northumberland's aunt, Lady Mary Percy, came to live at Blackfriars. The Master of the Wardrobe's steward, John Robinson, was a very active Catholic who later sent his sons to the new Jesuit school at St. Omer.*

But it was not only these powerful neighbours, it was the Gatehouse itself which baffled Topcliffe. Many and bitter were the complaints of spies and pursuivants about its 'sundry backdoors and byeways, and many secret vaults and corners', its 'many places of secret conveyance', and its 'secret passages towards the water'.

Climbing up from Blackfriars to Greyfriars, within the old wall, Robert passed the crowded west side of Paul's churchyard where his publisher lived, and where his friend Thomas Pormort was to die for reconciling a townsman who dwelt there. By the New Gate lodged his cousin Margaret and her husband John Gage, who had abandoned their crippled estate in Surrey; these two also were soon to be captured and condemned to death, but reprieved at the last moment.

Coming out of Newgate, where there were always prisoners to be visited, Robert stood on the north side of the square, and this too was a direction that he often took. It was the battered high road leading to Oxford and Warwickshire—by way of Tyburn. The road dropped steeply to cross the Fleet at Holborn Bridge,

* One of them, another John Robinson, took over the tenancy of the Gatehouse when it was bought by Shakespeare in 1613: perhaps the same John Robinson who witnessed Shakespeare's will.

and then rose in a long ribbon-built slope to Holborn Bars. On the way, by St. Andrew's Church, he passed the house of Swithin Wells, another notorious centre of recusancy, near which lived several others whose names were on Topcliffe's list. Just beyond the Bars was Southampton House where that strange lady, the Countess, maintained a determined piety along with undiminished worldliness; she continued to shelter missionary priests even during her brief married life with Sir Thomas Heneage. (9)

But, once in Holborn, Robert entered a new world, the World of the Law. Rising from the fields, the great Inns of Court and Inns of Chancery blocked all the west side of his square, reaching from Saffron Hill to the River; and joined by the 'Rents', little clusters of low-gabled lodging-houses. Here, too, as Francis Cowper shows in his *Prospect of Gray's Inn*, 'the old religion went underground, and nowhere could there be a better hiding-place than an Inn of Court, where intellectual freedom, independence of outside interference, and professional and personal comradeship were deep-rooted traditions.' In the maze of irregular buildings between Chancery Lane and Fetter Lane lived the two young Wisemans and many more of Southwell's friends and helpers, including his two Sussex cousins, Gage of Bentley, a noted lawyer, and Shelley of Michelgrove.

Nearly all these hosts belonged to the Sussex-Hampshire ring of Southwell's relatives; and it is possible to trace the names of six priests connected with him who frequented both the town and country houses of these or their kinsfolk. (10) 'They shift such persons between them', says one report, referring to Gilbert Wells of Brambridge (Swithin Wells's brother), and John Shelley and Robert Barnes who were in the service of Lord Montague of Cowdray.* This points to a relief system between town and country, of which probably Southwell was an organizer.

There is a trace of his own presence at Cowdray this summer.

---

* John Shelley of Buriton was a second-cousin of Southwell's who sent his sons to St. Omer's and later himself became a Jesuit. Robert Barnes will be met with again in Chapter 19.

Later on, when the old Lord Montague was dead and Southwell was in prison, Topcliffe raided the district and made gruesomely exhaustive inquiries about 'Father Robert', a Jesuit, who had been there, he said, 'the summer before the Queen's Majesty came to Cowdray', that is, 1590. One of the questions concerned a Jesuit conferring with Montague's son about a marriage to be arranged. (11) The point is of some interest because the young Earl of Southampton, then aged eighteen, was visiting at Cowdray that summer, and his grandfather, Lord Montague, was writing to Burghley to explain why the young man was not more forward in confirming his marriage-contract with Burghley's grand-niece, Elizabeth Vere.*

No doubt this particular inquiry was one of the many false scents followed by Topcliffe against Southwell. But the approximation to Southampton remains a probability, and is a reminder that Robert's fame as a writer was already, albeit anonymously, abroad. 'Yet since the copies thereof flew so fast and so false abroad that it was in danger to come corrupted to the print', he wrote in his preface to the 1591 edition of *Mary Magdalen's Funeral Tears* which he signed 'S.W.', 'it seemed a less evil to let it fly to common view in the native plume and with its own wings, than disguised in a coat of a bastard feather, or cast off from the fist of such a corrector as might haply have perished the sound, and imped in some sick and sorry feathers of his own fancies.'

The tone is the usual one of the assured gentleman-writer— Gerard, perhaps, had lent a hand with the falconry terms. When the Archbishop licensed this book,† he can have had no idea that 'S.W.' was the same as the outlaw for whom there was a mounting hue and cry, the notorious brain behind the London recusant organization, the 'Chief dealer for the Papists in England', as Southwell was afterwards exaggeratedly but significantly called.

---

* In November 1594, a letter from Garnet to Persons suggests that the Catholics did have some interest in the matter: 'The young Earl of Southampton, refusing the Lady Vere, payeth 5000 li. of present payment.'

† See Appendix 'D'.

There are only a few fragments of evidence to show how he earned this title of 'Chief dealer for the Papists' in London. But fragmentary as they are, they cover a variety of the tasks he was engaged in in 1590: finding accommodation for incoming priests; helping young men to escape overseas to be trained as priests; acting as spiritual guide to priests in difficulties; and being in general the sort of person whose authority was appealed to in a crisis.

Some of the evidence comes from a Rheims priest, Father James Standish, who represented the English Clergy in Rome in 1596, and again in 1602. He was answering the slanders of the small section which, with the support of Cecil and Bancroft, was trying to split the ranks of the English Catholics. The main story of that lamentable episode is fortunately right outside the time-limits of this book; but two of Standish's depositions throw retrospective light on Southwell's activities during this year. (12)

The first concerns his relations with the martyr Thomas Pormort, and the calumnies they were subjected to. The first half of the calumny—that Pormort was ill-treated at the English College during Southwell's tenure of office—has already been noted above in Chapter Five. The second half was that Southwell in England had turned Pormort away from his door in distress, and thus caused his subsequent capture and execution. This lie was indignantly exposed by Standish who had come to England in March 1590 a few months before Pormort.

The third lie . . . is against that glorious martyr Robert Southwell who was, when alive in England, as he is now in Heaven, on terms of the closest friendship with Pormort. He gave him a wonderful welcome on his arrival in England; he fed and clothed him, and brought him with honour into his own house, which is a mark of singular esteem in times of persecution. He also found him twenty crowns, introduced him to friends of very high rank, and established him in as safe a shelter as possible.

Father Garnet, writing in March 1593, before the slander was current, confirms the happy reconciliation of Pormort with South-well which preceded their final reunion in Heaven:

Entering this realm, and learning that Mr. Robert Southwell was then in London, he made it his first duty to renew with him a friendship which, he said, had been broken by his own fault; he had done the like in Italy with some other of our fathers. Having made a general confession of his whole life, he never ceased to follow Robert's advice in all things, until finally being arrested and pitifully tortured, 'he did not hesitate to resist unto blood'.

It may be taken for granted that Father Pormort was only one of many to whom Southwell proved an angel guardian and a friend in need.

The second incident shows him as helping escapes abroad, and also as having to dispose of a large sum of money. In 1589 or 1590, Edward Walpole, heir to the Houghton estate and many other properties, having made over his rights to his Protestant brother (ancestor of Sir Robert, the Prime Minister), came to London and lodged at the Blackfriars Gatehouse, prior to slipping overseas—perhaps by one of those 'secret passages towards the water'. Before he left, he presented Southwell with a hundred pounds to bestow as he thought best. According to Blessed Henry Walpole, Edward's cousin, Southwell sent part of this to the exiles in Flanders and the rest to the College of Rheims. (13)

The third incident illustrates Southwell's talent in an unexpected direction. It is best told in the words of Father Standish:

Robert Charnock, who had been one of the more troublesome students at the Roman College, afterwards came to England where he gave an example not only of intrigue but also of loose living. For in one of the most distinguished Catholic houses, he began to make desperate advances towards both the mother and the daughter. The greatest harm might have resulted if Father Southwell of the Society of Jesus (afterwards gloriously martyred) had not managed by his skill and foresight to get him quietly moved away.

Such an incident could be more serious than it may sound. Moral laxity was often followed by yielding to Government pressure. A hostess who found herself blackmailed by the very priest she was sheltering was in the most ghastly predicament imaginable.

Southwell was only too painfully aware how vital it was for a missionary priest to have a secret haven of tranquillity at the heart of the whirlwind of dangers and temptations. He felt a special responsibility towards those who had been students under him at Rome. Almost certainly it was to one of these that he addressed his *Letter to a Wandering Priest*, of which the first and last paragraphs, translated from More's Latin, are here quoted:

> I am grieved when I hear of your unsettled way of life, the guest of many and at home with none. We are all pilgrims, I know, but not vagabonds; we must risk our lives, but not our destiny. To be a vagabond and fugitive was the Curse of Cain, a sordid punishment to suit his crime. A mind inconstant is like one diseased, twisting and turning always, and finding no resting-place for quiet and holy thoughts . . .

> Set nature herself before your eyes; in the seasons of the year, in the succession of day and night, you may read continually the praise of order. There are times which call us abroad, and times which beckon to retirement. Learn when you are at home how to behave among men. And teach your own mind how to cherish in seclusion those thoughts which would make the practise of virtue to you a pleasure beyond all delights; and so may you live the long and holy life which from my heart I wish you. Farewell.

Exercising all these different functions, he could not hope to remain unknown indefinitely to the government.

It is interesting to try and estimate how his shadowy figure took shape in the calculations of Sir Robert Cecil, pieced together, at first, bit by bit, and then isolated and marked down. Cecil had virtually succeeded to Walsingham's office in 1590, and his chamber swarmed with spies offering the latest sensational discovery in exchange for a modest employment. As he patiently checked one rigmarole against another, three variations of the same man emerged. (A): There was a 'young Mr. Southwell', one of these boy-priests, some sort of cousin of his, who had

caused trouble in 1586 and early 1587; but he had disappeared
since and not been heard of again. For lack of other evidence he
was assigned in a 1588 list to Norfolk or Suffolk. (14) (B): Then,
in a different category, there was evidence of some brain behind
the London organization which sheltered incoming priests on the
way to their destinations, and—what was perhaps worse—enabled
young men to slip overseas to be trained as priests. The name
'*Robertus*' had been assigned to this underground leader; at one
time it had been thought to signify Robert Persons himself,
returned to take charge. (15) (C): Finally, in a quite different
category, there were reports from the raffish literary crowd on the
South Bank of a new writer who was stealing the affections of
promising patrons and reawakening sympathy with the old
religion. Two spies who kept their ear to the ground in these
circles were Robert Poley and Richard Baines. Baines, who
afterwards accused Marlowe of both 'popery' and 'atheism', had
brought the same sort of accusations at an earlier date against
one of Marlowe's associates, a ballad-writer and former Government spy called Richard Cholmeley: (16)

> That he had a certain book (as he saith) delivered him by Sir Robert
> Cecil of whom he giveth very scandalous reports; that he should
> incite him to consider thereof, and to frame verses and libels in the
> commendation of constant priests and virtuous recusants. This book
> is in custody and is called AN EPISTLE OF COMFORT and is
> printed at Paris.

What this obscure statement appears to mean is that Cholmeley
was using Southwell's book as a quarry for ballads in praise of the
old religion, and that, when threatened with arrest, he replied
impudently that Cecil had given him the book and authorized
him to use it.

It is useless to inquire what his real relations with Cecil were.
Scores of needy gentlemen were plying the same dubious trade.
But it was unfortunate for Southwell that, without any action or
intention on his part, his works were being read and quoted in
such circles.

When it became definitely known that (A) was the same person as (B); and when it was discovered with a shock of surprise that (AB) was none other than (C), then the hunt was up, and even wider and more overriding powers were given to Topcliffe to lay Robert Southwell by the heels once and for all.

It was a buccaneering flank-attack by Robert Persons that led to the first revelation of Southwell's identity. From the new college at Valladolid eight priests came to England in a most unorthodox manner. The names of four—Cecil, Fixer, Blount, Warnford—may recall Chapter Five. They were indeed all members of that difficult year, '84, and Persons had taken them off with him to help found his new college, in the belief that responsibility would bring out the best in them. As will be seen in a moment, he was half right and half wrong.

CHAPTER SIXTEEN

The Year of Challenge, 1591

For a considerable time after the 1589 expedition to Portugal
—England's counter to the Armada—stragglers and released
prisoners continued to trickle home. In the early spring of
1591 came six weatherbeaten sailors, remembering carefully who
they were and what they must say to the questions put them.
Two of them avoided the ordeal by landing in an out-creek near
Plymouth and making off into the interior. The others were
taken in charge at Portsmouth and sent up to the Lord Admiral
Howard in London. On the way, two more avoided the ordeal,
one falling grievously sick and the other being told off to look
after him. But the last two faced the Admiral across the Council
table. They answered frankly and satisfactorily the questions
about what ship they had sailed with, how they had been captured and how released. They were well-set-up young fellows;
and the chief spokesman of the two, in particular, made a very
good impression. It was an impression he continued to make
throughout his long and adventurous career, the last twenty
years of which, ending in the reign of Charles I, were spent as
Provincial of the English Jesuits. His name was Richard Blount,
and his companion was James Younger. (1)

Having been sent off to collect the Queen's bounty for dis-
tressed seamen, they presented themselves instead to Robert
Southwell's chief helper in London—successor it would appear to
Henry Vaux—young Thomas Wiseman, now a law-student at
Lincoln's Inn. At Wiseman's lodgings they were fitted out with
clothes and money—there is mention of 'a white satin doublet

and black-tuffed taffety hose'—and lay hid for three days. Then Younger was stationed at Upton Park, Lady Throckmorton's house in Essex; and Blount made his way down to Mr. Darrell of Scotney Castle on the borders of Kent and Sussex—a place he was to render famous by an epic escape in 1598.

The sight of Blount must have been an immensely cheering one to Southwell. But about Younger it is not possible to be so certain. He changed his residence several times in the next few months and became restive to retire to his native county of Durham. It is most likely, since he was an aspirant to the Society, that he is the person addressed in Southwell's *Letter to a Wandering Priest*. Hazardous though the assertion may be, it seems true that Robert Southwell was a better judge of character than Robert Persons. Persons, contrary to what is generally thought, was extremely simple and forthright in his dealings with men. Being himself utterly single-minded, clear-headed and resolute, he was a splendid leader of strong men, but he had not much sympathetic contact with the tortuous struggles of a weak nature trying to be strong.

Poor Younger, having begun so well, had nothing to fall back on when he was finally captured—or gave himself up. He made a complete revelation of all the secrets that he knew, and promised to find out more if he were released. On being released, he played the spy for a little, and then retired to Douai where he became a disgruntled lecturer and a supporter of the secret faction of Dr. Gifford. But among much matter against Persons in his confessions, there was one true sentence which deserves to be noted in view of what follows:

> On their departure from Spain to England, Parsons did *not*★ counsel them to comfort Catholics in England with hope of help from Spain shortly, but persuaded them to be resolute and not to fear death, and to withstand the opinion of some priests in England, that it was lawful to resort to Church at the command of the Prince.

That, however, was in the following year. Meanwhile, the crucial instance of Persons being deceived has still to be related,

★ Italics added.

though he is perhaps hardly to be blamed for it, since he was up against the machiavellian brain of John Cecil, who for the past eighteen months had seemed to be his devoted helper in Spain.

Cecil and his friend Fixer, having separated themselves from their companions, had proceeded to the Low Countries where, as a security, they deposited their important papers and letters in packages addressed to the Lord Treasurer. Crossing over in May, they were arrested, as they had intended to be, and taken before Sir Robert Cecil. The first thing they did was to expose the manner in which their companions, and others from Rome and Rheims, had landed. It was the most shocking news that Sir Robert and his father had received for a long time. All the details that their namesake told them, and their horror at this new depth of Jesuit duplicity, were revealed in the rising accents of the *Proclamation* published five months later:

And furthermore, because it is certainly known and proved by common experience, upon the apprehension of sundry of the said traitorous persons sent into the Realm, that they do come into the same by secret Creeks and landing-places, disguised both in their names and persons. Some in apparell as Soldiers, Mariners, or Merchants, pretending that they have been heretofore taken prisoners and put into Galleys and delivered. Some come in as gentlemen with contrary names in comely apparell, as though they had travelled into Foreign Countries for knowledge: And so generally all, or the most part, as soon as they are crept in, are clothed like gentlemen in apparel, and many as gallants, yea in all colours, *and with feathers,** and suchlike disguising of themselves, and many of them in their behaviour as Ruffians, far off to be thought or suspected to be Friars, Priests, Jesuits, or Popish scholars. And of these many do attempt to resort into the Universities and Houses of Law from whence in former times they departed; many into services of Noble men, Ladies and gentlemen, with suchlike fraudulent devices to cover themselves from all apprehension or suspicion: and yet in process of time, they do at length so insinuate themselves to get themselves credit with hypocrisies, as they infect both the Masters and Families, and consequently adventure also yea secretly to use their offices of

* The italics are not in the original.

priesthood and reconcilements: Whereby all such as do retain them are worthy to be suspected, and may be charged by law to their great danger.

Cecil's and Fixer's informations were naturally followed by a furious search through London which pressed Southwell hard. But their further dealings with the Government threatened him even more directly. John Cecil was no common informer. He nursed big ideas of a 'National Catholic' sect on the Henrician model; he purveyed his information in order, as he explained to Sir Robert, 'to work the dissolution or diminution of the Seminaries' with Government assistance; and he gave a very falsely swollen list of priests who sympathized with the faction of Monsignor Owen Lewis and Doctors Bagshaw and Gifford.

Sir Robert seems to have listened coldly to this Seminary gossip; he passed them on to his father with the comment that they might prove useful if they avoided suspicion. Lord Burghley, wiser and kindlier, gave them a much more flattering attention. Fixer was kept in England to spread corruption there. But John Cecil was reserved for more ambitious intelligence work in Scotland. Meanwhile, continuing to write devoted letters to Persons, he betrayed the routes by which those letters were to go, and the names of two Catholic tradesmen whose shops were used as post-offices. But to follow their further careers would be a digression. What is of importance here is how they helped the Government to identify and incriminate Robert Southwell.

They identified him beyond doubt as 'Robertus' by producing a copy of his letter on the death of Christopher Bailey, quoted in the last chapter, which, they said, had done much harm to the English name in Spain. It is endorsed in the State Papers, 'Extract of a letter from Robert Southwell the Jesuit. . . . This relation was translated into Spanish and presented to all the grandees to make them conceive the number and persecution of the Catholics was great.'

On being asked for a description of him, they were unable after six years to say much more than that he was of medium height, with auburn hair; as to his beard, said Cecil, 'he went without beard when I knew him'.

On Southwell's side, his judgement of Cecil was more vivid. Before the winter of that year, a strong report from London went out to Cardinal Allen that Cecil and Fixer were false brethren; and Southwell in his answer to the *Proclamation* was almost certainly referring to the two priests who supplied information for it, when he wrote grimly: 'that the Penitents that made this Confession knew well enough that they were not with their right ghostly Fathers, or else they would never have committed such a Sacrilege in abusing the Sacrament with such untruths'.

But by far the most damaging weapon that they supplied against him was contained in a letter which they said Persons had written to them when they were at Lisbon. In this (according to their version of it) they were urged to get in touch with Ferdinando Lord Strange, the Earl of Derby's son, and find out if he were still disposed to claim the crown after Elizabeth's death. This highly delicate and dangerous commission was to be entrusted to no one except to Southwell or to Garnet, 'the principal priests in England'.

It is hard to decide whether this letter is authentic or not. (2) But much worse than the letter was the interpretation of it, which they said had been given to them verbally by Persons. They said that Lord Strange, if he accepted, was to start corresponding with the Cardinal, and was to be assured that his cousin, Sir William Stanley, would be ready to land an army in his support. Thus, what was only a tentative inquiry in the letter was altered into a definite plan of campaign which involved Garnet and Southwell in *political* High Treason.★

Fictitious as Lord Burghley and his son (almost certainly) knew this information to be, yet it did provide them with a *political* pretext for torturing Southwell to extremity. As long as

★ Lord Strange was the son of Henry the Seventh's great-granddaughter. Because of Henry the Eighth's will which excluded foreigners from the Succession, and because of Hertford's dubious marriage, the Stanley claim to succeed the Tudors was better than any other.

he was known for a holy and learned priest who did nothing but good, and as long as his works were read and enjoyed by influential persons, his reputation was a blinding exposure of the Topcliffian persecution against which the Cecils were already conscious of a growing volume of protest. But as soon as his reputation could be stained with an apparently genuine charge of political treason, this vague body of protest would draw in its horns and retire.

This is the climate of opinion which surrounds his activities in the next few months, between the priests' landing in April and the *Proclamation* of October.

A long report by a renegade priest (identity unknown) was headed by Robert's name, now published for the first time:

'Mr. Southwell, a Jesuit about London, apparelled in black rash'—a kind of velvet.

There followed a list of the new priests from Valladolid and Rheims with details of their disguises. There was news (but too late) of Henry Bell, a future Jesuit, 'lean-faced with auburn beard', who had been fitted up with 'a russet fustian doublet with silver lace, and leather hose'; and of one Mr. Marten 'a young man, somewhat high-coloured', garbed in 'a plain yellow fustian doublet, his netherstocks red and his hose the same'. There were lists also of the priest-shelterers: tradesmen, professional men, and several magnates, hitherto unsuspected, in the far suburbs, such as Sir Edward Stanley (Lord Strange's cousin) at Battersea. (3)

Among those arrested for harbouring priests were John and Margaret Gage. Both were condemned to death as felons under the Statute of 1585. Then two priests, veterans of great holiness, George Beesley and Monford Scott, fell into Topcliffe's hands. They were treated with the same barbarity as Edward Jones, and, on 1st July, hanged and quartered in the same place as he had been, that is to say, by the Conduit in Fleet Street, at the end of Shoe Lane, beside St. Bride's Church.

The object of these executions in unusual places was to strike terror into the surrounding inhabitants; and this triple repetition of the scene in Fleet Street was altogether exceptional. One cannot help wondering whether it was Sackville House, just opposite, which Topcliffe had in mind to overawe. It will be remembered that Lord Buckhurst's daughter-in-law was Margaret, the Earl of Arundel's half-sister and a close friend of the Countess.

Thomas Sackville, Lord Buckhurst, afterwards Earl of Dorset, is an enigmatic figure. A very considerable poet in his youth, and a pioneer of blank verse, he had said goodbye to all that and devoted himself to politics; but in spite of his high talents, it was only towards the end of his long life that he achieved more than a respectable mediocrity in that line. He was frequently to the fore as a persecutor, but nearly always in response to some stimulus from higher quarters. He had been a good friend to Robert Persons when Persons was planning his flight overseas for conscience sake; and for some reason the English Catholics continued perseveringly to repose a certain trust in him. (He is said on good authority to have been reconciled on his death-bed by Father Richard Blount.)

His daughter-in-law, whom he had protected in a somewhat tortuous fashion, fell sick and died in the August of that year; and 'On the last of September 1591', Robert Southwell, signing himself boldly 'R.S.', completed his funeral elegy of her under the title of *Triumphs over Death*. It is in a fine, clipped, philosophic style, unsympathetic to modern ears but suitable to a fashion that was changing from the manner of Lyly to that of Bacon. He wrote it for her brother Philip, but foresaw in the dedication that Philip would never see it in his imprisonment, and that it might serve to comfort others who knew her. It was published a year after his death with a dedication by John Trussell to the Sackvilles which took it for granted that the name of Southwell was well known in that family. (4) Thomas Sackville, Buckhurst's younger son, became a Catholic about 1590 and a great friend of the Society; so it is a reasonable conjecture that he was one of the 'many principal persons' whom Southwell is said by his earliest biographer to have converted.

The ambiguity in Buckhurst's career—Southwell's connections

with the family—the mutual esteem implied in the writing and publishing of the elegy—the repeated executions in front of the house: these things come together in an outline which suggests that Southwell found a precarious foothold for his work in Sack-ville House, with Buckhurst either turning a blind eye or pretending to know him only as a writer; and that Topcliffe came up against a barrier of influence he was still not powerful enough to break through. It was a precarious foothold, because as soon as another national crisis, real or imaginary, were to blow up—like the Babington Plot or the Armada—at once all the defences would be down, and no one would be more thorough than Buckhurst in purging his household.

But in the late summer of 1591 there were other signs that Topcliffe had come up against a temporary check. His recent boastings about the tortures he used had caused murmurs at Court. It was among the Essex Circle, apparently, that 'Topcliffian' was first used as a term of opprobrium; although Essex himself was supposed to favour the Puritans, among his intimate friends were Sir Christopher Blount and the young Earl of Southampton, both by way of being Catholics, and also Charles Blount, afterwards Lord Mountjoy, whose regard for Southwell will appear in a later chapter. It was at this time that Topcliffe was obliged by public opinion to confine his practices to his own house—a hypocritical but significant restriction.

Another check occurred when John and Margaret Gage with their hands bound were being taken in the cart to execution. (5) As they reached the scaffold, a reprieve for both arrived from the Queen, through the influence of Lord Howard of Effingham. In this may be traced a special plea by the Countess of Arundel to her kinsman on behalf of Robert's cousins; it is also worth remembering that his other cousin and namesake was Howard's son-in-law. Margaret's youngest brother, who describes the incident, attributed it to cupidity on the part of the old Admiral, keeping them alive so as to enjoy their estate which would be forfeited by death. This may well be so; but it is not the only instance of Howard exerting himself on behalf of Papists. (6)

What had probably caused a slight pro-Catholic reaction was the 'Hackett conspiracy' which caused a great stir in London on 19th July 1591. Two respectable Puritans, Coppinger and Arthington, had the misfortune to go off their heads. Styling themselves respectively Prophet of Mercy and Prophet of Judgement, they proclaimed that only those whom they signed on the forehead would be saved. Before a great concourse in Cheapside, they produced a third deranged minister called Hackett whom they crowned King as 'Jesus Christ', and in whose name they pronounced the damnation of the Archbishop of Canterbury and the deposition of the Queen. The affair was hushed up as much as possible, and Hackett was made its sole scapegoat. 'The death of one man', wrote Southwell in his *Supplication* four months later,

> shut up in silent oblivion that open offer to an uproar, and most blasphemous impiety against God and your Majesty, though it be generally known that there were more favourers and abettors of that party than could ever be touched by Babington's offence.*

Nevertheless the affair had a modicum of the same effect as the Babington Plot on the Puritan fortunes; and it drew attention temporarily away from the Catholics. Indeed, for the first time since 1585, they were conscious of a swing-back of public opinion in their favour. Revulsion from Puritanism still led straight either to Rome or to atheism, because Hooker's *Via Media* was not yet in working order; and Bancroft, the real engineer of the Established Church, had still to establish *himself* first, by winning over the Cecils to his side. Meanwhile, as the number of Seminary priests grew, and the core of their organization held firm, so did the conversions increase and multiply by leaps and bounds. The Topcliffian war of extermination was being held up by the connivance of anti-Puritan magistrates with what went on in the districts around them and even in their own households. It was this last menace which the Queen's Government—that is, the

---

* It may be regretted that Southwell never made contact with that very appealing Puritan personality, John Penry, a martyr to his beliefs in 1593. As it was, the only side of the movement that he saw was its hideous anti-Popery, its crafty backing in high places, and its sporadic lunacy.

Cecils—were urgently preparing to counter by the new *Proclamation*: a document whose chief claim to distinction has been that it drew from Robert Southwell, like a flash of fire, his fighting answer, *An Humble Supplication to Her Majesty*.

In this biography there has always been a danger of wresting the facts by concentrating all the attention on one man. Yet it does seem true that Robert Southwell epitomized all that the Government was most afraid of and determined to crush. He was the living embodiment of that piety and culture which the Church of England longed to possess, but which in his case led inflexibly to Rome.

It is fascinating to reflect that during these hectic and harried months he was not only writing the *Triumphs over Death*, but was quietly putting the finishing touches to his new preface to *Mary Magdalen's Funeral Tears* which was due for publication in November; and that in this preface, without a trace of sectarian bitterness, he appealed to men of letters to enlist their talents on the side of moral beauty and religious truth. The effect of his appeal, especially upon the 'University Wits'—as the bohemian intellectuals of the South Bank were called—will be seen in a later chapter. It must be largely a matter of inference; yet the fact that he had publishers anxious for his work shows that he had already a footing in this literary world. His choice was Gabriel Cawood, probably a secret Catholic (his father had been publisher to Queen Mary); and to him he seems to have given the copyright of his prose (except for the private pieces) and of his verse.

It may be wondered whether he felt any of the thrill of the author on seeing his work actually going into the press; and the answer, however regretfully, must be 'No!' The publishers' offices around St. Paul's were in a locality that allowed no time for complacency; and the South Bank for him held other memories. Two more priests had just been taken. One of them, thrust into Newgate with seven malefactors, converted six of them before they were all taken out to die. The other priest, caught in September reconciling a townsman who dwelt in Paul's Churchyard, was Thomas Pormort. The thought of this sensitive, questing spirit lying at Topcliffe's mercy was hard to bear.

No, what weighed on Southwell next to his heart this autumn was the burden of his own relative security, precarious though it was. Five years had passed since he first stood on the South Bank and looked up at the towering Gatehouse of London Bridge with its circle of pikes and heads. To this autumn may be assigned a little incident recorded afterwards by Garnet:

A certain nobleman has told me that when he was going for a walk with Father Robert by London Bridge, he saw his face light up with an extraordinary gaiety. He was looking up at the Martyrs' heads and he said 'Oh, my Lord, if God grants it, you will see *my* head sometime on one of those'. (7)

At the hinge of the year, through the oak-forests still in leaf, Robert Southwell and John Gerard rode together into Warwickshire. A much larger company than usual was converging from different parts of England on Baddesley Clinton: eleven priests, all told, each in charge of a district, and several laymen. The numbers showed that Garnet's plans, outlined on the eve of the Armada, had succeeded beyond expectation. Yet once more, as on the eve of the Armada, there were bloodthirsty rumours of a foreign invasion and foreign spies, and of a fresh Proclamation to deal with them. No doubt the implications of this threat formed part of the agenda for the meeting.

It was a most hazardous thing to gather in such large numbers; but, after a preliminary alarm, Garnet had decided that, if a raid were being organized, they would get warning in time. 'We ought not to meet all at the same time', he told them, 'now that our numbers are growing every day. But we are gathered for God's glory. Until we have renewed our vows', he continued, with that calm accuracy that had won him the trust and veneration of them all, 'the responsibility is mine. After that, it is yours.'

The meeting began on 14th October, and was due to end with the renewal of their vows on the 18th, the Feast of St. Luke the Evangelist whom they had taken as their patron.*

It was a day charged with the tenderest recollections for Robert

* This was the last meeting of the kind that was held until February 1593.

Southwell: the anniversary of his entry into the Society and of his own vow-day on which he had written: 'Unto the Crucified my soul is spouse.' He was just thirty years old, and it was to be the last time he would eat and talk and pray together with his brothers in religion whom he loved so strongly.

Not a breath of trouble disturbed their five days. But at dinner on the 18th Father Garnet smilingly withdrew his protection. 'At table on the feast of St. Luke', he wrote in a letter afterwards, 'I know not what inspiration made me address them as follows: saying that, though up to now I had taken on myself all responsibility, I was no longer willing to guarantee them their safety, when dinner was over.' Four priests accordingly rode off, thus considerably diminishing the congestion and the danger.

Next morning at five o'clock, when the priests were at Mass or at prayer, and the servants were laying out their things for departure, inexplicably and without warning, the avenues round the house were blocked, the great door swung open, and the pursuivants were banging at the entries within the courtyard. Servants with pitchforks rushed up and drove them back. Word ran through the house; and the occupants, men and women, moved to action stations and went through their drill. Gerard gives this description:

Father Southwell was beginning Mass and the rest were at prayer, when suddenly I heard a great uproar outside the main door. Then I heard a voice shouting and swearing at a servant who was refusing them entrance. . . . Father Southwell heard the din. He guessed what it was all about, and slipped off his vestments and stripped the altar bare. While he was doing this, we laid hold of all our personal belongings: nothing was left to betray the presence of a priest. . . . Some of us went and turned the beds and put the cold side up to delude anyone who put his hand in to feel them. Outside, the ruffians were bawling and yelling, but the servants held the door fast. They said the mistress of the house, a widow, was not yet up, but was coming down at once to answer them. This gave us enough time to stow ourselves and all our belongings into a very cleverly built sort of cave.

Underneath the west wing ran a long tunnel intended to convey sewage into the moat. But Nicholas Owen had diverted the sewage by building a *garde-robe* tower projecting on to the moat; and had fitted up the tunnel so that it could be reached by a shaft from the room used as a sacristy; exit to the moat was blocked as tightly as possible by a slab fixed into vertical grooves. (8)

The men slid down the shaft in quick succession into the dank depths and caught the things that the women threw after them. Garnet says:

Doors were bolted, everyone warned, books collected, pictures, Rosaries, chalices, vestments, and all other signs of our religion were thrown into the culvert, together with the men. The mistress of the house [poor Eleanor] was stowed away in a separate hiding-place of her own, both to prevent her being torn away from her children and carried off to prison, and also because she is rather timid and finds it difficult to deal with the threats and evil looks of the searchers. On this occasion, as often before, when this same pursuivant paid us a visit, her younger sister posed as the mistress of the house. . . .

Then they set about searching the house. Everything was turned upside down; everything was closely examined—storerooms, chests, and even the very beds were carefully ransacked, on the off chance of finding Rosaries or pictures or books or *Agnus Dei* hidden in them. I have no idea with what patience Ladies in Italy would put up with this!

Garnet adds that by a strange oversight they did not search the stables, where they would have found an alarming number of horses saddled for the road. He described Anne Vaux's behaviour: 'Though she has all a maiden's modesty and even shyness, yet in God's cause, and in the protection of his servants, *virgo* becomes *virago* . . .'

After several hours of contest, Anne invited the exhausted pursuivants to breakfast. After breakfast and a final fruitless search, they exacted a bribe and departed. ' When they had done', concludes Gerard,

. . . and gone a good way, so that there was no danger of their turning back suddenly, as they sometimes do, the lady came and called us out of our den, not one but several Daniels. The hiding-place was below ground level; the floor was covered with water and I was standing with my feet in it all the time. Father Garnet was there, also Father Southwell and Father Oldcorne (three future martyrs), Father Stanney and myself, two secular priests and two or three laymen.

So we were all saved that day. The next day Father Southwell and I rode off, as we had come, in company.

Garnet had described it as 'a particularly rigorous search'. But when Robert parted from John Gerard and approached the capital once more, he may have sighed with some envy for the hierarchic solidity of the shires.

He had not been back long before this was exemplified. His old friend, Swithin Wells, played his last round with death. On 7th November Mass was being said at his house in Holborn when the door was violently broken in. A layman, Brian Lacey, tried to stop the leading pursuivant from desecrating the priest at the altar (it was Polydore Plasden, one of Southwell's students from Rome). The pursuivant brandished his sword. In the scuffle that followed he was thrown from the top of the stairs to the bottom, and sustained a bloody coxcomb. The equivalent of 'Now you've done it!' must have dropped from the lips of the other catch-polls, for their leader was none other than Topcliffe himself. Topcliffe took personal charge of the torture, trial and executions that followed—gaoler, judge and hangman in one. ('Brian Lacey', the Martyrs Catalogue reads, 'pitifully tortured in Bridewell.') Swithin Wells had not been at his house, but when he heard that his wife had been carried off for sentence, he went to the magistrates and took full responsibility, only regretting that he had missed the Mass.

On his way to the scaffold he called to a friend in the crowd, 'Farewell, dear friend, farewell all hawking and hunting and old pastimes. I am going a better way.' To Topcliffe's railing on the scaffold he replied, 'Dispatch, Mr. Topcliffe, dispatch: are you not ashamed to keep an old man standing in his shirt here in the cold?' To the usual taunt about 'roaring hellish Bulls', he made the rather plebeian but not inapt reply that a roaring bull was better than a diseased cow. But at once he apologized for that, and anxious that all should end in charity, as they put the rope on him, he said: 'I pray God for you, Mr. Topcliffe: may he make of you, a Saul, a Paul.' A letter of his written in prison shows that beneath his jovial exterior lay a mystical love of Christ Crucified.

Seven persons altogether, three priests and four laymen, suffered on that one day, some at Holborn, opposite Gray's Inn, and the rest at Tyburn.

They had been arrested on 7th November, arraigned on 4th December, and executed on the 10th. Between the arrest and the arraignment, on 20th November, appeared the great *Proclamation*. (9)

The sequence of dates is important because it shows that almost as soon as a copy was available Southwell began his famous answer, and that by 10th December, writing with tremendous drive, he had nearly finished it. It began: 'Most mighty and most merciful, most feared and best beloved Princess . . .'

CHAPTER SEVENTEEN

'Best Beloved Princess'

In the summer just past, when the searching had been at its height around Fleet Street and Holborn, Southwell and his fellow-priests had a secret hiding-place in quite a different district. In June or July, Garnet had hired a little holiday cottage in the ground north of the City—either in Moorfields or beyond Houndsditch, where, as Stow lamented, 'there is now made a continual building throughout of garden houses and small cottages: and the fields on either side be turned into garden plots, teynter yards, bowling alleys, and such like . . .'

Garnet in a later letter described the nature and function of this special hiding-place, and the rules that governed it:

> Most of the London townsfolk have little gardens outside the City Walls and many have built cottages there, where they betake themselves to enjoy a sweeter air. At quite a low price we hired one of these small gardens, very well placed for our purposes, and in it a tiny cottage with a kitchen, a dining-room, and a third room set apart for a chapel and for other special purposes. It was at the disposal of our friends who were obliged to visit the City or to reside there permanently. It was generally believed to be untenanted, so it was free from molesting officials who came round, as they regularly do, to inquire whether all had been to the heretics church. We had a rule that no one must speak except in a very low voice, so as not to be heard in the street nearby, and a fire was never to be lit there, even in the depth of winter, but all provisions had to be cooked at night and eaten cold the next day. The house was reserved, for the following occasions of special need: when there was an unusual reign of terror in the City; when there was writing to be

done of great importance; when a special meeting had to be called with secular priests or laymen. It proved a help to many in their necessities. (1)

The house, however, as he goes on to relate, was discovered in the spring of 1592; so that the only winter it was used in was this one. Hence his clause: '*When there was writing to be done of great importance . . .*' seems to have a special reference to the writing of Southwell's *Humble Supplication*.

The 'military' (so to call it) understanding between Garnet and Southwell was that Garnet gave him general directions what to do, and left him complete liberty as to how he did it. Southwell was sometimes distressed by this liberty, as Garnet related after his death:

He was so strict in his obedience that secular priests, as they told me have found him actually in tears, because (he said) I had left every-- thing to his own choice, and he was afraid that this must be the result of his spoiled and froward humour. But in truth it was just the opposite. For he was so gifted by the Lord with prudence that he managed everything well, and there was no need of anyone else's guidance or inspiration. And so for all those years, in times of the greatest difficulty, we lived together in such harmony of mind that not the slightest shadow ever fell between us. And to *his* virtue I declare that this was due. (2)

It is a fair conclusion from this that Garnet and Southwell had agreed, at the October meeting, what line to adopt in the con- tingency that might arise; and that with the assurance of Garnet's approval, Southwell betook himself to the little garden-house in the winter, with a copy of the *Proclamation*, and settled down to answer it.

It was a shock to discover that a solemn declaration by the Queen in Council was written in the language of a less reputable pamphlet. Although its occasion appeared to be the landing of a Spanish Army in France to help the Catholics against the Hugue- nots, its bulk was a diatribe against priests and Jesuits. It was a surprise for one who had heard the cheers over the prostrate

R

Armada, and seen the great counter-expedition to Portugal, to learn that the King of Spain and his 'Milanese vassal' (the Pope) were coming again with larger forces than before—at the request of the two traitors Allen and Persons. It was a confirmation of his worst fears to read, in words that supported Topcliffe up to the hilt, that the forerunners of this invasion were the seminary priests, 'a multitude of dissolute young men who have, partly for lack of living, partly for crimes committed, become Fugitives Rebels, and Traitors . . .'

Beneath the abuse, the note of panic was discernible; and Southwell at once knew the reason why. The persecution had not been a notable success materially; and morally it had been a complete failure. The national conscience, or what was left of it, had been scraped and gored. Independent men and women were asking themselves: 'If every dog in office has such absolute power to lie and rob and murder, where will this persecution end?' Southwell picked on this at once, assuming as a forensic device, after a suitable flourish to the Queen, that some underling had got out of hand and abused her authority:

> We verily presume that none of your Majesty's honourable Council would either show so little acquaintance with the Prince's style as to deliver in your name a discourse so full farced with contumelious terms as better suited a clamorous tongue than your Highness's pen; or be so slightly affected to the regard of your honour as to defile it with the touch of so many false assertions. Yet all men justly marvel that any Inditor durst adventure to disgorge private ill-will rather than to observe decency in so public a thing. Yea, they lament their own case when these abuses make uncertain what to credit in serious points importing their Country's and their own safeties, when they see in this (which seemeth to be but a prologue to future tragedies) the strongest foundations to human belief applied to all men's minds to support mere improbabilities.

and he added boldly, that

> the injury offered to your Majesty, and nearly all concerning your Realm, might in equity challenge all men's pens to warn you of so perilous courses. . . .

The 'perilous courses' he feared seem to have been: *both* the wresting of the royal prerogative to violation of the natural law, *and* the pandering to what was already coming to be known as the *mobile vulgus*—later anglicized to 'mobile' (pronounced 'mobble') or 'mob'.★

On this latter menace in the hands of influential paymasters he has a passage which is the more interesting in that its information comes straight off the London streets where he had spent the greater part of the last five years:

Our slanders are common work for idle presses; and our credits are daily sold at the Stationers' stalls, every Libeller repairing his wants with impairing our honours, being sure that when all other matters fail any Pamphlet against us shall be welcomed with *Seen and allowed.* . . . If any displeasing accident fall out, whereof the Authors are either unknown or ashamed, Catholics are made common fathers of such infamous orphans, as though none were so fit sluices as they to let out of every man's sink these unsavoury reproaches. Not so much but the Casual Fires that sometimes happen in London†—the late uproars between the gentlemen and the apprentices were laid to our charge, though the occasioners of both were so well known that the report against us could not but issue from an undeserved malice. Yea, even *Hackett*, a man so far from our faith as infidelity itself, and a little before so notorious a Puritan that he was of chief reckoning among them, when his blasphemies grew so great, and his Articles so impious, that they made all Christian ears to glow and his adherents to blush, then was he posted over to us for a Papist, and so named to the vulgar sort: so common a practise it is to bestow upon us the infamies of all offenders.

The *Proclamation* was framed deliberately to make this state of things incredibly worse. They were 'perilous courses' indeed on the long view which would see in the space of a century

---

★ cf. Watson: *Decachordon*, 1602, and perhaps also, with a double meaning, Shakespeare in *Hamlet*: 'the mobled Queen'. By the *mobile vulgus* was not meant the people at large, but shiftless gangs of ne'er-do-wells at the service of influential paymasters.

†Southwell gave an instance of one such false alarm in his letter of 7th September 1588.

the overthrow of the monarchy and the apotheosis of Titus Oates.

But Southwell did not perhaps appreciate, could hardly be expected to, that the Queen's immediate policy was to shatter both Puritans and Catholics, and to shepherd the middle sort into the Church of England. The *Proclamation* was not so easy to answer as his opening flourish suggested.

Though its dominant note appeared to be panic-stricken mendacity, it was panic with a purpose. The 'Big Lie' for the apathetic majority, especially in the thickly-populated South-east, was based on a sure and cynical estimate of their lower instincts: their readiness to buy a reputation for loyalty at the easy price of cruelty to a defenceless foe; while for the very considerable minority (a third of the nation, in Southwell's estimate) that was still deeply attached to the old religion, but not deeply enough to be starved or disembowelled for it, there was the cold threat of a felon's death brought right inside their front door.

The sting in the tail of the *Proclamation* was the appointment of 'Commissioners' with absolute power to overhaul the households of all 'Noblemen, gentlemen, Lords, Ladies, Master or Mistress or owner whatsoever . . . yea, the very officers of our own household . . .' 'Wherein we are resolutely determined to suffer no favour to be used for any respect of persons, qualities or degrees, nor shall allow or suffer to be allowed any excuse of negligence for not detection, or for not due examination of the qualities of such dangerous persons according to the order hereafore prescribed.'

The voice which whined through the main part of the *Proclamation* might well be the voice of Burghley in sheep's clothing, but the hand which devised and signed the conclusion was undoubtedly the hand of Elizabeth giving complete support to Topcliffe. This was the fact that Southwell had to face before he began his answer, and the decision he had to make was whether to go on advising loyalty to such a Queen. Obviously if the answer were 'No', there was nothing to be done except keep silence; so in effect the decision was whether the *Supplication* was

worth writing at all. Three motives for the answer 'Yes' can
be discerned running through his tract.

The first was that the *Proclamation* had once more brought
up the 'Bloody Question' as a proof that Catholics suffered for
their politics, not their religion; so he wanted once more, as at
the time of the Armada, to comfort the recusants with the certainty that religion only was the cause at stake and that they could
fling back the odious epithet of 'traitor' which they hated worse
than death—'An infamed life being to free minds more irksome
than an innocent death, we had rather put our uttermost hazards
to your Highness's Clemency, than seem with our silence to give
credit to our obloquies: to which if we do not, it may be imagined
that we cannot answer.'

Moreover, the acknowledgement of the Queen's temporal
supremacy gave him a free field to expose the intrinsic viciousness
of the 1585 Statute. He could show that it was the priesthood
only—and therefore the Holy Mass, England's most precious
heirloom—that was the object of this wicked law; for there was
no difference between the seminary priest and the priest of any
Christian age, no additional oath or promise was made at ordination, only the priestly Vow of Chastity—'a thing', he added,
with solemn courtesy, 'a thing rather pleasing than offensive to a
virtuous Queen, who hath for herself made choice of a single
life'. He could quote the Lord Chief Justice at the recent trial of
the priests with Swithin Wells: 'that though many things had
been urged, yet he was to pronounce sentence of death against
them only upon that Statute.' And in a brilliant scene he could
confront Elizabeth with all the Kings and Statesmen of England
rising from their graves and finding themselves liable to the same
penalties of felony for the Cathedrals they had built and the
Masses they had endowed—'if it should please God to allot the
day of General Resurrection in your Majesty's time, a thing not
so impossible as uncertain . . .'

This is Southwell in his very happiest vein, and there is the same
dancing blade in his defence of the Seminary priests—a Clergy
that might have put England at the top of the world for piety and

Christian culture—and in his reply to the grotesque charge in the *Proclamation* of 'baseness of birth', which he tosses back to the Cecils with the ease of a true-born gentleman:

And for the *baseness of their birth* (which among other like points is interlaced with as impertinent as scornful a parenthesis, and a fitter note for this penner's than your Majesty's observation) I mean not to dwell long upon it; for the thing neither importeth any offence to God, nor crime against your Majesty, nor greatly abaseth them whom excellent virtues (the only true measures of worthiness) have ennobled. Yet this without disparagement to any may truly be avowed, that the Cardinal's Grace is of as good and ancient a house, and every way as worshipfully allied, as some of the highest Councillors were in their meaner fortunes, till your Majesty's favour and their rare abilities made them steps to climb to their present honours. . . . As for other Priests, how many of them are Knights' and Esquires' sons, and otherwise allied both to worshipful and noble houses, and heirs to fair revenues, let their own friends and parents dispersed through the whole Realm bear witness! This only we may say in answer of our objected *baseness*: that in the small number of the Catholic Priests of our Nation (which reacheth not to the tenth of the Protestant Ministry), there are very near as many, yea happily more gentlemen, than in all the other Clergy of the whole Realm.

But his next motive for insisting on due obedience was a more difficult one to handle. It was a plea for toleration; and its argument was that Catholics by training and tradition were more reliable defenders of the monarchy and of law and order than the powerful forces that were hoping to exploit the Puritan opposition. The plea had in mind not only the large numbers of 'schismatics' (Catholics who put the State before the Church when the test came), but certain influential persons—such as, perhaps, Lord Howard of Effingham and Lord Buckhurst—who believed that the followers of the Pope were better to come to terms with than the followers of Calvin.

All the middle part of the *Supplication*, pages 15 to 27,* seems

* In the recent edition by R. C. Bald: Cambridge University Press.

designed for this purpose, and it seems to be a part on its own, since it is inserted between sections seven and eight of the whole, and begins with numbered sections of its own, one, two, etc. On page sixteen there is a claim which was to be amply justified in the reign of Charles I:

> It is a point of the Catholic Faith (defended by us against the Sectaries of these days) that subjects are bound in conscience, under pain of forfeiting their right in heaven and incurring the guilt of eternal torments, to obey the just laws of their Princes; which both the Protestants and Puritans deny with their Father Mr. Calvin. And therefore if we were not pressed to that which by the general verdict of all ages was judged a breach of the Law of God, we should never give your Majesty the least cause of displeasure.

And on page twenty-seven there is a further warning against certain unnamed forces which can cause the popular tides to swell and roar suddenly, and as suddenly to disappear:

> If, being so freely permitted to use their consciences to themselves, and to enjoy their honours, offices and favours in the Commonwealth without any taste of scourges, they notwithstanding sparkle out such tokens of a concealed flame, it cannot but be seen and known how much more cause there is to look into their actions, and to fear their attempts, than to wreak such anger upon us that were never chargeable with so huge enormities.

He makes it clear that he is not advocating the persecution of any Sect ('being too well acquainted with the smart of our own punishments to wish any Christian to be partakers of our pains'), but only emphasizing by contrast the good dispositions of the Catholic body.* He seems to be placing its hopes (though 'hopes' is too strong a word) in that moderate conservative trend which was enamoured neither of the Cecilian dictatorship, nor of its new rival, the young Essex, who was beginning to attract to himself adventurous and discontented spirits among both Catholics and Puritans. It is interesting to note that the attitude adum-

---

* It is a point overlooked by historians of this reign that the Church, although rejecting 'toleration' as an *ideal*, was prepared to accept or concede it on a contractual basis.

brated by Southwell was the one steadily maintained by Garnet as the crisis of 1600 drew nearer, and it was the attitude approved and recommended by Father Persons. Though the Jesuits were bound by personal ties to several of Essex's Catholic adherents, they kept the main Catholic body clear of all attempts to involve it in that ill-fated rising.

Although these events lay far beyond Southwell's view, he was consciously appealing to moderate and well-informed non-Catholic opinion when he devoted his middle pages (seventeen to twenty-five in the recent edition) to a detailed exposure of the myth that the Catholic body was responsible for plots against the Queen's life. His most valuable and exciting—though necessarily rather breathless—account of the Babington Plot cannot be discussed here, except to say that it is a serious reproach to Dr. Conyers Reade's wonted impartiality that he should have dismissed it in a single line as unworthy of attention.

Southwell was *involved* in the Babington Plot; he was intimately connected with friends and relatives of the duped conspirators; he believed initially the worst of them; and then by patient study and inquiry he came round to a completely different verdict as to who were the real conspirators. Moreover, he was acquainted, indirectly at least, with a vital source of information which has been closed ever since: that is to say, the papers of the renegade Gilbert Gifford, who had been arrested in a Paris brothel just after his counterfeit letter against Cardinal Allen in 1587. A *prima facie* notion of Southwell's value can be had by carefully comparing his account, first with Reade's (which is notably fair), and then with that of any previous academic English historian; there is no question but that Reade's is far nearer to Southwell's than to his own predecessors. The main difference is that Southwell proves his point a good deal more convincingly than Reade. Reade judges Mary by the iniquitous standards of her trial, and pronounces her 'Guilty!'—because she was not allowed the means to prove herself not guilty; but to Walsingham he gives all the benefits of a modern court of law—and gets him off with a bare 'Not Proven!', on the strength of the verdict already presumed against Mary: a doubtful proceeding both in logic and in justice. Southwell, on the other hand, does not allow his devotion to Mary ('your Majesty's more infamed than faulty sister'), nor any hostility to Sir Francis (to whom he refers very pleasantly throughout) to sway him from his main point, which is that the Catholic body, and particularly the Jesuits and Allen's seminary priests, had nothing whatsoever to do with the conspiracy. He proves this triumphantly, and by so doing he exposes the foundation for the whole edifice of lies which was being built up, and which has continued to stand in violation of the known truth, right up to our own day.

It is a fairly safe guess that his exposure of the Babington Plot was the item in his *Supplication* which most exacerbated the Government against him. It was this which Topcliffe stressed particularly in a description of a copy of it captured from a priest in prison in 1596: 'a most traitorous written book, dedicated to the Queen, (about) her Government's proceeding in justice against Papists by laws, against the Scottish Queen, against Babington and Bullerd, etc.' (3)

His third motive for dedicating his answer with all devotion to the Queen was at once the most obvious and the most delicate of the three. He really believed that there was a chance of moving her. He must have known that it was a very slender chance, since it was by now notorious that Topcliffe was her private employee. But, as long as the chance existed, it was his duty as a priest to try it; for—

> if our due care of our Country be such, that to rear the least fallen soul among your Majesty's subjects from a fatal lapse, we are contented to pay our lives for the ransom: how much better should we think them bestowed, if so high a pennyworth as your gracious self, or the whole Realm, might be the gain of our dear purchase?

So much was obvious, and, unconsciously it winged his words to her with a peculiar and almost friendly charm.

But from a controversial point of view, his task was an extremely difficult one, because only by unspoken implications could he allow his real conviction to appear: that the Queen having been horribly misled from the start, the only remedy was an abrupt change of counsellors and an honourable peace with Spain. These were the points that Father Persons was to make more bluntly in his widely-read answer to the *Proclamation* in the following year. (4) Like Southwell, Persons believed that Elizabeth's persecution of the Catholics was dictated by fear, not by malevolence. But he was also convinced that the only way to overcome that fear was by a stronger fear: by the conviction that toleration for the Catholics was a less dangerous alternative for the monarchy than a long and crippling war with Spain. (5)

The task Southwell had set himself was to remove the fear by proofs of loyalty. But he found himself returning always by implication to the same conclusion as Persons: 'Change your counsellors, and make peace with Spain.' For he was not in the least inclined to make apologies for the leaders whom he so revered.

His reply was a splendid, and by no means exaggerated, eulogy of the Cardinal (pages 5–6), the purport of which was that if the Government had forced a breach between such a man and his Queen, it was the Queen that had been put in the wrong box, not the Cardinal; and the calumnies against him which the Government had had to resort to in this *Proclamation* were sufficient proof of that. The unspoken conclusion was obvious: 'Change your government!'

His defence of Persons came mostly at the end of the *Supplication* (pages 36–9). Persons' credit with the King of Spain, he says, so far from needing an apology, was a matter for the Queen to congratulate herself upon, since it had been used tirelessly for the benefit of his countrymen, her subjects. The ancient friendship between Spain and England had been broken by aggression on England's part, and there was no knowing how a protracted struggle between two such mighty monarchs would end—

Yet this without presumption may be truly said, that if ever he should prevail in that designment (as the casualties of war are most uncertain to us, and only overruled by God) Father Persons assisted with Cardinal Allen's authority hath done that in our Country's behalf, for which his most bitter enemies, and generally all your Majesty's subjects, shall have cause to thank him for his serviceable endeavours; so hath he inclined fury to clemency, and rage to compassion.

It was an appeal to the older tradition of patriotism, vested in the concord of Europe, not in naked national greed.

Yet even as he wrote, he was conscious of a wall of misunderstanding that shut him out, the wall of the new National State, within which absolute values lost their nature and became instruments of policy. It was the Copernican revolution reversed in the order of morality; heavenly virtues were made the satellites of an earthly throne; truth was 'what the Government says' and goodness was 'what the Government does'. What hope was there of proving loyalty in such a context, when the most solemn proof of all had been tried repeatedly and had failed?—

since we daily in our lives, and always at our executions, unfeignedly pray for your Majesty: since at our deaths we all protest upon our souls our clearness from treason, and our loyal and dutiful minds, subscribing our protestations with our dearest blood . . .

In the last pages of his *Supplication* (40–5) he practically flung aside the pretence of 'supplication'; his voice came as it were from the bowels of a tortured people, and mingled with the blood of innocents crying to the throne of heaven, not of earth, for vengeance. His description of the loathsome physical tortures practised to extort evidence makes truly terrible reading. But since these pages are already unavoidably filled with that sort of thing, and since his *Supplication* can now be read in a modern edition, they may be taken for granted. What is more worth noting is his account of the *harrying* process that stopped short of death. The priests and recusants who endured extremest agonies were men who had counted the cost and relied on supernatural strength to sustain them. But what oppressed him was the multitude of plain folk, husbandmen, farmers, and simple squires, who were not cut out for martyrdom and were not given the chance of it. Burghley's policy of tearing these people from the millenary roots of their religion by a relentless pressure of lawless brutality and humiliation was more horrible to his mind's eye than the butcheries at Tyburn. As one generation followed another, these people, whose sturdy piety had always been reckoned the backbone of the nation, would either die out altogether, or would turn from all religion in cynical disgust. And this was the policy which had just been confirmed by the Queen's hand in a gruesome mockery of truth as 'agreeable to the most ancient laws and usages of our Realm'.

In his final petition, with a resignation more piercing than any insult, he shut his eyes to any less favourable picture of Elizabeth, and forcing himself to see instead *Gloriana*, the ideal Queen, he begged briefly that if the tortures she had ordered were to continue, she might at least deign to acknowledge their existence and their true cause:

> We presume that your Majesty seldom or never heareth the truth of our persecutions, your lenity and tenderness being known to be so professed an enemy to these cruelties that you would never permit their continuance, if they were expressed to your Highness as they are practised upon us. Yet, since we can bring the ruin of our houses, the consumption of our goods, the poverty of our estates, and the weeping eyes of our desolate families for the palpable witnesses of the truth of these complaints, let us not be so far exiled out of the limits of all compassion, as besides all other evils, to have it confirmed under your Majesty's hand, *that we suffer no punishments for Religion*—suffering in proof all punishments for nothing else.

It was mid-December when he finished writing, having averaged a thousand words a day, in that little house where, in Garnet's words, 'a fire was not allowed, and all food had to be cooked at night and eaten cold the next day'. But Garnet was not writing here with his usual clarity; for if the food was cooked at night, presumably a fire was lit at night; and this is confirmed by his further description of the mysterious 'third room' when it was

searched by Justice Young in the ensuing spring. It was an underground cellar where evidently Nicholas Owen had been at work,
for it contained a hiding-place large enough to hold six or seven
persons, where all the secret Jesuit writings were stored. But all
that Mr. Young found was a little heap of coals, some kindling-
wood, and a barrel of ale. The ale seems to have been of good
quality, for Mr. Young, having taken a copious draught of it in
the way of duty, went off in quite a cheerful temper, though his
search had been unsuccessful. It also appears that there was a
gardener who came to work there occasionally and was on good
terms with the neighbouring squatters; he was in reality a Jesuit
lay-brother who ministered to the needs of whoever happened
to be hiding in the house.

So the setting in which Southwell signed what was virtually
his own death-warrant was a more homely one than appeared
from the outside. There may have been a little coal fire—with a
concealed vent—for him to flex his hands at when he could write
no more, and a little burnt sack to warm his vitals at night.

The last person who had presented a Catholic petition to the
Queen had been his kinsman, Richard Shelley, in 1585. It had
been a protestation by representative Catholics of their innocence
of conspiracy and their complete loyalty. But the only answer
had been to throw Shelley into prison, where he rotted to death
without trial. Such a fate left no doubt as to what would happen
to the author of this so much more mettlesome protest. He took
up his pen to add a last paragraph which would draw the responsibility for it upon no one but himself:

We are forced to divulge our petitions, and by many mouths to open
unto your Highness our humble suits. For neither daring ourselves
to present them in person, being terrified with the precedent of his
imprisonment that last attempted it, nor having the favour of any
such Patron as would be willing to make himself Mediator to your
Majesty, we are forced to commit it to the multitude, hoping that
among so many as shall peruse this short and true relation of our
troubles, God will touch some merciful heart to let your Highness
understand the extremity of them . . .

But from this it is clear that in fact he had the help of many in 'divulging'—that is, in broadcasting it among the general public. One of the surviving transcripts is dated 'December 14', and another 'This last of December'. Probably the intervening period was spent with his friends and faithful lay-helpers in revising details, making many copies, arranging for simultaneous distribution at strategic points (6)—but breaking off to keep the Feast of Christmas with that peace of soul and detachment from earthly cares that was the secret of their moral victory:

> If you would foil your foes with joy,
> Then flit not from this Heavenly Boy.

Some time in January the distribution should have taken place. But there is no means of telling how successful it was, whether it reached the Queen, or what was its general effect. What may possibly be the earliest reference to it comes in a letter from Francis Bacon to his brother Anthony, the same Anthony who had secured a copy of Southwell's poem on Mary Queen of Scots.

> Good Brother—I send to you the *Supplication* which Mr. Topcliffe lent me. It is curiously written, and worth the writing out; though the argument be bad. But it is lent me but for two or three days. So God keep you. From Gray's Inn, this 5th of May. Your entire loving Brother, FR. BACON. (7)

Unfortunately he did not put in the year. The date which naturally suggests itself is 5th May 1592, when the *Supplication* was still hotly topical. In any case it is of interest that Bacon's guarded terms conceal a very real tribute. 'Curious' was the term then in vogue for fine and intricate workmanship, and the 'argument' means the cause for which it was written, so that Bacon's purport in modern language is: 'It is a lovely bit of writing, even though it is on the wrong side.' Bacon had been 'Mr. Topcliffe's' assistant in the examination of Catholic prisoners since 1588. But he had begun to rebel at this sordid task, cold-blooded though he was, and to hope for higher employment through the rising influence of Essex. In 1592, Anthony was installed as Essex's party-manager, and was beginning to attract easy young Catholic swordsmen to his service in return for religious tolerance.

It is interesting in this connection, whether Francis's letter is placed in 1592 or some years later, that Anthony should have been apparently anxious to have the whole *Supplication* copied out in the space of two or three days. It suggests that he was hoping to turn it into pro-Essex propaganda—with the same disregard for its main drift as Essex's supporters afterwards showed towards Shakespeare's *Richard the Second*. The after-history of the *Supplication* lends some confirmation to this suggestion. It was towards the end of 1600, that is, between the disgrace of Essex and his desperate rebellion, that the Appellants printed and published the *Supplication* in a deliberate attempt to embroil the Jesuits with the Government. (8)

A more immediate sign of the Government's reaction to the *Supplication* is contained in a short letter of Father Garnet's written from London, under conditions of great stress, on 11th February 1592. In it he says that he has taken over Robert's duties in London, and sent him off to the country to enjoy a brief respite. 'The latest storm we are being tossed by is the worst we have yet suffered in this Ocean.'

An alarming reference to betrayal seems to apply to John Cecil and the part he played in supplying matter for the *Proclamation*:

Suspicions and outspoken rumours are rife here about a certain person who recently asked to be admitted into your family. If only he had stated his case plainly and honestly to us or to you! But if he is in truth a double-dealer, Good God, what havoc he will wreak—or rather, what havoc he is already wreaking, and we suffering!

The intensity of this new wave of persecution can be gauged by Garnet's concluding sentence:

It is not worth sending any more over to us for a while yet— unless they are willing to run straight into the direst poverty and the most atrocious brigandage: so desperate has our state become, and so close, unless God intervenes, to utter ruin; for more often than not there is simply no where left to hide.

It was under these circumstances that he insisted on Southwell leaving London, and on himself taking his place.

Verstegan's dispatch of the same month speaks of 'a new Cecilian inquisition', eight commissioners, house to house searches, and the torture of servants. 'The afflicted state of Catholics was never such as now.'

Among those caught in the drag-net of this January was Anne, the eldest daughter of Richard Bellamy of Uxendon. (9) In this unfortunate woman Topcliffe saw a possible instrument for at last laying by the heels the man who was beginning to make a mockery of his reputation as a priest-hunter.

In January there had been information from a reliable source that Southwell was in Cotton's house in Fleet Street, and using his name.★ But the house had been found empty. Once more the man had eluded him by slipping out of London. But it was not long before Topcliffe picked up his tracks again.

★ The information seems to have come from Cholmeley. Did he send it in late on purpose?

CHAPTER EIGHTEEN

'Master W. S.'

ROBERT was in Sussex. The light-blue sky and the light-green turf with its wiry harebells was the setting of his last free springtime on earth. He began his holiday with the Copleys at Horsham. At least so one gathers from Topcliffe's last information about him before his return to London. (1)

'Young Anto. Copley and some others', he wrote, referring to some escapade at Horsham, 'be most familiar with Southwell. . . . There liveth not the like . . . upon whom I have more good grounds for watchful eyes, for his sister Gage's and his brother-in-law Gage's sake, for whose pardon he boasteth he is assured.'*

When Topcliffe got wind of Robert's presence at Horsham, no doubt he had to move elsewhere. But Sussex was a friendly county to him. The Lieutenants of the district, Buckhurst and Howard of Effingham, still lagged behind in the necessary ruthlessness. And he would have been a welcome guest at any of the numerous families, already often mentioned, that were grouped around the still powerful houses of Montague and Southampton.

It seems likely that he used this rare period of leisure to draw together his poems into the book-forms in which he intended

---

* Anthony, having finally disgraced himself at the English College (by appearing in the pulpit to preach a sermon with a rose between his teeth) had returned to England after various adventures, in 1591, on promise of a pardon. Such a pardon often led to employment as a spy. But in fact, probably owing to Southwell's influence, he spent the next six years in seclusion, writing poetry and trying to cultivate a philosophic calm.

them to be published. 'Dear eye that dost peruse my muses style',
he wrote in one dedication:

> Of mirth to make a trade may be a crime,
> But tired spirits for mirth must have a time. (2)

There are three dedications (two in verse and one in prose)
doubtless corresponding to a threefold division of his poetry.
The first dedication belongs exclusively to his long poem *St.
Peter's Complaint* (often shortened to *Peter's Plaint*):

> Dear eye, that deignest to let fall a look
> On these sad memories of Peter's plaint . . .

Although it is off the main beat of this chapter, a little must be
said about this poem.

He had begun work on the Italian original as early as 1584, and
he kept on refurbishing it at different intervals, so that in length
and in effort, it must be considered his masterpiece. But the
branches are much too heavy and luxuriant for the trunk; and,
as a whole, it droops. Yet in some details it is perfect, and its
wealth of imagery was a treasure-trove for contemporary poets
and poetasters.

The two stanzas on sleep, with their contrast of lovely peace
and nagging strife, were anticipated by Sidney and emulated by
many others, but not surpassed in precision even by Shakespeare:

> Sleep, Death's ally, oblivion of tears,
> Silence of passions, balm of angry sore,
> Suspense of loves, security of fears,
> Wrath's lenity, heart's ease, storm's calmest shore:
> Sense's and soul's reprieval from all cumbers
> Benumbing sense of ill with quiet slumbers.
>
> Not such my sleep, but whisperer of dreams,
> Creating strange chimeras, feigning frights;
> Of day-discourses giving fancy themes
> To make dumb-shows with worlds of antic sights:
> Casting true griefs in fancy's forging mould,
> Brokenly telling tales rightly foretold.

A special quarry for poets of his own and of succeeding generations, as late as Andrew Marvell, was the long section on the
Sacred Eyes of our Redeemer, in which he plays over theo-
logical depths with a sensuous ardour that cedes nothing to
Crashaw:

> Sweet volumes stored with learning fit for saints
> Where blissful quires imparadize their minds,
> Wherein eternal study never faints,
> Still finding all, yet seeking all it finds:
> How endless is your labyrinth of bliss,
> Where to be lost the sweetest finding is . . .
>
> O pools of Hesebon, the baths of grace,
> Where happy spirits dive in sweet desires,
> Where saints rejoice to glass their glorious face,
> Whose banks make echo to the angel choirs:
> An echo sweeter in the sole rebound
> Than angels' music in the fullest sound!
>
> O Bethlehem-cisterns, David's most desire,
> From which my sins like fierce Philistims keep;
> To fetch your drops what champion should I hire
> That I therein my withered heart may steep:
> I would not shed them like that holy king,
> *His* were but types, *these* are the figured thing.

The reason why he spent so much labour on this poem was,
frankly, an apostolic one: to attract imaginative souls to repentance and the life of the spirit. A concluding stanza, by its marked
reversal of stress and independence of the regular beat, seems likely
to have been written at the very end of his period of freedom:

> Christ! health of fevered soul, heaven of the mind,
> Force of the feeble, nurse of infant loves,
> Guide to the wandering foot, light to the blind,
> Whom weeping wins, repentant sorrow moves:
> Father in care, Mother in tender heart,
> Revive and save me, slain with sinful dart.

So much for *Peter's Plaint*. The drift of this chapter has a different scope, though it returns to the poem at the end.

The second dedication was to the same person as the first, and was probably added when a group of his poems was added, to make one volume with *Peter's Plaint*: much the same, perhaps, as that eventually published by Cawood immediately after the author's death. (3)

The third dedication is a letter in prose evidently intended for a different group of his poems. This group may be connected (though not identically) with those omitted by Cawood and published immediately after by John Busby under the title *Maeoniae*, with the bold addition of the author's initials. Busby's preface makes it plain that he was complying with the demands of several 'Gentlemen Readers', presumably influential ones. (4)

It is this third dedication that begins the main thread of this chapter. Its salutation was printed until 1616 in an abbreviated form, 'The author to his loving cousin'. But there is no doubt that what Southwell originally wrote was: 'To my worthy good cousin, Master W.S.', and he signed it 'Your loving cousin, R.S.' (5)

Vague though this dedication is, it is the only documentary contact between Robert Southwell and any actual person in that literary world which he hoped to convert. It is vague because there is no known W.S. among his cousins-german (except William Shelley who had been many years in close imprisonment) and therefore the word 'cousin' must be taken in its looser sense.

The content of the letter tells us nothing about W.S., except that he was a devotee of poetry and perhaps of the stage. Southwell chides him humorously for urging him to present these verses to the public; then, in more serious vein, says it is time that poets ceased to abuse their talents and remembered their noble ancestry. 'Christ Himself by making a hymn the conclusion of His Last Supper and the prologue to the first pageant of His Passion, gave His Spouse a method to imitate . . . and to all men a pattern to know the true use of this measured and footed style.'★ All he hopes from his clumsy efforts, he says, is that they may incite some finer poet to show 'how well verse and virtue suit together'.

To suggest that 'Master W.S.' was William Shakespeare is a thing that anyone sensitive to ridicule will naturally shrink from. Yet in this case the probabilities seem so reasonable that it would be wrong not to expound them. There is the probability that Southampton's was the influence that caused publishers to accept Southwell's work in spite of his being a proscribed 'traitor' at the time—this is a social reason; secondly, the probability amounting to certitude that Southwell was well-known, at least by repute, to other contemporary poets and dramatists less likely than Shakespeare to have had contact with him—this is a literary reason; and thirdly the conjunction of the literary and social reasons in the case of Shakespeare fits in with the change of theme from *Venus and Adonis* to the *Rape of Lucrece*.

At the outset there is a welcome fact. But to mention it means leaping forward to Southwell's last evening on earth. He was visited in prison by a nobleman who was either Lord Mountjoy or one of Mountjoy's friends enjoying an equal favour with the Queen. This nobleman drew from him a solemn assurance that he had never intended any treason against the realm. He and his friends attended the execution very noticeably on the following day; and afterwards, in a private audience with the Queen, he showed her a written book of Southwell's verse with the author's *Preface* which urged poets to cherish their talents and use them for good ends.

This story has a good authority; (6) and it does not strain it too far to conclude that the preface in question was Southwell's prose-letter to W.S. But leaving aside these initials, one finds that his verse-book was in the possession of Mountjoy or one of his friends. No doubt it could have got there by way of a pursuivant's raid, but the more likely way under the circumstances

---

★ The same stage metaphor occurs in the *Humble Supplication*, 'a prologue to future tragedies', indicating perhaps that the two phrases were written at no great interval of time.

is that it came either directly or indirectly from Southwell himself. The obvious way for Mountjoy, who was a Protestant, was through his Catholic friend Southampton.*

The links between Southwell and the Wriothesleys have been noted in different parts of this book. He was connected with them by marriage and very closely related to their dependants in Hampshire; and his missionary duties could not fail to bring him to Southampton House in Holborn. One might say that if Southwell knew Mountjoy, as he seems to have done, *a fortiori* he knew Southampton.

During the years 1591-5 both became influential literary patrons. That is strictly relevant, because it is difficult to see how, without such influence, respectable publishers would have risked bringing out no less than *ten* editions of Southwell's work during those five years.†

The next step in this staircase of probabilities is one approved by many Shakespeare-theorists: that about this date (1592) Shakespeare was acting as a 'schoolmaster', or librarian or something of the sort, in the Southampton household. We are here upon an elevation that was reached as a mere conjecture by Grosart and others: namely, that Southwell's second verse-dedication was an exhortation to someone (on the present theory, Southampton) to deflect Shakespeare from Venus to a higher theme:

> This makes my mourning Muse resolve in tears,
> This makes my heavy pen to plain in prose;
> Christ's thorn is sharp, no head his garland wears,
> Still finest wits are stilling Venus's rose:
> In paynim toys the sweetest veins are spent,
> To Christian works few have their talents lent.

---

* It might have been Southampton himself who visited Southwell and then saw the Queen. But Mountjoy is the only name actually mentioned among the small group of noblemen, clearly members of the 'Essex Circle', who attended the execution.

† It is significant that Gervase Markham who dedicated books to both, was author of a devotional poem on Mary Magdalen which was copied wholesale from Southwell's *Funeral Tears*. See Herbert Thursdon, 'Father Southwell, the Popular Poet', *The Month*, vol. lxxxiii (1895), p. 383.

License my single pen to seek a phere;
You heavenly sparks of wit show native light;
Cloud not with misty loves your orient clear,
Sweet flights you shoot, learn once to level right.
Favour my wish, well-wishing works no ill;
I move the suit, the grant rests in your will.

This would mean that Shakespeare in 1592 had already written *Venus and Adonis*; and that is not improbable, because, when he actually published it a year later, he already had in hand a 'graver labour'—for his patron.

Finally it must be said that from the social point of view there was nothing odd about Southwell addressing Shakespeare as 'cousin'. To be a cousin need mean nothing more than to be a neighbour belonging to the same wide group of families. Shakespeare was a neighbour of the household at Baddesley Clinton;* and he had the same distant connection with the Vaux family through the Ardens and Throckmortons, as Southwell had through the Anthony Southwells and the Lestranges. Southwell and Shakespeare may have had other common acquaintances from the past: Edward Throckmorton, Simon Hunt, and the Jesuit missionary (Campion or Persons) from whom John Shakespeare got his copy of the 'Spiritual Testament'.†

These circumstances are not arguments that Southwell *did* know Shakespeare, but that he *could have* known him—to meet the initial prejudice of most readers that such an acquaintance would be beyond the bounds of likelihood.

From 'could have' to 'did' the transition can never be more than a probability. But a mere probability becomes a greater probability when it is reinforced from an independent angle. In

---

* There was in fact a distant blood-relationship between Southwell and Shakespeare. Both were sixth in descent from Sir Robert Belknap. See page 5 n., and G. R. French, *Shakespearian Genealogies* (Cambridge 1869), p. 489.

† Both Campion and Persons stayed with Edward Arden in Warwickshire in the same year that Persons wrote to Allen for more copies of the 'testament'. See Herbert Thurston, *The Month*, November 1911 (vol. CXVIII, p. 487). Also Persons's *Memoirs* (*CRS*. IV. p. 115.)

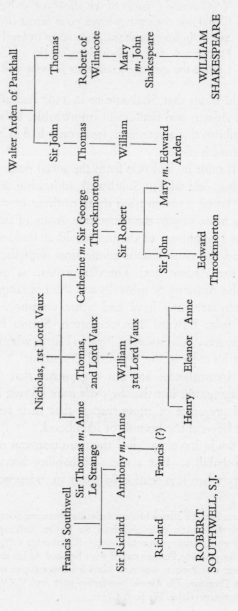

Remote connection of the Vaux family with Robert Southwell and with William Shakespeare.

this case the new angle is that of Southwell's influence on other writers who were socially more remote from him than Shakespeare was. It is a subject which would have to be dealt with in any case in a biography of Southwell.

The main evidence arises out of two of the most sensational literary events of 1592-3: 1. The controversy between Gabriel Harvey and the University Wits, first with Robert Greene and then with Thomas Nashe; 2. Greene's pamphlet about his death-bed repentance, which was accompanied or followed by other 'conversions' among the University Wits.

The controversy was one which Gabriel Harvey, whose mind was made for better things, should never have got involved in. But instead of breaking it off when Greene died in September 1592, he thought this was an opportunity for dealing a final blow. Greene died in squalor, leaving behind him this extraordinary pamphlet which warned his friends that their hour of fame and licence was over, that 'an upstart crow' (identified as Shakespeare) was overreaching them, and that their only hope lay in repentance.

In parenthesis it should be said that as regards the wave of 'repentances' (personal or conventional) which marked the next few years, Greene's example may better be likened to a weather-cock than to an efficacious wind. Thomas Lodge, Greene's collaborator, was already reported to be leaving the stage and turning to Papistry. And Christopher Marlowe, the most gifted, violent and mysterious of the University Wits, was said to be producing a morality-play very different from his previous master-pieces of 'atheism'.

Harvey's comment on the situation was a horrible but carefully circumstantial account of Greene's death. This provocation brought a hornet's nest about his ears from Thomas Nashe, the most nimble and scurrilous of the University Wits. But just as Harvey was girding himself for another ponderous reply, Nashe too, of all people, announced his conversion in a pamphlet entitled *Christ's Tears over Jerusalem*: 'To God and man do I

promise an unfained conversion'—with a special apology to
Gabriel Harvey. Harvey was thus left after all with the last word,
and did not fail to take it, in a *New Letter of Notable Contents*,
16th September 1593, which contains the references to Southwell.

This is the strangest of all companies in which to find the Jesuit
poet. Yet the only explanation for the wave of repentance that
Gabriel Harvey could think of was the influence of *Mary Magdalen's Funeral Tears*. Scoffing at Nashe's abrupt change from
Aretino to Divinity, he wrote: 'Now he hath a little mused upon
the *Funeral Tears of Mary Magdalen*, and is egged on to try the
suppleness of his Pathetical vein . . .'; and he recurred, twenty
pages later, in his disjointed manner, to the same charge, when
contrasting Nashe unfavourably with the pagan philosophers:
'I know not who weeped the *Funeral Tears of Mary Magdalen*:*
I would he that sheddeth the Patheticall *Teares of Christ*, and
trickleth the liquid Teares of Repentance were no worse affected
in pure devotion . . .'

And he seems to be levelling the same accusation of being
influenced by the *Funeral Tears* against the dead Marlowe's *Doctor
Faustus*; though he can only have known of it by repute: 'Greene
and Marlowe might admonish others to advise themselves: and I
pray God the promised Teares of Repentance prove not the
Teares of the Onion upon the Theater.'

The abrupt change of heart, or at least change of theme, on
the part of Greene, Marlowe, Lodge and Nashe—all within the
same short space—was certainly a notable phenomenon. No
doubt the Plague, together with other reasons, was partly responsible. But there is enough internal evidence to show that Harvey's
obscure references to Southwell were well-founded.

In the case of Thomas Lodge, whose conversion was complete
and lasting, the probability of direct influence by Southwell is
very considerable. In his *Tears of . . . the Mother of God* (1596)
there is an open acknowledgement of *Mary Magdalen* and *Peter's*

---

* But Harvey probably did know; for earlier in the year he had coupled
Southwell's book with Robert Persons's *Book of Resolution* as being both of them
'elegantly and pathetically written'. (*Pierces Supererogations*, 1593, p. 191.)

Plaint; and his marriage with a Catholic waiting-woman of the Countess of Arundel (whose physician he afterwards became) is as likely to have been arranged while Southwell was still at liberty as later. (She was the unfortunate young wife, and fortunate widow of Solomon Aldred.)

With Thomas Nashe, it is a question of influence rather than conversion. His *Christ's Tears over Jerusalem*—which is a fine if somewhat indisciplined bit of moralizing—has very strong and thinly-veiled Catholic leanings. A careful study puts it beyond reasonable doubt that he had been reading Southwell's *Epistle of Comfort*, which, as we have seen, was being circulated by Cholmeley before 1593. (7)

About Marlowe's *Doctor Faustus*, even if the date 1592–3 is accepted as certain, there is too much uncertainty regarding the authenticity of the clowning scenes to make discussion worthwhile; and the rest of it is too much a work of genius to betray any verbal influences from other poets. Yet the supreme line:

See, see, where Christ's blood streams in the firmament . . .

is so utterly unexpected that it might conceivably have taken wing from the poem which was so admired by Ben Jonson:

A pretty babe did in the air appear all burning bright . . .

in the same way as Shakespeare's sudden vision in *Macbeth*:

And pity, like a naked new-born babe
Striding the blast . . .

For it was not the phrasing of Southwell's poem that struck his fellow-poets, but its blindingly simple conception of the Son of God appearing through the veils of earthly qualities and earthly feelings.

Apart from Marlowe's connection with Nashe and Lodge, and his association with the ballad-writer Cholmeley, already mentioned, there was another alley-way in which a meeting with Southwell would have been likely. An intimate friend—not just a literary acquaintance—of his was the elder poet Thomas

Watson. Watson, a student *in utroque iure*, had been resident at Douai at the same time as Southwell; (8) but, though a roysterer, he does not seem to have been a spy; and his sugary sonnets were of the type that Southwell in his early days tried to emulate for a better end. The prison of Newgate where Watson and Marlowe lay in February 1590 was one which Southwell often visited. Another vague but portentous approximation of Southwell to Marlowe is that both were shadowed by Robert Poley. The accusation of Papistry that accompanied Marlowe's arrest and death indicates certainly a surprising change from the tone of his *Massacre at Paris*.

The object of these surmises is not to build a theory, but only to suggest that Southwell's literary apostolate need not be imagined within too narrow limits. He knew the streets of London thoroughly, and the seamier side of London was not closed to his ministrations.

Nevertheless, it remains true that the regard he was held in by patrons such as Mountjoy and Southampton was the most probable reason of his becoming known to the other writers of that period.

The end of 1591—the period of Southwell's emergence into print as a writer and of his retirement to avoid capture—coincided with the emergence of three new poets, who, though friendly with Nashe and Lodge, were soon to eclipse them in the struggle for the limited favours of patrons; with the emergence, too, of a very *barocco* style of poem: *The Complaint of Rosamund* (1592) by Samuel Daniel, *Lucrece* by William Shakespeare, and *Matilda the Fair* by Michael Drayton—both published in 1594 but written probably a year earlier. This change in taste created the situation partly described and partly prophesied by Southwell in his 1591 preface to *Mary Magdalen's Funeral Tears*:

> It is a just complaint among the better sort of persons that the finest wits lose themselves in the vainest follies, spilling much Art in some idle fancy, and leaving their works as witnesses how long they have been in travail, to be in fine delivered of a fable. . . . Yet this incon-

venience might find some excuse, if the drift of their discourse
levelled at any virtuous mark. For in fables are often figured moral
truths, and that covertly uttered to a common good which without
mask would not find so free a passage.

His last sentence is of peculiar interest because 'fables—figuring
moral truths—covertly uttered for a common good' is an apt
description of at least two of these three poems. Their common
theme is the rape of a beautiful lady, but their inspiration is
repentance; the rape becomes an allegory of the violation of a soul
by sin.

Drayton's poem—though much the least inspired of the three
—is interesting, not only because he was very consciously following in the footsteps of Daniel and Shakespeare, but because his
borrowings from Southwell's *Peter's Plaint* are quite flagrantly
obvious. (9) Of his previous poem *The Shepherd's Garland* (1593),
whose debt to Southwell is by comparison negligible, Bernard
Newdigate has written in his *Michael Drayton and his circle*:
'There are passages which suggest both the thought and manner
of Robert Southwell. His *St. Peter's Complaint*, which is written
in the same metre and verse-form . . . though not yet in print,
was circulating in manuscript.' It is impossible, therefore, not to
suspect that Southwell was partly responsible for the type of poem
which he had desired (as a lesser evil) in his preface.

We have thus returned, by an independent route, to the same
question as in the first half of this chapter. What relation does
Shakespeare's *Lucrece* bear to Southwell's *Peter's Plaint*? A careful
comparison leaves little room for doubt. If there are resemblances
between Daniel's *Rosamund* and Shakespeare's *Lucrece* (as there
ought to be, because of the similarity of theme), the resemblances
between *Lucrece* and *Peter's Plaint* are both more numerous and
more impressive, despite the *dissimilarity* of theme. Seventy years
ago Hales wrote in his preface to Ward's *English Poets*: 'St. Peter's
Complaint* reminds one curiously of the almost exactly contemporary poem, Shakespeare's *Lucrece*. There is a like inexhaus-
tibleness of illustrative resource. . . . *St. Peter's Complaint* reminds
one of *Lucrece* also in the minuteness of its narration, and in the

unfailing abundance of thought and fancy with which every detail is treated.'

There are indeed any number of similar antitheses and apostrophes, and there is a common store of similes—the swan singing and dying, the lamb pleading with the wolf, the mutinous troops sacking a town, the stream befouling the ocean, and so on. But beneath these well-worn conceits, as they chink and chime together, a deeper note is heard: one which is more natural to Southwell's theme than to Ovid's story in which there was no dialogue of temptation and no analysis of remorse. Southwell's emblematic but much-alive image of temptation—

> Where fear my thoughts candied with icy cold,
> Heat did my tongue to perjury unfold

—is quickly taken up and condensed by Shakespeare:

> Thus graceless holds he disputacion
> 'Tween frozen conscience and hot-burning will.

And Southwell's aphorism on the barrenness of sin—

> Servéd with toil, yet paying nought but pain,
> Man's deepest loss, though false-esteeméd gain

—is caught up lithely into Shakespeare's narrative:

> Having no other pleasure of his gain,
> But torment that it cannot cure his pain.

Both compare sin to a wound, but what they are trying to express is the delayed effects of the wound in consciousness.

> Shot without noise, wound without present smart,
> First seeming light, proving in fine a load

—wrote Southwell; and Shakespeare:

> O unseen shame! invisible disgrace!
> O unfelt sore! crest-wounding private scar!

Eventually it becomes clear that Shakespeare is beating Southwell at his own game. Southwell had set himself to probe 'the anatomy of sin':

This fawning viper, dumb till he had wounded,
With many mouths doth now upbraid my harms;
My sight was veiled till I myself confounded,
Then did I see the disenchanted charms:
Then could I cut the anatomy of sin
And search with lynx's eyes what lay within.

Shakespeare is doing the same thing, but doing it more dramatically:

O deeper sin than bottomless conceit
Can comprehend in still imagination!
Drunken desire must vomit his receipt
Ere he can see his own abomination . . .

Even in this thought through the dark night he stealeth,
A captive victor that hath lost in gain;
Bearing away the wound that nothing healeth,
The scar that will, despite of cure, remain.

There is a deeper resemblance here than a 'common storehouse' of imagery; and even in their use of common images and conceits, there is a peculiar resemblance. It derives from the humanism of the Fathers, not from contemporary fashion. Southwell himself supplies an obvious example in his *Epistle of Comfort*, quoting Chrysostom on Eutropius:

Our life, sayeth the same saint, was a shadow and it passed. It was a smoke and it vanished. It was a bubble and it dissolved. It was a spinner's web and it was shaken asunder. No wise man lamenteth that he lived not a year sooner than he was born, and why should he lament that within a year or less, he shall live no longer?

It was the homiletic tradition that shaped Southwell's rhetoric in passages like these:

Ah life, sweet drop drowned in a sea of sours,
A flying good posting to doubtful end,
Still losing months and years to gain new hours . . .

A flower, a play, a blast, a shade, a dream,
A living death, a never-turning stream

—and Shakespeare's in one closely parallel:

> What win I if I gain the thing I seek?
> A dream, a breath, a froth of fleeting joy.
> Who buys a minute's worth to wail a week?
> Or sells eternity to get a toy?
>
> The sweets we wish for turn to loathéd sours
> Even in the moment that we call them ours.

The real debt of Shakespeare to Southwell, however, would seem to be an inspiration rather than a set of conceits. The intuition of the soul in grace as a consecrated virgin ('Thy ghostly beauty offered force to God') runs right through a great part of Southwell's verse, though it is only glanced at in this poem, in the imagery of the temple:

> Christ, as my God, was templed in my thought,
> As man, He lent mine eyes their dearest light;
> But sin His temple hath to ruin brought,
> And now He lighteneth terror from His sight:
> Now of my lay unconsecrate desires,
> Profanéd wretch, I taste the earnest hires.

This is the image which Shakespeare has taken up in the strongest part of his poem, that part in which the seed of his future Tragedies can be most clearly discerned. He is more concerned with Tarquin's soul than Lucrece's body. There is a rape within a rape, Tarquin has done violence to the divine spark within him, his immortal jewel and his princess:

> For now against himself he sounds this doom,
> That through the length of time he stands disgraced:
> Besides, his soul's fair temple is defaced,
> To whose weak ruins muster troops of cares
> To ask the spotted princess how she fares.
>
> She says her subjects with foul insurrection
> Have battered down her consecrated wall,
> And by their mortal fault brought in subjection
> Her immortality, and made her thrall

To living death and pain perpetual:
Which in her prescience she controlled still,
But her foresight could not control their will.

Apart from that special inspiration, the general impression one gets—quite independently of any external evidence—is that Shakespeare pricked by Southwell's example, had tried his hand at tapping a loftier and more metaphysical vein.

Now, if one fits that to the tentative conclusion of the first half of this chapter, a situation emerges which may be put crudely (and with some ambiguity as regards exact dates) as follows:

In 1591–2 there was a general 'complaint among the better sort of persons' that poets were abusing their talents. Not only Southwell, but Spenser in his *Tears of the Muses*, had borne witness to this complaint. Young Southampton, who was one of 'the better sort of persons', found that he had an erotic poem dedicated to him by Nashe, and another—though of finer calibre, *Venus and Adonis*—in progress from the hand of Shakespeare. Ignoring Nashe, he addressed himself to Shakespeare, and showed him a written book of Southwell's poetry, with the plea in the dedication: 'I move the suit, the grant rests in your Will.' Shakespeare, who had already a considerable admiration for Southwell, readily acceded, and chose Daniel's type of poem, with excursions into Southwell's, as the theme of his 'graver labour'. Southwell, in anticipatory gratitude, wrote to him his last dedication: 'To my worthy good Cousin, Master W.S.'

Lucrece may not be a great poem, but it is an important one. In its central image—the haunted face of Tarquin in the flickering rushlight—is the shadow cast by many mighty dramas to come, *Macbeth*, *Othello*, *Hamlet*, and *Measure for Measure*.

Thus, it may be claimed with some probability, that Robert Southwell's last service to English letters, before he returned to London, was to rouse Shakespeare to a loftier conception of the divine spark within him.

T

CHAPTER NINETEEN

Arrest and Torture, 1592

GARNET'S cry from London in February had sounded desperate: 'There is simply nowhere left to hide!'; and, since then, the little garden-house in Finsbury Fields had fallen—betrayed by James Younger who had been captured in March and released as a decoy. Nevertheless that search had been carried out with surprising laxity, and not by Topcliffe. There is reason to believe, in fact, that Topcliffe was keeping quiet and watching his step at this time. And that, if it is a fact, must be attributed to the strange heroism of Thomas Pormort.

Pormort, under question by Topcliffe that winter, had either begun to weaken or had feigned to do so. Topcliffe, hoping for the credit of having 'converted' a priest, and hoping also apparently for a chance to blackmail Archbishop Whitgift (though the connection of this with Pormort is obscure), became genial and confiding. Pormort listened, and afterwards put all he had heard on a piece of paper which he managed to smuggle out of prison. It contained not only Topcliffe's scandalous remarks about Whitgift, but also and principally his salacious boastings about indecent familiarity with Queen Elizabeth. There is no need to repeat them here; but it should be emphasized, as Pollen says, 'that Pormort did not allege Topcliffe's words to be true; the charge was that he did utter them; Topcliffe, not Elizabeth, was the person incriminated.' (1) As a result, Pormort had to suffer such torture that he would have died in prison if an old man had not lent him a truss to bind his rupture; and at his execution, he 'was enforced to stand in his shirt almost two hours upon the ladder in Lent time upon a very cold day, when Topcliffe still urged him to deny the words, *but he would not.*' Moreover, at his trial he had boldly reaffirmed them, and his paper had circulated among members of the Council. They viewed it with stony faces; but there can be little doubt that its information was stored away for the occasion when Topcliffe should first slip from favour.

The obscene favourite had another reason for walking carefully within the law this Easter-time. He had committed one of those actions which the Queen seems genuinely to have disapproved of. Robbery, extortion, perjury, even murder she might countenance in her favourites, but against rape she set her face sternly.

Anne Bellamy had entered the Gatehouse prison on 26th January with her head held high, a potential Dorothy or Cecilia. 'Her youth', says More, 'had been grounded in such firm and lively faith and piety, that for religion's sake she was ready to defy both the horrors of prison and the assaults of evil men.' But after three months' close imprisonment, she was found 'in most dishonest order'; and by the end of April it was certain that she was pregnant. Richard Bellamy's damning indictment, (2) afterwards presented to the Council, leaves no doubt that the author of the crime was the sexagenarian Topcliffe himself.*

The complicated scheme that followed for ensuring his credit seems to have issued from the brain of his servant and familiar, Nicholas Jones, a weaver's son—'my boy Nicholas, who first set him [Southwell] into my hands', as he afterwards handsomely acknowledged in a letter to the Queen. Like Topcliffe's other scheme, for ruining the Fitzherbert family, its effects dragged on for seven years, necessitating crime after crime on his part, and finally proving a millstone round his neck.

One of its victims was Mr. Robert Barnes of Mapledurham near Petersfield. After five years of hard usage in prison, Barnes was brought to the bar in 1598. He was allowed to speak freely,

* Later writers have deepened Topcliffe's guilt by describing Anne as 'a child'; but in fact she was a woman of twenty-nine—not that that makes her plight any the less tragic.

and delivered a meticulous and crashing indictment of Topcliffe's methods and misdeeds, supported at every turn by witnesses, non-Catholic as well as Catholic. (3)

Barnes's speech is the most detailed exposition of the scheme set on foot by Topcliffe and Jones. Its main object was the capture of Southwell, but its corollaries were to cover up Topcliffe's guilt and to provide Nicholas Jones with an estate. Anne, in her misery, was to be offered the hope of saving her family from all future vexation by enticing Southwell to spend one night under their roof, informing Topcliffe meanwhile of the time and hiding-place. Thus the Bellamys would be caught in a position where only Topcliffe's personal favour could preserve their lives and property. And so, well before her child was due, Anne would be married to Nicholas Jones—but married in church with the blessing of her parents, and with the rich Manor of Preston from the Bellamy lands as her dowry. In the event, five innocent people, three men and two women, died in great pain, and several others were ruined, in order to provide the weaver's son with a country-house.

In his evidence Barnes said:

The first original of all my troubles proceeded from Anne Bellamy . . . who about the twenty-sixth day of January . . . was committed to the gatehouse . . . where she lay not the space of six weeks but was found in most dishonest order, and before six weeks more, being with child, was delivered by Mr. Topcliffe's means, upon bail not to depart above one mile from the city: at which time she lay at the house of one Mr. Basforde in Holborn until midsummer day following; being in the meantime practised withal by Mr. Topcliffe and Nicholas Jones for the apprehension of one Mr. Southwell, one of the society of Jesus, upon promise (as she affirmeth in a letter to her mother) from some of the Council, and also a letter under Mr. Topcliffe's hand, that none should be molested in the house where he should be taken. . . .

By April or May, Robert had returned to London. He was back in his old haunts between Fleet Street and Holborn; and no doubt it was for that reason that Anne was lodged in a house at

Holborn 'hard by' his hiding-place, as Barnes's speech goes on to say. Her approach to Southwell was on the most natural pretext possible: to win back her brother Thomas who, sick of continual browbeating by his inferiors, was beginning to put in a nominal appearance at the Protestant church. When her two younger sisters came to visit her, she told them to tell their mother of Southwell's return and to persuade him to Uxendon to revive their drooping faith.

> One Thomas Bellamy, a brother of hers, upon midsummer day coming to London and going to see his sister, she was importunate with him to have him go with her to a seminary priest which, she told him, did lie hard by; terming him by the name of a young man, giving great praise of his virtue and learning, the like whereof she had done to her two sisters immediately before. . . . (4)

It may be wondered, if she was able to locate him in Holborn, why Topcliffe missed the chance of arresting him there and then. Why the complicated scheme to entice him uncertainly out of London? The answer would seem to be that his lodging at Holborn was one which Topcliffe at that time did not care to run the risk of invading by storm. Since the only relatively 'safe' place for Catholics in Holborn was Southampton House, this explanation fits in well with the literary conjectures of the previous chapter.

It was midsummer, therefore, before the trap was properly set. Topcliffe, in the meantime, had retired ostentatiously to the Court at Greenwich, fifteen miles from Uxendon, leaving the coast apparently clear.

By an ironic coincidence, what decided Robert to accept the invitation was a move by Garnet to ensure his greater safety. Seized perhaps by one of his premonitions, he sent him word to leave London and come into Warwickshire. 'He had actually planned his journey to us', wrote Garnet, 'when he received an invitation to the honoured household of the Bellamys which had long lacked a consoler, and so he arranged to spend his first night there.' (5) The bearer of the message was probably Robert

Barnes who acted often as courier for the priests. By the same messenger Southwell had sent word to Father Richard Blount in Sussex to meet him on the morning of 26th June at Uxendon, the object being either that Blount should accompany him into Warwickshire, or should take his place in London. If Blount, by a fortunate mischance, had not been disappointed of a horse and so arrived later than he intended, both he and Barnes would also have been trapped. (6)

On Sunday morning, 25th June, at ten o'clock as arranged, Robert met Thomas Bellamy in Fleet Street, and they took horse and rode out of London together. Shortly afterwards, Nicholas Jones set out at speed for Greenwich, where Topcliffe for the last three weeks (or so he himself boasted) had had horses saddled and men waiting in readiness.

It was seven and a half miles to Uxendon from the north-west fork at Tyburn, through one of the fairest and fattest parts of England. The great sea of forest that was St. John's Wood still threw out a foam, as it were, of glades and thickets; but the land that enclosed them was crammed to bursting with crops and gardens. Passing through Westbourne Green and Kensal Green and Holsden Green, the two horsemen reached the River Brent, which they crossed by a stone bridge, and came to Wembley Green.

As they turned off the Harrow road and moved up a little tributary of the Brent, the country grew somewhat wilder, though still very prosperous. They were on the rim of a large shallow cup formed by Sudbury Heights to the south-west, Harrow-super-montem to the north-west, and, just in front of them, two miles east of Harrow, a third wooded hill, whose name has changed frequently in the intervening centuries. In the lee of this hill, from terraced gardens surrounded by trees and watered by two large ponds, rose the roof and chimneys of Uxendon.

Its name has long since vanished from the maps of Middlesex; in the eighteenth century it was replaced by Preston. But when John Speed was planning his atlas in Shakespeare's time, Uxendon and Harrow were the only two names he knew of in this district,

and he drew his little pictures to represent the mansion house of
the one and the parish church of the other. Preston was a rich
manor of the Bellamys, tenanted until that year (the year of his
death) by their very good friend and neighbour, John Lyon, a
wealthy yeoman, who had founded the free school for children
of the parish at Harrow-on-the-hill. It was Preston, the cradle
so to speak of Harrow School, that Topcliffe had marked down
for Nicholas Jones.

At midday, when Southwell was seen approaching, the last
preparations were made for the long-awaited Mass. Richard
Bellamy was away from home; among those of the family mentioned as present were his wife and two daughters, Mary Bellamy
and Mrs. Audrey Wilforde, a nineteen-year-old widow. In the
long years of cruel imprisonment that were to follow, during
which their mother died of ill-usage, these two young women
confessed unfalteringly that they had never been to a Protestant
church and had no intention of going. To them and to a large
number of tenants and retainers Southwell preached and gave
Holy Communion, celebrating his last Mass.

'He used to come here', says More, 'sometimes when he had
the chance to recreate himself with a freer and purer air'; and
that was what he did for the rest of this day. Despite intense
suspicion in the past, no priest had ever been captured in this
house. Danger, on this occasion, seemed utterly remote; and on
the morrow there was waiting for him the warm and friendly
West.

But in the middle of the night he was startled wideawake by
a noise of dreadful familiarity: pounding feet, crashing glass,
splintering wood, and above it all the animal voice of Topcliffe
howling insane threats. Sick at heart, but patiently neat as always,
he collected everything to do with his priestly office, and spoke
some cheering words to those who came breathlessly in with
other evidence to hide. (7)

Topcliffe's troop—'a vast swarm' says Garnet—was composed
of gaol-birds wearing the Queen's escutcheon, and courtiers of
the meaner type; hounds to whom harrying women was cheaper

and more sensational than stag-hunting. Among them was the wretched young Fitzherbert who, four years before, had offered Topcliffe £3,000 to remove all of his family that stood between him and the estate of Padley, and who in three years' time was to be prosecuted by Topcliffe in the open court for breach of contract to pay for murder.

A motley gang, armed to the teeth, they had careered through the soft midsummer evening, gathering in on the way a local magistrate with still more men. At nightfall Topcliffe had disposed his forces around the house; and at twelve o'clock the assault was launched.

Soon the great hall was thronged to overflowing. Heavily guarded, the household stood with stiff, contemptuous faces, while searchers stormed through the building, and Topcliffe raved up and down calling Mrs. Bellamy a string of filthy names. Suddenly, like a blow in the face, they realized that he was talking sense. He had a paper in his hand from which he was reading a fairly accurate description of the hiding-place.

'Now will you hand over this *Cotton*' (for that was Southwell's *alias*), 'or shall I pull this foul nest about your ears, beam by beam?'

Mrs. Bellamy repeated, 'I know no man of that name', but her voice faltered, and the changed countenances of all were obvious. No one but a member of the family could have written the words on that paper. Topcliffe began to laugh.

His position, however, was not as secure as he feigned. He had to be away with his catch by daybreak, for Uxendon was an honoured house in the neighbourhood, and an inquiry into the source of his evidence might prove complicated. So he changed his tone to one of hearty good-sense, and appealed to Mrs. Bellamy to save her husband's credit by a free surrender, relying on his own influence with the Queen to shield her.

She still refused, but she managed somehow or other (though Garnet does not understand how) to convey the situation to Southwell and to '*leave him the free choice* of what should be done'. It is difficult to see how she could have done this without revealing the place and leaving him *no* choice; but it may be that this was the sort of situation which Southwell had constantly envisaged, and that there was some sort of prearranged signal. At any rate Garnet's words are definite enough to be accepted: 'He judged, for a certainty, that the game was up, and presented himself before Topcliffe there and then.' It was, after all, what he had been preparing for, these last six years almost to a day. But there were still a few moments of the game to be played out.

Topcliffe paused in his harangue as the newcomer entered the hall. He had probably never seen Southwell in the flesh before, but the description tallied. The slim, straight build, the auburn hair, the famous eyes with their arched brows, the finely-cut lips set in a slight smile that might be called mockery if it were not so mild and courteous; and not the description only, but a certain air of something indefinable, something *absolute*, proclaimed that this was the man. (8)

An ungovernable fury began to swell and shake the old man's frame.

'Who are you?' he managed to say.

'A gentleman,' was the reply.

The word released a stream of epithets from Topcliffe. 'Sir', said the man, 'these are hard words. By what right do you use them?'

'Priest! Traitor!! JESUIT!!!'

'Ah, but that is what you have to prove.'

These things he said, wrote Garnet, not to save himself, but searching some way to avert ruin from the family. Their immediate effect, however, was to remove the last vestiges of self-control from Topcliffe. He drew his sword and rushed at the figure before him. The magistrate and another standing by had to hurl themselves upon him and hold his arms. The struggle continued for some time. Once he nearly broke away from them, but they dragged him back. For one mad moment it may have looked as if the impossible would happen; as if Topcliffe might have to be carried away in a fit, and the arrest held up for lack of identification.

But it was not to be. Robert's quota of miraculous escapes was finished, and he knew it. Renegade Catholics in Topcliffe's troop came forward to swear that he was Southwell and that they had seen him saying Mass. It may have been then that he made the curious remark recorded by Garnet: 'I see. It is my blood you are after. You may have it as freely as my mother gave it to me'; and he turned to speak some consoling words to the family. Topcliffe, who had now regained control of himself, interrupted shortly, 'We came here to arrest you, not to listen to you gabbling. Take him away!' He then despatched young Fitzherbert to Greenwich with news of his success for the Queen, 'who heard it, I am told', says Garnet (whose information came straight from the Court), 'with unwonted merriment'.

Before sunrise the ransacking of the house was completed; and the church furniture was thrown into a cart, along with Southwell bound hand and foot. As quickly and as secretly as possible the cart trundled back along the wooded road of the day before, as far as Tyburn, and then continued in the same direction to Topcliffe's house in Westminster.

Garnet continues:

With the first light of morning he was taken to London; and though they had only the least-frequented streets to traverse, yet immediately the report of his capture spread through the City; and, more swiftly than one would believe, it was bruited abroad through the whole kingdom. It is not possible to describe the sorrow of the Catholics (and not of Catholics only); as if each one had lost a dear kinsman. . . .

And yet he is so well prepared that, stricken as we are, we feel that God by his sufferings will increase his glory and the good of the Church. . . . But a very special kind of courage is needed to endure these tortures. . . . Our hope is in the Mystical Body of Christ and in the mutual compassion of its members.

In Robert's life up to this moment, sometimes he had been threatened by blind panic, and at other times by black depression. As he bumped up and down now in the cart, it would not be surprising if both these enemies joined forces more formidably than ever before. The last barrier to heaven, which had seemed so blissful at a distance, was now the ghastly cliff-face of another world. Mountains of agony joined together by troughs of despair. He must call on his pale spirit and leaden limbs to quicken themselves for the encounter with sheer pain: a labyrinth that would divide and multiply for ever in new dimensions. The Angel of Death would despise him, and the Angel of Oblivion would hang back.

> Sleep, death's ally, oblivion of tears . . .
> Not such my sleep, but whisperer of dreams . . .

There remained only the Angel of Silence. The silence of the grave. He must be so silent that Death, for very shame, would come and take him.

When Topcliffe had refreshed himself for the loss of his night's sleep, before settling down to the main task in front of him, he wrote a preliminary report to the Queen which deserves to be studied in all its implications, though its almost paranoiac spelling is here modernized:

Most Gracious Sovereign, Having F. Robert Southwell (of my knowledge) the Jesuit in my strong chamber in Westminster . . . I have presumed (after my little sleep) to run over this examination enclosed, faithfully taken and of him foully and suspiciously answered, and, somewhat knowing the nature and doings of the man, may it please your Majesty to see my simple opinion. Constrained in duty to utter it. Upon this present taking of him it is good forthwith to enforce him to answer truly and directly, and so to prove his answers true in haste, to the end that such as be deeply concerned in his treacheries have no time to start or make shift. To use any means in common prisons either to stand upon or against the wall (which above all things excels and hurteth not) will give warning. But if your Highness' pleasure be to know anything in his heart, to stand against the wall, his feet standing upon the ground and his hands stuck as high as he can reach against the wall, like a trick at Trenshemeare,* will enforce him to tell all, and the truth proved by the sequel.

* Trenchmore, a boisterous dance of the period.

The answer of him to the question of the Countess of Arundel, and that of Father Persons deciphereth him. It may please your Majesty to consider that I never did take so weighty a man: if he be rightly used. . . .

So humbly submitting myself to your majesty's directions in this, or in any service with any hazard, I cease until I hear your pleasure here at Westminster with my charge and ghostly father this Monday the 26th of June 1592. Your majesty's faithful Servant.

RIC. TOPCLIFFE. (9)

Did they really hope to get political secrets out of Southwell? The 'question of Father Persons' may possibly be Persons's letter, with Southwell's name in it, which Cecil and Fixer had brought over, and the stories they had added to it about Lord Strange and the succession. The 'question of the Countess of Arundel' may possibly be another of Fixer's informations about a plan to have Philip's son and heir educated by Catholics overseas. No doubt they expected Southwell to supply details of how students were sent abroad; but the only questions of which there is actual evidence turned upon the names of his many friends who sheltered priests. Topcliffe's letter implied that he hoped to get a detailed confession without much difficulty. He consistently despised priests as ladies-men who sheltered in boudoirs; and Southwell, being a poet as well, looked like being particularly vulnerable to physical assault.

Topcliffe was also very conscious, not only that the Queen's eyes were on him, but that the ears of many thousands were straining for the issue of his struggle with this man whose name had been whispered so often in unflattering contrast with his own. 'The Goliath of the Papists' Southwell was considered. In the context he was more like David, or, in his own words—for now that the ordeal was upon him, his training told, and he pitched all the wealth of his consciousness in a single point upon the wheel of Prayer—

> Like Abraham ascending up the hill
> To sacrifice . . .

In the torture-chamber, which faced the street, the windows had been boarded up, and only a little skylight let in the air. Of the methods employed only one can be identified with certainty. It was the new one of the 'manacles' or 'gauntlets', which had proved itself more efficient than the rack. While inflicting the maximum amount of pain, it was easy to employ and left no visible wound or dislocation. Gyves, with a point pressing on the wrist, were fitted to the victim, and he was simply left to hang by the hands. Modern experiments with ropes have shown that a brave man cannot endure this posture for more than ten minutes; and if protracted much beyond that time, it would result in severe internal injuries, and finally in death.

In the case of those English priests who were hung for many hours, and many times, death was avoided and the pain prolonged either by allowing the wall to take a little of the body's weight, or by having a stool which the toes could just touch and which could be removed and replaced at intervals. It is instructive to compare Father Gerard's very short account of 'hanging by the hands' with a modern analysis of its effects.

Hanging like this I began to pray. The gentlemen standing around asked me whether I was willing to confess now. 'I cannot and I will not', I answered. But I could hardly utter the words, such a gripping pain came over me. It was worst in my chest and belly, my hands and arms. All the blood in my body seemed to rush up into my arms and hands and I thought that blood was oozing out from the ends of my fingers and the pores of my skin. . . . The pain was so intense that I thought I could not possibly endure it, and added to it, I had an interior temptation.

A modern writer, Dr. Hynek, has argued that this 'hanging by the hands' was the essential pain of crucifixion and the cause of death on the cross. Whether or not this is so, his description of the effects of 'hanging by the hands' can be read as an accurate analysis of Gerard's simple words:

In a short time the arm muscles became stretched to the limit of their capacity, which culminated in a spasmodic contraction and in cramp. The extreme contraction of the muscles prevented the blood from circulating as it should. One defective condition increased the other, until the muscle reached its maximum of activity and of irritation in the conditions known as *tetanisation*. . . . The bacillus of this terrible infection attaches its poison to the central nerves, and irritates the muscles into convulsive spasms, which reach a point at which the sufferer, while remaining fully conscious, becomes almost demented with pain. . . .

This was very much what took place in the case of those suffering on the cross. Their arm muscles were contracted in an extremely exhausting manner, which gave rise to spasms that affected the arms, the shoulders, and the muscles of the back, as well as the thighs and the legs.

. . . There is another point to consider . . . in this position even the liver, that great reservoir of blood, which is attached by strong bands to the diaphragm, sinks with the sinking of the diaphragm: in other words, the liver also obstructs the free circulation of the blood. This obstruction affects chiefly the catheters of the intestines and the lower limbs. For this reason the tissue of the muscles is still further deprived of the blood it needs. All these circumstances give rise to spasms of increasing severity which sooner or later must lead to death. . . .

This means that the crucified man died, fully conscious, in the most terrible pain. (10)

From this it may be gathered that Southwell was speaking with perfect accuracy when he said at his trial that he had been tortured ten times—'*each one worse than death*'. For each time that death seemed to be hovering near, the torture was relaxed, and death retired. On one occasion, however—according to both Garnet and Verstegan—Topcliffe nearly went too far. (11) Impatient perhaps at getting no results, he strapped the prisoner's heels behind his thighs, and went away leaving him like that. A terrified servant had to summon him back with the news that the prisoner was barely conscious and seemed to be expiring. When he was taken down and revived, he threw up a great quantity of blood.

Forty hours, day or night making no difference, he spent in Topcliffe's house; and during that time he endured the first four of his hangings, according to Verstegan, who adds that Topcliffe had tormented him in other ways also. Later, at his trial, when challenged to show the marks of his torture, he replied in one terrible sentence: 'Ask a woman to show her throes!' And he added that he did not say these things for himself, but for others, that they might not be driven to despair.

But before dark on the first day Topcliffe was already worried. According to Garnet, he sent a second message to the Queen to say that the prisoner was behaving with brutish obstinacy and would not even confess his name.

> The Queen called Topcliffe a fool, and said she would put the matter in the hands of her Council who would soon finish it. So on the next day, or the day after, the two Clerks of the Council arrived to help Topcliffe in his inquisitions. Yet still, they say, 'the prisoner remains obstinate'. (12)

One of the Clerks was William Wade to whose skill and cruelty as a torturer the Hatfield Calendar bears abundant witness. At nightfall on Tuesday, or early on Wednesday, he had Southwell removed next door to the Gatehouse Prison where the inquisition could be conducted in a more scientific manner. From now on, it may be presumed, the hangings were at much longer intervals, employed only as a last resort, and the emphasis was on cross-questioning and the deprivation of sleep.

Members of the Council came to take part in the examinations, and among them Sir Robert Cecil himself. As he and others spoke about it afterwards to friends and courtiers, some scraps of information reached Garnet from one or other of his reliable sources. Topcliffe's accounts had prepared the distinguished visitors to meet the surly obstinacy of a wild beast. But the sick, strained figure in front of them answered their first questions with ready courtesy and affability. Cecil, or one of the lords, complimented him on his manner of answering, and asked why he did not show a like reasonableness to Mr. Topcliffe.

'Because', he answered—perhaps showing his hands, like Saint Paul, with a faint smile—'I have found *by experience* that the man is not open to reason.' (13)

But when they began to ask him where he was in London on a certain day, or the colour of a horse that he rode in the country, he apologized in advance for any apparent discourtesy, and said that he found the best way to avoid misunderstanding and to safeguard the rights of others, was to say nothing at all.

'What', said one of the lords sharply, 'what harm can it do to anyone if you say that you passed through Paul's on this or that day?'

But the answer was silence, and again silence. So there was nothing for it but to resort once more to Mr. Topcliffe's methods. In the ruined body in front of him, Robert Cecil, for perhaps the first time in his life, had met someone who was his master in suavity of manner, quickness of thought, and cold intensity of will. It was a strange meeting of the two cousins who were almost of the same age. When Robert Cecil left the sweating torture-chamber, he was shaken and even moved.

Later, when travelling with a friend, he turned to him and said: 'They boast about the heroes of antiquity . . . but we have a new torture which it is not possible for a man to bear. And yet I have seen Robert Southwell hanging by it, still as a tree-trunk, and no one able to drag one word from his mouth.'

Another remark, passed on to Garnet, indicates that the questioning of Southwell turned always on the houses of his friends: 'No wonder they trust these Jesuits with their lives, when, from a man ten times tortured, not one word could be twisted that might lead others into danger.' (14)

It is not known at what date the tenth torture ceased. Some time in July, he seems to have been thrown aside as useless for further examination. Towards the end of that month he was still lying helpless and neglected in the Gatehouse Prison, utterly emaciated, too weak to fend for himself, covered in his own filth, and swarming with maggots.

But this state of degradation which, in prospect, had been one of the things that he most dreaded, now meant nothing to him. In the depth of his consciousness he was aware that the battle was won, the mountain scaled; and strange, strong hands were leading him, step by faltering step, to the last resting-place before the end.

It may be taken as a proof of the extremities he had been in that his transference to solitary confinement in the Tower of London was hailed by his friends with sighs of the profoundest relief. The order, dated 28th July (15) in the *Privy Council Registers* requires the Lieutenant of the Tower 'to receive Rob. Southwell priest to be kept close prisoner so that no one may be suffered access to him but such an one as Topcliffe shall appoint as his keeper'. And there was an addition which sounds like Topcliffe's own words: 'Herein we require you to take order for his close restraining, he being a most lewd and dangerous person.'

The form was grudging enough, but the issue seems to have been a triumph of his friends on his behalf. According to Yepez's *Istoria*, which relied mostly on first-hand reports from England, indignation broke out when, at the end of the month, he was actually brought before a court of Justice to be charged; but there is no other evidence for this appearance. The Spanish historian may be simply amplifying Verstegan's dispatches of August and September which state that

it was observed by some that saw him, that with close keeping and hard usage, wanting linen to shift himself, he was much troubled with lice. But since his being in the Tower, his father hath obtained leave of the Council to send him some necessary apparel whereby he findeth himself in far better state than before he was, being in the custody of a merciless monster, one Topcliffe. . . .

The petition of Richard Southwell is given by Yepez in a form that sounds authentic:

That if his son had committed anything for which by the laws he had deserved death, he might suffer death. If not, as he was a gentleman, that her majesty might be pleased to order that he should be treated as such, even though he were a Jesuit. And that as his father, he might be permitted to send him what he needed to sustain life. This petition was granted, and thus his people visited him, and thenceforth sent him meat, and a Bible, and the works of St Bernard, which he himself wanted for his solace. (16)

U

It was the Countess of Arundel who sent him his volume of Saint Bernard, along with a loving consignment of clothes and bedding.

Since Richard Southwell was virtually bankrupt at this time, it may be presumed that he had powerful backing for his bold plea. According to More, the only person who was actually allowed to visit Robert, before his transfer to the Tower, was his sister Mary Bannister. But she represented many others who offered their services. The story of his victorious resistance was now common property; and, in spite of violent official propaganda against him, the details of his sufferings were matter for indignation not loud but deep.

For the first time, perhaps, Elizabeth became aware that this Jesuit about whom there was so much fuss, for and against—the man who had written that impudent *Supplication* which began with the same flourish as Philip Sidney's—belonged to a family that was well known to her; he was the son of the girl she had been brought up with and learnt Latin from. At any rate, the petition was granted.

More politic motives than clemency may have played their part; there was nothing like solitary confinement in the Tower to make a man forgotten and to reduce his fighting spirit. Still, it was a clemency to allow him his books.

For the next two and a half years they were his only companions: the Bible, a breviary which Garnet managed to send him, and the works of Saint Bernard 'which he wanted for his solace'.

CHAPTER TWENTY

The Interval, 1592–5

'LET *him kiss me with the kiss of his mouth.* What does it mean, this sudden and abrupt opening, taken as it were from the middle of a speech? As if someone had already spoken, and this was a reply, made by some other person desirous to be kissed.'

So does Saint Bernard begin his discourses upon the Canticle of Canticles. (1)

It was a speech being held (he continues) between the Angels and the Spouse—that is, our human nature.

'Do you not recall', say the Angels, 'when you were an outcast and stained with sinful wandering, how it seemed to you supreme felicity to crouch before his feet, and how to kiss those feet seemed a prize beyond your hope?' 'I do recall it,' says she. 'And when at last with long and racking sobs you had expelled the evil vapours of your past, how overwhelmed you were when he held out his hands to kiss. To be admitted into the company of his loyal and trusty servants seemed to you then the highest honour possible.' 'I grant it.' 'Well, then, you have been allowed to kiss his feet; he has even given you his hand to kiss. What more can you desire to content you?' '*Let him kiss me with the kiss of his mouth.* . . . I have no right to kiss his feet, I am not worthy to kiss his hand. I have received far more than I deserve. Yet it is less than I desire. For I am not born by reason, but by desire. Shame indeed cries out to me, go back; but love orders me on. Judgement is against me, but love is head-long: heeds not judgement, overreaches counsel, throws aside shame and defies reason. I beg, I supplicate, I demand: *Let him kiss me with the kiss of his mouth.*'

As Robert turned over the pages that he knew so well—but had imitated only in very muted accents—he read them no longer with shamefast awe, but with a new lightness of heart. In discourse after discourse, proceeding slowly through the verses, the Saint outlines the virtue and contemplation that a devout soul must acquire before it can be one with the Spouse, the Church of the Elect: with many applications of the Biblical imagery, some happier than others, and with many warnings against presumption. Why then should he, who had always judged this imagery too high for him, who knew himself so destitute of virtue, so arid in contemplation, why should he find the Spouse's words so perfectly his own: 'My beloved to me, and I to him, who feedeth among the lilies.'

As was his custom, he turned away from them as an invitation to rest, and took them instead as an incentive to effort. With a pin (for he had no writing materials) he pricked out the words for himself several times: *Deus tibi se dedit: tu te Deo.* 'God hath given himself to thee; do thou give thyself to God.' But even as he braced himself for what fresh tortures might be in store, the sense of strain was charmed away. He had only to glance up at the bars of his cell, and the words came singing through: '*The voice of my beloved, behold he cometh leaping upon the mountains, skipping over the hills. . . . Behold he standeth behind our wall, looking through the windows, looking through the lattices. Behold my beloved speaketh to me: Arise, make haste, my love, my dove, my beautiful one, and come. For winter is now past, the rain is over and gone.*'

Perhaps when he reached the thirtieth verse of the Canticle, in the sixty-first discourse of the Saint, he knew the truth. '*My dove in the clefts of the rock, in the hollow places of the wall, show me thy face, let thy voice sound in my ears: for thy voice is sweet and thy face comely.*' Christ is the Rock, says St. Bernard, and the clefts of the Rock are his precious wounds. To one who shares those wounds he says: 'Let thy voice sound in my ears', in fulfilment of his promise: 'Whosoever shall confess me before men, I will also confess him before my Father who is in Heaven.'

Why then should the faithful soldier fear when his gentle captain calls to him: 'Show me thy face. Lift thy eyes to my wounds.' Why should he fear to lift his bruised, discoloured face to his, by whose bruises he is healed. . . . He who looks upon those wounds can think no longer of his own. The martyr stands; he stamps the ground in triumph, though his body is all torn. When the knife rips open his sides, blithely as well as bravely he sees the blood well forth. . . . It is no drug, but love that causes this. The senses are not lost, but lifted up. The pain is present, but it is subdued, it is despised. From the Rock, therefore, is the martyr's strength, strong as the rock to endure, and valiant to drink the chalice of his Lord. And that inebriating chalice, how glorious it is!

And so, albeit slowly at first, he opened his whole consciousness to this great well of joy that was being pumped through him. 'The joy of the Lord is our strength.' With it came a peace such as he had never known in his life before. Always before, there had been one deep corroding barb: the fear of *not* dying, the fear of living on with a gradual loss of vision and decline into sin. During his tortures, that fear had done its worst. Death had indeed hung back. But a greater than death had come to rescue him and had cast out fear for ever.

He knew now with certainty that whether he was martyred or not, he would die of love. In the extraction of fear, he had received a wound that would never cease to flow. But it was a life-giving wound which nourished him night and day with peace and consolation. As Garnet wrote:

It truly seems that with a special providence Our Lord willed to keep him all that time as it were in a good noviceship, to prove him like gold in the furnace, to make him worthy of Himself. Certainly, so long a perseverance, such a multitude of sufferings, such a lack of all human means and aids, shows clearly how fortified was that holy soul and furnished with spiritual weapons, and at the same time with what power and love Our Lord spoke to his heart in that blessed solitude, giving him vigour and freshness, and making him display in public such a peace and tranquillity that the heretics themselves stood in awe of him. (2)

As the months passed he recovered in some measure his bodily strength also—though here too he had received a wound from which it is unlikely that he would ever have recovered wholly. It seems that at the time when he hung for so long that he spewed a great quantity of blood, he had suffered a grave intestinal injury. Two and a half years later, when he was moved to his third and last prison, and found a friendly gaoler—'he asked the gaoler not to be too far away in case some accident should happen to him, or he should be in need of anything, because (as a result of his bitter tortures) his sides were not strong enough for him to shout'. (3)

Garnet, who never tired of adding new details, says again about his thirty months of imprisonment:

> Notwithstanding that all the aforesaid time he was never once able to celebrate Mass or confess himself or speak with anyone who might bring him a like consolation, yet he came forth to judgement and execution with such an undaunted spirit, so calm and settled, that it seemed as if he had just been with a company of angelic souls, and was going to enjoy himself at the rarest banquet. (4)

Garnet also believed that he practised in prison a devotion which he often recommended to his penitents when they could not get to Mass: to stand before God at a fixed hour, and to join oneself in desire with the Sacrifice of the Eucharist being offered in all parts of the globe.

Strange though it seems, then, there is no other way of regarding these thirty months except as a very happy period in his life. In the absence of actual torture, the regime of the Tower was harsh rather than positively cruel. Bad food and water, bad air, and nervous oppression were the prisoners' worst enemies; but Robert, though he felt those as much as others did ('I am decayed in memory with long and close confinement', he said at his trial), had found a *modus vivendi* with such companions long ago. The Lieutenant of the Tower, Sir Michael Blount, whom other accounts present as a coarse and unfeeling man, was quite won over by this gay and gentle captive; he spoke of him often as 'that saint', saying what an honour it was to have had converse with him.

This report of Garnet's is confirmed unintentionally by the *Life* of the Earl of Arundel, whose author, describing the love and veneration which Philip had for Robert, says:

> For when the said Father after some years was apprehended and imprisoned in the Tower, whensoever the Lieutenant made any mention of him in his presence, as oftentimes he did, he [Philip] used ever to speak with great respect of him, calling him often 'Blessed Father'.   And when once the Lieutenant seemed to take exceptions thereat, saying: 'Term you him Blessed Father, being as he is an enemy to his country?' the Earl defended him, saying: 'How can that be, seeing yourself hath told me heretofore that no fault could be laid unto him but his Religion?'

Once when the Lieutenant was visiting Robert, Philip's dog, which had strayed from its quarters, came wagging its tail into his chamber. When Robert learned whose dog it was, he seems to have given it his blessing to take back to its master; for when Philip heard about it from the Lieutenant, he recalled 'Saint Jerome's writing how those Lions which had digged with their paws Saint Paul the Eremit's grave stood after waiting with their eyes upon Saint Anthony expecting his blessing'.

But though Southwell might see the little dog, he could never see its master. As far as friends and fellow-prisoners were concerned his confinement was absolute. In March 1593 there was a rumour, reported by Verstegan *as* a rumour, that he had been tortured again and was to be brought out for trial at Easter. But at the risk of the wish being father to the thought, one may incline to the view that the 'ten times' of his torture were completed in the Gatehouse prison. He was certainly interrogated at intervals by Privy Councillors, Sir Robert Cecil among them; but a story relayed by Garnet in a letter of just the same month, March 1593, suggests that this particular questioning was humanely conducted. It concerned Thomas Bell, a fairly prominent priest in Lancashire, who had apostatized at the end of 1592 and offered his services to the Government. The Government, anxious to assess the value of their new acquisition, bethought themselves to ask Southwell's candid opinion.

Southwell replied, with that admirable terseness which he could command when he chose, that from what he knew of the man, he thought they would find him of average ability, but much given to quarrelling. 'And so indeed we did', said one of the Councillors to Garnet's informant, 'for he turned out to be a most trivial and pestilent fellow, in contrast with this Southwell who is so plainly earnest and devout.'

This, however, could not have been the only question in 'the many examinations' to which, as Garnet says, 'he answered always with great shrewdness as well as prudence'. These years when the plague was devastating London were years also of deep political malaise, of a widening rift between the Cecilian party and the supporters of Essex. Each side was casting around for useful foreign agents; Phelippes was working for Essex at this time, whereas Poley had been taken on by Cecil. There was much coming and going of messages between Poley and his friend Moody, who was working with the Morgan-Paget faction. From these murky crossings, and from the Essex-Cecil rivalry, was bred a monstrous procession of plots, each new one surpassing the others in absurdity, until finally with the Squire plot of 1597 they were clapped off the European stage for the rest of the reign.

Since the English Jesuits, it is hardly necessary to say, were the alleged authors of all these plots, Southwell could not have escaped attempts to incriminate him, especially as the first two concerned the Stanley succession claim with which John Cecil's information had connected him. In 1592 there had been the condemnation of Sir John Perrot, on the evidence of a letter forged by his accuser, for treasonable correspondence with Sir William Stanley. In 1593 there was the execution of the Protestant adventurer, Richard Hesketh, who, according to Burghley, 'persuaded Lord Strange (then Earl of Derby) to undertake . . . all the treasons and purposes aforesaid'; the evidence in this case would appear to have been a letter planted on Hesketh by a Government agent. The death of the young Earl of Derby in the following year put an end to this fruitful source of spy-stories; but others took their place. (5) In 1594 a number of needy Irishmen came over from Flanders bursting with information; but all of them (except one genuine fanatic who desired to kill Antonio Perez) turned out to be *provocateurs* uncertain who was supposed to accuse whom and of what. Then there was the Lopez plot which revolved round the almost metaphysical question whether the unfortunate Jew was a Spanish spy who had taken money from Elizabeth to betray King Philip, or an English spy who had taken money from Philip to betray Queen Elizabeth. Finally the Yorke-Williams plot in which Yorke's story—that it was concocted by the Jesuits *in consultation with Dr. Gifford*—caused Lord Burghley to shake his head in disapproval: the fellow had got the story all muddled up. (6)

Many were the revelations made 'to Mr. Topcliffe in my lord Burghley's house in the Strand'. John Daniel, the leader of the needy Irishmen, who had come over with a passport from Lord Burghley, later averred that he had come over to advertise not only the plot of his compatriots, but that of Lopez as well; 'and at the arraignment of Yorke, Williams, *and Southwell the Jesuit*, I was nominated to have been the first discoverer of these late practises intended against her highness'. (7) Topcliffe was very active in Sussex also at this time, pursuing evidence against a 'Father Roberts' who was said to have been there in 1590 and 1592; in the course of these proceedings, from which he hoped an estate or two would fall into his lap, two men and an elderly woman died in prison as a result of his diabolical ill-treatment. (8)

But as the year 1594 wore on, and from all this farrago of horrible nonsense no overt accusation materialized against Southwell, his friends began to be certain that he would never be brought out for trial; and suggestions passed between Rome and London that an offer should be made for his ransom, and for that of Father Weston, and for their banishment out of the realm. (9)

But the two persons who, it might have been supposed, would

have been most forward in this respect, seemed strangely to demur. These were Claudius Aquaviva and the Countess of Arundel. Aquaviva knew very well that if he could procure the ransom, Southwell would accept banishment with his usual resignation, but it would be the bitterest blow he could possibly have dealt him. The Countess of Arundel knew the same; for she had promised him solemnly 'never to concur to the hindering of his Martyrdom, in case Almighty God did call him to that high honour; therefore she contained herself and did not strive therein'. (10)

But in that same autumn she had a ray of news from him in a strange manner. Two gentlewomen had obtained the unusual favour of being allowed to buy some of the rare flowers that grew in the Queen's Privy Garden. The Privy Garden (which is now a garden no longer) was a little triangle or quadrangle at the east end of the lane that runs along the river-front inside the moated wall. It was flanked by four turrets: the Cradle and the Lanthorn on either side of the gateway into the garden, and the Well Tower and the Salt Tower at the far end, the Salt Tower being joined to the Lanthorn by the long Queen's Gallery.

In the Salt Tower at that time lay Father Henry Walpole in terrible pain, having suffered, it would seem, even worse tortures than Southwell. The Lanthorn Tower was where Philip Arundel had been, and perhaps still was.* The Cradle Tower was that from which Gerard was to escape in 1597, having first put up a prayer to Father Walpole, and 'to Father Southwell who was imprisoned near here'. All things considered, it seems most likely that Southwell's prison was on one of the storeys of the Lanthorn Tower.

The two women, having presented their petition at the main gate, slipped in and advanced along the lane that led past Traitor's Gate to the Privy Garden where their flowers were being picked. It was a brave thing to do, because there was a general belief and dread that those who entered the Tower precincts irregularly

---

* The incident of his dog would be more natural if he had been here, and not back in the Beauchamp Tower.

were never allowed out of them. But they were rewarded by the sign that they had hoped for. From between the bars of one of the tower-windows they saw a hand come out and reach towards them in blessing. Emboldened they returned once more, and this time there was no doubt; it was Father Robert who was blessing them. (11) So they were able to bring back to the Countess the news that he was in the same tower as her husband, or very near it.

The close proximity of these three Norfolk men, Robert Southwell, Henry Walpole, and Philip Howard, who were all to die martyrs in the following year, recalls a letter written on 23rd June 1591, which may have been taken later on as recording a portent, though there is no evidence that it was. On Saint George's Day of that year, says the letter-writer, between nine and ten in the evening, those who were in Norwich and round-about saw three suns in the sky enclosed by a great white and cloudless circle, and between the suns a shadowy St. Andrew's Cross which seemed to the eye about twelve arms in length. Not all, adds the letter-writer, saw the shadowy cross in the centre, but of the three suns there were many eye-witnesses in Norfolk. (12)

In the winter of 1594 Robert sent a personal petition to Sir Robert Cecil that either he might be brought to trial to answer in public all the things that had been urged against him in private, or else, if he were not to be tried, that his friends might have access to him. Cecil is said to have replied that if he were so anxious to be hanged, he would have his wish very soon. It was an answer out of keeping with the Secretary's usual suavity; but perhaps, in an inverted sort of way, it was a more sincere one than usual. Its very brutality was a confession of defeat and perhaps even of self-disgust. But one is left with the problem of why the Government should have decided at this particular time upon an action which they had been postponing for so long.

According to Deckers, Elizabeth was encouraged by the example of Henry IV of France who had temporarily banished the Jesuits. But this is only a conjecture on Deckers' part, and it seems far from likely. Elizabeth of England was not in need of the example of Henry of Navarre.

Yepez was on surer ground when he reported that the decision was connected with the capture of several boys from the new school at St. Omer who were sailing to the seminary at Seville. The connection, fortuitous but real, was that the discovery of this new nest of young papists was the occasion of a furious tirade from Topcliffe to the Council; and Topcliffe's violent insistence on Southwell's condemnation is the only reason given for it by Garnet, who adds, however, that this alone would not have caused the decision, and that the main reason for it must rest simply with the divine disposal.

While this is undoubtedly true, there is another subsidiary reason, not yet mentioned by anyone, which seems to accord with the facts. A sentence blurted out by Topcliffe at the trial reveals that Southwell in one of his examinations in prison had expounded to Sir Robert Cecil the theory and practice of 'equivocation'. This was the opportunity that the Government was looking for. It was their custom never to arraign a well-known priest unless they had some charge which they reckoned would disgrace him and distract people's attention from the unpopular Statute. They had failed to find a colourable charge of treason against Southwell, but they had stumbled on this one of 'equivocation' which he had frankly admitted; he had not realized how easily it could be distorted by a skilful prosecutor.

It was this charge which formed the brunt of the Attorney's attack on him at his trial; and from that time forth it was one of the chief accusations against the Society. Right up to the Gunpowder Plot it was Southwell's reputation which had to sustain the full odium of the charge; and it was a charge vociferated not only by Government propaganda, but even more by the anti-Jesuit faction, particularly by his old enemy Bagshaw—'these good fellows', as Persons wrote, referring to Bagshaw and his friends, 'who, conspiring with the persecutors, have sought to disgrace him (. . . Mr Southwell of blessed memory against whom this calumniation was first urged . . .) ever since for the same,

and not only him but his whole Order'. (13) It is a charge which
has been echoed frequently down to our own day, and there is
no doubt that Southwell's example was the beginning of it. That
being so, it seems necessary to say something in his defence, since
he was not allowed to say it for himself at his trial.*

It seems that the Puritans of the Classis movement were the
first to employ equivocation in England. They did so in consultation with lawyers and with a good conscience. ' The Minute Book
of the Dedham Classics', writes Usher, 'proves that they had actually
compassed very nearly everything of which they were charged,
but by means of playing upon words they had been able to avoid
the legal terms.' It seems likely also that the Marprelates had
recourse to the same; otherwise it is hard to explain how no
individual, despite rigorous questioning, was ever convicted of
the authorship of their Tracts. (14)

What has to be borne in mind in the case of both the English
Catholics and the Puritans is, first, that they were up against a
system of forced self-accusation worse than the Spanish Inquisition; and secondly that they would not allow lies. 'He that
sticketh not at lies', as Persons said pointedly in his defence of
Southwell, 'need never to use equivocation.'

Southwell's alleged advice to Anne Bellamy ('alleged' because
it may not have been given to her personally) is the first quoted
instance of the practice among the English Catholics.† What
exactly the advice was will never be known, because he was not
allowed to state his version of it; but it tended to the effect that a
Catholic, who was asked with evil intent by a pursuivant, 'Have
you a priest in the house?' could answer 'No' with a good
conscience, meaning, 'No, you have no right to know.' The
pursuivant would not be deceived—he would search the house
in any case—but the householder, in the event of the priest not
being found, would be protected from having convicted himself.
It is certain that times before this Catholics had answered 'No'

* For a theoretic discussion of 'equivocation', consult Appendix 'C'.

† A letter of Garnet's of March 1593 shows that he was still in some perplexity
about the rights and wrongs of the question.

when there was a priest in the house, and it is equally certain that the pursuivants had interpreted the denial as a challenge to find out. The only novelty that Southwell introduced was to relieve the Catholic conscience of what before, by the books, had seemed a sin of lying.

But to the Government the implication of this new moral sanction was much larger and more alarming. It meant that the chief weapon of Tudor law, self-accusation, was being countered by the older and banished principle, now restored to life: that no man is bound to incriminate himself. Unless the Government could discredit it thoroughly at the outset, it might prove a serious threat to what Lord Burghley had called the 'execution of justice'.

In defence of the Government, it should be admitted that there is certainly grave danger in any subject making himself judge of the law. Moreover, the ability to play with words possessed an attraction for that age which it is hard for us to appreciate. There was the further danger that the moral sanction for equivocation would be usurped, without its safeguards, for less worthy motives than religion. Southwell's answer to that, however, had already been made in his *Humble Supplication*: give us the barest elements of justice, and you will have no loyaller or more docile subjects. For, as Persons insisted, under a proper system of justice there is no need and no justification for the practice. He concluded his treatise (1607) in defence of his fellow-Jesuits:

> And now, gentle reader, having brought this Treatise to an end and justified, as I hope, our Catholic doctrine from the odious imputations of Rebellion and Equivocation, there remaineth nothing but that I conclude with an exhortation to all Catholic people not only to abstain from the first, which is utterly unlawful (I mean the attempting of anything against their loyal duties in subjection, be their pressures never so great): but also from the practice and frequent use of the second, though in some cases most lawful . . . except some urgent occasion do force them to the contrary.

There may seem at first a discord between the controversies that were to occupy the last act of Robert's life and the mystical union with God hinted at in the beginning of this chapter. But there was a connection. He had been given 'the joy of the Lord' in order to make him strong for the part he had to play. Left to himself he would have asked nothing better than to die quietly, at peace with all. But he had offered his life for England as well as for the Church; and his last hours were claimed to make that offer good. He had to walk the last stretch, almost up to the very end, exposed to the equally trying ordeals of hostility and admiration. He was a man marked for sacrifice, a Jonah, who had to trouble the belly of that great Leviathan, the State, for three days and three nights, before he was thrown up as a sign of the eternal resurrection of God's Church.

Three days and three nights it literally was. On 18th February, without any warning, he was transferred to Limbo. Garnet takes up the story, rich in detail:

By a special warrant of Sir Robert Cecil he was removed from the Tower of London to Newgate, the most severe of the twelve London gaols, so as to be always at hand when he should be called for trial. He stayed there for three or four days: in *Limbo*, as they call it, a subterranean cell of evil repute where condemned felons await the hangman's stroke, (yet a place honoured by many martyrs and by the conversion of several criminals through the converse they have had there with some valiant soldier of Christ).

But through the loving foresight of a Catholic, and by the kindness of the Keeper, he found it fitted with a bed and a fire and a constant supply of candles—for there is no other means of light in that place. All the time that he was there, no felon was condemned, so he was alone with the worms—except that the Keeper came to visit him several times, a most unusual thing.

On the first evening that he arrived, and all the time that followed, he was given such good fare that he said he had never eaten like this all the time that he was in the Tower—for the Tower, being the City Fortress, the Catholics do not dare to put their heads inside it. He was greeted with a cup of wine, which he accepted, saying that it was the first he had drunk for two years and more. It was the Catholics who procured these things for him, as a sign of the great love they bore him; and they would gladly have done much more if it had been allowed them.

Just before he was brought out for trial, he was visited by a little old woman, sent by his friends with a cup of soup, who said to him: 'O Sir, God comfort you, you must appear today before the judges. But drink up this, it will make you brave and merry.' He drank it, and said to her: 'This is a broth for champions, not for condemned men.' And that was the first news that he had that his hour had come.

He was then conducted to that same tribunal, called the King's Bench, where so many years before had stood his blessed predecessor —Edmund Campion. . . .

CHAPTER TWENTY-ONE

'Like a Giant to Run his Race'

'THE Father, being brought along with halberds and bills and his arms tied with a cord, pressed with the throng, at the length came to the bar; and then, having his hands loosed, put off his hat and made obeisance.'

In the dusty light and shadow of the court-room three presences took shape: one he guessed, the second he knew slightly, and the third more than slightly. Sprawling above him was the Chief Justice of the King's Bench, Sir John Popham, with huge ungainly body and uneasy pendulous face. (1) Over against him, handsome, smiling, and alert, was the richest lawyer at the Bar, Sir Edward Coke, the Attorney-General, with the trump card of 'equivocation' up his sleeve. The third man was Mr. Topcliffe. There were other actors seated around, but between himself and these three—with the pack of people almost on top of them straining to hear—the main scene rested.

The Chief Justice was addressing the Jury. The prisoner, he said, was to be judged on the Statute of Anno 27—by which to be a priest was in itself treason—but they must bear in mind the wise and just grounds on which this Statute had been enacted. It had been proved by experience that as long as a priest or Jesuit was at large in England, Her Majesty's life was not safe, and no honest man could be sure of his lands and goods. He continued:

The Rebellion in the North, by whom was it stirred but by Cardinal Allen, a Jesuit, and the College of Jesuits and Priests? Throckmorton's action was by Jesuits and Priests. And that of Parry likewise by Jesuits and Priests.

Having reached 1585, the Chief Justice, for some reason, omitted the Babington Plot. Perhaps he had read *An Humble Supplication* and was taking no chances. His summary of official history was resumed with the period when Southwell was in solitary confinement:

> Hesketh's action to set up a subject for King was their practice. And lastly that of Yorke and Williams, to murder the Queen, was practised by Holt a Jesuit and others, who on his soul and by the Blessed Sacrament warranted it. And Stephano Hara, Agent for the King of Spain, gave assurance for payment of 40,000 gold pieces, as mounted to 12,000 English pounds, upon the performance of it.

He concluded that these were the sort of facts that the Jury must bear in mind in pronouncing their verdict upon the prisoner.

There was no likelihood of the Jury doing otherwise. It was taken for granted on both sides that they were men picked for their unquestioning Protestantism. The real Jury who were to pass the real verdict were the people who sat strangely silent in the packed court. The legal verdict was a foregone conclusion. But the moral verdict was still in doubt. It depended on how the prisoner comported himself.

The Bill of Indictment was then read. It asserted no actual contrivance of treason, but only the three facts: that he was a subject of the Queen, that he was a priest ordained since the Queen's accession, and that he had been present 'like a false traitor' at Uxendon on 26th July 1592. Did he confess the indictment?

The hearts of some at least of the spectators sank as they heard, or failed to hear, the slow gasping voice that came in reply. He was going to try and distinguish the charges, and in the inevitable wrangle to follow he would lose much strength and gain nothing.

'I confess I am a Catholic priest, and I thank God for it, but no traitor; neither can any law make it treason to be a priest.'

'You must answer the whole indictment, and either confess it, or say Not Guilty.'

'I do not deny that I was at Uxendon, for the whole house saw me apprehended there, drawn and brought thither as a mouse to the trap. But I never intended, God Almighty knoweth, to commit any treason to the Queen or State. Only to minister the Sacraments to those that seemed willing to receive them.'

'Mr. Southwell, you must either confess the indictment or say Not Guilty.'

'Not guilty of any treason,' amended Southwell, and Popham let it pass. But on the next point it was Southwell who gave way, quickly and easily, after a play on words that was not without its effect.

'How will you be tried? By God and by your country?'

'By God and by you, for I would not lay upon my country the guilt of my condemnation.'

'We are not to try you. You are to be tried "by God and by the laws".'

'By God I will be tried, but not by the law, for the law is contrary to the law of God.'

Popham cut this short, saying: 'If you refuse the trial, it shall be a sufficient condemnation, and then we are to proceed with you otherwise.'

'I am loth that these poor men [indicating the Jurors] should be guilty of my death. But if you will needs have it treason that I must lay upon them, I will be tried by God and the country.'

He was then asked if he wished to challenge any of the Jurors before they were sworn in. 'I know no goodness in any of them, neither do I know any harm,' he replied, 'but according to charity I judge the best, and will challenge none.'

To defend himself was like running the gauntlet. But his mind was recovering a little of its old quickness; and, with his mind quickening, he cared less about the pain of raising his voice. A set speech was impossible. But his hope was in the Holy Spirit, prompting him when and how to interrupt with best effect.

The preliminaries were over; and the Attorney-General, who had seemed to take no interest in them, now occupied the floor. He was in the prime of manhood, still anxious to win favour and not yet wholly prone 'to insult over misery and to inveigh bitterly against persons' as an unknown admonitor later described him. Heavily backed by the Cecils, he knew exactly how he was expected to handle this case; the prisoner must be shown as a silly little man, yet dangerous, deluded by vanity and superstition.

He began, quietly and lucidly, playing with the indictment's three points:

They shall be proved, Mr. Southwell, if you deny any of them. For the first, I think he will not deny that he was born within this land? For the second, Mr. Southwell having acknowledged himself to be a Catholic Priest, and thanking God for it, you need not any further proof. He must likewise confess that he was made a priest since the first year of Her Majesty's reign, for he was not born when Her Majesty began to reign.

At this point, Popham contributed his solitary witticism to the trial. Casting his eyes upon the prisoner, and 'seeming to scorn his youth', he asked: 'How old *are* you?'

Southwell replied—almost dreamily, it would seem, and half to himself—'I think that I am near the age of Our Saviour who lived upon the earth thirty-three years.'

Here came Topcliffe's first interruption. He 'made a great exclamation, saying he compared himself to Christ'.

'No, no,' cried Southwell, startled and abashed, 'Christ is my Creator and I am a worm created by Him.'

'Yes,' sneered Topcliffe, 'you are Christ's fellow.' (Apparently this insult, alternating with that of 'boy-priest', was meant to carry an odious meaning.)

'For the third point', resumed the Attorney, 'I think he will not deny that he was at Uxendon, for he came thither "to minister the Sacraments". But did he not know the Act of Anno 27 that has made this same a treason?'

'I know the Act', said Southwell, 'but it is impossible to make any such law agreeable to the word of God.'

The Attorney threw off his quiet manner, and his voice rolled with menace.

I had not purposed to speak much on my coming hither. But Mr. Southwell has let slip a word that *I* may not let slip: that the laws are not according to the word of God. Yet, even at this time, to my great astonishment I have heard such a point of doctrine proved against the prisoner, as many shall wonder at, and I will afterwards deliver.

This was what the people were waiting for. At no trial of a priest did the prosecution rest solely on the Statute of 1585. There was always some pseudo-revelation of personal depravity which made it seem a good thing to get rid of such persons, however harsh the law might be. For Southwell's trial, after so long, something very special of the sort must surely have been found against him. But Coke kept the people in suspense while he galloped back over the same ground as Popham's initial speech, but more picturesquely.

Every fresh attack, he said, of the Pope and the King of Spain had to be met by a fresh law. He circled very close to Southwell when he made a special point of a new weapon of corruption: *books*.

'And them likewise we met withall, and made it a felony to publish them, and a felony to keep them. A good point, my masters, to be observed', he added, his eye travelling over the people. 'Beware how you read them!'

Most of the lies he was rehashing had been already exposed in *An Humble Supplication*. Whenever his voice paused in a period, Southwell kept trying to interrupt; but the voice flowed on. At last Popham, who was showing the prisoner a very fair consideration, said sharply:

'Hold your peace, until the Queen's Counsel hath spoken, and then you shall be heard.'

Quick as a flash Southwell changed his ground. The intrusion of Topcliffe had proved a godsend in disguise. It gave just the spur that was needed to his tortured sides, and it lent colour and vibration to his voice.

'My Lord, let me answer forthwith. I am decayed in memory with long and close imprisonment, and I have been tortured ten times. I had rather have endured ten executions.'

The effect was instantaneous. The entire prosecution was thrown back on to the defensive.

'I never heard that you were tortured', said Popham.

'I never knew that you were racked', said Coke, with a neat—but illicit—use of the 'equivocation' he was about to scarify.

Topcliffe caught the point, and, anxious to show it, joined in with a bellow:

'If he were racked, let me die for it!'

'No,' shot Southwell, 'but you have another kind of torture, I think, worse than the rack.'

He began to describe it, the people hanging on his words. But the Chief Justice cut him short. 'Such things are done among all nations', he said uneasily. 'I confess that other nations have the like', replied Southwell, 'but when by torture nothing can be got, I wish there might be some measure therein, lest by extremity of pain a man be driven—if it were possible—to despair.'

He turned to the people, and, with that gesture, stamped on the minds of all their dominant impression of the trial. 'I speak not this for myself, but for others, lest they be handled so inhumanly as I.'

In a wild effort to retrieve the situation, Topcliffe shouted:

'Show the marks of your tortures!'

In the torture-chamber, when he had hoped to find a poet, he had found a Spartan. But it was the poet who turned on him now:

'Ask a woman to show her throes!'

The eye-witness accounts say nothing about the reactions of the people, except at the end of the trial. But there can be little doubt that at this stage there were rising murmurs of indignation. One sign of it is that Topcliffe became thoroughly disturbed and even frightened. 'I did but set him against a wall', he babbled, making things worse, 'I had authority to use him as I did. So that I did not hurt life or limb. I have the Council's letters to show for it'; and he used 'much other speeches to clear himself of the rigorous dealing wherewith he was charged'.

'Thou art a bad man', said Southwell, and left him.

At this point, the Attorney cut in. He was very angry, and understandably so. He 'took the speech from Topcliffe'—and not in the deferential manner Topcliffe was accustomed to.

'Mr. Topcliffe has no need to go about to excuse his proceedings in the manner of his torturings. For'—he wheeled upon Southwell—'think you that you will not be tortured? Yea, we will tear the hearts out of a hundred of your bodies.'

Topcliffe again interrupted; and a brief shouting-match seems to have ensued between him and the Attorney, with ironic interjections from Southwell.

'I would blow you all to pieces!' shouted Topcliffe.

'What, all?' asked Southwell, '*Soul* and body too?'

'He meant not the soul', interposed the Attorney angrily. But at length Topcliffe was authoritatively silenced; and the Attorney, gathering again the skirts of his discourse, swept on to his climax. 'The Rotten Chair' of the Papacy was his recurrent theme. The lawfulness of murder was one of the doctrines that maintained this 'rotten chair'; and now another had come to light, equally heinous, which would make an end of all honest dealing.

'Conscience!' he exclaimed. 'They pretend conscience, but you shall see how far they are from conscience.' And, turning, he called the first and only witness: Mrs. Nicholas Jones.

It was Anne Bellamy. The contrast between the two names is sufficient. There is no need to elaborate it.

'And she, being sworn, said that Father Southwell told her that if, upon her oath, she were asked whether she had seen a priest or no, she might lawfully say "No", although she had seen him that same day—keeping in her mind this meaning: that she did not see him with intent to betray him.'

'The Rotten Chair will down', thundered the Attorney, 'which by this doctrine is maintained, a doctrine by the which all judgements, all giving of testimonies, shall be perverted.'

Southwell was badly hit. The appearance of his penitent against him was a cruel and shocking blow; and her testimony took him completely by surprise. He might have questioned her credentials as a witness, the wife of his gaoler, and exposed her past life, but he did not choose to do so. He said that his words were not altogether as she reported, but he admitted the substance. If they would give him leave to interpret his own meaning, he would show—but 'his utterance was somewhat unready', says Leake's account,* 'and they always cut him off when he began to speak'.

'Perjury!' stormed Coke, sweeping him aside. 'This is the doctrine of the Jesuits: "It is lawful to commit perjury"!'

Topcliffe, whose prize piece of evidence this was, joined in with glee: 'And to Sir Robert Cecil he confessed it, and sought to excuse it from the Scripture!'

The tide which had begun to flow strongly in Southwell's favour at the passages about torture, seemed to turn abruptly and rush back at him. His arguments were too feebly spoken and too arid in substance to resist the torrent. He abandoned argument, and prayed silently.

The answer to his prayer came, an impish inspiration.

'Mr. Attorney,' he slipped in, 'you must admit my doctrine, or else I will prove you no good subject or friend of the Queen.'

The Attorney paused. It was an impertinent challenge. But the Candid Friend who, years later, warned him not 'to insult over misery', had to warn him also against another temptation: 'You will jest at any man in public without respect of the person's dignity or your own; this disgraceth your gravity more than it can advance the opinion of your wit. You make the Law lean too much to your opinion, whereby you show yourself to be a Legal Tyrant, striking with that weapon where you please, since you are able to turn the edge any way.'

Yes, he could turn the edge any way, as this shaveling would soon discover. He smiled the smile of a shark. 'Yea?' he drawled, leaning forward. 'Let me hear that!'

Suppose that the French King should invade Her Majesty's realm, and that she (which God forbid) were enforced to fly to some

---

* See the end-notes on this chapter for the documentation of its sources.

private house for safety from her enemies, where none knew her being but Mr. Attorney? Suppose that Mr. Attorney, being taken, were put upon his oath to say whether she were there or not? And suppose (for such would be the case) that Mr. Attorney's refusal to swear should be held as a confession of her being in the house? Would Mr. Attorney refuse to swear? Or would he say: 'She is not there,' meaning 'I intend not to tell you'?

There was silence. Deckers' comment on the dialogue seems here quite justified: 'The Attorney remained as one struck by apoplexy.'

Very gently the prisoner drew the strings of the bag together over the head of the prosecutor:

'If Mr. Attorney should refuse to swear, I say he were neither Her Majesty's good subject, nor her friend.'

The Attorney still stayed silent; the comparison that suggests itself is of a highly armoured tank, caught in an elephant-trap. Popham came to the rescue; but he does not seem to have been quite abreast of the argument: 'He should refuse to swear,' he said.

'Then,' said Southwell sweetly, 'that were by silence to betray his Sovereign.'

It was a flagrant *argumentum ad hominem*. But it worked. Most of the audience had probably no clear idea what was the question in dispute, but only a secret amusement that the Attorney's much-heralded engine had back-fired so disconcertingly. They were thus left with their earlier and more serious impression, which was the dominant memory carried away from this trial, the phrase repeated to and fro in various forms: 'Ten times tortured by Topcliffe, and each one worse than death.'

Coke, meanwhile, had recovered his power of speech but not his temper. 'The Attorney said that the case was not like, and, being moved in choler, did often call Mr. Southwell "Boy-Priest", and told him that he had not read the Doctors.' 'I have read those that have read them', replied Southwell easily, 'and you, Mr. Attorney, in the study of your laws, do not go always to the grounds and principles of the law, but take other men's reports.* Deckers notes well here that this answer of Southwell's was a proof of his effortless superiority; 'he was in truth very learned in the Doctors, having studied them closely for twelve years; he preferred, however, not to waste the fine steel of his mind in a war of insults, but instead, like David with Goliath, wrested away his enemy's sword and cut his throat with it'.

'Aye,' rejoined Coke, 'you have studied the Doctors. You have studied Doctor Allen, Doctor Parsons, Doctor Holt, *Doctor Traitor* . . .' Topcliffe, recognizing his element, waded in with more insults; 'and thereafter', says Garnet's Italian letter, 'many times they called him "boy priest" '—*sacerdote putto*—'with much railing'.

Popham however broke in upon this unseemly duet of Coke and Topcliffe. He seems to have been belatedly but seriously interested in the matter of equivocation. 'Mr. Southwell', he said, 'if this doctrine were allowed, it would supplant all Justice, for we are men and not Gods, and can judge but according to men's outward actions and speeches, and not according to their secret and inward intentions.' It was a very fair and honest objection, and Southwell tried fairly and honestly to satisfy it.

'Two things are to be presupposed in this cause', he explained, 'first, that the refusing to swear is held as a confessing the thing, and second, that the oath is ministered by such as have no lawful authority; for every oath ought to contain judgement, justice and truth, and no man is bound to answer every man that asketh him, unless it were a competent Judge . . .' But, says the *Brief Discourse*,† 'as he was going forward to explain his meaning, he was continually interrupted, so as they would by no means permit him to say any more . . . and here again Topcliffe began to be earnest in most railing manner, as is always usual with him'.

Wearily, the Chief Justice restored order, and, very peremptorily, bade Topcliffe hold his peace. Then after a brief speech to

---

* Coke was, in fact, heavily indebted to the great Catholic lawyer, Edmund Plowden.

† See the end-notes to this chapter.

the Jury, he sent them into a house apart to consider their verdict.

It is not surprising that, after this exhibition, there was little love lost between Topcliffe and the law officers. A few weeks later they held an inquiry into the Fitzherbert blood-money; and Topcliffe, very arrogantly, asked why he should not have taken a bribe of three thousand when the Lord Keeper had taken one of ten. This was the occasion of his first downfall and brief imprisonment, but the occasion only; the real cause seems to have been the disgraceful scene at Southwell's trial which brought both the law and the Government into such disrepute. (2)

The Jury were absent for a quarter of an hour. Meanwhile the prisoner, like an exhausted swimmer, drowned in waves of pain, clung to the wood in front of him, gasping but happy.

The Chief Justice, who had behaved like a gentleman throughout, gave him leave to retire and restore himself with a drink of cordial. But he begged leave to stay. After thirty-two months of solitary confinement it was a joy to let his eyes rest on the landscape of faces, smiling or tear-stained, and to see the fluttering hands; he could recognize friend after friend, and feel their love and congratulation radiating out to him.

When the Jury had returned with their verdict, 'the Clerk asked Mr. Southwell what he could say why the judgement should not be given'. The people, says Garnet's informant, were longing for him to speak further. But 'Mr. Southwell answered, and said nothing but this: "I pray God forgive all them that are any way accessories to my death".'

Incredible though it seems, Topcliffe again broke in, trying at the last moment to raise a laugh against the prisoner: 'I found him hiding in the tylles!' (3) Under the circumstances, Southwell's reply could not have been happier. 'It was time to hide', he said, 'when Mr. Topcliffe came.'

The rest is soon told in the words of the *Brief Discourse*:

Topcliffe being not suffered to reply, the Lord Chief Justice . . . gave judgement that he should be carried to Newgate from whence he came, and from thence to be drawn to Tyburn upon an hurdle, and there to be hanged and cut down alive, his bowels to be burned before his face, his head to be stricken off, his body to be quartered and disposed at Her Majesty's pleasure.

Mr. Southwell thereunto made low and humble reverence and gave great thanks for it. The Chief Justice wished that some minister might have Conference with him, and said he would send a learned preacher unto him. Mr. Southwell answered: 'As for that, you need not take any care.'

His arms were then tied again, and he was led away. The Attorney—according to Leake's account—had instructed his guards to take him by the River, so as to avoid the throng of people waiting to greet him.

But—continues the *Brief Discourse*—

The officers consulting whether they were better carry him by water or by land, they all concluded he would go quiet enough, and so he went joyfully with them through the streets, where many of his friends and acquaintances awaited his coming only to see him, which they did to their great comfort, ('deeming themselves happy,' adds Garnet's informant, 'to obtain one glance from him'), 'perceiving him full of consolation, his countenance nothing dismayed, they never knowing him to look better or more cheerfully.'

Back in the little cave that was called 'Limbo', there followed the visit of the preachers, who stayed for three hours, discoursing upon points of religion. How the discourses ran, and how he answered them, was kept very secret. But the Catholics got an indication of them from Southwell's friend, the Keeper, who came out swearing that he had never heard so rare a man and that he himself henceforth would lead a better life.

When the ministers had at last gone, he hoped for solitude to prepare himself. But it was not to be. It was borne in upon him that he had no need to be solicitous for the morrow; that, to be more perfectly like his Saviour, he must spend a great deal of his remaining time in the giving and receiving of human consolation.

It is not certain that the Catholic prisoners were actually allowed to visit him—at least not in any great numbers—but he was very conscious of their presence and their prayers. They hovered around, sending in a succession of tasty dishes they had contributed to provide. He ate as heartily as he could, and sent back messages to say that it was royal food and that he had never fared so well in the Tower as here in Limbo. The only harsh note was struck by the Head-Keeper who came to warn him that any attempt at suicide would be easily prevented. 'Did you ever hear of a Catholic Priest that hurt himself so?' he asked in reply. 'Why should we add the destruction of our soul to the death of our body?'

When the Head-Keeper had gone, the other Keeper came back again, offering every attention he could, and asking for spiritual counsel in return. There were other comings and goings, also, it would appear. 'What was further done and said that night', says the *Brief Discourse*, 'was kept very secret and known to very few.' But one story did transpire. It seems that at nightfall the door of his cell opened again, and a last mysterious visitor was ushered in. The incident, since it has a wide historical interest, had better be given as Janelle relates it.

Regarding that last night, however, something more is known through Yepez, whose biography is almost contemporary, and rests on documents received from England. He reports an extremely curious and suggestive incident: 'After the Father had been sentenced to death, there came to him in his prison an English nobleman of high rank, who besought him earnestly, as he was now to quit this life, to tell him whether that was true which he had been charged with, namely that he had come to detach subjects from their obedience to the Queen. To this the Father replied that his intention had never been anything but the eternal good of souls; that so far from repenting what he had done, he would do it again if he could; that he would come again, and many times more, not only from Rome but from the farthest parts of the world, to procure the salvation of the Queen, which he desired no less than his own; that he had always asked the Lord God to enlighten her, and her Council also, as to the error they were in, and not to hold them guilty for his death.

'The noble, very much moved by his answer, departed; and he went and told the Queen (we must here anticipate, says Janelle, the latter part of this narrative) all that had passed at the death of the Father, praising him very much, and the rare parts he was gifted with. When the Queen had heard him, she replied that they had deceived her with calumnies telling her that the Father had come to the realm to raise sedition; and she showed signs of grief for his death, especially when she saw a book that he had composed in the English tongue on different topics, pious and devout . . . a book designed to teach Poets how to safeguard their talent and employ it as befitted.'

The story is a curious pendant to the remote relations between Robert Southwell and Queen Elizabeth, beautiful, but unsatisfying because of the shadows of unknown thoughts that shroud it. But, at least, it is possible to infer the identity of the nobleman. It seems clear from the story—though not explicitly stated—that the nobleman was himself present at the death-scene on the following day, and that it was he who showed the Queen the book 'that taught Poets . . . to use their talents as befitted them'. But the nobleman who was most obviously present at the execution, and the only one mentioned by name (though others of his friends were there also), was Lord Mountjoy. He was very much favoured by Elizabeth, in a personal but straightforward way, and he was deeply interested in literature. It is not possible to think of anyone else who fulfils all the conditions so closely.

When Robert's last visitor had left him, sleep was still not possible because of scorpions or some such creatures in his cell. (4) He stayed awake, praying and waiting for the knock on the dark shell of his prison that would tell him the daylight had come. It was his friend the Keeper who came at last to say that the horses were standing at the gate. The last uncertainty was over. He threw his arms round the Keeper and embraced him. 'No man ever brought me such good news before. And, alas, I have nothing to give you except this——' He took off his cap. 'If I had anything better to give, you should have it.' Naturally there were many offers afterwards from Catholics for such a relic; but—

'this cap the Keeper, albeit a Protestant, maketh such account of that he can be brought by no means to forgo it'.

Before Robert left the prison, they brought him a posset. He did not refuse it, but drank it all, and said: 'It was good. It has made my heart glad.'

Outside, in the raw morning air, with a catch in his throat, he saw the hurdle on the cobble-stones; and remembering how many of his heroes and companions had gone this way before him, he could not help exclaiming: 'How great a preferment for so base a servant!' And as he lay down and was tied to it, he said again: 'How great a preferment for so base a servant!' From the throng of people waiting outside the gate, an old peasant raised his voice: 'God bless you and give you the strength!' He was told violently to cease, but he cried out all the more: 'God bless you and give you the strength!' Perhaps some unknown story of Robert's childhood or priesthood lay behind the old countryman's words.

According to Garnet, in order to deflect the crowds and prevent any disturbance, the Government had advertised the hanging of a famous highwayman on this same day. But the effect of this had been to increase the proportion of friends and Catholics among the people along the route and at the gallows. Their behaviour, however, took its cue from his own: firm and devout, but friendly and decorous.

Outside St. Sepulchre's the procession halted before the steep descent over stones and puddles to the roaring brook swollen by winter streams and Smithfield sewage. A young woman, his cousin, slipped between the guards and fell on her knees beside him for his last blessing. 'Father Robert, pray for me that I may go forward in the way you have taught me.' He blessed her as well as he could with his bound arms, and said: 'Dear Cousin, I thank you, and I pray you pray for me.' Then he begged her lovingly to be careful of the mud that was flying again from the horses' hooves. But she followed beside him for some time, 'beautiful in her grief', till he besought her not to risk her liberty: 'For they will take you and put you in prison again.   So she saluted him once more and slipped away. It seems most likely that this was Margaret Gage.

Slowly they went: across the bridge and up the long, heavy slope to the chains of Holborn Bars: past St. Giles-in-the-fields and into the open, windswept countryside. And then more quickly: bumping and racketing along the last stretch of what is now Oxford Street, till the horses drew to a standstill at what is now Marble Arch, and looked over their shoulders, with steaming nostrils, at the load behind.

It seems incredible that after such an ordeal anyone could still have the stomach to make a brave show at the gallows. Yet this was the supreme moment that every man or woman who came to Tyburn Tree, priest or cut-purse, sacred or profane, hoped and expected to be judged by: a sort of rehearsal of the General Judgement. The victim on the scaffold or the cart was that much nearer to heaven, and the people who looked up at him, looked to be edified as well as entertained.

Throughout his journey Robert, by a muscular effort, had kept his head clear of the road. Indeed, as he neared the Tree, he had raised both head and shoulders to greet it. Now, as soon as they had cut the ropes, he rose from the hurdle, shapely and debonair. 'His courage and nobility and gentleness, the beauty of his face and form', wrote Garnet, 'so won the hearts of all that even the mob of sightseers gave it as their verdict, that this was the properest man they had ever seen that came to Tyburn for hanging.'*

The hangman leant over and drew him up to the cart. With a handkerchief between his bound hands he wiped his face and neck, and let his eye travel over the throng. There was still one office of friendship to perform. He saw the face he was looking for. Kneading the mud-soiled cloth into a ball, he threw it with both hands straight into the crowd. (5)

When the hangman came to loose his doublet, he asked, 'May

---

* But perhaps the crowd always said that sort of thing. See *The Beggar's Opera*:

> Beneath the left ear do fit but a cord,
> A rope so charming a zone is,
> The youth in his cart hath the air of a lord
> And we cry, There dies an Adonis!

I speak to the people?' and the hangman said, 'Why, yes', and stepped back. Then he made the sign of the cross and began with the words that he often used in danger: 'Whether we live, or whether we die, we belong to the Lord.' But as he was continuing, 'I am brought hither to die——' the under-sheriff interrupted him, shouting: 'Make an end! Cry God-a-mercy and make an end!' 'To whom he used this speech: "Give me leave to speak, it will not be much, and I will say nothing offensive to the Queen or State." '

It was evident that the people desired to hear him, so leave was given, and he began again:

> I am come hither to play out the last act of this poor life. I pray and supplicate Our Saviour Jesus Christ, by whose dear passion and death I hope to be saved, that he would deign to pardon all the sins of all my life. I do profess myself to be a Catholic priest of the Holy Roman Church, and of the Society of Jesus, and I do thank God eternally for it.

But here again he was interrupted. This time it was the Chaplain of the Tower:

> You hold the decrees of the Council of Trent, wherein is decreed that no man shall presume to believe that he is sure to be saved, but is to doubt. Now, if you believe to be saved, you contradict the Council; but if you doubt, being to die, your case is hard, and you doubting, we must needs doubt.

Southwell's reaction reminds one of the tight-rope of effort on which he was walking. There is no reason to think that he was supernaturally freed from the pain in his chest and sides which racked him when he raised his voice. And the worst part, the disembowelling, was still to come. 'Good Mr. Minister', he pleaded, 'give me leave and trouble me not.' And then, more urgently: 'For God's sake, let me alone. Notwithstanding your words, I hope to be saved by the death and passion of Our Saviour.'

The minister, obtuse and dutiful, was sawing on; but from the crowd came growls and cries of protest: 'Let him alone! He will pray for the Queen, let that suffice!'

Y

So, taking his cue from the crowd, Robert began again:

Concerning the Queen's Majesty, God Almighty knoweth that I never intended any harm against her. I have daily prayed for her; and in this short time which I have yet to live, I do beseech Almighty God for his tender mercy sake, for his precious blood sake, and for his most glorious wounds sake, to grant she may so use her gifts and graces, which God and Nature and fortune hath bestowed on her, that with them all she may both please and glorify God, advance the happiness of our Country, and purchase to herself the preservation and salvation of her body and soul.

Next, into the hands of Almighty God I commend this my poor Country, desiring him for his infinite mercy's sake, to reduce it to such perfect insight, knowledge, and understanding of his truth, that thereby they may learn to praise and glorify him, and gain for their souls health and eternal salvation.

And lastly, I commend into the hands of Almighty God my own poor soul, that it would please him for his great mercy sake to conform and strengthen it with perseverance unto the end of this my last conflict. And this poor body of mine, as it shall please Her Majesty to dispose thereof.

This is my death, my last farewell to this unfortunate life, and yet to me most happy and most fortunate. I pray it may be for the full satisfaction of my sins, for the good of my Country, and for the comfort of many others. Which death, albeit that it seem here disgraceful, yet I hope that in time to come it will be to my eternal glory.

At last his duty to the public was done, and he turned to his own private prayer. But the chaplain and the officers would not let him be. They cried to him that he had asked no pardon of the Queen for his crimes. A little wearily, he said: 'If I have offended the Queen with my coming hither, I humbly desire her to forget it, and I accept this punishment for it most thankfully. And now I desire all Catholics to pray with me, so that whatsoever be said to trouble and distemper me in this conflict, I may yet, the little while I have to live, live a Catholic and die a Catholic.'

One notices again the wearing-thin of a body too anxious for solitude and the dark, while for the mind there was still the child's terror, at the last moment, of losing the way.

But the hangman saved him from further interruption by coming forward with the halter. Gratefully he turned to him, and obediently helped to strip his doublet and tuck back his shirt. He lifted his chin for the noose to settle. With his eyes on the restful sky and in his ears only the infinite murmur of air, he prayed softly: 'Blessed Mary, ever a Virgin, and all you Angels and Saints assist me . . . *In manus tuas, Domine commendo spiritum meum.*' These were to have been his last aspirations, his viaticum, before the steep plunge into suffocation and the twisting passage to the cauldron by ravenous blade and fire.

But the hangman delayed. At first there was only a rough little jerk. The rope was being readjusted above him; and the knot, which was tied too large, slipped right behind his head, forcing it forward and down. He closed his eyes and said '*In Manus Tuas, Domine* . . .', making the sign of the cross.

Then suddenly, he opened his eyes and looked at the people with great love—'*con . . . volto graziosissimo*, with a countenance most lovely'—or 'like the sun', as another account has it, 'when it breaketh forth after it hath dispersed the clouds'. They heard his voice, firm and clear, reciting the psalm *Miserere*: 'Restore unto me the joy of thy salvation, and comfort me with a perfect spirit.'

For the third time he said '*In Manus Tuas, Domine* . . .' and made the sign of the cross; and at last the cart lurched clear.

The crowd below saw his face unchanged, the eyes still open, his body motionless except for the bound hands knocking at his breast in the motions of the *Confiteor*, or as if urging the heart within to break the stranglehold and force a passage.

A sergeant came forward to cut the rope as prescribed, so as to begin the butchering alive. But there was a little knot of noblemen standing by the gallows; and from among these Lord Mountjoy stepped forward and waved the sergeant back, while from the crowd came murmurs of approval. (6) Uncertainly the sergeant turned to the Sheriff, who ordered him angrily to cut the rope. But again the noblemen with Lord Mountjoy shouted in scorn and protest; and the crowd found its voice in a great confused cry: 'Let him hang till he be dead!' and 'Pull his legs!'—

so as to hasten death. Furiously the Sheriff drew his sword and rode up to the gallows to sever the rope. But such a full-throated roar of hostility met him that he blenched.

Then the hangman, seeing what was wanted of him, leant with all his weight and felt the body above him grow limp and still. He lowered it very gently into his arms—'a most unwonted courtesy'—and laid it on the block.

On the edge of the crowd, a pursuivant stirred himself and said to his companion: 'You have deceived me! I never saw a man die so well as this man.' A minister—perhaps one of those who had disputed the night before—talked of his rare charity, and very much blamed the other minister, the chaplain. Later, when the hangman, having cut off the head, held it up as was customary saying: 'God save the Queen!' and 'Here is the head of a traitor!', there was silence. The people bared their heads, but they held their caps low. No one echoed, 'Traitor! Traitor!', and many signed themselves with the cross.

White with mortification, the Sheriff shouted at the group of noblemen: 'I see there are some here who have come, not to honour the Queen, but to reverence a traitor!' (7)

But Lord Mountjoy, the future conqueror of Ireland, who perhaps had the Queen's secret authority for what he had done, cried out in a voice full of emotion:

'I cannot answer for his religion, but I wish to God that my soul may be with his.'

Meanwhile the hangman went on methodically with his work, chopping off members, hacking at joints, and tearing back the ribs to grope for the heart, which fluttered a little in his hand, and seemed to leap of its own accord to join its faithful henchmen in the cauldron.

A few men and women, seeming to pass him by casually, dipped handkerchiefs in the sprayed blood, and offered him money for a piece of bone or a lock of hair. But for the most part the people stood still and silent, looking upwards.

It was not yet too difficult for them to see the heavens opened, and a ladder of Angels ascending to the Son of Man.

APPENDIXES

The Jesuits and the English College

It is hard to write about the 'stirs' in the English College without being drawn to one side or another of what Fr. Philip Hughes has called 'that rooted antagonism which for generations was to split the Catholic effort in England'. (1) Although the seminary disputes were so small in comparison with the major rift, yet they were a sort of rehearsal for it. Several of the chief participants were the same in both cases.

Those who hold that it was the main body of the Secular Clergy that complained at the end of the sixteenth century about attempts to 'Jesuitize' them, and who agree with the complaints, will naturally form the same sort of judgement about the students in 1585 and 1596. Such a judgement alights particularly on the later stirs of 1596; but it also leads to those of 1585 being treated perfunctorily as an earlier instance of the same radical complaint.

After reading Cardinal Gasquet's *History of the Venerable English College*, one has the impression—an impression made all the more devastating by the distinguished historian's urbanity of style—that the two centuries of Jesuit rule in the College were an unfortunate interlude in its history. In keeping with this attitude, his narration of the stirs of '85 accepts quite calmly the terrible charges against the Jesuits (charges of criminal negligence and dishonesty) as being those of the entire student body. (2) The present writer, however, has been obliged to treat the incident on its own evidence, and he has found that Gasquet's assumptions are not tenable.

In the first place, the Cardinal has completely ignored the counter-protest of loyalty to the Society signed by a majority, nearly three-quarters, of the students. It is true this evidence cannot be pressed unreservedly, for among the forty-nine signatories are four who were afterwards hostile to the Society, while among the eighteen absentees are two who afterwards became distinguished Jesuits. But as a general manifestation of feeling it was wrong of Gasquet to ignore it.

Another point is that the Cardinal shows no interest in tracing the subsequent careers of students who are known by name to have been troublesome. He could not be expected to treat the matter in detail, but to get an insight into what was happening it must surely be borne in mind. Had he made any sort of study of it he would not have alluded to Hugh Griffin (who was a notorious agitator by all accounts) as 'one Hughes'; and he would not have included William Tedder the apostate among a list of 'shining confessors'. (3) The truth—of which examples are given in the text—is that among the majority who found Jesuit rule beneficial were those of whom the English Catholics have most reason to be proud, while among the minority were several whose characters afterwards proved exceptionally rancorous or deceitful.

That is not to deny that there may have been good and honest men who resented the Jesuit discipline. An interesting backward light on the troubles of '85 is cast by John Cecil in a report of 1591 to Lord Burghley. (4) He is giving a list of priests who—he thinks—may be won over to the Government. Among them are eight names which coincide with absentees from the protest of loyalty and include two or three specifically mentioned in Sega's report as discontented. 'They are of modest, mild and temperate disposition', wrote Cecil, 'and have been much molested by the Jesuits, especially in Rome, for endeavouring in the year '85 to alter the government of the college there and exclude the Jesuits.' Of the eight, one was an informer like himself, Fixer; three were apparently worthy missionaries of whom little else is known, Dudley, Roberts and Almond; two had already renewed their old attachment to the Society, Woodward and Pormort; and two were shortly to become Jesuits, Warford and Blount the future provincial. It seems a fair conclusion that there *was* some honest resentment of Jesuit rule, but that it was not more serious than was to be expected from high-spirited young men under any good rule in those trying circumstances, and that the more vicious charges were of outside fabrication.

Southwell's letter of 1585 to Aquaviva is important evidence in favour of this conclusion. His opening remark that 'the growth of the students in piety and learning is a matter for gratitude to God rather than emendation' might be queried as a pious generalization. But he goes on specifically to attribute this success to the universal respect in which the Rector is held, to his tactful handling of individual students and to his deep knowledge and love of things English. The main part of his letter, however, is an implicit criticism of Agazzari that he has gone too far in *discouraging* students who have a vocation to the Society; and in this connection Southwell seems to take it for granted that the serious opposition to the Society was coming from outside, not from within the College.

There is indeed evidence that Agazzari was very disturbed when students wished to join the Society, and Allen had gently to reassure him on this point. (5) Allen's whole-hearted approval of the Jesuit rule in his college might also be cited in its justification. But there is no need to insist further.

Burghley's Memorial of 1584

Its title in the Petyt MSS. (Series 538, vol. 43, ff. 304 etc.)* is *An Antidote against Jesuitism written by the Lord Treasurer Burleigh to Queen Elizabeth*, and the date of composition, by internal evidence, is about 1584. It is written in a characteristically prosy style, but the thought is clear, cold and brutal; and it sheds a flood of light on the secret workings of Burghley's religious policy.

He places Elizabeth's dilemma fairly before her. Her Catholic subjects (he says) are so great in numbers and influence that to increase her pressure against them would be as unsafe as to relax it. To massacre them 'in such numbers as they are, would be as hard and difficult as impious and ungodly'; but to come to terms with them would mean changing her government—which is unthinkable, because the last persons a Prince can afford to trust are those whom he has already injured.

The only way out of the dilemma is to divide them in their loyalties by a new oath of allegiance—for they are so simple that 'they make conscience of an oath'. They should be forced to answer 'yes' or 'no' to the question: 'If the Pope were to send an invading army, would you take up arms against him?' Those who would hesitate to say 'yes' can then be dealt with as traitors; but on no account should the charge against them be their religion, for that only leads the common people to esteem them more, 'persecution being ever accounted as the badge of the Church'. The majority (as he hopes) who would say 'yes', being thus weakened in their loyalty to the Pope, the source of their strength, may be dealt with at leisure by a process of guile and attrition: by inciting their tenants against them—'though there may hereby grow some wrong'; by taking their children as hostages—'under colour of education'; by stripping them of their armour so that

* In the Inner Temple Library, quoted by courtesy of the Librarian.

twenty thousand of them will be helpless before one thousand Protestants; in short, by all those old oriental devices which never seem to fail against large-hearted simpletons.

One other point, a delicate one: the Queen should put more trust in the zeal and fervour of the Puritans, even as 'that excellent Emperor Frederick II', in order to attack the Pope, made use of Saracens where Christians would have hung back.

Burghley has exposed the situation so clearly that there would be no need to add anything further here—if it were not that his authorship has been questioned by Francis Bacon's biographer, James Spedding, who with a severe stretch of his critical apparatus annexed the piece for Bacon, then aged twenty-three. Spedding, a great literary advocate, was well aware of the flimsy ground he was on. Not so S. R. Gardiner, who arrived later to write the life of Bacon in *DNB*. With no authority except a vague reference to Spedding, and with no indication of any evidence to the contrary, the myth that 'Bacon's views on the political situation were embodied in a *Letter of Advice* to Queen Elizabeth', sprouted forth from what Spedding had carefully italicized as '*possibly and not improbably* his composition'. (6)

In reality, however, *all* the documentary evidence is in favour of Burghley's authorship, and there is not a single manuscript assigned to Bacon.

Spedding's two main arguments are both nugatory. The first is that in a volume of 1651 the tract is printed *as Burghley's*, but included along with some pieces by Bacon. All that this indicates is that the tract may have passed into Bacon's possession later on—which is not improbable, for it was certainly used again in Stuart times. Spedding's other argument is that Burghley after such long service of the Queen would never have apologized—as he does in his tract—for offering her his advice. How empty is this sort of reasoning is shown by *Bacon's* own description of how Lord Burghley tendered his advice:

> . . . There was never counsellor of his Lordship's long continuance that was so appliable to her Majesty's princely resolutions; endeavouring always, after faithful propositions and remonstrances (and those in the best words and the most grateful manner), to rest upon such conclusions as her Majesty in her own wisdom determineth, and them to execute to the best; so far hath he been from drawing her Majesty into any his own courses. (Spedding, *Letters and Life of Bacon* (1861), I, pp. 198-9.)

It so happens that in the next page of Spedding's volume, following the tract, there is a neat refutation, both external and internal, of his hypothesis. In a letter of August 1585 to Walsingham, Bacon laments that a pressing suit which he presented to the Queen through Burghley *five years earlier* has not yet even been acknowledged by her. Yet this is the young man who is supposed to have been summoned in 1584 to advise her on the highest matters of State.

Here is the tract-writer of 1584, ponderous but deadly:

Your strong factious subjects be the Papists: strong I account them, because both in number they are (at the least) able to make a great army, and by their mutual confidence and intelligence may soon bring to pass an uniting: factious I call them, because they are discontented;—of whom in all reason of state your Majesty must determine, if you suffer them to be strong, to make them content, or if you will discontent them, to make them weaker: for what the mixture of strength and discontentment engender, needs no syllogisms to prove. (p. 47.)

And here is the letter-writer of 1585, incisive but nervy:

I think the objection of my years will wear away with the length of my suit. The very stay doth in this respect concern me, because I am thereby hindered to take a course of practice, which by the leave of God, if her Majesty like not of my suit, I must and will follow: not for any necessity of estate, but for my credit sake, which I know by living out of action will wear. (p. 57.)

One is Polonius before his dotage; the other is the new generation that had Hamlet for its prototype.

But this sort of reasoning, though persuasive, is really beside the point. The deciding argument in favour of Burghley's authorship is the Petyt manuscript—in vol. 43, and there is also an apparently later version in vol. 37. Both these are in an Elizabethan hand, and the ascription to Burghley in the former is exact and unequivocal. It was printed as Burghley's in the volume of 1651, as stated; and in *Somers Tracts*, from which it was quoted in part by Hallam (1846). (7)

Spedding, however, did a useful service in printing a good version of it, *Letters & Life of Bacon*, I, 47–56.

Equivocation

The problem, what to do when truth seems to be on one side and justice or charity on the other—for example, when a plain answer or a misinterpreted silence will betray another's right to secrecy—is no new one. It goes back at least fifteen hundred years.

Some of the Greek Fathers allowed the telling of an untruth when it was in legitimate self-defence. They made the same distinction between a lie and a *justifiable* untruth as between murder and justifiable homicide. But Saint Augustine, followed by the great Scholastics, refused to admit this distinction. They held that a lie was *intrinsically* evil, because it was a *locutio contra mentem*: it corrupted the natural function of language. Every untruth, therefore, was a lie. It was an offence against veracity, not primarily against justice or charity; and since it was intrinsically evil, no external causes could ever justify it. Pope Alexander III (1159–81) spoke for the Middle Ages when he took it for granted, writing *De Usuris*, that an untruth was never lawful, even to save the life of another. Towards practical dilemmas no tenderness was shown.

But by the sixteenth century it had become a matter of urgency to safeguard the conscience of honest men in dilemmas between justice and veracity. Martin Luther, on the principle of *Pecca Fortiter* (tell a lie and have done with it), said that untruth was always evil, but sometimes excusable: a natural view-point, perhaps, but ethically quite hopeless. On the Catholic side, the Augustinian Navarro (1493–1587), taking his cue from existing practice in the law-courts, suggested the theory of 'equivocation' as a means of safeguarding a man's rights and duties without falling into the intrinsic evil of lying. A man who was unjustly questioned (he held) might reply in words that were ambiguous —ambiguous either in themselves or in the context in which they were uttered—provided that one of their meanings corresponded to what he believed to be true. Later theologians, including the Jesuits Suarez and Toledo, accepted this suggestion with cautious and qualified approval. A necessary qualification was that the purpose of the reply should not be deception but legitimate self-defence.

In the next century, Protestant writers (Jeremy Taylor, Milton, and Paley in the following century) went a good deal further by maintaining that a plain untruth—a *locutio contra mentem*—is lawful under certain circumstances. 'The great Anglican writers', says Cardinal Newman, 'who have followed the Greek Fathers in defending untruths when there is a "just cause", consider that "just cause" to be such as the preservation of life and property, defence of law, the good of others. Moreover their moral rights: defence against the inquisitive, etc.'—*Apologia Pro Vita sua*. NOTE G. (8)

The grounds of latitude are the same in both theories, but they differ in principle and in practice. In principle, the equivocation theory refuses to admit that a flat untruth can ever be lawful; and in practice it insists that the speaker should intend a true meaning which it should be possible for his hearer to collect, either from the words themselves or from the context. But since ambiguity in words is bound to break down before skilled questioning, it is the ambiguity derived from the context which is more important in the present issue.

Obvious examples of such ambiguity are 'Not Guilty' and 'Not at home', where the context advises the hearer to look for another meaning. In the case of unjust questioning, the context is the right or duty that every man has to keep certain secrets. Since this right and this duty are obvious and admitted by all civilized societies, any answer that a man makes *should* be accepted by his questioner with the implicit qualification: 'apart from certain secrets which I am justified in keeping'.

At this point there may seem no difference between the two theories. But the difference becomes clearer when the element of deception is considered. A theory which justifies plain untruth allows wide scope for invention, and allows the speaker deliberately to deceive his interrogator. But on the equivocation theory the speaker must not have the intention of deceiving his interrogator, but of leaving him in as much doubt as he was before the reply. John Gerard, for example, warned his examiners in advance that their questions were unlawful; it was 'his regular practice, which he taught his friends, to add to the denial some remark which made it clear that he regarded the occasion as a privileged one and was making his answer in the sense allowed by modern law and practice'. (9) The deliberate deception, which St. Thomas defines as the natural consequence of a lie, was allowed in the one theory and disallowed in the other.

Both theories were honest attempts to answer a real problem, and it may be admitted that neither is altogether satisfactory. But it should be a matter for admiration, not for contempt, that the English Jesuits, hunted and haggard, with all the burden of their friends' agony urging them to laxity, were more tenderly scrupulous to avoid untruth than the Protestant writers of the next century whose reputation for honesty has never been questioned.

APPENDIX 'D'

Licensed editions of Southwell's works published in London 1591–5

1. 1591. *Mary Magdalen's Funeral Tears* (*STC*,* no. 22950).
   Printed by John Wolfe for Gabriel Cawood.
   (*Stationers Register*, ii, 598, 8 November 1591: 'Master Cawood Entred for his copie under the hand of the Lord Archbishop of CANTERBURY A Booke entituled MARY MAGDALEN's funerall teares.')

2. 1592. The same, by the same. Not in *STC*.†

3. 1594. The same (*STC*, no. 22951).
   Printed by Abel Jeffes for Gabriel Cawood.

4. 1595. *Saint Peter's Complaint* (*STC*, no. 22957).
   Imprinted by John Wolfe.

5. 1595. A larger edition of the same.

6. 1595. *Saint Peter's Complaint, with other Poems* (*STC*, no. 22956).
   Printed by James Roberts for Gabriel Cawood.

7. 1595. *Maeoniae* (*STC*, no. 22955).
   Printed by Valentine Sims for John Busbie.
   (*Stationers Register*, iii, 50, 17 October 1595: 'John Busbie Entred for his Copie under the wardens handes *meoniae*/ The spirituall Poems or hymnes of R.S.')

8. 1595. The same, by the same (*STC*, no. 22954).

9. 1595. *The Triumphs over Death* (*STC*, no. 22971).
   Printed by Valentine Sims for John Busbie.
   (*Stationers Register*, iii, 53, 20 November 1595: 'John Busby Entred for his copie under the wardens handes a booke intitled The Tryumphes over Deathe ... by R.S.')

10. — *A Short Rule of Good Life* (*STC*, no. 22969).
    (No date or name of printer.)
    In the next four years, 1596–9, there were six more editions, three of the poems and three of prose works.

* *STC* = 'A Short-Title Catalogue of Books printed ... 1475–1640.' Compiled by A. W. Pollard and G. R. Redgrave. *The Bibliographical Society*, London, 1926.
† See J. Macdonald, *A Bibliography of Robert Southwell*, Roxburghe Club, 1937.

LIST OF ABBREVIATIONS
(in alphabetical order)

—by title or place of origin:

Arch. Rom. S.J.: Roman Archives of the Society of Jesus.

CRS: Catholic Record Society Publications.

CSPD: Calendar of State Papers Domestic.

DNB: Dictionary of National Biography.

Epistle: An Epistle of Comfort, undated edition marked 'Imprinted at Paris', copy in private hands.

Hat. Cal.: Calendar of Hatfield Manuscripts.

PRO, SP, 12: Public Record Office, State Papers, Elizabeth.

PRO, SP, 53: Public Record Office, State Papers, Mary Queen of Scots.

VCH: Victoria County History.

—by author's or editor's name:

Allen: Letters and Memorials of Cardinal Allen, ed. T. F. Knox (London, 1882).

Anstruther: see *Vaux.*

Bartoli: Daniello Bartoli, *Istoria della Compagnia di Gesù, Inghilterra* (Roma, 1667).

De Buck: *Spiritual Exercises and Devotions of Blessed Robert Southwell S.J.,* ed. J.-M. de Buck S.J. (London, 1931).

Foley: *Records of the English Province of the Society of Jesus,* ed. Henry Foley S.J., in 7 volumes (London, 1877).

Hamilton: *Chronicle of the English Canonesses of St Monica's, Louvain,* 1548–1625, ed. Adam Hamilton O.S.B. (London, 1904).

Janelle: Pierre Janelle, *Robert Southwell the Writer* (London, 1935).

Macdonald: James H. Macdonald, *Poems and Prose Writings of Robert Southwell S.J.,* a bibliographical study (Roxburghe Club, 1937).

Meyer: A. O. Meyer, *England und die Katholische Kirke unter Elizabeth* (Rom, 1911).

z   337

More: Henry More, *Historia Provinciae Anglicanae*, 1660.

Morris: *Troubles of our Catholic Forefathers*, in 3 volumes, by John Morris S.J. (London, 1872).

Pastor: Ludwig von Pastor, *History of the Popes* (English edition, London, vols. xix–xxi—1930, 1932).

Strype: J. Strype, *Annals of the Reformation*, in 4 volumes (Oxford, 1824).

Tierney-Dodd: M. A. Tierney, *Charles Dodd's Church History of England* (1739), in 4 volumes (London, 1840).

Trotman: *Southwell's 'Triumphs over Death' together with 'The Epistle to his Father'*, ed. J. W. Trotman, Catholic Library VIII (Roehampton, London, 1914).

Vaux: Godfrey Anstruther O.P., *Vaux of Harrowden* (Newport, 1953),

Verstegan: Despatches of Richard Verstegan in the Stonyhurst MSS. *Anglia, Collectanea B* (transcripts at Farm Street, W.1.)

Yepez: Diego Yepez, *Historia Particular de la Persecucion de Inglaterra* (Madrid, 1599).

Notes

CHAPTER ONE
England: the Fading Portrait

1. *DNB*, xvii, 700–1. *VCH*, Norfolk, II, p. 348. E. W. Tristram, *English Mediaeval Wall Paintings in the Thirteenth Century* (Oxford, 1950), p. 361 and plates 205–7.

2. Hamilton (see Abbreviations), I, 111–14. This *Chronicle* contains narratives of recusant families by their sisters or daughters who became nuns at the convent. T. C. Christie, *The Letters of Thomas Copley* (Roxburghe Club, 1892). Nearly all information regarding the Copleys is derived from these two sources.

3. *Hat. Cal.*, iv, p. 533.

4. More, p. 172.

5. Trotman, p. 43. See also pp. 37, 62.

6. G. H. Dashwood, *Visitation of Norfolk*, 1563, I, 124–9 (Norwich, 1878). The editor has added the name of Mary and her marriage. Both are confirmed by the Jesuit historian More who mentions her visit to Southwell in prison.

7. Spelman, *History of Sacrilege* (2nd edition, London, 1853), 252, 253.

8. A catalogue description of the deed ('on vellum, with seals broken, 15s.'), which I have not been able to locate, was passed on to me among Fr. Pollen's notes. It is item 229. Item 225 is Philip Sidney's 'acquittance for the fee of Cupbearer at the Annunciation 1576'.

9. Dasent, *Acts of the Privy Council* (New Series), I, 112–19.

10. *CSPD*, 1547–80, 571, 576. *PRO, SP*, 12, cxx, nn. 26, 27.

11. See Chapter 2, note 1.

12. The evidence for this is from Copley's letter to Burghley, 18th May 1583: 'I beseech [Gatton] may be returned to my sister Southwell, her Majesty's old servant of nigh 40 years continuance, who had it before and did not leave it to my Lady Latimer but at your Lordship's request as I have before mentioned.'

13. *Epistle*, pp. 90–1.

14. Letter of Thomas Stephens, Stonyhurst MSS., *Collectio Cardwelli*, f. 16.

15. *PRO, SP*, 12, cxl, n. 40.

16. Richard Gough's edition of Camden's *Britannia* (1806) additions, p. 200.

17. Printed by Macdonald, p. 50. See *Gerusalemme Liberata*, canto xvi, stanzas 14, 15, and *Faerie Queene*, II, xii, stanzas 74–5.

18. The MS. is at Stonyhurst. Translation by Foley, IV, 289 ff. Persons makes Southwell the author (*CRS*, IV, p. 70). Yepez says it was Agazzari. Bartoli supposes it was both. A phrase (missed by Foley) in the original, '*in hac Anglia nostra*' ('*our* England') suggests that the early part at least was by Southwell.

19. Spelman, p. 253. Trotman, p. 62.

CHAPTER TWO
'The Beautiful English Youth', 1576–8

1. *Douai Diaries* (ed. T. F. Knox, London, 1878), p. 105. See also p. 106. It is not *absolutely* certain that Southwell sailed from the South coast with Cotton. The arguments are that he arrived in company with Cotton, a Hampshire boy, brought by Covert, Allen's agent in Paris, and that More had first-hand evidence of his presence at Paris with Cotton over a period of two years, presumably June to June 1576–8. More knew nothing of Southwell's schooling at Douai, except what he gathered from his letters now lost to us: 'Some of his letters indicate that he withdrew to Belgium.'

2. Janelle, pp. 19–22. The French professor, however, is judging from a 'romantic' standpoint when he concludes that Robert's early lyric gift was 'damped with frigidity by the literary theory which the Jesuits had evolved . . . a repellent and absurd theory indeed which is the very negation of poetry'. The Jesuits had no special theory of poetry distinguishable from those in general currency. Bencius, of the Roman College, seems to have held the same sort of views about 'delight' and 'inspiration' as Sir Philip Sidney. Every English poet at this period had to go through a prolonged apprenticeship in the manipulation of words.

3. *CRS*, V, p. 316 (unpublished documents relating to the English Martyrs, edited by J. H. Pollen).

4. The authority for Southwell's early dreams of India is his friend Deckers, *Narratio Martyrii* (*Arch. Rom. S.J.*), transcript at Farm Street.

5. See A. C. Southern, *Elizabethan Recusant Prose* (London, 1950).

6. For the MS. reference see Foley, IV, p. 345.

7. Alfred Poncelet, *Histoire de la Compagnie de Jesus dans les Anciens Pays Bas* (Bruxelles, 1927), gives an excellent background for life in the Jesuit College (II, pp. 37 ff.) and the troubles in Flanders 1576-8 (I, pp. 311 ff.).

8. *CRS*, V, p. 294.

9. Leo Hicks, *Archivum Historicum Societatis Iesu* (1932), I, pp. 276 ff. Fr. Hicks outlines the importance of this letter for Southwell's biography: 'It confirms what we know from his own *Querimonia* of his grief at his admission to the Society being deferred. . . . It shows moreover his determination notwithstanding this rebuff to go to Rome and press his petition there, though many opposed his purpose and even his friend endeavoured to dissuade him from it. The letter also corrects the statement of former writers that Deckers accompanied Robert on his journey to Rome.'

CHAPTER THREE
Rome: the Portrait Revived, 1578-81

1. *CRS*, II, p. 162 (Persons's Memoirs, edited by J. H. Pollen).

2. *CRS*, XXXIX, p. 4 (Persons's Letters, 1575-88), edited by Leo Hicks.

3. Ibid., p. 2.

4. *CRS*, II, p. 85. Archbishop Mathew in his sympathetic study, *The Celtic Peoples and Renaissance Europe* (London, 1933), suggests that Lewis's aim was to found a rest-centre for exiles, with a Celtic atmosphere.

5. C. C. Martindale, *The Vocation of Aloysius Gonzaga* (London, 1929), p. 137.

6. *Catalogus Primorum Patrum* (1640), Stonyhurst MSS.

7. De Buck. Passages are quoted from the following numbers in order: 56, 9, 11, 40, 50, 25, 30, 21, 31.

8. R. de Scoraille, *François Suarez* (Paris, 1911), pp. 169, 179.

9. *CRS*, XXXIX, pp. 5–28.

10. Sega's second Report (translation in Foley, III, pp. 3 ff.) cannot be lightly set aside. It was written for a keen-eyed Pope who was no favourer of the Jesuits. It is true that Allen maintained friendly relations with Lewis to the end; but Allen's tact and forbearance were remarkable. There is a memorial of 1588 bearing his name in which he passes a judgement on Lewis that goes far to confirm Sega's verdict. See T. E. Knox, *Letters and Memorials of Cardinal Allen* (London, 1882), p. 303d.

CHAPTER FOUR
The English College, 1581–3

1. The main source for this chapter is the Annals of the Venerable English College, generally called the *Liber Ruber*. *Liber Ruber I* consists of the names and particulars of the students, often with later biographical details added. It has been published: *CRS*, XXXVII. *Liber Ruber II*, unpublished, contains the Annual Letters, of which there are transcripts at Farm Street.

2. *CRS*, XXXIX, p. 226.

3. *CRS*, V, p. 303.

4. Ibid., pp. 56–62.

5. Ibid., p. 301.

6. *CSPD*, 1580–90, p. 52.

7. J. Pitts, *De Illustris Angliae Scriptoribus* (1619), p. 794.

8. Annual Letter 1583–4, enumerating Jesuit staff at the College, has the following: 'The first hears the confessions of the students. . . . The second, besides the task of writing letters for the community (*praeterquam quod communem rei literariae curam agat*) has charge of the daily exercises in theology. . . .' This public letter-writer and tutor in theology would appear to be Southwell—except that a Roman Catalogue for the beginning of 1584 calls him: '*Repetitor in Phil. ad duos annos*' ('tutor in philosophy for the past two years'). But this could refer to the past only. Jesuit Catalogues, even nowadays, are not always up to date.

9. *DNB*, I, p. 873.

10. *Douai Diaries*, Appendix, pp. 326–31.

11. *CRS*, IV, p. 133.

12. *CRS*, XXXIX, p. 200.

13. There seems no doubt that the playwright and the seminarist are one and the same person—both Kentishmen, both aged twenty-nine in 1583–4, and *DNB* leaves a gap in the playwright's life between 1582 and 1585. See also, with a query, *CRS*, II, p. 209.

14. *DNB*, XXII (Suppl.), p. 403.

CHAPTER FIVE
The 'Stirs' of 1584–5

1. *CRS*, V, pp. 315–16.

2. Ibid., 187–90. See chapters 15 and 19 of this book for Pormort's future.

3. The complaints against the Jesuits are all those listed in Sega's report of 1585 (see Meyer, appendix xix, pp. 348 ff.). I have considered them here as rising in a crescendo from 1584 to 1585.

4. Janelle's brief reference to Southwell's part in this affair is misleading (Janelle, p. 28).

5. *CRS*, XXXIX, p. 215.

6. De Buck, numbers 66, 61, 67, 57.

7. Conyers Reade, *Mr Secretary Walsingham* (Oxford, 1925), vol. III, p. 1.

8. *Douai Diaries* (ed. T. F. Knox, London, 1878), Appendix, p. 326.

9. See Leo Hicks, 'Solomon Aldred', *The Month* May–June 1945, p. 181, and 'The Strange Case of William Parry', *Studies* (Dublin), September 1948.

10. J. H. Pollen, *Queen Mary and the Babington Plot* (Edinburgh, 1922), p. lxxvii. Tyrrell's letter to Burghley retracting the lie, *PRO*, *SP*, 53, XIX, n. 67.

11. *CRS*, XXXIX, p. 244 and note.

12. De Buck, number 63.

13. More, p. 179.

14. *CRS*, XXXVII (*Liber Ruber I*), pp. 53–4.

15. *Douai Diaries*, p. 199.

16. 'Pilgrim Book of the English College', in Foley, VI, p. 556.

17. *CRS*, IV, p. 119 (Persons's 'Domestical Disputes', edited by J. H. Pollen).

18. *CRS*, XXXVII (*Liber Ruber I*), p. 43.

19. *Arch. Rom. S.J.*, *Fondo Gesuitico* 651. This is the reference for the letters to Aquaviva recently discovered at Rome.

20. Translated in Foley, VI, pp. 507–8. It is endorsed 'Fifty Students' but there seem to be only forty-nine names.

21. Pastor, vol. XXI, pp. 172–3.

22. De Buck, numbers 69 and 71.

CHAPTER SIX
Life in Rome, 1585–6

1. The first draft is among Robert's Roman papers, now at Stony-hurst (A.V. 4). Janelle by a happy discovery, also at Stonyhurst, was able to show that the draft though cast in the form of a sermon is really a paraphrase or translation of a late-medieval tract ascribed to Saint Bonaventure. But it is not possible to accept Janelle's remark that Southwell 'was but following in the wake of numerous contemporary writers and complying with contemporary fashions' (p. 189). All the works quoted by Janelle—except Valvasone's—were published well *after* Southwell's departure from Rome. Although Valvasone's work was published along with Tansillo's *Lagrime di San Pietro* which Southwell certainly used for his *Peter's Plaint*, yet it was not so published till 1587; and there is no indication, internal or external, that Southwell used the *Lagrime della Maddalena*. All that can be said is that *before* the fashion started, he chose an out-of-the-way medieval tract as his rough material and turned it eventually into a finished work of his own. That points to a personal choice independent of contemporary fashions, and the content of his work supports this view.

2. Petyt MSS., Series 538, vol. xliii, ff. 304. See Appendix 'B'.

3. Quoted by Pastor, XX, p. 559. Most of the Roman events described here are derived from this volume of Pastor, chapters 11 to 15.

4. *Epistle*, p. 185.

5. The story can be gathered from Copley's last letter (ed. Rox-burghe Club) and from Catherine Copley to Robert Southwell in the Stonyhurst MSS. A.I. 25.

6. *Archives Jesuitiques Flandro-Belges*, No. 1301. Transcript at Farm Street.

7. See for example the appeal of Birkett, the future Archpriest, to Agazzari, *CRS*, IV, pp. 152–3.

CHAPTER SEVEN
The Road to England, 1586

1. Persons's impression of the scene is recorded in a fragment by an unknown hand attached to a letter of Garnet's, 10th March 1594.

2. Persons, *Life of Campion*, c. 18. Quoted *CRS*, XXXIX, introduction.

3. *CRS*, XXXIX, p. 279.

4. See, for example, his *Manifestation* (1602), p. 46. Also Cajetan's report from Madrid printed in Meyer, Appendix XXII, pp. 460–1.

5. See Appendix 'B'.

6. *CRS*, XXXIX, p. 318, n. 19.

7. For George Gifford, see Pollen in *The Month*, XCIX, p. 607.

8. The facts about the Babington Plot are taken from the standard works *Queen Mary and the Babington Plot* and *Mr Secretary Walsingham*, by J. H. Pollen and Conyers Reade. But it must be urged with all deference that neither has said the last word about this affair. Pollen was too intent on incriminating Walsingham, and Reade on clearing him, for either to bother with the possibility of Morgan's treachery. Yet the case against Morgan is a strong one. To take one point only: had he been a genuine devotee of Mary, no one should have seemed to him more loathsome, after her death, than Robert Poley. Yet in 1593 he was banished by the Archduke from Flanders for spying *in collaboration with Poley* (see *Douai Diaries*, p. 404). English Catholics who were convinced of his treachery to Mary were amazed that he got off so lightly: 'Tis marvel that Morgan escaped only with banishment, which is an encouragement to Pooly and other spies.' (Verstegan, August 1593. Stonyhurst MSS. Coll. B, transcript at Farm Street.)

9. *CSPD*, 1580–1625, p. 174.

10. Conyers Reade, *Mr Secretary Walsingham*, II, p. 433.

11. J. H. Pollen, *Queen Mary and the Babington Plot*, pp. cxix, cciii, and 172.

12. *CRS*, V, p. 307.

13. *Archives Jesuitiques Flandro-Belges*, n. 1529.

14. *PRO, SP*, 53, XVIII, n. 31. Pollen: *The Month*, CXIX, pp. 302–3.

15. More, pp. 182–3.

16. Prison lists for June–July 1586, *CRS*, II, pp. 243–56.

17. Lansdowne MSS. 50, n. 74 (British Museum).

18. Garnet to Aquaviva, 30th July 1586. *Arch. Rom. S.J., Fondo Gesuitico* 651.

CHAPTER EIGHT
'The Birds of the Air Have their Nests—'

1. Southwell to Aquaviva, 25th July, intercepted letter printed by Strype, *Annals*, III, appendix 12. It is only conjecture that Southwell met the Catholics under arrest precisely at London Bridge; but it suits well with the vicinity, and with the symbolic importance which he attached to the place.

2. The sources of evidence for this paragraph are: *Middlesex County Records* (ed. J. C. Jeaffreson, Clerkenwell), I, 158–67; *PRO, SP*, 53, XIX, n. 76; Strype, *Annals*, III, appendix 14; *PRO, SP*, 12, CXCII, n. 18.

3. J. H. Pollen, 'Robert Southwell and the Babington Plot', *The Month*, vol. CXIX, p. 303.

4. *William Weston* (ed. Philip Caraman, 1955), chapter 9. Weston's narrative gives them a night in London after their meeting and then 'eight full days' in the country terminating on 23rd July. Subtraction gives the 13th as most likely date of meeting.

5. *PRO, SP*, 12, CLXXXVII, n. 37.

6. *Calendar of Scottish Papers* (ed. W. K. Boyd), vol. VIII, p. 598. Poley's report on Babington (here turned into direct speech) can be relied on since it was for Walsingham who was in a position to check it.

7. Weston's narrative is here collated with Poley's report. It is clear that Babington's visit to Weston occurred after his last interview with Walsingham—which was 13th a.m.—because Weston was out of town for a long period before this; he left again next day and 'never saw Babington again'. This makes 13th p.m. or 14th a.m. the only possible time. It is not surprising that Weston does not connect

Babington's visit with his own hurried departure. He deliberately shut out from his mind all surmises about the plot; and when he wrote his narrative thirty years later he grouped his reminiscences by personal memories.

8. *PRO, SP*, 12, CXCI, n. 23.

9. *VCH*, Buckinghamshire, III, p. 72. See *William Weston*, notes to chapter 9.

10. *Calendar of Scottish Papers*, VIII, p. 542.

11. There is a reminiscence in the *Annual Letters* of 1635 (quoted Foley, VII, p. 1136) which is interesting from more than one point of view: 'A man of high position died this year. He had once heard Father Robert Southwell preach a sermon full of divine fervour, exciting the souls of young men to virtuous life. He used often to recall this sermon which was regarded as miraculous. The face of the preacher, then nearing the end of his life, appeared radiant with light, and his head seemed to be surrounded by bright rays. From that time forward this gentleman became a totally changed man.'

CHAPTER NINE
' And the Foxes have their Lairs . . .'

1. The most useful reference-source for Tyrrell is Morris, 'The Fall of Anthony Tyrrell', in *Troubles of our Catholic Forefathers*, II (London, 1872). See also C. Devlin, *The Month*, December 1951.

2. Garnet to Aquaviva, March 1593, a long reminiscent letter, *Arch. Rom. S.J.*, transcript at Farm Street.

3. *CRS*, V, p. 318; and prison lists in *CRS*, II, 257–75.

4. *CRS*, V, p. 310.

5. The name in the text appears to be 'Sale', but since there was no known priest of that name or *alias*, it looks as if Tyrrell had indistinctly heard or seen the name of Southwell in some abbreviated form, e.g. 'S——l'. Persons, who edited but did not publish Tyrrell's retractions, notes that he was set to spy out Southwell in the winter of 1586. Morris identified 'Sale' with 'Sayer'; but this cannot be so, since 'Sayer' is mentioned by Tyrrell elsewhere.

6. Reconstruction of the raid is made from: (a) spies' accounts and description of the house, printed in *Vaux*, 153, 170–1; (b) Southwell's

letter of 21st December; (c) Frances Burrows's story in Hamilton, II, 164–6. Fr. Anstruther (*Vaux*, p. 181) is of the opinion that the raid described by Frances took place in the midlands; but he has overlooked the threat of the pursuivant to take her to the *Bishop of London*, which indicates her home with the Vaux family in Hackney. It is reasonably certain that the raid described by Southwell is the same one. He sheltered at Hackney during his first months in England (More, p. 184; Bartoli, p. 357); and there are several points of connection mentioned in the text.

7. Its endorsement remains: 'The writer was Parsons the Jesuit, now come secretly into England to promote the Catholic cause.' Strype, *Annals* III, app. 12.

8. *Epistle*, p. 182. Compare the account by Thomas Platter of Basle, printed in E. K. Chambers, *Elizabethan Stage*, II, p. 365.

9. *CRS*, II, p. 266. Although the Christian name is different, Harris's arrest or re-arrest may be connected with a spy's recommendation to Lord Burghley the previous day, 29th, 'There is one Thomas Harris, a trusty servant of Mr Henry Vaux. Much might be found out in him if he were apprehended.' (Printed in *Vaux*, p. 171.)

10. Although I have a clear memory of the substance of this report, I have lost my note of the reference, and cannot now trace it.

11. *PRO, SP*, 12, CCXVI, n. 77.

12. *The Lives of Philip Howard, Earl of Arundel, and of Anne Dacres his Wife* consists of two seventeenth-century manuscripts by an unknown Jesuit who was the Countess's chaplain for the last fourteen years of her life. Published by Hurst & Blackett for the Duke of Norfolk in 1857. The important chapter, 'Of Father Southwell's coming to live with her', from an earlier manuscript in the same library at Arundel but not used in the published version, was printed for the first time, along with a useful account of the manuscripts, by C. A. Newdigate *The, Month*, March 1931.

CHAPTER TEN
The Secret Printing Press, 1587

1. To Aquaviva, 21st December '86. *CRS*, V, 314.

2. Done Bushell, 'The Bellamies of Uxendon', *Harrow Octocentenary Tracts*, Cambridge, 1914.

3. To Aquaviva, 12th January '87. *Arch. Rom. S.J., Fondo Gesuitico* 651.

4. Quoted from Conyers Reade, II, p. 312.

5. The wicked design of January '87 to precipitate Mary's death is uncovered by Pollen, *The Month*, vol. C, p. 86. He comments: 'it shows us the shameful features of an Elizabethan sham-plot without any disguise'.

6. David Rogers, 'Papist Thackwell and Early Catholic Printing in Wales', *Catholic Biographical Studies*, II, 1 (1953).

7. *Epitome*, p. 23, in Ames, *History of Printing* (Herbert's edition, London, 1790), III, p. 1466.

8. The phrase 'this 29 years' (p. 197) fixes the limits, 17th November '86 to 16th November '87, the twenty-ninth year of Elizabeth's reign. See Janelle, p. 147.

But Chapter 15, 'A Warning to Persecutors', suggests a closer limitation. Southwell is citing cases where officials suffered as a result of executing martyrs. His latest instance is the execution of Fr. Ingleby at York, June 1586, after which his chief persecutor dropped dead outside the Bishop's palace exuding an unbearable stench. But in March 1587 there were other cases of the same sort even more striking, following immediately the martyrdom of Fr. Thomas Pilcher at Dorset, 21st March. Now, Southwell was kept very well posted in news of this sort; and since his friend Fr. Stanney was working in the Dorset region it is virtually certain that the incidents attending Pilcher's death would have been reported to him at least by the following April. He would certainly have included them in his fifteenth (and second-last) chapter had it still been unfinished at that date. So internal evidence lends support to the Marprelate date of February for the printing of the *Epistle*—a printing which, as its preface suggests, followed hot-foot after its hasty revision. Perhaps it should be added, in case Fr. Pollen is wrong about 'imprinted at Paris' being fictitious, that there is nothing intrinsically improbable in an edition of the book being smuggled from France in February or March 1587.

9. Ames, *History of Printing* (Herbert's edition) II, pp. 1031, 1033.

10. *PRO, SP*, 15 (*Addenda*), XXI, n. 97.

11. 'Remembrances of wordes and matter against Richard Cholmeley', British Museum, Harleian MSS. 6848, f. 190. For the connection between Cholmeley and Christopher Marlowe see F. S. Boas, *Marlowe and his Circle* (Oxford, 1929), chapter 4.

12. Lambeth Palace Library, Bacon Papers, MS. 655.

CHAPTER ELEVEN
Rumours of War, 1587–8

1. The four letters of Southwell and the one of Garnet used in this chapter are from those recently discovered at Rome, *Arch. Rom. S.J., Fondo Gesuitico* 651.

2. M. M. Knappen, *Tudor Puritanism* (Chicago, 1939), pp. 294, 477.

3. Holinshed, *Chronicles* III (1587), p. 1359, col. 2. Lingard, *History of England* (London, 1854), vol. VI, p. 170.

4. Sir Robert Southwell is found interceding in May 1592 for two humble London recusants, perhaps at his cousin's instance (*Hat. Cal.* IV, p. 201). His daughter Elizabeth, a maid of honour, having eloped disguised as a boy with the Earl of Warwick (Sir Robert Dudley) became a Catholic.

5. See 'Ralegh's *Discourse of War* and Machiavelli's *Discorsi*' in *Modern Philology*, 1950, XLVII, 217–27.

6. Printed in *Letters of Cardinal Allen*, 299–301, by T. F. Knox who accepts it as genuine. But for a detailed demolition of its authenticity see Leo Hicks, *The Month*, June 1934.

7. The facts and quotations about Bellarmine and Whittaker are taken from James Brodrick S.J., *Blessed Robert Bellarmine* (London, 1928), I, 138–40.

8. For Tyrrell references see chapter 9, note 1. The Government's revenge on Fr. Leigh for distributing Tyrrell's recantation was to pretend that the spurious *Letter . . . to . . . Mendoza* (see next chapter) was found among his papers after his arrest.

CHAPTER TWELVE
The Spanish Armada

1. Southwell to Aquaviva, 10th July, *Arch. Rom. S.J., Fondo Gesuitico* 651. For internment of leading Catholics, see *Vaux*, pp. 172–8.

2. For correlation of naval and political events with religious situation, see Pollen, *CRS*, XXI, 165–75.

3. See Hicks, *The Month*, April and May 1948.

4. See Appendix 'B'.

5. *PRO, SP*, 12, CCXI, n. 15, printed in *CRS*, XXI, p. 169.

6. See Pollen, 'An Anti-Catholic Forgery', *The Month*, 1911, p. 300.

7. Printed in Strype, *Annals*, III, 2 (Oxford, 1824), pp. 87–92.

8. P. Caraman, *John Gerard* (London, 1951), p. 98.

9. Garnet to Aquaviva, 11th July, *Arch. Rom. S.J.*, *Fondo Gesuitico* 651.

10. Southwell to Aquaviva, 31st August, *CRS*, V, p. 322. Garnet to Aquaviva, 29th October, *Arch. Rom. S.J.*, *Fondo Gesuitico* 651.

11. *CRS*, V, p. 119.

12. *PRO*, *SP*, 12, CCXII, n. 70, printed by Pollen, *CRS*, V, p. 151.

13. Harleian MSS. 6998, f. 232, printed as above, pp. 154–5.

14. T. W. Baldwin, *William Shakespeare adapts a hanging* (Princeton, 1932).

15. In the introduction to *CSPD*, 1595–7, the editor of the Calendar has this impression of its contents: '. . . Religious opinions unsettled, a deep and general discontent prevailing, waiting only the opportunity of the Queen's death for development, an exchequer almost bankrupt, and heavy loans from all classes of people still unrepaid.'

CHAPTER THIRTEEN
A Wandering Minstrel

1. Southwell to Aquaviva, 21st and 29th December, *Arch. Rom. S.J.*, *Fondo Gesuitico* 651.

CHAPTER FOURTEEN
Philip and Anne, 1589

1. A rising churchman, Richard Bancroft, chaplain to the Chancellor Hatton, had not only hunted down the marprelates but was engaged with the Queen's support in crippling the presbyterian Classis movement; his weapon was the High Commission transformed from a random tool of the Privy Council into an all-powerful ecclesiastical machine. See R. G. Usher, *The Reconstruction of the English Church*, I (New York, 1910).

The sources for nearly everything in this chapter are: for the trial,

Pollen's *Philip, Earl of Arundel, CRS*, XXI; for Southwell's relations with the Countess, her *Life*, see Chapter 9, note 12; for his 'Letter to his father', Trotman, *Catholic Library*, VIII (1914).

CHAPTER FIFTEEN
The Rise of Topcliffe, 1590

1. Southwell to Aquaviva in *CRS*, V, pp. 329, 330.
2. P. Caraman, *John Gerard*, p. 15.
3. For a sketch of Topcliffe, see C. Devlin, *The Month*, March 1951.
4. Garnet to Aquaviva, 16th July 1592, *Arch. Rom. S.J., Fondo Gesuitico* 651.
5. *PRO, SP*, 12, CCXXX, n. 57.
6. *CRS*, V, pp. 183–5, 291.
7. Most of the information for the next few pages is drawn from the 1591–2 Recusant Lists in *PRO SP*, 12, CCXXXVIII, n. 62 and CCXLI, n. 35, and *Hat. Cal.* IV. Also from Stow's *Survey* (ed. C. L. Kingsford, Oxford, 1908), II, pp. 45, 87, etc.
8. Stonyhurst MSS. B. VI, 1 (Macdonald, p. 15).
9. Since I have seen it denied that the Wriothesleys used Southampton House at this time, the reference is *CSPD*, 1591–4, pp. 463, 503— where the Jesuit Lister (*alias* Butler) is reported as coming up there from Hampshire and lodging with one of her gentlemen. Puckering commented, p. 510, 'Southampton House, where priests frequently come together.'
10. Fennell is found in Sussex and the Blackfriars Gatehouse in 1590–1, Gray at Cowdray and Southampton House in 1593; Lister and Baldwin come from Buriton (Shelley) and Bambridge (Wells) to Southampton House and Chancery Lane in 1594. See the same volume, *CSPD*, 1591–4.
11. *PRO, SP*, 12, CCXLV, n. 138. See also Barnes's speech in Tierney-Dodd, III, app. 27.
12. They are in the Westminster Archives, V, p. 369 and VI, n. 51, p. 183 (transcripts at Farm Street). In *CSPD*, 1593, p. 357, Standish is reported by the renegade Younger (see next chapter) as 'resorting to Mrs Gardiner's in Fleet Street'; so he was evidently in close touch with Southwell.

13. For the slanders against the Jesuits in the matter of alms-distribution, see L. Hicks, *Letters of Thomas Fitzherbert*, CRS, XLI, 131–4.

14. *CRS*, XXII, p. 127.

15. 'Roberts' was the natural form which the spies gave to '*Robertus*'. Garnet was credited with it at his trial, but he was certainly not using it as his alias at this date; he may have acquired it later on when he took over Robert's duties in London.

16. See Chapter 10, note 11.

CHAPTER SIXTEEN
The Year of Challenge, 1591

1. The story of this expedition and its various sequels can be gathered from John Cecil's own two-faced reports to the Government (*SP*, 12, CCXXXVIII, nn. 160–3), and to Persons (in *CRS*, V, 199–203). Similarly from Younger's very detailed and interesting relations, anti-Catholic in PRO, SP, 12, CCXLIII, n. 11 etc., and pro-Catholic in *The Acts of the English Martyrs* (Stonyhurst, *Anglia*, VI).

2. Burghley withdrew this letter from Cecil's other informations and put it in his private papers, see *Hat. Cal.*, IV, p. 104. In favour of its authenticity is that, though the handwriting does not claim to be Persons's, the signature appears to be his. But that cannot be taken as decisive since forgery of signatures was a regular habit with Government spies in that decade. Against it are the facts that Persons did *not* support the Stanley claims, that he never allowed missionary priests to dabble in politics, and that in a letter written two months before this alleged one he betrays ignorance of Cecil's whereabouts and no anxiety to repair the deficiency. It is possible, of course, that he was simply gathering information for the *Conference on the Next Succession*, then being written. But that would mean—what is true in any case—that Cecil's interpretation of it was wholly and deliberately false. For its further connection with the future Earl of Derby, see C. Devlin, 'The Earl and the Alchemist', *The Month*, January, February, March, 1953.

3. *PRO, SP*, 12, CCXXXVIII, n. 62.

4. See Trotman for the dedication and a sketch of Trussell. But the editor's further lucubrations baffle comprehension.

2A

5. Foley, I, pp. 186-8. See also Topcliffe's note on first page of Chapter 18.

6. Both Howard and his son-in-law Southwell are found exercising themselves on behalf of recusants in May 1592; see *Hat. Cal.* IV, 201, 203.

7. Garnet to Aquaviva, 1st May 1595, *Arch. Rom. S.J., Fondo Gesuitico* 651.

8. See *John Gerard*, 41-3, and *Vaux*, 186-92.

9. About two-thirds of the way through, Southwell mentions the arraignment but *not* the execution, which indicates that he had finished two-thirds of his tract between 4th and 10th December. This agrees well with the date of completion, 14th December, on the earliest manuscript. See the edition by R. C. Bald, p. xi, who also prints usefully the *Proclamation*. '*An Humble Supplication to Her Majestie*' by *Robert Southwell* (ed. R. C. Bald, Cambridge, 1953). But since Bald's edition is the one referred to in the next chapter, it must be said that it is marred by an introductory thesis that is gravely misleading. See C. Devlin, *The Month*, December, 1953.

CHAPTER SEVENTEEN
'Best Beloved Princess'

1. Garnet's long letter of March 1593 (transcript at Farm Street).

2. Garnet's letter of May 1595, *Arch. Rom. S.J., Fondo Gesuitico* 651.

3. Salisbury MSS. XLIII, n. 41. Transcript at Farm Street (cf. *Hat. Cal.* VI, p. 311).

4. Persons however cannot be held responsible for the English version of it known as the *Advertisement*. It is very doubtful whether this version was 'made by some of his colleagues' (Bald, *op. cit.*, p. x). It contains some mistranslations which make nonsense of Persons's Latin, notably the oft-quoted passage about Ralegh spelling GOD backwards.

5. It seems likely that Persons's judgement was perfectly sound on this point. Certainly nothing is more false than the repeated assertion that the only effect of his writing was to increase the persecution at home. The facts are quite the contrary. In January 1593 Persons's

book had had its full effect in England. In March of the same year Garnet reported a distinct relaxation in the persecution.

6. A weird and distorted reminiscence in John Donne's slovenly pamphlet, *Pseudo-Martyr* (1610), might be explicable if his brother Henry, a law-student who died for the faith in Newgate in 1593, had been one of Southwell's helpers in the revision and distribution. See Bald, Appendix III.

7. James Spedding, *Letters and Life of Bacon* (London, 1861), II, p. 308.

8. See C. Devlin, *The Month*, December 1953, p. 348.

9. *Not* the youngest daughter as is commonly affirmed. See the Harrow Baptismal Registers entry printed by Done Bushell, *Harrow Octocentenary Tracts*, 'The Bellamies of Uxendon' (Cambridge, 1914), p. 34.

CHAPTER EIGHTEEN
'Master W. S.'

1. Lansdowne MS. 72, f. 113. 'Burghley Papers 1592', printed by Christobel Hood, *The Book of Robert Southwell* (Oxford, 1926), p. 48.

2. All verse quotations are from Grosart's edition, 1872.

3. The first 1595 edition was actually published by Wolfe, not Cawood. Macdonald (p. 74) conjectures that Wolfe had an incomplete stolen copy and that he raced Cawood who had the copyright. We hear of one such copy seized in a raid on the Wisemans' house in 1593.

4. It was Busby also who published the *Triumphs over Death* with Trussell's dedication to the Sackvilles. Busby and Trussell are probably the best clues for further research into Southwell's literary associations.

5. Macdonald, p. 91. The full form first appeared from the St. Omer's Jesuit Press in 1616. But its content proclaims intrinsically that it was the original form—unless we are to accuse the Jesuits of an utterly pointless forgery. Earlier publishers would naturally have shrunk from exposing the initials of a well-known literary man alongside those of an executed Jesuit. But for a foreign edition in the year of Shakespeare's death (and 'he dyed a papist' in a district served by Jesuits) there was no such deterrent.

6. See Janelle, pp. 85–6.

7. For the internal evidence see C. Devlin, 'Robert Southwell and Contemporary Poets', *The Month*, September 1950, pp. 172–5.

8. *Douai Diaries*, p. 121.

9. See C. Devlin, *The Month*, November 1950, pp. 311–13.

CHAPTER NINETEEN
Arrest and Torture, 1592

1. See Pollen in *CRS*, V, 209–11, 292.

2. Lansdowne MS. 73, n. 47. Printed in *The Rambler* (New Series, London, 1857), vol. VII, p. 111.

3. Stonyhurst MS., *Anglia*, II, 41. Printed in Tierney-Dodd, III, app. 27. Although Topcliffe was never finally disgraced (he passed into honourable retirement on the sequestered Fitzherbert estate of Padley), this trial signified his dismissal and the virtual triumph of the Catholic resistance. 'If you would convert them,' the Queen is reported as saying, 'do it by your good lives. For I will persecute no more than I have done.' (*CSPD*, 1601–3, p. 86.)

4. Barnes in his speech deliberately kept up the pretence, first introduced by Topcliffe himself, that there was no previous acquaintance between Southwell and the Bellamies.

5. Garnet to Aquaviva, 16th July 1592. *Arch. Rom. S.J.*, *Fondo Gesuitico* 651.

6. See Morris, I, p. 192, and *The Rambler*, VII, p. 110.

7. The Bellamy hiding-place remains a mystery, though it must have been a good one, for up to Southwell's time no priest was caught in the house. Topcliffe said it was 'in the tylles', or Tiles, which would mean the attics of the house. Later writers speak of trap-doors and secret passages, but without evidence. Janelle also errs (p. 83, n. 69).

8. There is no reliable likeness of Southwell. An engraved portrait pasted into the 1630 edition of his poems (British Museum copy) seems to be only a conventional likeness; it is marked '89', one of a series of the English martyrs; it has been reproduced in Marguerite Fedden's *Blessed Robert Southwell S.J.* (Bristol, 1954). There is also a drawing at Stonyhurst done by Charles Weld about 1830, which is said to have been copied from a portrait once at Fribourg; this portrait vanished when the Jesuits had to leave Switzerland; but it seems likely that it

was the original of the engraving mentioned above. The drawing is now too blurred to be faithfully photographed; it was reproduced, with the features slightly altered, in Christobel Hood's *Book of Robert Southwell* (Oxford, 1926).

From the written evidence all one can say is that his appearance was such as his personality would naturally suggest.

9. See Chapter 18, note 1.

10. B. W. Hynek, *The True Likeness* (London, 1951), pp. 61–2.

11. Verstegan to Persons, August and September 1592, *Arch. Rom. S.J., Anglia*, 38, ii. Garnet to Aquaviva, 7th March 1595, ibid., 31, i, ff. 109–13 (transcripts at Farm Street). The remaining facts in this chapter, unless otherwise noted, are from one or other of these sources. Verstegan gave the news as it first came out, Garnet as it was after being sifted and collated.

12. This is from Garnet's earlier letter, 16th July 1592.

13. More, p. 193.

14. From another reminiscent letter of Garnet's, 1st May 1595.

15. Dasent, XXIII, p. 71. 28th July agrees with Garnet's evidence that he was moved to the Gatehouse on the night of 27th–28th June; for Pickering, the Gatehouse Keeper, charged him maintenance for 'four weeks and two days'—though the dates he gave were 30th June to 30th July. 'It is not known', as Richard Simpson in *The Rambler* wrote, 'what honest Pickering charged for starvation,' but he may have been more concerned to get the number of days right than the exact dates.

16. Quoted in Janelle, p. 68, n. 35.

CHAPTER TWENTY
The Interval, 1592–5

1. Migne (1862), CLXXXIII, p. 787. The echoes of Saint Bernard in Southwell's early writings are often transparent.

2. 7th March 1595, see Chapter 19, note 11. Garnet references in this chapter, unless otherwise stated or noted, are to this letter.

3. Garnet, May 1595. *Arch. Rom. S.J., Fondo Gesuitico* 651.

4. 22nd February 1595. *Arch. Rom. S.J., Anglia*, 31, i, ff. 107–8 (transcript at Farm Street).

5. See Devlin, *The Month*, January, February, March, 1953.

6. See *Hat. Cal.*, IV, p. 601.

7. *CSPD*, 5th August 1595.

8. See Barnes's speech, reference in Chapter 19, note 3.

9. Persons to Aquaviva, 10th May 1594 (transcript at Farm Street).

10. From the missing chapter in the *Life*, *The Month*, March 1931. See Chapter 9, note 12.

11. Garnet, 7th March 1595, as before.

12. Stonyhurst MS., *Anglia*, Coll. B, 30.

13. Persons's *Apologie*, p. 199. See T. G. Law, *Jesuits and Seculars* (Edinburgh, 1889), p. 108. Persons's information was partly derived from a treatise written by Garnet to correct distorted versions of Southwell's opinion.

14. See R. G. Usher, *The Presbyterian Movement* (Camden Series, Third, vol. VIII, pp. xxii, xxiii; and *The Notebooks of John Penry*, Camden Series, Third, vol. LXVII, introduction).

CHAPTER TWENTY-ONE
' Like a Giant to Run his Race'

The last twenty-four hours of Robert Southwell's life are magnificently documented. Almost everything in this chapter is taken from one or other of these four sources:

i. *A Brefe Discourse of the condemnation and execution of Mr Robart Southwell* . . . by an unnamed eye-witness, copied by Verstegan in 1595, and now at Stonyhurst, *Anglia*, A, ii, 1.

ii. Garnet's Italian letters of 22nd February and 7th March 1595 (*Arch. Rom.*, *Anglia*, 31, i), identical in some passages, complementary in others.

iii. Leake's Relation: autograph (probably), by a secular priest; Thomas Leake, Stonyhurst, *Anglia* VI; printed in *CRS*, V, 333–7. Though written later it sheds new light from an independent eye-witness.

iv. A further letter of Garnet's, hitherto unused, 1st May 1595, which adds many interesting details, *Arch. Rom. S.J.*, *Fondo Gesuitico* 651.

Deckers's *Narratio Martyrii* (1595) is based entirely on the *Brefe*

Discourse, and adds only, as it were, 'stage-directions'—often redundant but occasionally valuable as from one so close in time and so familiar with Southwell's early life.

Other additions by Yepez and Verstegan are noted in their place.

1. See Aubrey's hostile account of Popham, quoted in *DNB*.
2. Verstegan, 3rd May 1595, is quite positive on this point.
3. See Chapter 19, note 7. Deckers's Latin version is '*in tegulis*'.
4. This is a later detail from Garnet's Annual Letter of 1601 (in Foley, VII, p. 1361)—presumably told him by the friendly Keeper.
5. Garnet adds in his May letter that he has the handkerchief by him as he writes.
6. All three accounts mention Mountjoy's presence.
7. Garnet, 1st May 1595 (*Arch. Rom. S.J.*, *Fondo Gesuitico* 651).
8. Robert Southwell was declared 'Blessed' by Pope Pius XI in 1929. In the Society of Jesus his feast is celebrated on 21st February.

APPENDIXES

1. Philip Hughes, *Rome and the Counter Reformation* (London, 1942), p. 287.
2. F. A. Gasquet, *History of the Venerable English College* (London, 1920), pp. 88, 89.
3. Ibid., pp. 81, 150.
4. *PRO, SP*, 12, CCXXXVIII, n. 180.
5. *Letters of Cardinal Allen*, ed. T. F. Knox, p. 153d.
6. J. Spedding, *Letters and Life of Bacon* (London, 1861), I, p. 46. *DNB*, I, p. 801.
7. H. Hallam, *Constitutional History of England* (1846), I, 148–50. *Somers Tracts:* Somers collected his 'tracts' towards the end of the seventeenth century. They were published in 1748, and again by Sir Walter Scott in 13 volumes beginning in 1809. I do not know from which edition Hallam was quoting.
8. J. H. Newman, *Apologia Pro Vita Sua* (London, 1881).
9. *John Gerard* (ed. Philip Caraman, London, 1951), p. 95, note 1.

NOTE
on the pronunciation of the name

The initials 'S.W.' which Robert used for his surname suggest that he pronounced it with the 'w': South-well. In the next century Fr. Grene once wrote it as 'Southall'. That the 'w' was pronounced in the Elizabethan era and then began to be dropped in Stuart times is what one would naturally expect.

Index of Persons

Agazzari, Alphonsus, 49, 54, 59, 60, 64, 70, 71, 74, 87, 97, 122, 327
Aldred, Solomon, spy, 49, 50, 62, 70, 75 n., 94, 95, 267
Alfield, Thomas, martyr, 169
Allen, Cardinal William, 17–18, 23, 24, 27, 49, 50, 57–8, 59, 60, 69 n., 70, 88, 90, 92, 95, 132, 133, 154–5, 161, 229, 242, 248, 327; *Declaration*, 163, 164, 165, 166–7
Alvarez, Fr., 13, 14
Aquaviva, Claudius, General of the Jesuits, 58, 68, 69, 75, 88–9, 90, 94 n., 110, 128, 149, 151, 157, 168, 172, 176, 189, 207, 298
Arden, Edward, 18, 263 n.
Array, Martin, 133
Arthington, 233
Arundel and Surrey, Countess of, 95, 131, 134–5, 142–3, 198–201, 232, 284, 290, 298
Arundel and Surrey, Earl of (Philip Howard), martyr, 95, 131–2, 133, 190, 191 ff., 295, 298, 299
Arundell, Dorothy, 118
Arundell family, 108, 117
Atslow, Dr., 144
Audley family, 8, 29
Audley, Katherine, 7, 8, 9

Babington, Anthony, 101, 110, 111–12, 113
Babington Plot, 71, 94, 95, 96, 100–1, 110, 121, 138; Southwell's account of, 248, 249
Bacon, Anthony, 147 and n., 254, 255
Bacon, Francis (later Lord Chancellor), 254, 255, 329–30
Bacon family, 4

Bagshaw, Dr. Christopher, 61, 62, 64, 65–6, 71, 74–5 and n., 117, 161, 228, 300
Bailey, Christopher, martyr, 59, 208, 212–13, 228
Baines, Richard, spy, 223
Baldwin, Professor T. W., 174
Ballard, John, 71, 92, 95, 100, 117, 121, 122
Bancroft, Archbishop, 220, 233
Bannister, Edward, 13, 217
Bannister, Mary (Southwell's sister), 6, 109, 217, 290
Barnes, Robert, 128, 218, 275–6, 277–8
Barrett, Dr., 60, 61, 70
Beesley, George, martyr, 230
Belknap family, 5, 263 n.
Bell, Henry, 230
Bell, Thomas, 295–6
Bellamy, Anne, 256, 275 and n., 276–7, 301, 311
Bellamy, Mary, 279
Bellamy, Richard, 140 n., 256, 275, 279
Bellamy, Thomas, 277, 278
Bellamy family, 138
Bellarmine, Robert (saint), 46, 156–7
Bennet, 191, 192, 193, 194
Berden, spy, 95, 111, 113
Blake, Saunder, martyr, 213
Blount, Charles. *See* Mountjoy, Lord
Blount, Sir Christopher, 26, 232
Blount, Sir Michael, 294–5
Blount, Richard, 224, 225–6, 231, 278
Bold, Richard, 114, 115, 121
Bolton, Edmund, 187
Borromeo, Cardinal (St. Charles), 48
Bost, John, martyr, 190
Brinkley, Stephen, 53

361

Nihil obstat
Joannes M. T. Barton, S.T.D., L.S.S.
Censor deputatus
Imprimatur
E. Morrogh Bernard
Vicar General
Westmonasterii, die
2a Septembris, 1955

From the time when, as a boy, Robert Southwell slipped illegally overseas, his chosen path led through strange and dangerous places. The years in Paris and Rome were the preparation for the day when he was to return to England, with the noose of the Babington Plot already, as it were, round his neck. To spies and pursuivants he was "Chief dealer for the Papists in England"; while to the literary world of the day he was the new poet in whom "verse and virtue" sang together with unrivalled sweetness. The London that saw Shakespeare's rise to fame saw also ten licensed editions from the pen of this proscribed "traitor". At last, by a bold and deeply moving appeal to the Queen, he signed his own death warrant. There followed the scenes in Topcliffe's torture-chamber, the amazing duel of wits at Southwell's trial, and his last triumphant journey to the Tree of Tyburn.

To capture the spirit of such a man as Robert Southwell is no easy task, but Christopher Devlin's insight and scholarship, with the aid of much important new material, have framed this bright and elusive personality in its true setting. Robert Southwell's humility, courage and unselfishness soar above human explanation; but, as this fine biography shows, they were grounded in human qualities which all can appreciate. This is a book which will take its place, for many years to come, as the standard biography of Robert Southwell.